SOCIAL CLASS DIFFERENCES
IN BRITAIN

Ivan Reid was born in Hackney and went to technical school in Walthamstow. He trained for two years
as a teacher at St John's College, York, and taught
mathematics and history in a comprehensive and
secondary modern school. Later he read a first degree
in sociology at the University of Leicester and
part-time higher degrees at the universities of Liverpool and Bradford. His career has been mainly in
teacher education and particularly in-service educa-
on. He taught main-course sociology at Edge Hill
College of Education and tutored in the discipline at
the University of Liverpool. For a number of years he
taught the sociology of education at the University
of Bradford, where he was Chairman of the School of
Applied Educational Studies. He currently teaches
in the School of Education, University of Leeds, and
is Pro-Dean of the Faculty of Education.

His other books include *Sociological Perspectives
on School and Education* (Open Books, 1978), *The
Sociology of School and Education* (Fontana, 1986)
and *Sex Differences in Britain* (with Erica Stratta;
second edition, Gower, 1989). He is joint editor of
Research in Education and an executive editor of
the British Journal of Sociology of Education.

is married and has two daughters, and his
ests are running, travel, live-steam model rail-
ays, photography, and industrial and cultural
archaeology.

SOCIAL CLASS DIFFERENCES IN BRITAIN

Life-chances and life-styles

THIRD EDITION

IVAN REID

Fontana Press

First published by Fontana Paperbacks in 1989
Copyright © Ivan Reid 1989

Set in Linotron Trump Mediaeval

Printed and bound in Great Britain by
William Collins Sons & Co. Ltd, Glasgow

Fontana Press is an imprint of Fontana Paperbacks,
part of the Collins Publishing Group

This book is dedicated to
the three Marys in my life

CONTENTS

TABLES

FIGURES

ACKNOWLEDGEMENTS

Surprisingly enough, writing a third edition of a book is no easier and in some ways much harder than the first. The author is therefore particularly grateful to all those who, directly or indirectly, helped and supported him during the preparation of this book, whether or not they are mentioned by name. Pride of place must be given to his family, and especially Pat, for yet again providing a support system well beyond expectation, let alone desert. Many people have been kind enough to comment on the earlier editions and their comments have been most useful. Many of my colleagues in the School of Education at Leeds deserve thanks for sustaining in difficult times an environment in which writing can take place. In particular I am grateful to Sylvia Vallance for her help in sustaining my role there. I have reason to thank a number of library staff for their patient, cheery help. I continue to be stimulated by my students' challenging combination of interest and scepticism over what I try to set before them. This book owes much to generations of students not only at Leeds, but also Bradford and Liverpool universities and Edge Hill College. All those researchers and writers who have contributed by their work to this book are thanked. Generous help was provided by Tony Wornell and Mary-Ann Reynolds of Social Surveys (Gallup Polls) Ltd, Martin van Staveren and Philip Mitchell of British Market Research Bureau, Darren Marshall of National Opinion Polls Market Research Ltd and Janet Mayhew of National Readership Surveys.

The author and publisher thank the following for permission to use data presented in this book: Basil Blackwell, Oxford, for data from Le Grand (1978); Professor Brian Abel-Smith for data from Abel-Smith, Zander and Brooke (1973); the British Broadcasting Corporation for unpublished data from the BBC Daily Survey, British Audience Research Bureau and Audience GB audience research for 1987; the British Market Research Bureau for data from their *Target Group Index* (1987); the British Tourist Authority for data from *The British on Holiday*; The Centre for Educational Sociology, University of Edinburgh, for data from Burnhill (1981); Century Hutchinson Publishing Group for data from Lomas and Monck (1977); Croom Helm Ltd for data from Victor (1987); the editor of *Health Bulletin*, Edinburgh, for data from Carstairs (1966); The Health Promotion Research Trust, Cambridge, and Dr B. Cox for data from *The Health and Lifestyle Survey* (1987).

The Controller of Her Majesty's Stationery Office, the Office of Population Censuses and Surveys and the Cabinet Office for unpublished data from the 1981 Census and the General Household Survey of 1982 and for data (HMSO Crown Copyright) from *Birth Statistics 1985* (1987), *Britain's Workforce* (1985), Cartwright (1987), *Country of Birth, Census 1971, Great Britain, Supplementary Tables* (1978), *Demographic Review 1984* (1987), *Economic Activity, Census 1981, Great Britain* (1984), *Education for All* (1985), *Education Statistics for the United Kingdom* (1987), *Employment Gazette* (1982), *English Life Tables 14* (1987), *Family Expenditure Survey 1986* (Revised) (1988), *General Household Survey 1976, 1977, 1979, 1980, 1982, 1983, 1984, 1985* and *1986*, Haskey (1983, 1984, 1986, 1987), *Higher Education* (1963), *Household Composition Tables, Census 1971, England and Wales* (1975), *Household and Family Composition, Census 1981, England and Wales* (1985), *Immigrant Mortality in England and Wales 1970-78* (1984), *Labour Force Survey 1985* (1987), McDowall (1985), Macfarlane and Mugford (1984), Martin and Monk (1982), *Mortality Statistics 1985* (1987), *National Dwelling and Housing Survey* (1979), *New Earnings Survey 1987* (1988), *Occupational Mortality* (1978), *Occupational Mortality* (1986), *Royal Commission on the Distribution of Wealth and Income* (1979), *Royal Commission on Legal Services* (1979), Shaw (1988), Sillitoe (1969), *Social Trends 16* (1986), *Social Trends 17*

(1987), Werner (1985).

The Gower Publishing Group, for data from Airey and Brook (1986) and Brown (1984); the editor of the *Jewish Journal of Sociology* for data from Prais and Schmool (1975); The Joint Industry Committee for National Readership Surveys, London, for data from their *National Readership Survey 1987*, the Longman Group Ltd for data from Davie, Butler and Goldstein (1972); Macmillan Ltd for data from Butler and Stokes (1974); and Routh (1980), Methuen and Co. Ltd for data from Kelsall, Poole and Kuhn (1972); National Opinion Polls Market Research Ltd, London, for published and unpublished data from their surveys; Oxford University Press for data from Douglas, Ross, Hammond and Mulligan (1966), Halsey, Heath and Ridge (1980) and Goldthorpe, Llewellyn and Payne (1980); Penguin Books Ltd for data from Townsend (1979); Pergamon Press for data from Heath, Jowell and Curtice (1985), Professor Ken Roberts for data from Roberts, Cook, Clark and Semeonoff (1977), Social Surveys Gallup Polls) Ltd, London, for published and unpublished data from their surveys; The Tablet Publishing Co. Ltd for data from Moulin (1968); Tavistock Publications for data from Abbott and Sapsford (1987); Tyrell Burgess Associates Ltd for data from Edwards and Roberts (1980); The Universities Central Council on Admissions, Cheltenham, for data from *Statistical Supplement to the Twenty-fifth Report* (UCCA, 1988); Unwin Hyman Ltd for data from Mack and Lansley (1985) and Newson and Newson (1963, 1968 and 1978); Georg Westermann Verlag, Braunschweig, for data from McIntosh and Woodley (1974).

Full details of these publications can be found in the Bibliography.

PREFACE

In my preface to the first edition I pointed out that the idea for that book arose from my teaching experiences and my recognition of the need of students and teachers for a review of contemporary British social class reality based on empirical research. The reception of the first edition (and, indeed, the second) was such that my belief was more than vindicated, and established that others, beyond academia for which it was written, had a use for the book. The present edition therefore has essentially the same aim and approach, which are fully outlined in Chapter 1.

This edition is, however, a complete revision of the last and very substantially rewritten. There are two major salient reasons for such changes. First, part of the book's usefulness rests on how up-to-date its data are. While the basic facts of social class differences are far from dynamic, most data, and particularly those affected by inflation, age rapidly. Wherever possible all data have been revised from those available up to mid-1988. Second, the growth in sustained research and public interest in other forms of social stratification – mainly sex and ethnicity – has encouraged me to widen further the scope of this edition. Available data and space do not allow for a balanced, comprehensive treatment of the forms of social stratification across the various aspects of life in Britain, let alone to address fully their interrelationships. However, wherever available, data on sex, ethnicity and age have been included within the canons of selection and presentation of the book.

In applying these limitations I have been aware of how much has had to be left unsaid. For this I make no apology, trusting that interested readers will move on to literature that is more specific to their interests. I have deliberately maintained much of the original and singular concern with the empirical reality of social class differences. Consequently, this edition is clearly a commentary on social differences in Britain in the 1980s – for all practical purposes the here-and-now. Social class is taken as the fundamental form of stratification and used as the focus through which to view social differences.

Somebody remarked about the first edition that its publication was timely. My feeling is that, given the social and political changes of the last decade, the present edition may be even more so. The book provides, I believe, considerable food for thought and reflection, not only in academic, but also in social and political terms. I trust that readers and users will find it even more useful than previous editions.

IVAN REID
September 1988

CHAPTER 1

Social Differences
and This Book

> This booklet is . . . to meet a need which has been
> put something like this: 'You have in your office a
> great store of facts. . . . Some of your publications
> are costly, and it isn't too easy for the plain man
> to find his way through them to what he ought to
> know. Why not produce a short simple statement
> of the main facts?'
> It is not so easy. Much must be left out. Exact-
> ness in detail must give place to brevity, but with-
> out sacrifice of essential truth in the broad picture
> presented. The urge to use footnotes, parentheses,
> qualifications must be resisted.
>
> GEORGE NORTH (1948)

This book is about social differences and inequalities in
contemporary Britain. In particular it examines in detail
one aspect of the vast, complex and controversial topic
of social class – the empirical evidence concerning class
differences in Britain today. As such it follows its earlier
editions (Reid, 1977a and 1981). At the same time it provides a review of some of the empirical data on the other
main forms of social differences that occur in our society,
those of sex (or gender), age and ethnicity. Sociologists
see these fundamental social groupings as related forms
of what they call social stratification.

The differences, and attendant inequalities, between
social strata in Britain could be, and often are, viewed separately. In this book they are not only seen as interrelated

1

aspects of the same phenomenon, but social class is taken as the main focus through and from which to view social differences and inequalities in contemporary Britain. This introductory chapter has three purposes. First, it describes what social stratification is, and how its use in research relates to the everyday. Second, it places social stratification in its public context by outlining something of the breadth of usage of the ideas of social differences. Third, it describes, in some detail, this book's distinctive and particular approach to social stratification.

WHAT IS SOCIAL STRATIFICATION?

In general terms social differences, based on social class, sex, age and ethnicity, or allusions to such, are very familiar and frequent in our society. At the everyday level they can be discerned in conversation, attitudes and behaviour both public and private. Differences are recognized in people's appearance and speech, where they live and come from, what they do for a living, how they spend time and money and what their interests are, to name but a few examples. Such differences provide much rich material for discussion, emulation, condemnation and, indeed, humour. In turn these differences are used to characterize, or make assumptions about, people of different types. This area is explored at greater length in the next section below. Our concern here is with their more formal definition.

Put as simply as possible, social stratification is an arrangement of society into layers. In some ways the idea is very similar to that of layers or strata of rock. However social stratification usually also implies some form of differentiation between, or comparative evaluation of, the layers; reference is being made not only to different groups within society, but to a hierarchy or ranking of these groups. This implied evaluation and ranking can be seen in the definitions of social class outlined in

2

Chapter 2. These are ordinarily ranked by number or letter and listed from the 'highest' to the 'lowest'. The very common use of contrasting terms such as 'middle class' and 'working class', 'non-manual class' and 'manual class' reveals the same evaluative connotations.

The number of criteria on which social stratification (or categorization) could be based is theoretically infinite. Any culturally recognizable difference – forms of skill, type and amount of knowledge, religious practice, strength, length of hair, beauty, and so on – could be such a basis, depending on the social context. Some kind of social stratification seems almost universal, or even inevitable, in social life. Even among groups of peers certain hierarchies are likely to be perceived. In any group – whether of fellow students, colleagues, or even a family – we are likely to categorize the members by some such differences. To some extent the recognition of such criteria affects people's behaviour towards each other and their behaviour and organization as a social group. In turn this may mean differences in people's use and control of resources, in their power and status within the group. The more visible the criteria of differentiation, the more strict the social stratification, and the more regulated the relationships between the strata. Extreme examples are the armed forces and hospitals, where the wearing of uniform ensures recognition of differences and hence regulates relationships and behaviour.

In society, social stratification is essentially about groups' relationships to social wealth – used here in the generic sense of anything in society which is both scarce and valued by society. Hence it encompasses not only wealth, income and the ownership of property, but also power and prestige, together with a large number of associated factors including style of life, education, values, beliefs, attitudes and patterns of behaviour. Since our society, like all Western societies, runs on a cash nexus, many of these differences can be seen to have an economic basis. This is not to say that the differences

3

are necessarily economically determined, but rather that most aspects of social life are directly and/or indirectly affected by economic circumstances. Therefore most social analysts see social class, which has an economic basis, as the most important and fundamental form of social stratification.

Many sociological treatments of stratification contrast social class with the comparative and historical examples of caste and estate. It is much more meaningful, however, to compare it with other forms of stratification in our society, such as the two almost universal forms of stratification – age and sex. To a great extent people of different ages, or different sex, are given, and expect, differential treatment; they have different rights, privileges and duties, have differing levels of access to forms of social wealth, and they hold views of the world and of themselves which are related to such differences.

Our understanding, and even our recognition, of female and male comes from our culture – what we have learned as a member of society. In other words, we use what amounts to generalized stereotypes, which involve inaccuracies and unwarranted assumptions. In reality, all the supposed social characteristics of each sex exist in both females and males, although their display and recognition are differently encouraged or discouraged. A whole series of social forces, ranging from the law, through custom and norms, institutions and the media, to humour, affect the situation. So we can all recognize in ourselves and in others, for example, that ways of behaving, thinking and feeling are very complex and not simply divisible into two, discrete categories of the sexes. At the same time we are aware of how society shapes and affects not only these, but a whole range of aspects of social life, in terms of gender.

That there are objective, distinct social differences between the sexes in a range of factors including wealth, rights and opportunities cannot be denied. It was to attempt to overcome some of the disadvantages of

4

women in our society that equal opportunity legislation was introduced and the Equal Opportunities Commission set up. Current interest and research suggest that sex differences are somewhat similar and indeed related to class differences (see, for example, the appendix to EOC, 1978). Aspects of sex difference and the interrelationships between social class, sex and age are viewed in the chapters that follow.

A further obvious, basic form of stratification is that of skin colour and/or ethnic group, sometimes inappropriately referred to as race. While such differences are almost inevitably recognized by most, in some societies they are at the basis of social, economic and political organization. The most blatant example is apartheid in South Africa, though there are numerous other more subtle forms of discrimination and disadvantage. Again this type of stratification has to do with inequalities on a very broad front as well as differences. In much the same way as in the case of sex, our society displayed its concern in legislation – the Race Relations Act and the setting up, first, of the Community Relations Council, and subsequently the Commission for Racial Equality. Similarly, aspects of colour/ethnic group/race/country of origin are interrelated with social class, sex and age. However, since, unlike sex, these matters are regarded as sensitive and delicate, not much research has included them as variables. For instance, such was the controversy over the use of questions about ethnicity in the census that the government decided to exclude them from the 1981 census schedule. Hence, only limited data are available on the basis of ethnicity, which seriously curtails its examination in this book.

Obviously, social class and ethnicity have much more elusive characters than age or sex. Indeed, there appears to be a good deal of discussion, or even confusion, in sociological literature about the nature and meaning of social class. Crisp definitions of social class rarely appear, and the concept is generally seen to be problematic. Even

5

O level sociology textbooks, not unknown for their pat, meaning-defying definitions, treat the concept with caution. Such caution is well advised, since social class is a multidimensional concept, involving not only the identification of categories that are partly invisible in society but also an understanding of the effects of these on the people involved. Fortunately, for the purposes of this book, we can afford to be bolder, and accept as a working definition the following: social class is a grouping of people into categories on the basis of occupation. This is not to suggest that social class is simply or only based on occupation, or for that matter any other single criterion such as income or education. In any case, as will be seen in Chapter 2, occupational classifications of class involve fairly elaborate consideration of a number of associated factors.

The main reason why an occupational definition of class can be accepted here is that our exclusive concern is with empirical research. In British research, as will be seen in Chapter 2, occupation is almost the sole criterion of social class which has been used. While British researchers have expressed some reservations about the use of this single factor, it appears to be accepted as a reasonable general-purpose tool for classifying people into social classes. Or, as Monk (1970) has argued, 'Occupation remained the backbone of social grading because no better methods have been found, and because it has still remained a powerful and useful stratification factor, even though the interpretation has become more complex.' Interestingly, until very recently British researchers have shown limited concern with the development and use of scales of social class based on other factors, or on multidimensional measures. In some contrast, American sociologists and social anthropologists have developed a number of multidimensional scales. Some of these have been based on combinations of factors such as occupation, income and education, while others have involved more unusual factors such as participation in the community, family prestige, and contents and condition of living rooms. Several British classifications which combine occupation with other variables from the census exist – for example Madeley (1978), Osborn and Morris (1979), ACORN (1979) and Carstairs (1981).

However, it is true that most of these scales have been developed for a particular study, and their general use in other studies has been limited. This is because using such scales costs time and money. There is also the potential problem of relating to each other and to the existing body of knowledge findings based on different class scales. In terms of research use, occupation, almost certainly because it is easily collected and simple to treat, has remained universally the most popular criterion. Moreover, occupation has been consistently shown to be highly related to most other factors associated with social class, particularly income and education.

Occupation, then, is recognized as an element of social class in all sociological and other treatments of the concept. The reasons for this are very simple and can be dealt with briefly. In all societies based on a cash nexus occupations are differentially rewarded. Income is obviously an important determinant of possessions, style of life and place of living. Since earned income is for nearly everyone the main form of wealth, occupation is a good indicator of the economic situation of a person and a family. Furthermore, holding down an occupation takes up a considerable amount of people's time and life, and typically involves them in interaction with particular groups of people in particular ways. It would be surprising if the experience of work did not affect in some way a person's view of the world, attitudes and opinions. Broadly speaking, too, people are residentially segregated by occupation. People with similar incomes are likely to be able to afford similar housing, and will thus share many other aspects of life with each other. Dockers, for example, are likely to have more in common with other dockers than with doctors.

As has been suggested above, social differentiation is a common and essential characteristic of day-to-day life, the nature of which varies from place to place. At work the distinction between employers and employees and, within these, differences of rank and skill, can be seen as a more formalized idea of social class. This idea is especially exemplified by the use that parties to industrial relationships – trade unions, employers' associations and the government – make of the concept 'them and us' and the behaviour they adopt. In politics it is difficult to escape social class connotations in what the parties and politicians stand for, or in their words and actions.

Everyday life provides many further examples. One of the earliest and most common inquiries made in a casual meeting is, 'What job do you do?' – a question which usually brings a response, and rarely leads to an end of the conversation, or to embarrassment. From this 'knowledge' (of another's occupation) people are likely to make a number of assumptions about that person, their interests, attitudes, and so on. These assumptions, which will be based on one's previous experience of similar people and/or what one has read, seen or heard about them, affect the conversation and one's reactions to it. Surprises and mistakes do occur. One could meet a stockbroker who raced pigeons, for example, or a docker who drank only Pernod, but on the whole our assumptions are borne out. Significantly, when they are not, we do not discard them, but merely dust them off and retain them for the future. We are unlikely to inquire of the next stockbroker we meet how his pigeons are. The experience is accommodated as an oddity. This happens because our categories are resilient, and indeed they probably need to be. Life would become socially and psychologically intolerable if every new encounter had to be built up from scratch.

Outside the purely social encounter, many commercial

and government organizations require to know our occupations. Since few of us change our jobs dramatically, we may not realize what a crucial role our job plays in the way people and organizations react to us. It is possible to test this by pretending to be something other than what we are, say at a dance or on a rail journey in the company of others. Assuming we are convincing enough, this allows us to compare the responses we get with those we normally receive. Categorization of people on the basis of small snippets of information is common in social life. One's outward appearance can often affect the treatment one receives in places like banks, garages or large stores. Most of us pay some heed to this – for example, when we go to an interview for a job.

What is happening here is clearly not far removed from what social scientists do when they classify people in terms of social class. They are assuming that this single piece of information – occupation – is a good general predictor of a host of other factors such as income, education, style of life, attitudes, interests and beliefs, which together form their concept of social class. Their research is likely to be based on hypotheses (which can be seen as informed guesses, or hunches) rather similar to those used in face-to-face situations. Their categories are just as crude and resilient as our 'real-life' ones, but they are likely to be more systematic in collecting data, and their judgements can thus be rationally appraised.

General interest in social stratification is reflected in, and probably fuelled by, the mass media. The news programmes make full play of people's occupation, age, sex, ethnicity and status (not to mention titles), even when these can be seen as irrelevant or marginal to a story. Social class as an issue in itself is newsworthy, almost to the same extent as sex and crime are. Hence wide coverage is given even to academic books on the topic – for example, editions of this book have 'basked' in it for several days, and a more popular account (Cooper, 1979) was serialized for a week in a national newspaper. At the same time aspects of social stratification provide a fertile and constant theme, or subplot, for plays, films, novels and humour.

In each form of social differentiation there appears a clear tendency to highlight the trivial at the expense of the fundamental and to indulge in rhetoric rather than review the evidence. In the case of social class, for example, great play is made of such aspects as snobbery, political views, interests and opinions, with far less, if any, attention being paid to the underlying economic inequalities affecting not only life-styles but life-chances. A further deflection from serious consideration is the regular claim that things have changed and become better – that we no longer live in a class society, since the classes have merged or become very similar; that equality between the sexes has gone as far as necessary, or has almost been achieved. An added gloss to this sort of argument is that those who appear to be disadvantaged, be they the working class or women, either actually enjoy their situation or do not want any change, and would not know what to do with it. Such views may sound to readers to be those of the advantaged in the situations – that is, the middle class or men, since they represent those parties' interests in the maintenance of the status quo, or its minimal change.

However, we need to remember that ideas and values do not necessarily have discrete boundaries and that the disadvantaged may also hold such views. Shared, general views of social reality, apparently supporting a particular group's interests, are common, especially in social situations where one party has control or influence over information, knowledge and ideas, or where power in its general sense is unequal between the parties. This is certainly true in respect to social class and sex, where such views continue to be supported by those who have nothing to gain and, indeed, may be losing, from their continued acceptance.

The importance of entrenched values, beliefs or ideologies is almost impossible to overestimate, to the extent that they are not necessarily affected or changed through experience or exposure to facts. Hopes that people would realize the injustice or unfairness of social situations merely by being told 'the facts' have often been dashed because of resistance to their acceptance caused mainly by participants' 'understandings', based on deeply rooted cultural assumptions. Despite, and because of, these cautions, it is valuable for society to have as many facts as possible readily available, to facilitate informed discussion and understanding, if not action.

Clearly, too, social class and stratification feature in a whole range of academic disciplines – such as history, economics, politics, psychology, medicine – indeed all the social sciences and literature, and, above all, sociology, where social class has to be seen as one of the central concepts and concerns and arguably, granted the time, energy and space devoted to it, *the* central concept. This is witnessed by, for example, the number of books on the subject to be found in the sociology section of any library and the impossibility of finding any introductory textbook, or syllabus, in the subject which does not include it. Social stratification, and particularly class, feature prominently too in journal articles and in research, demonstrating their acknowledged importance as a vital variable.

This is not to suggest that the significance of social class and other forms of stratification as a variable in research is limited to the social sciences. Other institutions concerned with human social behaviour and its possible prediction, notably the government, industry and commerce, have long and considerable involvement. Many governmental agencies, particularly the Office of Population Censuses and Surveys (OPCS), collect, record and publish a whole variety of material on such bases. Similarly the significance of such social factors in marketing, advertising and selling commodities and services, in creating and servicing needs, has

11

given risen to what amounts to an industry of market research.

The great interest and involvement in social differences has generated a considerable range of opinions about them. These range between the extremes – from denying that they matter to seeing them as the sole explanatory variable for a whole host of situations. For example, while some people dismiss social class completely, others believe that is *the* vital factor that explains all spheres of social life, including relationships between the sexes and within families. The shades of opinion in between are too numerous and subtle to recount here. Discussions about social class, gender and ethnicity, both face-to-face and in the literature, take on many of the same characteristics as those about religion. Subtle differences of belief and emphasis and the interpretation of facts and events become the grounds of major division. The avid devotion and zeal of believers is equally matched by those who reject any possibility of its existence. Such debates appear to change in popularity. Currently, sexism and racism seem more popular concerns than classism, which has enjoyed greater popularity in the past, and ageism, which has yet to be a major public concern in Britain.

Some people react to social differences with lack of interest or even with delight, seeing them as adding to the richness and diversity of life. Certainly, social differences do not in themselves present society, or its members, with a problem. Perhaps few people would see the ideal world as one in which everybody was identical, while nearly all would reject one in which groups were denied their basic rights and the wherewithal to exist. Most are probably concerned by the fact that some groups in our society can be shown to be materially deprived through no fault of their own, and others disadvantaged in terms of length of life and health, and access to services like health and education (and the quality of what they receive when they get it), which are supposed to be provided fully and freely for all on the basis of need.

In turn these issues are based on questions of social equality and justice. Here the prime concern appears to have been not so much with attempts to achieve general equality, as with changing the legitimate criteria for inequality and extending equality of opportunity rather than equality of treatment or outcome. In the field of education, for example, the grounds of the debate since the Second World War have shifted from social class to sex and ethnicity, and have been concerned mainly with attempts to remove barriers to the various types of schooling, education and achievement for members of those groups. The goal has been to extend the opportunities for children from different classes, sexes and ethnic groups to gain educational achievements – and hence be differentiated on educational rather than social grounds. For some the provision of equal opportunities is a sufficient end in itself, for others the end is equality of outcome, which is only achieved when the educational attainment of the classes, sexes and ethnic groups is identical. As can be seen in Chapter 8, there is a considerable way to go to achieve either of these ends, though progress has been made in some respects in terms of gender.

We need to bear in mind that all evidence and data have limitations, and must be so viewed. In the present case limitations arise from several sources:

First, in looking at differences, precisely these are emphasized, and similarities are overlooked or played down. Social group differences are rarely, if ever, total, since while the majority of one may differ from others in a certain respect, some of both may well be alike. In turn this raises the question of within, rather than between group gender differences – why are some different to others? In some instances, the first type of difference may be of the same order and interest as the second. It is useful, then, to review the data in this book along such lines, though the explanation of similarity between, and differences within groups is not treated in any detail. It may well be that explanation of differences within groups is more complex than differences between groups.

Second, limitations arise because much of the data presented were collected for purposes other than displaying or exploring social differences. The result of using available, mainly 'official' data is that some interesting areas are left unexplored and criticisms can easily be raised about the data's collection, classification and presentation. These may be seen to incorporate particular values and assumptions. Since we live in a clearly stratified society, we must expect that the identification of problems and the conduct of research into them, let alone attempts to resolve them, will display at least elements of sexist, classist, racist or other forms of cultural assumption and imperialism. Sometimes these may be blatant, but more frequently they are subtle and implicit. The EOC, having considered the portrayal of women, commented, 'The assumptions underlying the statistical portrayal of women (as contained in official publications) are, at points, so divorced from reality as to be dangerously misleading' (EOC, 1980).

Third, and perhaps most serious, is that much of the data can be seen as theoretically inadequate. As Halsey (1972) has argued in another context,

A recurring problem is one which arises particularly in interpreting data relevant to social policy and the provision of welfare services. This is the difficulty of gaining from the statistics any idea of quality or adequacy. Obviously any analysis of health or welfare services or of housing should include some statement about how far the standard or amount of service supplied meets the need for it. But for the most part the figures are concerned with supply; independent measures of need which would be required to judge adequacy are virtually nonexistent.

Similarly, the data in this book often lack any clear or consistent conceptual framework of equality and/or justice within which to judge and interpret them. At present they do not match Halsey's call for a measure of need in order to make evaluation. Ideally, the answer to theoretically inadequate data is for research to be explicitly related to theory. As yet such research is piecemeal – though there are developments in some areas; see, for example, poverty, pages 179–86 below. In any case, it is by no means apparent that adequate theories for research have yet been developed.

This does not mean that this book and its approach are atheoretical except in the formal sense. The forms of social stratification are seen as cultural products within a societal and historical setting. Consequently, differences between them are clearly related to societal organization and capable of almost infinite form and change. Basically, then, the position of any strata in our society is constrained by, or the result of, their assumed role within the social structure. The fundamental assumption is that differences between strata are caused and persist because of their differing access to almost all social resources, to power positions and to opportunities that, in general, are to the decided advantage of some and the decided disadvantage of others.

Finally, it needs to be appreciated that the variety of ideas about, and involvement with, social differences are interrelated. For example, everyone, or so it seems, has their own ideas and theories about social class. A consequence of the popularity of class in our life and literature, therefore, is the difficulty in presenting a comprehensive and satisfactory account. As Giddens (1973) remarks in his acclaimed text, 'Anyone who has the temerity to write about the theory of social class is immediately plunged into controversy by the very way he approaches his subject – by the materials he chooses to consider and by what he ignores.' This book is no exception, despite having been written from a sociological standpoint and being devoted exclusively to the presentation of contemporary empirical material. Hence the rest of this chapter outlines my own particular approach and the criteria used for the selection of the material presented.

15

ABOUT THIS BOOK

A major aim of this book is to continue to fill a gap identified in the considerable literature on social class. That gap, recognized in the first edition, lay between the rather grand generalizations concerning social class differences found in introductory texts, and the very detailed, though often inaccessible, data and findings of empirical studies. Even given the audiences for whom they were written, many textbooks are misleading about social class, their oversimplification amounting to misrepresentation or even to total inaccuracy when compared with contemporary sources. Moreover, statements on social class can be, and are, presented simultaneously from vastly different sources. For example, differences in school attainments by social class (based on a number of large national surveys) can be followed by explanations couched, say, in terms of social class differences in values (based on small-scale studies from another society – typically the USA). Their juxtaposition implies a similar degree of reliability and importance, which may well be inappropriate. To take an extreme case, the applicability of dated American material to contemporary Britain is obviously limited. The overall effect of much of such literature is misleading and confusing, and can lead to the rejection of the concept of social class because of a lack of really appropriate data. Contact with contemporary statistics and research findings demands not only access to a university library or its equivalent, but also very real efforts of searching and interpretation. Even given the opportunity and motivation, most students and some sociologists would find difficulties in using certain original sources, even, for example, census material. This is because their presentation is normally designed for purposes other than communication with, or use by, students or the public.

This situation is also true of ethnicity and age, though sex is catered for in a manner similar to the present

16

texts in Reid and Wormald (1982) and Reid and Stratta (1989). This book alleviates the overall situation and is particularly comprehensive on social class. This it does by presenting a review of semi-digested empirical data on social class and other strata using a standardized format (see pages 20–1). More importantly, however, it provides not only the basis or vehicle for discussions about how the concepts of social class and other strata have been used in empirical research (operationalized) and the nature and extent of social differences, but also reveals something of the actual state of knowledge in the field. In so doing it should lead to a more realistic appraisal by a far larger audience than has been possible.

To achieve this aim within a single volume it has been necessary to limit the scope of the work. The obvious, intentional omission is any direct considera-tion of sociological and other theory about social class or stratification. Theories in these fields are dynamic and constitute a vast literature. The following short selection is almost exclusively sociological and British. Readers will find that the works listed contain abundant further references.

Social class A very good, brief introduction is pro-vided by Salaman (1972), who outlines and contrasts the works of three major sociologists, Marx, Weber and Parsons. The controversy centring on the func-tional explanation of social class is well summarized in the debate between Davis and Moore, and Tumin, which is to be found in Bendix and Lipset (1966). A good, clear and brief introduction to the sociological concept of class and its place in Marxist theory is that by Bottomore (1965). Thompson and Tunstall (1971) have most usefully brought together well-edited extracts from the original contributions to the concept of social class of Marx, Engels, Weber, Parsons, Bottomore, Marshall, Runciman, Lipset, Goldthorpe and Parkin. Together these extracts cover a historical period of some 120 years and provide a basis for comparison. Probably the finest contemporary text in the field is that of Giddens (1973), an extremely good critique of theories and theorists. Marx's basic ideas are best read in the original: see Marx and Engels (1848). An interesting book written from a clear Marxist perspective, which views some data from Britain and other societies in relation to theory, is that by Westergaard and Resler (1975). Similarly, Roberts, Cook, Clark and Semeonoff (1977) discuss a number of theories of change in the British class structure in the light of their investigations in Liverpool in the early 1970s. The complexities of Marxist and Weberian thought, which shape most current sociological considerations, are well covered in Abercrombie and Urry (1983), Cottrell (1984) and Giddens and Mackenzie (1982).

Ethnicity Stone (1985) provides a sound and readable introduction. The works of Rex (1986, 1983) reflect his long and active involvement in the field and place it well in the context of British society and sociology. A good reader in the field is Husband (1984). For those wanting to get nearer the frontiers, Rex and Mason (1986) contains explorations of Marxist, Weberian and pluralist approaches to race and ethnic relations by a range of academics.

Sex and gender Section 5 to Bilton *et al.* (1987) and section 4 to Abercrombie and Warde (1988) provide useful introductions to this field. Oakley's work (1972, 1981) is generally recognized as an excellent contribution and may well become classic. Cooper (1989) reviews current theoretical debates within sociology and feminist sociology. Crompton and Mann (1986) have brought together contributions which cover current issues from those involved. Brittan and Maynard (1984) tackle both sexism and racism.

Age The major emphasis currently in gerontology (study of ageing) is with the elderly. Victor (1987) combines a useful theoretical outline with an extremely good and comprehensive coverage of empirical data on the elderly in Britain, including a good deal of unpublished GHS data. A most comprehensive survey of the field which includes comment on the original work on age stratification (Riley, 1971, of interest in itself) is that by McPherson (1983).

Social stratification and inequality As for class, most introductory textbooks contain sections on this. A straightforward introduction is Kelsall, Kelsall and Chisholm (1984). Turner (1986) presents a short but comprehensive and very readable introduction to the sociology of equality and inequality. Tawney (1931) is a classic which continues to commend itself.

The empirical data in this book are sometimes directly limited by the nature of available sources. It is surprising, for example, that some areas of social differences, which one would judge from their treatment in the literature and media to be well catered for, turn out to be otherwise. Similarly, even where information is collected and recorded on a social stratification basis, it is not always published in that manner. This is particularly true of census material. Conversely, in some areas it has been possible to choose from a number of similar sources. It is therefore necessary to spell out the criteria upon which data have been selected and used.

Only British data have been used. The vagaries of research and publication do not allow the consistent use of data for Britain as properly defined. For example, official statistics are often published for the UK, Great Britain, England, Wales, England and Wales, Northern Ireland and Scotland, and are not always identical in content. As a rule of thumb, it may be assumed that wherever a choice was available the data and studies chosen are those which covered the largest part of Britain.

There is a bias towards the presentation and exposition of social class data. This reflects not only the emphasis of the book, which is based on the assumption of the fundamental role of class in the creation and perpetuation of social differences, but also the quantity of research which has used class as a variable.

Wherever possible the most up-to-date and large-scale research figures obtainable have been used. A selection has been made from available sources up to June 1988. The object is to present, as far as possible, a picture of contemporary British social differences. This is not to deny the importance of the historical/developmental perspective in the study of social differences but merely to assert that use, or particularly the overuse, of dated material without access to the contemporary is misleading and confusing. In any case, historical treatments of many of the areas dealt with in this present volume exist elsewhere. (For example, Halsey, 1972 and 1988, 1978, 1981 and 1986; Marsh, 1965; Routh, 1965, 1980; Sampson, 1982.)

Large-scale studies have been used, since a wider spread of samples and data probably better reflects social class and other differences in Britain as a whole. At the same time it is true that some of these studies suffer, in comparison with smaller-scale research, from superficiality, and disguise some illuminating trends and variations. Smaller-scale and/or greater-depth studies have been used where large-scale studies do not exist or where smaller studies, in the author's opinion, make a significant contribution to the aim of the book. Similarly regional variations, where these are central to the concern of the book (for example, the geographical distribution of the social strata), have been included (see Chapter 3).

Data have been presented in a straightforward way but without oversimplification. Data have been recast into standard-format tables. In the case of social class, class has always been used as the top axis. As a general rule figures and percentages have been rounded to the nearest whole number for the sake of clarity. Wherever available, an average of the percentages for the whole sample has been provided to facilitate comparison. In no cases have the social categories used in a piece of research or a publication been collapsed. The common combination of social classes in manual/non-manual or middle-class/working-class categories has thus been avoided. Not only does such a dichotomy oversimplify differences, but it typically disguises variations and trends between social classes. Similarly, ethnic groups have not been collapsed, though it has not been possible to avoid the grossness of some of the classifications used, including 'White' (see pages 75-82).

The text has been designed to be a commentary on the data. Apart from necessary introductory and linking passages, there has been little attempt to provide any exposition of the topics under consideration. This has been done because it is assumed that readers will have access to other appropriate descriptive and explanatory sources, or that their immediate interest centres, like that of this volume, on the phenomena of social class and other social differences rather than on the nature of their contexts and the processes involved.

Data have been organized around topics commonly found in textbooks and syllabuses. This strategy was adopted to make for cogent chapters, and also to facilitate references to, and from, the type of sources referred to above. At the same time a system of cross-referencing (see Chapter 2, subject index and text) enables readers to make comparisons between different approaches, to review aspects of research methodology and social institutions, together with social class, ethnicity, sex and age, as well as social differences.

Areas with few available data have not been ignored. Since part of the aim of the book is to illustrate the state of knowledge regarding social differences, comprehensive coverage has been an objective. To some extent this implies not only a review of the available data but also asking what ought to be or might be available. The author has pointed out the lack or paucity of data at places where he felt it necessary or where readers might have expected evidence to exist.

At one level this book is a collection of some of the existing empirical knowledge concerning social class, and other social differences in contemporary Britain. At another it is a textbook, not, however, simply a traditional one, since it is also a sourcebook – which complements and supplements existing books, knowledge, courses and teaching. This section describes in general terms the layout of the book, and some of the uses to which it can be put.

The bulk of the book, Chapters 3 to 10, consists of data on British social differences grouped around typical syllabus topics such as work, health, family, education, leisure. These are supported by a running commentary on the data. Each chapter constitutes a useful source of information on specific topics. Used with introductory texts in sociology and texts on particular topics, they provide a basis on which the reader may evaluate the evidence and arguments used both here and elsewhere.

Chapter 2 reviews the use of the forms of social stratification in empirical research. Together with a review of research on the subjective existence of social class, it contains all the operational classifications of social class used in the studies reported in the book. These are coded so that reference can be made to the definition involved wherever social class is used in the main body of the book. This avoids the misunderstandings which can arise from the simultaneous presentation of sets of social class differences based on different categories of social class. Similar treatment is afforded to the classifications of ethnicity.

It should be borne in mind that one of the virtues of the format used, and the major axis and emphasis of the book, is that it should encourage the reader to move outwards from an initial interest in a particular topic. It is hoped that the cross-referencing will encourage this. This book should generate in the minds of readers some interesting connections or correlations between data in different areas. Readers should be aware both of the value of this – in some ways it is the essence of sociology – and also of its dangers, since correlations are not necessarily causations. Indeed, in this area they rarely are since social differences, on their own, generally have no explanatory power. To produce data to show social class (or sex, or ethnic) differences in children's performances at school is merely to present a statement. To evaluate that statement, we have to ask certain questions such as, 'What does social class mean in this context?', 'What were the criteria of achievement?', and 'How and where was the evidence obtained?' While this book attempts to provide answers to such questions, it does not attempt to explain the reasons why such results should be obtained. It does not approach questions which seek to identify the actual factors, or to describe the processes involved. For these the readers must turn to other literature.

It is also necessary to point out that categorizing knowledge in any field is problematic. Chapters 3 to 10 provide cogent accounts of social differences observed in particular scenarios, and it is therefore possible that an impression of separateness may be deduced. This would be false, since differences feed into and out of the different topics and should be viewed as a single phenomenon. I hope that readers will appreciate these interrelationships, and that the cross-referencing in text and index will help them to explore and understand this important point.

Exploring differences

Since in a book about social differences these are emphasized, similarities can be overlooked. A valuable exercise is to review the data, looking for similarities between the social strata. These similarities, or what might be called 'non-data', lead one to speculate why such 'deviance' exists. Does it reflect the crudeness of the social classification used (especially in the case of social class and ethnicity) – or are other factors, specific to the topic under consideration, responsible?

Since this book is a commentary on data about social differences, it presents material in a relatively objective way – that is, independently of the observer's attitudes, values and beliefs. Though this is how many sociologists and others try to approach social reality, it is, generally speaking, a somewhat unusual approach.

While I cannot claim to be without values and beliefs, I have avoided, at least consciously, presenting data from any particular political or philosophical standpoint, preferring that the reader brings his or her own to the material, and perhaps develops it while in contact with the book. In no way am I subscribing to the common fallacy that facts speak for themselves. That they do not is witnessed by the endless debates and controversies aroused by almost all facts, but particularly social ones. For most people, their beliefs, feelings and ways of understanding are as important as the facts themselves. It is a valuable exercise, therefore, to attempt to appreciate the variety of ways in which the social differences outlined in this volume can be interpreted. The extremes of these interpretations are marked, on the one hand, by the view that the individual is completely responsible for his or her situation and, on the other, by complete economic and/or social determinism; and there are countless shades in between.

No mention is made in this book of the statistical significance of the social differences reported. Briefly, statistical significance is a mathematical concept used to decide whether a difference which has been observed is likely to have happened by chance – or, to put it the other way around, the degree of confidence one can have that the difference is a real one and would therefore be found again in further research. Social scientists are usually happy if a test shows that the likelihood of their results having occurred by chance is only one in a hundred, and reasonably content if it is as high as one in twenty.

The lack of reference to statistical significance in this text is, of course, intentional. In the first place, the large size of the samples used in most of the research reported means that quite small differences are in fact significant. For example, Newson and Newson (1968) point out, in reference to their sample (N = 700), that 'a difference of the order of about 10 per cent between any two percentages will usually prove to be significant statistically' (at the 0.01 level; that is, it is only likely to have occurred by chance one in a hundred times). This study had one of the smaller samples of the studies surveyed. In the second place, statistical significance does not tell one much about the importance of an observed difference in real terms. Very small differences in voting behaviour which are not statistically significant can, and indeed often do, have vitally important outcomes; while much larger differences elsewhere – say, in choice of washing powder – may be totally irrelevant except to washing powder manufacturers and sellers. It is, then, in 'commonsense' terms that the social differences in this book ought to be viewed and considered.

The differences presented in the chapters which follow vary considerably in size, but their importance stems not from that but from interpretation. For example, a difference of 0.6 per cent between female and male school leavers gaining two or more A level GCEs or equivalents, is capable of being viewed as insignificant or as an example of female disadvantage in education. Readers will undoubtedly interpret differences according to their own predisposition, values and beliefs. At the same time it is again a valuable experience to bear in mind the range of interpretations that may be used by others while viewing the data which follows and to review them in that light.

Few people will read this book without in some way identifying with its contents. Looking at the data relevant to oneself, one's family, acquaintances and experiences is likely to provoke agreement, amazement, disagreement or amusement. One interesting exercise for readers is to compare their own reactions with those of others; do one's friends, colleagues or fellow students have concepts of social class – and what are they? Are they willing to identify themselves as being members of a social class? Do their opinions, habits and actions fit their social class ascriptions? And what about ethnicity, sex and age?

In order to economize on space, nearly all the data in this book have been presented in the most straightforward way, that is, in tables of figures. Many people find that graphical presentations help understanding, though for others they are a distraction. Data can be presented in several graphical ways, including simple bar graphs and straight-line graphs, both of which can easily be produced from the tables in this book using, for example, social class as one axis and the other variable as the other axis. A very useful scale for such purposes is provided by using 1 millimetre to represent 1 per cent. Pie graphs – circles cut into sectors, the size of each representing a percentage or actual number – can also be used. More artistic representations, using people or objects of proportionately varying size, are possible for the talented who are so inclined.

CHAPTER 2

Social Class, Ethnicity, Sex and Age in Empirical Research

Social class is a concept readily understood by the average man, but relatively difficult to define. . . . In recognizing that social class is not a simple factor, but an amalgam of factors that operate in different ways in different circumstances, such a person has arrived at the same view as the professional sociologist.

D. MONK (1970)

This chapter provides a framework within which the data contained in the rest of the book can be viewed. It examines the ways in which social strata are defined and used in empirical research. It explores further many of the issues raised in Chapter 1 and in particular those to do with social class and ethnicity, which are obviously the most complex forms of social stratification. The detailed listings of the classifications of these two forms of stratification enable readers to refer from any study in the text to the actual classification used. The chapter contains an outline of the basis on which the research reported has been conducted.

The topics dealt with in this chapter are extremely complex. Indeed, many volumes have been devoted to each of them. Our consideration is limited to that seen as relevant to review the contents of this book. Readers wanting more detailed treatments will find these readily

27

available, and the references mentioned in this chapter will serve as a starting point.

SOCIAL CLASS

No new idea

A commonly expressed opinion about social class is that, if sociologists, political scientists and the like did not actually invent the term, then they are certainly active in maintaining and popularizing it. This contention demands some consideration since it is untrue. There are many clear historical indications that divisions in society which exhibit most of the characteristics associated with social class have long been recognized. Plato, some three hundred years before the birth of Christ, wrote about gold, silver and tin people. The rights and privileges of these groups he saw as being based on inheritance, effort and worth to society. Aristotle wrote that the best-administered states had a large middle class – larger if possible than both the others – which is clearly a reference to the different degrees of political power enjoyed by the classes. Romans used the term *classis*, which was a division of people on the basis of property and taxation. According to the Roman historian Pliny, the classes were judged by wealth measured in asses of brass. In the twelfth century John Ball wrote in his Text for Sermon on the Peasants' Revolt,

> When Adam delved and Eve span,
> Who was then the gentleman?

A clause in the 1844 Railway Act read '. . . it is expedient to secure to the poorer class of travellers the means of travelling by railway at moderate fares . . . Companies shall . . . provide for the conveyance of third-class passengers.' Such historical allusions, and there are many more, suggest that all the usual concomitants of class – status, power, wealth, and so on – have been recognized as a basis for dividing people into groups probably for as long as societies have existed. Ossowski (1963), for example, traces the ideas of class and class consciousness from what he calls biblical legends through to contemporary society.

However, Briggs (1960) has argued that in Britain the term 'social class', as we understand it, started to be used only after the Industrial Revolution. Previously, in the eighteenth century, society was perceived in terms of broad bands, reflecting the comparatively simple social structure of what was basically an agrarian society. Industrialization not only broke up the existing order of society, but replaced it with a greater division of labour. People became much more differentiated in their occupations, which varied in terms of skills and rewards. These differences, together with the great migration to the cities (urbanization), also brought about separation in residence, style of life and interests. Certainly the Victorian era was characterized by what might be termed 'class consciousness' or 'awareness'. It was perhaps not by chance that Marx chose England as the model on which to base the development of his ideas. However, the flames of class consciousness were probably fuelled not so much by Marx as by the lingering fears created by the French Revolution, and the reaction to those fears on the part of established power. Hence the established Church of England sang:

> The rich man at his castle,
> The poor man at his gate,
> God made them, high or lowly,
> And order'd there estate,

and this was echoed in the literature of the day. Dickens wrote:

> Oh let us love our occupations
> Bless the squire and his relations
> Live upon our daily rations
> And always know our proper stations.

Marwick (1980) has comprehensively surveyed the use of the images of class through the recent history of our society to the present, and related these to the reality of inequalities. While certain classical sociologists, namely Marx and Weber, saw social class as a central concept in sociology, other sociologists did not. It was not so much sociologists who were initially involved in the systematic collection of social class data as medically inspired census workers (see Stevenson, 1928, and pages 122–4 below), empirically minded social reformers such as Booth and Rowntree, and social statisticians (see Cullen, 1975). Subsequently, government and commercial market researchers have played a major role in empirical research using social class. They have helped in shaping research fashions, but more importantly they have sustained the use of the concept and provided much of the data in the field.

Objective and subjective views

In much the same way, discussions about the reality and the utility of social class have a history. There are two different ways in which social class can be seen to exist. First, classifications in terms of social class are seen, to some extent, as comparable to those used by a scientist wishing to classify physical phenomena. Such a classification – for example of moths – needs only to fit the known instances of moths, and to be recognized as useful by other scientists. In this sense it has what can be described as 'objective existence'. It does not rely for its usefulness or legitimacy on whether or not the moths themselves agree with it! Social class too has objective existence, as is clearly witnessed by the data presented in this book: social class is accepted and used by social scientists and others as a classification of the population they investigate. The concerns of sociologists, however,

30

are rarely as straightforward as those of other scientists. As has already been suggested, ideas of social class, or social differences, appear to exist, and to have existed, among the general population (see also pages 32–52). Indeed it could be argued that sociologists have only systematized pre-existing knowledge of divisions in human society. Here the second way of looking at the existence of social class comes in. To the extent to which people in society perceive, or accept, social class, it has a 'subjective existence'. Hence we can identify two longstanding concerns of sociologists about the classifications they construct. They are:

How well do they fit the social reality they are designed to explain, or describe?

How meaningful are they to the people to whom they apply?

These concerns, which are interrelated, form the basis of much current discussion about sociology, both inside and outside the discipline. They are far from new. Marx, who is recognized by many as being father to the present interest in, and use of, the idea of social class, clearly recognized them both. His basic idea was that there were two social classes: the bourgeoisie, who owned the means of production, and the proletariat, who did not – as he saw it, the exploiters and the exploited. However, Marx recognized that in the social situation he was describing there was another group who, while not owning the means of production, were saved from exploitation because they had skills and knowledge which the bourgeoisie needed. He used the term 'petit-bourgeoisie' to describe such people as doctors and lawyers, who were evidently not being exploited to the same degree as the proletariat. In a similar fashion Marx was concerned that the proletariat did not share his concept of their position in society. They failed to recognize their exploitation because, while they were a class 'in itself' (objective), they were not a class 'for itself' (subjective). To put it more forcibly, as Marx did (but only once), they were suffering from 'false consciousness' – that is, they did not recognize their 'real' situation as he had defined it.

These sorts of concern continue, and would be seen by some to be of central importance for this book and for the researches from which it uses data. Some sociologists would argue that in the social as opposed to the physical world objective classifications have only limited utility. They argue that a proper understanding of social reality will be achieved only when social scientists use concepts which have real foundations in the consciousness of the people involved. Whether the efficacy of the concept of social class is dependent on the realization and acceptance by the general population that social class exists is open to debate. If it is so dependent, then the discussion which follows is vitally related to the rest of the book. If the evidence there is found wanting – which would suggest that the concept does not exist in people's minds – then possibly the utility of the rest of the book would have to be held in doubt. Other sociologists would be more concerned with social class in the objective sense. They would judge its utility by how usefully the concept performed in research: does it, for example, reveal consistent and illuminating facts about society? This volume provides the findings of empirical research upon which such a judgement might be made.

How the public sees social class

There are a number of ways in which research can be conducted to answer the question: does the public recognize class? The simplest is to ask straightforward questions, such as: 'How many social classes would you say there are in this country? Can you name them? Which of these do you belong to?' (Martin in Glass, 1954); 'Some people talk about social classes, others say that there is no such thing. Do you think there are different social classes in Britain today or not?' (National Opinion Polls, 1972);

'Do you think there are social classes in Britain today?' (Reid, 1977b); 'You hear people talking about social class. If you were asked what social class you belong to, what would you say?' (Townsend, 1979). In answer to such questions, more than 90 per cent of those asked will agree that there are social classes, and a similar percentage will place themselves in a class, of whom about four-fifths will use the terms 'middle class' or 'working class'. Such responses have continuity through time. In the following selection of studies, the figure that follows each is the percentage that identified themselves as a member of a social class: Martin (Glass, 1954), 96; Runciman (1964), 99; Rosser and Harris (1965), 93; Kahan, Butler and Stokes (1966), 96; NOP (1972), 91; Roberts *et al.* (1977), 96; Reid (1978b), 97; Townsend (1979), 94; Aircy (1984), 96; Abbott and Sapsford (1987), 93.

The results of Townsend's study, unusual in presenting figures separately for the sexes, are summarized in Table 2.1. Townsend reports that his respondents' replies to the question (see above) were mostly similarly worded and could be grouped without difficulty. As can be seen, few people used terms other than 'middle class' (42 per cent including 'upper' and 'lower' middle) or 'working

TABLE 2.1 Unprompted self-ratings of social class[1] (percentages[2])

	Upper/ Upper middle	Middle	Lower middle	Upper working	Working	Other[3]	Rejected class[4]	No/hazy concept
Men	1.7	32	5	1.6	50	5	4	1.3
Women	1.5	39	4	1.4	43	5	4	1.6
All	1.6	36	4	1.5	46	5	4	1.5

1. The categorized replies to the question on page 33 above.
2. Percentages over 2 are rounded.
3. Included poor, ordinary, lower, lowest.
4. Some of these subsequently acknowledged class and applied it to themselves.

Devised from table 10.1, Townsend (1979).

class' (48 per cent including 'upper working'), only four people claimed to be upper-class, while 4 per cent, at least initially, rejected the idea of class and 1.5 per cent had no, or only a hazy, concept of it. (Other studies – for example, Butler and Stokes, 1969 – found that, after prompting, nearly all respondents would use these terms; their 'refusers' were only 1 per cent.) Notice that a larger percentage of women than men placed themselves in the middle, and fewer in the working class. Some of the studies listed above have also invited their subjects to respond to further questions aimed at gaining finer definitions of social class. Kahan, Butler and Stokes, for example, asked their subjects whether they belonged to the upper or lower parts of the class they had chosen. Few chose to modify their identification; of those who 'were' middle-class, 4 per cent changed – equally in both directions – while of the 67 per cent who said they were working-class, 9 per cent modified this to upper and 4 per cent to lower. Townsend presented his sample with a list of class names, but three-fifths opted not to change and a further fifth merely to be more specific within their original choice. However, a smaller group changed fairly dramatically: 6 per cent from middle to working (half to upper working) and 2 per cent from working to middle. The first group of 'changers' tended to have lower incomes than those maintaining the middle-class choice and were similar in several other respects to those who originally chose working class. Those changing from working to middle class had two features distinguishing them from those who 'stayed' working class: a larger percentage had had eleven years or more education and owned their own homes.

A reasonable conclusion from this type of research would be that the term 'social class' has a good deal of currency among the population at large and that people are prepared to use it of themselves. More interesting, perhaps, is the extent to which the subjective social class (that which respondents gave themselves) related to the objective scales based on occupation used by the researchers. Table 2.2 presents three views of this relationship. At the extremes, the correspondence between subjective and objective ratings is quite high: around four-fifths of those in the variously defined classes 1

TABLE 2.2 The relationship between subjective[1] and objective[2] social class (percentages)

Subjective social class	(a) Objective social class (MR/B)					
	I	II	III	IV	V	VI
Middle class	80	60	57	46	26	20
Working class	20	40	43	54	74	80

	(b) Objective social class (RG 70)					
	I	II	IIIn	IIIm	IV	V
Middle class	74	71	48	37	21	29
Working class	11	23	42	56	66	62

	(c) Objective social class (HJ/B)							
	1	2	3	4	5	6	7	8
MEN								
Middle class	81	69	62	50	45	22	16	11
Working class	15	29	38	47	54	76	82	86
WOMEN								
Middle class	86	72	68	55	47	30	23	15
Working class	12	26	30	43	51	68	74	82

1. These have been grouped: e.g., 'middle' includes 'upper' and 'lower middle'; in the cases of (b) and (c), respondents using other self-ratings have not been included – hence columns do not = 100%.
2. For details of objective social class scales see below: (a) p.73–4, (b) 53–8, (c) pp.66–8. In the case of (a) this refers to class of head of household in which respondent was living; in (c) married women were classified by occupation of husband, even when they themselves were employed.

Devised from (a) table 4.3, Butler and Stokes (1974); (b) table 2.1, Roberts *et al.* (1977); (c) table 10.8, Townsend (1979).

saw themselves as middle-class and a similar proportion in classes VI, V and 8 viewed themselves as working-class. Notice, however, that in each case sizeable minorities of the respondents were at variance with the objective classifications, this being particularly pronounced in the intermediary classes (those in the middle of the scales). The table shows that the changeover from a clear majority self-rating middle class to one of working class occurs around the manual/non-manual divide in the objective scales (which lies between IV and V in [a], IIIn and IIIm in [b] and 5 and 6 in [c]). In studies (a) and (c), however, a bare majority of the lower/routine non-manual classes (IV and 5) rated themselves working-class. Roberts *et al.* argue that non-conformers perhaps enhance the value of the manual/non-manual divide, since they deviate not only in self-rating, but also from their objective class in other ways. In their study there were differences in terms of political affiliation, trade union membership and so on. Butler and Stokes (1974) demonstrated that income was related to self-rating, especially among those in classes III, IV and V, those with higher incomes being more likely to choose the middle class. What is clear, in all cases, is that a substantial majority of those in manual classes rate themselves working-class, and similarly those in non-manual ones, especially the 'higher', see themselves as middle-class. It can therefore be argued that the public's use of the terms middle and working has a fairly strong relationship with social scientists' non-manual and manual classes.

Similar conceptions of social class have been found among young people aged between fifteen and twenty-one (see Table 2.3A). The objective middle classes (AB and C1) had clear majorities identifying with that class, while among the working classes, though a majority rated themselves as such, it was lower than among adults (43 per cent), and a third saw themselves as middle-class. Clearly, however, the pattern is the same as for adults, the self-rating matching the non-manual/manual divide

TABLE 2.3A The relationship between subjective[1] and objective[2] social class among young people[3] (percentages)

| Subjective social class | Objective social class (MR) | | | |
	AB	C1	C2	DE
Middle class	78	58	37	37
Working class	14	29	43	43

TABLE 2.3B The relationship between subjective and objective[2] own and household social class (percentages)

| Subjective social class | Women | | | | Men | |
| | By head of household | | By own job | | | |
	ABC1	C2DE	ABC1	C2DE	ABC1	C2DE
Middle class	81	31	78	31	79	28
Working class	19	69	22	70	21	72

1. These have been grouped: respondents not responding or using other replies are not shown, hence columns do not add to 100.
2. For details of objective social class scale, see pp.73–4 for A and p.00 for B.
3. Aged 15 to 21.

Devised from table 96, National Opinion Polls (1978), and tables 28, 29 and 30, Abbott and Sapsford (1987).

of the objective scale. These findings are interesting in two respects. First, they suggest that social class recognition occurs at an early age in Britain. Second, since most of these young people were classed according to their parents' or head of household's occupation (for definition, see page 90), the findings suggest that class recognition is produced through association as well as by involvement. Table 2.3B shows at least on the basis of the non-manual/manual divide that female self-ratings are very similar in respect to objective class whether this is on the basis of the occupation or class of head of household or of their own, and that both match well male self-ratings. In each case over three-quarters of those classed as 'middle' and about 70 per cent of those classed as 'working' rated themselves the same.

The existence of some divergence between people's occupational level and their idea of which class they belong to can be taken to suggest that factors as well as, or other than, occupation count when people are classing themselves. Again a number of inquiries have been made into the criteria or bases used in the public's definition of social class. Kahan, Butler and Stokes (1966) asked their sample to describe the sort of people they regarded as belonging to the middle and to the working class (see also pages 40–1 below). From the replies they identified the implicit frames of reference used. The major factor was occupation. A majority of respondents (61 per cent) chose this as the criterion for describing the middle class, and a larger one (74 per cent) chose it to describe the working class. These findings are very close to those of Martin a decade before this study, where about three-quarters of the subjects viewed the working class in terms of occupation. However, as the authors remark, occupation cannot be seen as the sole basis of perceived social class. Other factors such as income and education (which are obviously, but not exactly, related – see Chapters 5 and 8), social graces, parentage, etc., were present. These factors were further emphasized by the respondents when they were asked what they saw as being important in relation to social mobility (that is, the movement of people between the social classes: see pages 207–18). It would appear, however, that occupation was seen as the primary basis for social class judgements.

A different picture emerges from other research. Table 2.4 contains the results from three studies in which people were asked to choose from a list of possible criteria for social class (the actual questions are in the footnote to the table). Occupation is far from being the overall favourite, though in study (c) it was ranked second by men and fourth by women. Such difference between the

TABLE 2.4 Rank order of social class criteria[1]

(a) Men and women	(b) Women only
1 The way they speak (33)	1 Appearance and behaviour (53)
2 Where they live (28)	2 Family background (50)
3 The friends they have (27)	3 Attitudes, beliefs and political views (45)
4 Their job (22)	4 Style of life (42)
5 The sort of school they went to (21)	5 Education (38)
	6 Occupation (31)
6 The way they spend their money (18)	7 House/area in which they live (13)
7= The way they dress (12)	8 Income (13)
7= The car they own (5)	9 Prestige/standing in community (11)

(c) Men	Women	Men and women
1 Way of life (29)	1 Way of life (33)	1 Way of life (31)
2 Job (22)	2 Family (21)	2 Family (18)
3 Money (17)	3 Money (16)	3= Job (17)
4 Family (15)	4 Job (12)	3= Money (17)
5 Education (10)	5 Education (11)	5 Education (10)

(a) is based on answers to 'Which two of these would you say are the most important in being able to tell which class a person is?' A card was shown listing the factors above (in a different order). Rank order shown is on both items chosen, treated equally.

(b) is based on answers to 'Ring a number in the first column to show which you think is the best single indicator of a person's social class. In the second column the next best and then the third.' Items were listed in a different order to that shown above. Rank order is based on the percentage of women using each item in whole response, each item treated equally.

(c) is based on the answers to 'What decides what class you are in? Is it mainly job, education, the family you are born into, your way of life, money or anything else?' Rank order based on principal factor identified from those mentioned in the question.

1. Figures in brackets following the criteria are the percentage of respondents using that item.

Devised from (a) p. 21, National Opinion Polls (1972); (b) table 2 and data, Reid (1978b); (c) table 10.2, Townsend (1979).

sexes may be due to the fact that employment is more frequent among men and, possibly, has greater importance to them. The low ranking of occupation in study (b) may well be due not only to the fact that the sample was exclusively female but also predominantly middle-class – in terms of their and their husbands' occupation, their education, political views and income. It could be, then, that they were assuming a similarity of occupation and choosing criteria for class differences within the middle class or else thinking of class with respect to other women. The table also reveals that the women set great store by the family or the family background as a criterion of class and, given traditional values and situation, this is not perhaps surprising. At first glance the top ranking given to 'the way they speak' and 'appearances and behaviour' – studies (a) and (b) – may appear surprising. However, this and many of the differences in the findings of this type of research may be accounted for by the difference in the questions used as well as the differences among the samples and the situations in which they were surveyed. In study (a), for example, the question refers to what is important 'in being able to tell which class . . .' This could have directed attention to obvious and outward indications such as speech and residence. Similarly the presentation of lists probably leads to consideration of a wider range of factors than open-ended questions. In study (c) the term 'way of life' is, of course, very broad in its meaning, and probably, in people's minds, includes economic factors which, in turn, are likely to be related to occupation. Townsend argues that the fact that almost half the adults in his survey chose 'way of life' or 'family' as the criterion 'testifies to the public consciousness of what are the underlying and long-term or life-long determinants'. Study (a) also included further questions. Asked what gave away a person's social class, respondents chose, perhaps predictably, aspects of speech – what they spoke about, the way in which they spoke and their ability to carry on a long conversation. Barriers between the classes were seen, in descending order, as money (27 per cent), education, the way you speak, job and family background (between 17 and 13 per cent each, though many people chose more than one). Middle-class respondents were more likely to choose speech and intelligence, while the working-class respondents stressed money.

The survey reported by Abbott and Sapsford (1987) asked, 'What sort of person do you mean when you talk about the middle/working class?', and the answers were subsequently categorized. In respect of middle class, respondents most frequently used 'style of life/attitude', followed by 'income/standard of life' and 'occupation'; for working class the order of the first two was reversed (and between them was 'all who work'). The three meaningful factors could be interpreted either as separate and different or as related aspects of occupation/economic situation. From all the studies mentioned and others in the field, it is reasonable to conclude that the public sees social class as an amalgam of factors, importantly including but not necessarily predominated by occupation. This is not, of course, contradictory to the way in which class is viewed by social scientists who classify classes on the single criterion of occupation (see also pages 3–7 and 49–52 below).

A good deal of debate about the sort of research described above, particularly about its meaning and reliability, is evident in the literature. This amounts almost to a suggestion that 'You asks your question, and you gets your answer' – in other words, that the question is the vital factor, different questions producing different responses. Webb (1973), in describing a small-scale study in Liverpool, contrasts findings from two distinct types of question. In response to the first – a straight-forward request for a self-rating of social class – the middle-class respondents appeared to have a stronger class identification than the working-class respondents. A further question asked, 'What type of person are you

thinking of when you talk about people like yourself?'
(Webb described this as 'free self-alignment'.) In response
to this question it was the working-class respondents who
were most likely to reply in terms of social class. Two
quite different pictures had emerged. In his conclusion,
Webb restates a point basic to the whole enterprise of
social science research:

> if [social] class is a meaningful term in their [the respond-
> ents'] normal day-to-day existence – which the interview
> best taps – it is perhaps advisable to let the respondents
> themselves select the term rather than to have it thrust
> upon them.

It is possible to explore people's ideas and use of social
class quite indirectly. For example, the author has interviewed teachers, asking them to talk about the pupils or
students they teach, their objectives in teaching, differences between the family they grew up in and the one
they now belong to, and the people they spend their
spare time with (Reid, 1980b). When tape recordings of
the interviews were analysed, both direct and indirect
references to social class or social class imagery were
discerned. Obviously, though, this type of research, apart
from being time-consuming, relies heavily on the understanding and interpretation of the researcher; different
researchers might draw different conclusions about the
same data. My impression was that the teachers had
spontaneously used a general awareness of social group
if not social class differences, with respect to both their
professional and their personal lives. The extent of this
awareness appeared related to their biography and professional experience, awareness being highest among those
who had experienced contrasts. Professional experience
appeared to colour their view and understanding in that
many saw education, ability and interests as important
elements in social differences. In response to a final, direct
question, the general picture to emerge was of three social

classes: a very large middle class (with which they identified themselves); a very small upper class (based on real money and power); a lower class based on poverty and ignorance.

Platt (1971), in reviewing some of the 'affluent worker' study material in this field (Goldthorpe, Lockwood, Bechhofer and Platt, 1969), makes a parallel, if somewhat different, set of points to those of Webb. In the affluent worker study the researchers attempted to gain a view of their respondents' 'image of class' with a number of open-ended questions. From the replies the researchers argued that there existed three basic images of social class:

1. A 'power' model, with two classes, based on power and authority.
2. A 'prestige' model, with three or more classes, based on life-style, social background or acceptance.
3. A 'money' model, with one large central class, and one or more small ones, based on wealth, income and consumption.

Among the affluent manual workers who were the subjects of this study, the 'money' model was found to predominate. Thus 54 per cent subscribed to model 3 above, 4 per cent to model 1, and 8 per cent to model 2; the remaining 34 per cent were classed as using 'other' models – which is itself perhaps remarkable. A further specific single question asked the respondents to rank six occupations, presented together with their incomes on a card, in order of their 'standing in the community'. A comparison of the respondents' ranking with what was called an orthodox status order (i.e. objective ranking) revealed considerable unorthodoxy. Moreover, in stark comparison with the findings above, in this second context 61 per cent of the affluent manual workers used a 'prestige' model; and only 2 per cent a pure 'money' model. Platt suggests a number of alternative explanations for this incongruence:

> Respondents distinguished between 'social class' and 'standing in the community'.
>
> Their responses were differently coded (analysed) by the researchers.
>
> The social range of the occupations presented was very narrow, and because of this respondents used criteria other than money in discriminating between them.
>
> Since the class questions were general, and the 'standing in the community' question was specific, the respondents used different frames of reference in answering them.
>
> The financial information (income) given in the second question directed the respondents' attention away from money.

Clearly one has to agree with the author that 'questions which are intended to refer to the same general area of a subject-matter may in fact vary and consequently create difficulties of interpretation. In particular caution is necessary in comparing findings from questions of different kinds, and in generalizing from them.'

Townsend (1979) identified two models within his sample's images of class.

1. A status model in which the population is arranged in at least three ranks – upper, middle and lower class – or more finely defined with subdivisions.

2. A power model in which there are two ranks – working class, and an employer, rich or prosperous class.

He argues that the two logically distinct models are crudely combined in public and scientific discussion and that the terms 'middle' and 'working' class are inconsistent. He suggests that people who ascribe themselves to the middle class are implying that there are three classes, and that they have advantage over one without superiority over the other. Those aligning themselves with the working class are resisting the acknowledgement of disadvantage of inferiority by using a term which carries the implication that other classes are non-working or non-productive and therefore inferior. He concludes that the illogical combination of terms from the two models produces a subjective distortion of reality in that very few people unreservedly believe they belong to the uppermost or lowest class in society.

Britten (1984) suggests that the sexes differ in their models of class. She found that working-class men saw two classes and themselves in the lower; middle-class men saw three classes and themselves in the middle. Women irrespective of class saw three classes and themselves in the middle. Abbott and Sapsford (1987) tentatively suggest that the majority of women in their study 'see society more in terms of a continuous hierarchy than in terms of bounded classes'. What is clear is that women's views on social class have in the past either been neglected or investigated in the same way as men's. This is currently being questioned, as is the applicability of existing social class classifications (see also pages 47–9). Indeed, more fundamental issues have been raised concerning the extent to which a woman's class position is determined by that of her husband/partner and whether class or sex is the more important axis of social differentiation – and even whether gender can be seen as class. According to Goldthorpe (1983), married women's class is appropriately determined by husband's occupation, both because of the women's different involvement in the labour market and because their disadvantage in most areas of social life makes them dependent. Others claim women have dual class, as housewife and as paid worker (Walby, 1986), or that women can and should be separately classified (Stanworth, 1984). What does seem pretty obvious is that class and gender qualify one another – relationships between the sexes are different in the different classes, being male or female in any class is also different. The debates on these topics are unresolved and ongoing and as yet have not directly affected the type of research reported in this book.

A second type of evidence on the existence of social class in the subjective sense arises from the interest of researchers in whether their social class definitions, based on occupation, have any commonly accepted basis. The most famous British study was that connected with the development of the Hall-Jones scale. Hall and Jones said to their respondents, 'We should like to know in what order as to their social standing you would grade the occupations in the list given to you' (Hall and Jones, 1950). Details of the scale can be found on pages 66–8 below. The question was basically that which Stevenson claimed to have answered, but presumably without the fieldwork, with reference to the Registrar General's social classification of 1921 (Stevenson, 1928). The list contained thirty occupations and the respondents apparently had no difficulty in ranking them according to the criterion supplied. A close correspondence between the standard (objective) classification of the authors and the undirected (subjective) judgement of the sample was found. Hall and Jones concluded that there were no major differences of opinion among those tested, and that the consensus was greater than they had expected.

A somewhat similar, though more sophisticated, approach was adopted by the Oxford Social Mobility Project. Part of this study was concerned with the construction of a grading scale for all male occupations on the basis of popular assessment (see Goldthorpe and Hope, 1974). In the initial inquiry respondents were asked to rank a list of forty occupations according to four criteria. These were: standard of living, power and influence over other people, level of qualifications and value to society. Once again the people involved had little difficulty, in general, in performing the task. The main findings were as follows. The four criteria were not treated as the same by respondents and the distinctions made between them were shared to an extent by all. The degree of agreement in ranking on the basis of the four criteria was very high indeed. Separate analysis of ranking by the sexes, three age groups and four occupational categories confirmed overall agreement with some minor differences. In repeating the exercise after two or three months, respondents displayed stability in their ranking. In the light of these findings the conventional criterion of 'social standing' was seen as the most useful. Hence, in the main study respondents were asked to rank representative occupational titles according to their social standing. From these rankings was produced the Hope-Goldthorpe scale, further details of which are on pages 68–72 below.

Such evidence suggests that the public can and will rank occupations with a fair degree of ease and similarity. This facility is not limited to British samples, being evident in other Western societies; there is also a similarity in rankings by people in different societies (see, for example, a review of studies in twenty-four countries: Hodge, Trieman and Rossi, 1966; and Trieman, 1977). However, nearly all these researches have involved 'nonconforming' respondents whose ranking has been at variance with the majority's. In the past there has been a tendency to dismiss such divergent views as being idiosyncratic, rather than socially or sociologically important. One might expect such differing views of the overall structure to arise from the fact that the respondents were occupying different positions in that structure. However, some studies have revealed these differences within the same occupational level. Young and Willmott (1956) even found a small minority of manual workers who thought that miners and other manual workers ought to rank alongside doctors and above lawyers and managers.

Some research has explored how different concepts of the occupational structure differ in socially significant ways. For example, Coxon and Jones (1974), reporting on a preliminary analysis of just such a study, suggest that 'it seems ... that people with similar occupational histories, rather than current occupational membership, make rather similar judgements'. Coxon and Jones have also questioned the meaning of the ranking of occupations. The fact that the public agree in evaluating occupations does not, they suggest, allow one to assume that people share the same perception (view) of, or cognition of (way of thinking about) the occupations involved. Or, as they illustrate:

> In discussing 'images of society' there is a danger of jumping from the fact that people talk about society in a particular way (say as a polarized dichotomy) to inferring that they *perceive* it that way. But this is by no means inconsistent with the hypothesis that such people are *just* as aware of social differentiations and gradations, and can equally make as fine discriminations around those positions, as a person who tends to talk in terms of graded hierarchies.

Coxon and Jones, influenced by cognitive psychology, have criticized the sociological use of occupational images and the ranking of occupations on the criterion of their general desirability. They contend that these are based on unwarranted assumptions and oversimplifications (Coxon and Jones, 1978), and have argued that what is necessary is a thorough examination of the cognition involved in ranking and a full exploration of the social meaning of occupations; this they have undertaken (Coxon and Jones, 1979; Coxon, Davies and Jones, 1986; and, for a similar exploration, see Davis, 1979). This type of research certainly reveals some of the thinking and values implicit in people's ranking of occupations and their use and concept of social class. Quite how this knowledge, with its depth and subtlety – long recognized by many social scientists – might be incorporated into an instrument for research on any scale has yet to be displayed.

There are some current developments in the operationalization of social class, which while they do not feature in the research reported in this book nevertheless are of considerable interest. These are attempts to produce women's social class classifications, in response to the perceived shortcomings of classing households solely by their heads (typically male) and classing women on the basis of classes developed in respect of men's paid employment, which both ignores unpaid work and fails to discriminate accurately women's occupations and part-time employment. Some new scales combine the class of spouses/domestic partners using existing classifications (Heath and Britten, 1984; Pahl and Wallace, 1985), as did for example that used in the NSHD (see pages 72–3), or include some aspects other than occupation (Osborn and Morris, 1979). Others have constructed separate classifications for women, which cover in more detail women's occupations and both full- and part-time work (Murgatroyd, 1982; Dale, Gilbert and Arber, 1985). Roberts (1987) and her colleagues are constructing a scale that is intended not only to distinguish occupations but also to allocate a class to housewives and measure both labour market and life-style position.

Some conclusions

This review has pointed to the complexity of the idea of social class. It has also outlined a variety of approaches to its understanding. Several general conclusions can be drawn. It cannot be, nor has it been, claimed that, simply because the public, when invited, is willing to recognize and identify with social class, therefore class is a fundamental and meaningful factor in their everyday life. To make such a claim empirically would require extensive observation of behaviour and exploration of language and thought. This clearly lies outside the scope of empirical research on any large scale and presents severe methodological problems in collection, classification and presentation. In any case it is very far from clear how such knowledge (some of which exists now) could be operationalized into a social classification capable of being used for survey purposes.

It is hardly surprising that deeper or indirect questions elicit increasingly complex or even conflicting shades of recognition and understanding of social class. This can be expected in any involved and emotional subject. Numerous examples might be used. People happily answer direct questions about the existence of God (interestingly enough, fewer agree here than about class; see Tables 9.3 and 9.4). However, if you probe people's ideas of God or deduce them from indirect questions or conversation, let alone behaviour, considerable differences will be observed. Not only is there a tremendous range of ideas, witnessed by differences in religions and denominations, but you would be led to consider whether some who claimed there was not a God in fact shared a great deal in common with those who believed. Without delving into psychology, it is obvious that what people declare is some sort of combination of what they think and feel in response to a given question or stimulus in a particular social context. Social survey techniques cannot be expected to go much further than to collect and classify these. Therefore, while it is not being suggested that social class classifications used in empirical research encompass the whole of people's subjective awareness, it can be claimed that they contain sufficient for their purpose. Social class is used in research to identify large, general groups in society. These groups are recognized by users as relatively broad and heterogeneous. Given this level of generality, the evidence on the public's responses to direct questions about social class in the early part of this review may be accepted as adequate support. Clearly a two-way process is at work here. While social scientists pay attention and perhaps respond to the public's subjective awareness, the public, in turn, responds to what it sees and understands of social science classifications. That the two are more than coincidental is, then, hardly surprising. In any case, as was pointed out in Chapter 1, social class classifications do not necessarily stand or fall by their research. The weight of the views expressed here is neatly summarized in the following:

> Many of the theoretical concepts which sociologists use – social class . . . [etc.] – are complex, intricate and rich in meaning. They do not lend themselves easily to being reduced to their elements, specified in terms of indicators and measured; yet if social scientists are to exploit the explanatory potential of large-scale survey research, using representative sampling and quantitative techniques to investigate causal relationships, this is a necessary step along the way (Bulmer, 1977).

This review should prevent readers from assuming that sociology's treatment of social class is as naive as some popular writings and the work of a few sociologists might suggest. Even though only empirical research was taken into account, the discipline was seen to have a continuing, active and deep concern with the notion of social class. While this has as yet borne little fruit in terms of new research methods – and most of the new scales of social class have yet to be used in any extensive research – this may be merely a matter of time. The continuing abundance in this field of theoretical and descriptive works, which have not been discussed here, reflects an imbalance between theory and research in British sociology. Further, readers have been enabled to compare the simplicity of the operationalization of social class with the complexity of its concept and understanding. Another contrast would be provided by comparing the contents of this book with those of the theoretical works referenced in Chapter 1, pages 17–9.

Finally, this discussion has also emphasized the discontent about social class shared by sociologists and the general public. Both groups, it would appear, subscribe to the existence of social class in broad general terms, while disagreeing to some extent about its nature, structure and meaning. Both groups share the basic idea that occupation is a factor in social class, but not the only one. They are therefore equally likely to be unhappy with the use of occupation as the sole criterion of social class, social standing or status in society. But neither party, apparently, can put forward any simple or complex alternative definition, and both are likely to resort to occupation as the best, the only or the most convenient 'shorthand' reference-point in terms of which to pin down this extensively used, though hazy, concept.

SOCIAL CLASS CLASSIFICATIONS

This section provides an outline of the common classifications of occupations into social classes used in empirical research in Britain. It also provides a referencing system (see Table 2.5). This allows the reader to refer from each table in this book to the classification of social class

TABLE 2.5 Key to codes used for social class classifications

Each code begins with letters (see left-hand column). Any numbers which follow refer to the year of classification, and a letter following an oblique stroke denotes a modification. The right-hand column shows the page(s) in this book on which details of the classification will be found.

Code	Source	See pages
DE	Department of Employment	64–5
FES	Family Expenditure Survey	65
HJ	Hall-Jones	66–8
HG	Hope-Goldthorpe	68–72
MR	Market research	73–4
NS	National Survey	72–3
RG	Registrar General's social class	53–8
RG SEG	Registrar General's socioeconomic group	58–63
UC	UCCA	65–6

used in the study in question. The following list is not exhaustive: inclusion signifies only that the particular classification has been used in a study referred to in the text.

The classification of occupations into social classes is an extremely complex business, because there are so many occupations. The Registrar General has a list of around 25,000 separate occupational titles, which are grouped into 350 occupational codes (*Classification of Occupations*, 1980), each one of which has a social class classification. Space dictates that only brief outlines of the classifications be presented below. Interested readers will find that the full classifications, and instructions for their use, are generally available, and sources for these are included below.

Registrar General

The census contains two forms of classification of occupations which are of direct relevance to the present text.

Social class (RG)

Since the census of 1911 it has been the practice to group the occupational units of the census into a small number of broad categories known as social classes. The present categories derive from the 1921 census (see Stevenson, 1928; and Leete and Fox, 1977). Indeed, as has been pointed out above, and as will be obvious from the rest of this section, the Registrar General's social classes form the basis of all the commonly used social class classifications in Britain. The basis and rationale of this categorization are as follows:

> The unit groups included in each of these categories (i.e. social classes) have been selected so as to ensure that, so far as is possible, each category is homogeneous in relation to the basic criterion of the general standing within the community of the occupations concerned. This

criterion is naturally correlated with, and its application conditioned by, other factors such as education and economic environment, but it has no direct relationship to the average level of remuneration of particular occupations. Each occupational unit group has been assigned as a whole to a Social Class, and is not a specific assignment of individuals based on the merits of a particular case (*Classification of Occupations*, 1970).

These categories have been selected in such a way as to bring together, so far as is possible, people with similar levels of occupational skill. In general each occupation group is assigned as a whole to one or another social class and no account is taken of differences between individuals in the same occupation group, e.g. differences of education or level of remuneration. However persons of a particular employment status within occupational groups are allocated . . . by the following rules (*Classification of Occupations*, 1980).

The social class appropriate to any combination of occupation and status is derived by the following rules:

(a) Each occupation is given a basic Social Class.
(b) Persons of foreman status whose basic Social Class is IV or V are allotted to Social Class III.
(c) Persons of manager status are allocated to Social Class II except for the following: Social Class I for General Admininstrators, national government [Deputy Secretary and above], Social Class III for club stewards, scrap dealers, general dealers, rag and bone merchants.

In 1970 (c) read, 'Persons of manager status are allocated either to Social Class II or III, the latter applying if the basic class is IV or V.'

Until the census of 1971 the social classes were titled as follows:

I	Professional etc. occupations
II	Intermediate occupations
III	Skilled occupations
IV	Partly skilled occupations
V	Unskilled occupations

The Registrar General recognized that social class I was wholly non-manual and that social class V was wholly manual (*Classification of Occupations*, 1960). The other social classes contained both manual and non-manual occupations. Researchers usually ignored the mixed nature of classes II and IV, normally treating II as non-manual and IV as manual. There was some concern about social class III, which clearly contained a large proportion of both types of occupation – some 49 per cent of the occupations of economically active persons in Great Britain in 1971. Researchers quite commonly subdivided this class into IIIn (non-manual) and IIIm (manual). This practice was sometimes indulged in by census and government researchers, who on occasion extended the process to classes II and IV as well. The 1971 census adopted the division of social class III as a standard procedure. Contemporary census material uses the classification on Table 2.6, which illustrates the types of occupation falling into each class.

It is important to appreciate that this classification, like most of those below (see particularly the next), is a combination of occupation and employment status. Hence when viewing the table bear in mind that foremen in occupations in classes IV and V are allotted to class III, and most types of manager are class II, though some are I or III. There have been changes from one census to another in the allocation of occupations to the social classes. Details of these changes are to be found in the relevant volumes of *Classification of Occupations* (1960/66/70/80). The most extensive changes occurred between the census of 1951 and that of 1961. The most important change in the classification was the total exclusion of members of the armed forces in 1961. The net result was to increase significantly the 'unclassified' groups. Other changes reflected a reordering of occupations. For example, aircraft pilots, navigators and engineers were changed from social class III to II, draughtsmen from II to III, postmen and telephone operators from III to IV, and

TABLE 2.6   Typical occupations[1] of each social class
(RG 80)

I PROFESSIONAL, ETC.
Accountant, architect, chemist, company secretary, doctor,
engineer, judge, lawyer, optician, scientist, solicitor, surveyor,
university teacher, veterinarian.

II INTERMEDIATE
Aircraft pilot or engineer, chiropodist, farmer, laboratory
assistant/technician, manager, proprietor, publican, member of
parliament, nurse, police or fire-brigade officer, schoolteacher.

IIIn SKILLED NON-MANUAL
Auctioneer, cashier, clerical worker, commercial traveller,
draughtsman, estate agent, sales representative, secretary, shop
assistant, typist, telephone supervisor

IIIm SKILLED MANUAL
Baker, bus driver, butcher, bricklayer, carpenter, cook,
electrician, hairdresser, miner (underground), policeman or
fireman, railway engine driver/guard, upholsterer.

IV PARTLY SKILLED/SEMI-SKILLED
Agricultural worker, barman, bus conductor, fisherman,
hospital orderly, machine sewer, packer, postman, roundsman,
street vendor, telephone operator.

V UNSKILLED
Chimney/road sweeper, kitchen hand, labourer, lift/car park
attendant, driver's mate, messenger, railway stationman, refuse
collector, window/office cleaner.

---

1. In alphabetical order. These are mainly basic occupation titles; foremen
   and managers in occupations listed are allotted to different classes (see
   pp. 53–4 above).

Devised from pp. 1–89 and appendixes B1 and B2, *Classification of
Occupations* (1980).

lorry drivers' mates from IV to V. These changes reflect the fact that the basic social gradient of the classifications is being retained within the changing economic and social structure of Britain. An important change in the application of the classification was the use of different age groups (twenty to sixty-four years in 1951) and fifteen to sixty-four in 1961). Obviously, therefore, straightforward comparisons between social class data based on the 1950 and 1960 scale are of dubious utility. Details of the effect of the reclassification in this way of economically active males can be found in Reid (1977a, Table 3.24) and in *Occupational Mortality* (1971, Table D1). Fortunately for the purpose of this book, the changes that occurred in the 1966, 1970 and 1980 classifications were comparatively minor. 'Social class and socioeconomic groups (see below) were retained unchanged and the only changes in the allocation of individual occupations have been necessitated by the revision of the classification of occupations' (*Classifications of Occupations*, 1980).

Wherever the code RG follows 'social class' in the tables and text of this book it indicates the direct use of the Registrar General's scale outlined above. The numbers which follow RG (60,66,70,80) refer to the particular year of the classification used.

Modifications

In some studies, for a variety of reasons, certain of the classes are combined. These combinations are clearly indicated in tables and text – for example, I and II. The descriptive terms 'non-manual' and 'middle' obviously refer to classes I, II and IIIn, while 'manual' and 'working' refer to classes IIIm, IV and V.

RG/A: a more substantial modification by Routh (1965, 1980) which divides RG classes into seven classes, two of which are further subdivided (A and B).

Routh class	RG class	Descriptive definition
1A	I	Higher professional
1B	II	Lower professional
2A	II	Employers and proprietors
2B	II	Managers and administrators
3	III	Clerical workers
4	III	Foremen, supervisors, inspectors
5	III	Skilled manual
6	IV	Semi-skilled
7	V	Unskilled

Socioeconomic groups and class (RG SEG)

Since the 1951 census, occupations have also been classified into socioeconomic groups. In 1961 the original thirteen groups were replaced by seventeen and these have been used since. The aim of the grouping is laid out as follows:

Ideally each socioeconomic group should contain people whose social, cultural and recreational standards and behaviour are similar. As it is not practicable to ask direct questions about these subjects in a population census, the allocation of occupied persons to socioeconomic groups is determined by considering their employment status and occupation (*Classification of Occupations*, 1960).

... to bring together people with jobs of similar social and economic status. The allocation of occupied persons to socioeconomic groups is determined by considering their employment status and occupation (*Classification of Occupations*, 1980).

The groups are as follows:

1. *Employers and managers in central and local govern-*

ment, industry, commerce, etc. – large establishments (with twenty-five or more employees).

2. *Employers and managers in industry, commerce, etc.* – small establishments (with fewer than twenty-five employees).

3. *Professional workers – self-employed* – in work normally requiring qualifications of university degree standard.

4. *Professional workers – employees* – in work as for 3.

5. *Intermediate non-manual workers* – employees engaged in non-manual occupations ancillary to professions but not normally requiring university degree standard qualifications; artistic workers not employing others; self-employed nurses, medical auxiliaries, teachers, work-study engineers and technicians; foremen and supervisors (non-manual), i.e. employees other than managers in occupations included in 6, who formally and immediately supervise others engaged in those occupations.

6. *Junior non-manual workers* – employees, not exercising general or supervisory powers, engaged in clerical, sales and non-manual communications and security.

7. *Personal service workers* – employees engaged in service occupations caring for food, drink, clothing and other personal needs.

8. *Foremen and supervisors – manual* – employees, other than managers, who formally and immediately supervise others engaged in manual occupations, whether or not themselves engaged in such occupations.

9. *Skilled manual workers.*

10. *Semi-skilled manual workers.*

11. *Unskilled manual workers.*

12. *Own-account workers (other than professional)* – self-employed in any trade, personal service or manual occupation not normally requiring training of university degree standard and having no employees other than family workers.

13. *Farmers – employers and managers* – persons who own, rent or manage farms, market gardens or forests, employing people other than family workers.

14. *Farmers – own account* – persons who own or rent farms, market gardens or forests and have no employees other than family workers.

15. *Agricultural workers* – employees who tend crops, animals, game or forests, or operate agricultural or forest machinery.

16. *Members of the armed forces.*

17. *Occupations inadequately described.*

The last two groups are generally disregarded, but the rest of the classification has been extensively used. Government research, particularly the *General Household Survey*, has also made use of a collapsed version referred to here as socioeconomic class. (Note that the *Classification of Occupations*, 1970 and 1980, also refer to socioeconomic class – in those cases a cross-classification between social class RG and socioeconomic groups – but that classification has not been used in this book.) This collapse is achieved, as shown below, by placing the fifteen groups into six categories. These categories are not identical with social classes, but are clearly parallel, particularly to RG 80. In some tables in this text, data collected for all the socioeconomic groups shown above has been presented according to the collapsed categories.

In the present text the socioeconomic classes above are referred to as social classes. They are distinguished both by a separate code, and by the use of ordinary numbers

Socioeconomic class	Socioeconomic groups	Descriptive definition
1	3,4	Professional
2	1,2,13	Employers and managers
3	5,6	Intermediate and junior non-manual
4	8,9,12,14	Skilled manual (with own account – professional)
5	7,10,15	Semi-skilled manual and personal service
6	11	Unskilled manual

as opposed to the Roman numerals used for social class (RG).

As in the case of social class above, a two-figure number follows RG SEG, indicating the particular classification used (60,66,70,80), and any letter indicates a particular modification.

Modifications

RG SEG/A: a five-group classification used by Sillitoe (1969) in a study of an urban population, hence excluding

Socioeconomic class	Socioeconomic groups	Descriptive definition
1	1,2,4	Professional, employers and managers – large establishments
2	2,5	Intermediate non-manual, employers and managers – small establishments
3	8,9	Skilled manual, supervisors, foremen
4	6	Junior non-manual
5	10,11	Semi-skilled, unskilled manual

agricultural occupations. A further characteristic that will be noted is that junior non-manual workers are placed between the skilled manual and the semi- and unskilled workers.

RG SEG/B: a fourfold collapsed classification used for example by Woolf (1971), which includes all seventeen groups.

Socioeconomic class	Socioeconomic groups	Descriptive definition
1	1,2,3,4,13	Managerial
2	5,6,7,12	Non-manual
3	8,9	Skilled manual
4	10,11,14,15, 16,17	Other manual and miscellaneous

RG SEG/C: a five-point classification used by the National Foundation for Educational Research. A notable characteristic of this scale is the inclusion of the armed forces (socioeconomic group 16), all of whom were classified as semi-skilled workers.

Socioeconomic class	Socioeconomic groups	Descriptive definition
1	1,2,3,4	Professional
2	5,6,7	Clerical
3	8,9,12,13,14	Skilled manual
4	10,15,16	Semi-skilled manual
5	11	Unskilled manual

RG SEG 50: This book also refers to two pieces of research which used a classification based on the original 1951 census's socioeconomic groups. These groups were as follows:

1 Farmers

2 Agricultural workers

3 Higher administrative, professional and managerial

(including large employers)

4 Intermediate administrative, professional and managerial (including teachers and salaried staff)
5 Shopkeepers and other small employers
6 Clerical workers
7 Shop assistants
8 Personal service
9 Foremen
10 Skilled workers
11 Semi-skilled workers
12 Unskilled workers
13 Other ranks in the armed forces

RG SEG 50/A: a five-group classification used by Butler and Bonham (1963):

Socioeconomic class	Socioeconomic groups	Descriptive description
1	3,4	Professional
2	5,6,7	Non-manual
3	9,10	Skilled manual
4	2,8,11,12	Semi- and unskilled
5	Residual and 1	Remainder

RG SEG 50/B: a four-group classification used by the Ministry of Education:

Socioeconomic class	Socioeconomic groups	Descriptive definition
1	3,4	Professional, managerial
2	5,6,7,8	Clerical and other non-manual
3	9,10	Skilled manual
4	2,11,12	Semi- and unskilled

Department of Employment (DE and FES)

This government department uses two quite different and separate occupational classifications for its research and publications.

DE: The first of these is extensively used in the *New Earnings Survey, British Labour Statistics Year Book* and *Employment Gazette*. It consists of a list of some four hundred occupations which are arranged into the following main occupational groups:

I	Managerial (general management)
II	Professional and related; supporting management and administration
III	Professional and related in education, welfare and health
IV	Literary, artistic and sports
V	Professional and related in science, engineering, technology and similar fields
VI	Managerial (excluding general management)
VII	Clerical and related
VIII	Selling
IX	Security and protective service
X	Catering, cleaning, hairdressing and other personal service
XI	Farming, fishing and related
XII	Materials-processing (excluding metal)
XIII	Making and repairing (excluding metal and electrical)
XIV	Processing, making, repairing and related (metal and electrical)
XV	Painting, repetitive – assembling, product-inspecting, packaging and related
XVI	Construction, mining and related not identified elsewhere
XVII	Transport-operating, materials-moving and storing and related
XVIII	Miscellaneous

The above groups are clearly different from social class and socioeconomic class as outlined above. They are not capable of translation into social classes as such. They can however be divided into non-manual (the first nine groups, left-hand column) and manual (the second nine, right-hand column). In this way they divide the working population along a commonly accepted basic dichotomy of social class. They are capable, then, of a rough comparison with the collapsed form of social class (RG) and socioeconomic class RG SEF mentioned above.

FES: The second classification is used in the *Family Expenditure Survey*. It claims to be derived from the Registrar General's classification (outlined above), but is clearly not identical with it. Until 1977 seven groupings were used; 1–5 were as below, 6 was manual workers, and 7 was members of Her Majesty's Forces. The present classification has eight groupings, as follows:

	Used in this text
1 Professional and technical workers	1
2 Administrative and managerial workers	2
3 Teachers	
4 Clerical workers	
5 Shop assistants	
6 Skilled manual	3
7 Semi-skilled manual	4
8 Unskilled manual	5

The unusual feature of this classification is the inclusion of individual occupations (3, 4 and 5). However, in this book these are omitted and of the resulting five categories, 1 and 2 are non-manual and 3, 4 and 5 are manual classes with different levels of skill.

UCCA (UC)

The Universities' Central Council on Admissions until recently used a four-category division of occupations devised from the Registrar General's classification in

Classification of Occupations, Appendix B, which lists twenty-seven orders. The unusual feature of the UCCA scale was its complete lack of differentiation of manual occupations, which the RG divides according not only to level of skill but also to employment status. Non-manual occupations were divided, however, so that there is some correspondence between these and the RG's non-manual social classes, though, for example, UCCA's class 1 contained occupations in RG classes I and II.

UCCA social class	RG's occupational order	Descriptive definition
1	XXV	Professional, technical and artists
2	XXIV	Administrators and managers
3	XXI–XXIII, XXVI	Clerical, sales, service, sport and recreation workers
4	I–XX	All manual occupations

Hall-Jones scale (HJ)

This scale was developed in the late 1940s and was based on a scale used in the pre-war Merseyside survey (Jones, 1934). Its development involved a consideration of the subjective social grading of occupations (Hall and Jones, 1950) which is discussed above on pages 46–48. Subsequently it has been used and modified by other researchers. The resulting classification of occupations was into seven social classes:

1 Professional and high administrative
2 Managerial and executive
3 Inspectional, supervisory and other non-manual higher grade
4 Inspectional, supervisory and other non-manual lower grade

5 Skilled manual and routine grades of non-manual
6 Semi-skilled manual
7 Unskilled manual

Modifications

HJ/A: the best-known modification · that by Goldthorpe, Lockwood, Bechhofer and Platt (1969, Appendix A) – involved both a more comprehensive classification into eight 'status levels' with subdivisions (shown in the left-hand column below) and a threefold classification (right-hand column below):

Occupational status level	*Summary classification*
1(a) Higher professional, managerial and other white-collar employees	
(b) Large industrial or commercial employers, landed proprietors	
2(a) Intermediate professional, managerial and other white-collar employees	White-collar
(b) Medium industrial or commercial employers, substantial farmers	
3(a) Lower professional, managerial and other white-collar employees	
(b) Small industrial or commercial employers, small proprietors, small farmers	
4(a) Supervisory, inspectional, minor official and service employees	Intermediate
(b) Self-employed men (no employees or expensive capital equipment)	

5	Skilled manual workers (with apprenticeship or equivalent	
6	Other relatively skilled manual workers	Manual
7	Semi-skilled manual workers	
8	Unskilled manual workers	

HJ/B: Townsend's modification was to divide Hall and Jones's class 5, producing eight classes, and to reallocate some manual occupations from their original coded level of skill to that given them in the Registrar General's scale.

1 Professional
2 Managerial
3 Supervisory – higher
4 Supervisory – lower
5 Routine non-manual
6 Skilled manual
7 Partly skilled manual
8 Unskilled manual

Derived from Townsend (1979, Appendix 6).

Hope-Goldthorpe scale (HG)

This scale was derived from a modified set of the 223 unit groups of occupations used by the Office of Population Censuses and Surveys (*Classification of Occupations*, 1970), ordered in relation to the results of ranking exercises according to their 'social standing' (see pages 46–8 above). From the complete scale of 124 categories a collapsed version of 36 was derived. These were achieved without combining major employment status divisions (employer/manager/employee) or types of occupation (professional/technical/non-manual/manual) and resulted in the following:

1   Self-employed professionals
2   Salaried professionals: higher grade
3   Administrators and officials: higher grade[1]
4   Industrial managers: large enterprises
5   Administrators and officials: lower grade
6   Technicians: higher grade
7   Large proprietors
8   Industrial and business managers: small enterprises
9   Self-employed professionals: lower grade
10 Salaried professionals: lower grade
11 Farmers and farm managers
12 Supervisors of non-manual employees: higher grade
13 Small proprietors
14 Managers in services and small administrative units
15 Technicians: lower grade
16 Supervisors of non-manual employees: lower grade
17 Supervisors of manual employees: higher grade[1]
18 Skilled manual workers in manufacturing: higher grade
19 Self-employed workers: higher grade
20 Supervisors of manual employees: lower grade
21 Non-manual employees in administration and commerce
22 Skilled manual workers in manufacturing: intermediate grade[1]
23 Skilled manual workers in construction
24 Smallholders without employees
25 Service workers: higher grade
26 Semi-skilled manual workers in manufacturing
27 Skilled manual workers in transport/ communications/services/extraction
28 Service workers: intermediate grade
29 Self-employed workers: intermediate grade

30 Skilled manual workers in manufacturing: lower grade

31 Agricultural workers

32 Semi-skilled manual workers in construction and extraction

33 Semi-skilled manual workers in transport/communications/services

34 Service workers: lower grade

35 Unskilled manual workers

36 Self-employed workers: lower grade

[1] Officers, NCOs and Other Ranks in the armed forces are assigned to categories 3, 17 and 22 respectively.

Based on Goldthorpe and Hope (1974, Table 6.6).

A social class scale has been derived by combining these thirty-six categories into seven classes, as follows:

Class	Hope-Goldthorpe categories	Descriptive definition
I	1,2,3,4,7	All higher-grade professionals, self-employed or salaried higher-grade administrators/officials in central/local government and public/private enterprises (including company directors), managers in large industrial establishments, large proprietors
II	5,6,8,9,10, 12,14,16	Lower-grade professionals/administrators/officials, higher-grade technicians, managers in small business/industrial/service establishments, supervisors of non-manual workers

III	21,25,28,34	Routine non-manual, mainly clerical, sales, and rank-and-file employees in services
IV	11,13,19,24, 29,36	Small proprietors, including farmers/ smallholder/self-employed artisans/ own-account workers other than professional
V	15,17,20	Lower-grade technicians (whose work is to some extent manual), supervisors of manual workers
VI	18,22,23, 27,30	Skilled manual wage-workers, all industries
VII	26,31,32, 33,35	All manual wage-workers in semi- and unskilled grades, agricultural workers

Derived from Goldthorpe, Llewellyn and Payne (1980, pp. 39–41).

Modifications

HG/A: an eight-class modification achieved by removing HG category 24 from HG class IV and category 35 from class VII. With these changes the modified scale then reads as the original with the addition of:

Class	Hope-Goldthorpe categories	Descriptive definition
VIII	24,35	Agricultural workers, including smallholders

Halsey, Heath and Ridge (1980).

HG/B: a collapsed version of three classes as follows:

	HG classes
Service class	I and II
Intermediate class	II, IV and V
Working class	VI and VII
	or VI, VII and VIII

HG/C: a collapsed four-class version, which separates the self-employed and foremen and technicians as classes.

	HG classes
Salariat	I and II
Routine non-manual	III
Petty bourgeoisie	IV
Foremen and technicians	V
Working class	VI and VII

Heath, Jowell and Curtice (1985).

National Survey of Health and Development (NS)

This survey used a rather interesting classification which, unlike the others quoted in this section, was not based solely on occupation. The families which reared the children who were the subject of this survey were classified by the occupation of the father together with the educational and social class background of the father and the mother. The initials in brackets which follow each social class title below are those used in the tables in this text.

Upper middle class (UM)
Father has non-manual occupation
and (a) both parents had secondary-school education and middle-class upbringing (i.e. had father with non-manual occupation)
or (b) both parents had secondary-school education and one parent had middle-class upbringing

72

or   (c) both parents had middle-class upbringing and one parent had secondary-school education

Lower middle class (LM)

All other fathers with non-manual occupations

Upper manual working class (UW)

Father has manual occupation

and   (a) either or both parents had secondary-school education

and/or (b) either or both parents had middle-class upbringing

Lower manual working class (LW)

Father has manual occupation

and   (a) both parents had elementary-school education only

and   (b) both parents had working-class upbringing (i.e. had father with manual occupation)

Market research (MR)

Most commercial social, advertising and consumer-research enterprises whose work is reported in this book use the following social grading of occupations originating from the Institute of Practitioners in Advertising. Fuller details of this grading can be found in Monk (1985).

A *Upper middle class*
Successful business persons (e.g. self-employed/manager/executive of large enterprise); higher professionals (e.g. bishop, surgeon/specialist, barrister, accountant); senior civil servants (above Principal) and local government officers (e.g. chief, treasurer, town clerk).

B *Middle class*
Senior, but not the very top, people in same areas as A.

C1 *Lower middle class*
Small tradespeople, non-manual, routine administrative, supervisory and clerical (sometimes referred to as 'white-collar' workers).

C2 *Skilled working class*
D *Semi-skilled and unskilled working class*
E *Those at the lowest levels of subsistence*
   Including OAPs, those on social security because
   of sickness or unemployment, and casual workers.

The national percentages of informants falling into
these classes are: A,3; B,14; C1,22; C2,28; D,18; E,15.

An interesting feature of this classification is the
inclusion of armed forces personnel, in contrast to their
exclusion by the Registrar General. Indeed it provides a
good illustration of the grading involved. For example,
army personnel are allocated: Lieutenant-Colonels and
above, A; Captains and Majors, B1; Sergeants, Sergeant
Majors, Warrant Officers and Lieutenants, C1; Corporals
and Lance Corporals, C2; Privates, D.

Modifications

The full classification of six classes is only rarely used.
Combinations of classes – for example, A and B, and D
and E – are clearly indicated in tables and text.
MR/A: a modification involving a division of class C1
producing seven classes, though the last is often omitted:

Butler and Stokes class	MR class	Descriptive definition
I	A	As for MR above
II	B	As for MR above
III	C1	Skilled supervisory non-manual
IV	C1	Lower non-manual
V	C2	As for MR above
VI	D	As for MR above
VII	E	As for MR above

Butler and Stokes (1969 and 1974).

ETHNICITY

This is the most problematic form of social stratification, in terms both of its conceptualization and operationalization. While occupation is an easily understood and gathered piece of information for research purposes, ethnicity has a wide range of meanings and connotations. Dictionaries provide a starting point, for example in stating that ethnicity 'relates to, or is characteristic of, a human group having racial, religious, linguistic and certain other traits in common' (Hanks, 1979). Essentially, then, ethnic groups are those identified by, or based on, cultural differences. Culture may be defined as all that is learned by an individual as a member of a group and society, and consequently covers nearly all aspects of human existence. Most important are distinctions of language (or linguistic style), religion, ways of living and behaviour, underlying which are such factors as values, beliefs and perceptions of the world. So theoretically the number of ethnic groups in a society could be infinite and depends on the strength of the criteria used to distinguish them. Only at an extremely high level of abstraction is it possible to talk of a (or the) British culture, since in reality it consists of a set of subcultures which belong to a series of groups. Hence in the general sense it can be seen that we are all part of an ethnic group, that the number of these groups is potentially large, and ethnic groups have always been a feature of society. Typically, however, the term is commonly applied only to minority groups whose identification is clearly visible, and has inappropriately become almost synonymous with those whose physical appearance/colour/way of life differs dramatically from the majority of society.

It is also clear that ethnicity and its basis are not only culturally defined, but also culturally specific. For example, differences between Roman Catholics and Protestants may appear as vital distinctions in Northern Ireland, but relatively unimportant, if not trivial, in other parts of the UK. The distinction between Jew and Gentile has displayed wide variation and importance across time in Britain, let alone world-wide. In essence, then, ethnic groups exist whenever and wherever (*a*) one group is seen by others as being different, (*b*) a group sees itself as being different to others, (*c*) both *a* and *b* occur. It is not often possible to discern which, or what balance of these factors are at work in a society or situation. In the case to hand, it can be argued that *a* operates when, for example, such groups are classified on the basis of answers to census questions on country of birth; that *b* is operative when individuals respond to questions about their ethnicity or ethnic origins (see next section), but obviously both take place within the context of *c*. Our considerations so far are neatly summed up by Yinger (1986):

> Thus ethnicity has come to refer to anything from a sub-societal group that clearly shares a common descent and cultural background . . . to persons who share a former citizenship although diverse culturally . . . to pan-cultural groups who, however, can be identified as 'similar' on the basis of language, race or religion . . .

Ethnicity can be seen to have a vital subjective element, since cultural, let alone national, origins or similarities do not necessarily of themselves lead to identification. In many ways, to class a British-born person whose family came from the Caribbean as West Indian is as appropriate/inappropriate as classing a Yorkshire-born person whose family came from Scotland as Scottish. In both cases either ascription may be right or wrong and, indeed, be dependent upon circumstance and intent. What is fact is that countless groups of immigrants from many differing origins have merged and all but disappeared in our society. By the same token many of those presently recognized as members of ethnic minorities may reject any classification other than British, particularly if they have lived their whole lives in Britain. Others, of course, may strongly identify with a very concisely defined group based on a number of well-defined criteria.

Looking at the use of ethnicity and ethnic group in social research, it is noticeable that both interest and definition have been almost exclusively concerned with the most easily recognized, relatively large groups of Asians and West Indians. Indeed, it might well be claimed that colour rather than ethnicity has been the major factor and that ethnicity has become the socially acceptable term to refer to colour (replacing the earlier, equally misleading, euphemism – immigrant). Certainly many other groups, such as the Irish, Jews and Poles, have been barely recognized, though a Royal Committee of Inquiry into the Education of Children from Ethnic Minority Groups did make mention of Chinese, Cypriot, Italian, Ukrainian, Vietnamese and travellers' children as 'examples of particular types of communities we considered to be particularly deserving of attention in their own right' (*Education for All*, 1985). Even so, almost all the report treats Asians and West Indians as if they were single and homogeneous groups. In fact, of course, each is composed of groups with wide differences in culture (including religion and language), origins, background, and residence in Britain. Placing such groups into a single category is similar to placing Britons (English, Welsh, Scots) into the category European. The West Indies comprise a series of islands whose cultures display a wide range much as does Europe, and not only is the subcontinent of India similarly varied, but some Asians in Britain have origins elsewhere, particularly in Africa.

At the same time there are compelling practical reasons why ethnicity in empirical research is often defined in terms of a small number of heterogeneous groups. All ethnic minorities are just that. A representative sample of the British population would include something of the order of 4.5 per cent of persons who could be included in all such groups (see page 117). To subdivide such a minority into precise groups, however based, results in group sizes not really suitable for analysis. For example, the *National Dwelling and Housing Survey* (1979), which covered almost seventeen thousand households, found only twenty-nine with heads who identified themselves as African. Specific surveys of ethnic minority populations that provide greater detail are relatively rare and sometimes do not allow for comparisons – though see PSI survey below.

As is the case with social class, so the utility of classifications of ethnicity can be seen to depend on how well they fit the purpose for which they are required. If this is to identify broad groups which share a location in society and have a similarity of access to social wealth, in order, for example, to identify inequality and monitor change and the effect of social policies, then their utility rests on how well they serve that purpose. That such a classification does not match the subjective understanding of those classified, in itself does not detract from its usefulness. However, if an ethnic group classification ignores or incorporates such a range that differences within groups are larger than those between them, then its utility is low or non-existent. Obviously this is true if we use White as an ethnic group, if only because it puts together all social classes, and it is also true for the other groups in common use. Such evidence as we have clearly suggests not only that there are class differences within the Asian group, but also that there are these and other differences between identifiable subgroups of Asians. For example, the social class and earnings of the occupations of the Indian, Pakistani, Bangladeshi and African Asian groups display differences (see Brown, 1984a, and pages 98–102 and 169–70 below). This both questions the suitability of the present classifications of ethnicity and, once again, illustrates the necessity of viewing forms of social stratification as part of a single phenomenon rather than in isolation. Unfortunately, existing data only allow this relatively rarely. Even so, the groupings in use do have utility for comparing the social circumstances of ethnic minorities and others in our society, recognizing that many of the differences that emerge amount to inequalities and addressing the question of whether these should exist and persist (and if not, how they might be relieved).

The identification of ethnicity and the collection of ethnic data are controversial and sensitive subjects. Ethnic minorities often form the basis of, and are subject to, social inequalities and injustices. Their members often face prejudice, discrimination and conflict from others. As a consequence some ethnic minority members object to and deny such categorization, while others emphasize and develop it. Politically, ethnic-based information may be seen as essential, in order to identify ethnic minority disadvantage, as a base on which to design social policy for its relief, and, subsequently, to monitor change. For the ethnic minorities involved it can, within the context of racial tension, immigration and citizenship law, and scepticism over political intent, arouse considerable suspicion. Summing up the protracted search for fully acceptable census questions on ethnicity, Sillitoe (1987) identifies a very small minority 'who feel it is objectionable in principle to include a question on race/ethnicity, of any kind . . .' He sees the only ways of resolving this issue as 'not only by assurances about confidentiality . . . but also by showing them, by practical examples, how the data will be used to the tangible benefit of the ethnic minorities'.

ETHNIC CLASSIFICATIONS

There are only two bases for ethnicity used in the research reported in this book – country of birth and self-identification of group membership from a set of provided alternatives. Of the five main surveys from which data have been used, two asked about country of birth and three about group membership (one of the latter also included visual identification). The questions and classifications used are as follows.

Census

Under the heading 'Country of birth' respondents were asked, 'Please tick the appropriate box.' The boxes were England, Wales, Scotland, Northern Ireland, Irish Republic, Elsewhere. (In Scotland, Scotland appears first.) 'Please write present name of the country.' Responses to the last box were subsequently classified under the following major heads and subheads:

Old Commonwealth (Australia, Canada, New Zealand)
New Commonwealth (Africa, Caribbean, Asia, Mediterranean, remainder)
Foreign countries (Africa, America, Asia, Europe – Community, remainder – rest of the world)

Full details of all countries involved can be found in *Definitions, Census 1981, Great Britain* (1982). Published analyses use a variety of combinations of countries.

At the time of writing it was announced that trials were to be held of the question on ethnicity with a view to its inclusion in the 1991 census. The recommended question was developed from a series of trials (see Sillitoe, 1987):

Please tick appropriate box. (If the person is descended from more than one group, please tick the one to which the person considers he or she belongs, or tick box 4 and describe person's ancestry in space provided.) (1) White. (2) Black. (3) Asian (please also tick one box below to show ethnic origin or descent: Indian, Pakistani, Bangladeshi, Chinese, Other Asian – please describe below). (4) Any other race or ethnic group (please describe below).

Policy Studies Institute (Third Survey)

The aim of this survey was to gain information from two representative national samples, one of black people of Asian and West Indian origin, the other of white people. The interviewer's schedule contained the following questions and instructions:

'In what country was . . . [each person in household]

80

born?' (If UK, Africa or other), 'What country did his/her family come from originally?' (If in doubt, code origin of father's father.) Codes available: UK, West Indies/Guyana, India, Pakistan, Bangladesh/East Pakistan, Africa (Asian origin), Africa (other), Other (write in), Don't know.

Published analyses (Brown, 1984a) use White, West Indian and Asian, with the last sometimes broken down into Indian, Pakistani, Bangladeshi, African Asian.

Labour Force Survey

In the course of an interview subjects are asked, 'To which of the groups listed [on a card] do you consider you belong?' The card lists: White, West Indian or Guyanese, Indian, Pakistani, Bangladeshi, Chinese, African, Arab, Mixed origin, Other. Those indicating either of the last two replies are asked to give more detail; if they use solely one of the other replies they are so reclassified. For some published analyses the groups listed are combined. The groups listed have varied somewhat between LFSs (see separate editions or Sillitoe, 1987). Published analyses normally use all categories.

National Dwelling and Housing Survey

Interviewers asked the following question:
'To which of the groups listed on this card do you consider . . . [person] belongs?' The card lists: White, West Indian, Indian, Pakistani, Bangladeshi, Chinese, Turkish, Other Asian, African, Arab, Other (please state), Mixed (please state). The interviewer's instructions note, 'This is an opinion and you should accept whatever the respondent says.' If possible 'Other' was subsequently recoded. Published analysis uses White, West Indian, African, Indian/Pakistani/Bangladeshi and Other. In analyses the following groupings were used: White (White and Turkish), West Indian, Indian/Pakistani/Bangladeshi, African, Other (Chinese, Other Asian, Arab, Other, Mixed). Of

the 16,824 households surveyed the numbers other than White were very small – 152, 186, 29 and 217 respectively.

General Household Survey

Household members are classified as white or coloured according to the interviewer's assessment of their skin colour. The percentage of those interviewed classified as coloured varies from year to year, e.g. 4.6 in 1984, 3.7 in 1985 (*GHS 1985*). Since 1983 the person answering the schedule has been asked, 'To which of the groups listed on the card do you consider . . . [each member of the household] belongs?' On the card is listed: White, West Indian/Guyanese, Indian, Pakistani, Bangladeshi, Chinese, African, Arab, Mixed origin, None of these groups.

GHS 1985 notes that the numbers in ethnic minority groups are small and as yet only population and age distribution of the combined 1983 to 1985 samples have been published.

SEX AND AGE

Within the context of empirical research these two forms of social stratification are almost entirely straightforward. Information on both is easily collected, being freely given and available. The level of accuracy in data on sex is almost complete, and while that on age may show some variation, this is most unlikely to be seriously misleading. It is possible however to raise certain questions about the terminology and categorizations used.

There is a continuing debate over the terms sex and gender. For some, sex refers only to the physical differences between male and female, all other differences being seen as culturally determined or affected. Such people prefer to use the word gender in reference to all but physical manifestations of men and women. As will be clear from our considerations in the first chapter, the author fully subscribes to the central importance of cultural production of such differences. However, he sees some fallacies in the use of sex to refer only to physical, and gender to refer only to social characteristics of female and male. In real life both aspects always coexist, so sex is never simply a difference of genitals or reproductive function but is inevitably and firmly set within a specific cultural setting. Sex, like all other human attributes, including intelligence, becomes meaningful and observable only when overtly expressed, at which point it is so interrelated with culture that it is for all intents and purposes inseparable. Hence in the following tables and text which compare or relate men and women on a host of social variables, sex is used as the major dimension, and the exposed differences are seen as gender.

The categorization of age is either done on the basis of numerical intervals, such as twenty to twenty-nine, or in respect to social or legal definition. Examples of the latter are: those related to compulsory school attendance, between the ages of five and sixteen; adulthood, eighteen; retirement, men sixty-five, women sixty. Choice is often related to the topic under consideration or in order to form groupings of a sample which will allow for comparison. Hence the age classifications in this book display variation, but are always stated in numerical terms. Descriptive age categories, such as children and the elderly, are defined in the same terms.

Both sex and age are then being used in what we have termed an 'objective' manner (see pages 30–2). This is not to deny the importance of their subjective reality and its interplay with the objective. In the case of age, the relationship between an individual's chronological age, his or her understanding of it and associated behaviour and its reception shows wide variation. Similar differences can be seen in respect to sex. In choosing not to explore these and other aspects of sex and age the writer is not ignoring their importance. He is rather recognizing and reflecting their more simplistic use than social class and ethnicity in the research that forms the basis of this book.

This section provides an introductory outline of the basis on which the reported data have been collected. Mainly because the studies reported are for the most part large-scale they use only a limited range of the methods available to the social scientist. Basically, social surveys are concerned with the answers given to questions by a large number of people (usually a sample), which are then combined and separated in various ways.

Sampling and research methods

The census is the only survey which attempts to collect information about an entire population – in the everyday meaning of that word – in this case all the inhabitants of Great Britain. In social science 'population', or sometimes 'universe', can also be used to mean all the members of an institution or group, for example a population of university students, of mental-hospital patients, of adolescents, or workers etc. A population can therefore vary considerably in size – from, say, all schoolchildren in Yorkshire to the children in the fourth year at Frog Island Secondary School. Most studies in this book have used a sample – that is, a proportion of the population which is representative of that population.

Social scientists adopt a number of sampling techniques with the aim of reducing the numbers involved while retaining as accurately as possible the characteristics of the whole group or population. It needs to be borne in mind that sampling in social surveys involves the possibility, if not the probability, of error – that is, failure to gain complete accuracy. This is not to suggest that a survey of the whole population is necessarily superior or preferable. The larger the study, the longer the likely lapse between collection and publication of data, which gives rise to its own inaccuracies. For example, material from a census continues to be published years after the event. Similarly the larger the survey, the more likely it is to be limited in the extent and scope of its investigation.

Technically the purest form of sampling is pure random in which each person in a population has an equal chance of being selected for the sample. This could be achieved by numbering each member and drawing out (bingo style) the required number or percentage (say 10 per cent). The most commonly used form is systematic random sampling, which is much more straightforward and time-saving. It involves starting at a random number and then selecting every nth person. All random sampling assumes that the list of the population involved (called a 'sample frame') has no particular order or arrangement which could have any bearing on the investigation. It would be the ideal method for producing a sample to test the quality of beer in bottles leaving a production line. However, most sample frames used in social research are not of this type, but typically have a definite order. Consider, for example, an investigation into schoolchildren: the most readily available sample frame would be their class registers, where the children's names might well be recorded by class (and hence by age and/or ability), by sex (boys first), and in alphabetical order. In such a case it is usually more appropriate to take a sample from each part (called a 'stratum') of the list – for example, a proportion of the boys and girls from each class – than to treat all the registers together as a single sample frame. As Conway (1967) points out, 'stratified samples have smaller sampling errors than simple random samples of the same size. Also each stratum is adequately represented in the sample . . .' For these reasons, together with convenience, speed and accuracy, nearly all the surveys reported in this book have used a form of what can be termed indirect sampling, often involving sampling strata at more than one level.

Obviously the value of any investigation depends to a certain extent on what proportion of the sample, and hence the population, are contacted and actually co-operate in the research. Clearly a low response rate, particularly in a specific part of a sample, is likely to produce distorted or dubious findings. To avoid this, replacements to non-respondents can and often are sought – indeed, most researches include the identification of substitutes in their sampling design.

Quota sampling – sometimes called representative sampling – is a non-random form of sampling. Whereas in random sampling interviewers may well work from a list of names and addresses, with a quota sample they would have a list of characteristics of the people to interview. The list might contain, for example, 'five married, middle-class women between the ages of forty-five and sixty-five'. They would then set out to find such women and interview them. Obviously their choice would be affected by the availability of people, and would depend upon their diligence and honesty. Quota sampling is dependent on previous knowledge of the population – that is, given the proportions of, say, sex, age and occupation of a population, a quota sample is drawn up by scaling down these proportions to a convenient size. Random sampling works on the assumption that careful sample constructions would lead to the same result. Quota sampling does not have replacement problems, since the interviewer can continue approaching people until his or her quota, and hence the sample, is completed. In fact, both types of samples, when completed, are often justified by being compared to known population characteristics – known, that is, from the census. Quota sampling is widely, but not exclusively, used by commercial social research enterprises.

Even using the best sampling techniques does not guarantee a properly representative sample. There may be unseen or unexpected bias or circumstances. In such cases, or to allow for meaningful comparison of unequally represented subsamples or minorities, weighting is commonly used. This is a straightforward mathematical technique which weights up and/or down certain parts of a sample, and hence their responses, so that they more accurately reflect the known distribution of a given population.

Finally there is volunteer or opportunity sampling which is sometimes used when research interest centres on a particular, identifiable group. Examples would be the readers of a publication, audiences at an event, the 'captive' samples of pupils or students in educational establishments, patients in hospital, and so on. The method is particularly economic and useful where the group involved is relatively small and widely dispersed among the population, when few would be found in a sample using either of the other techniques outlined above. At the same time problems may be caused through lack of knowledge of differences between volunteers and the rest, or of peculiarities of those subjects 'found' in a particular place or institution.

With few exceptions the acquisition of information from respondents in large-scale research is by questioning in one of two forms: either an interview, used here to refer to a situation in which the questioner is face-to-face with the respondent, and in which the questioner records the answers; or a questionnaire, used here to refer to a situation in which respondents record their replies on paper in response to written questions.

There are basically two types of questions: *Open-ended* are designed to elicit respondents' feelings, attitudes or knowledge in their own words, which may be recorded verbatim or on tape, or categorized according to a schedule provided. *Pre-coded* are those provided with a set of alternative answers from which a choice is expected. These alternatives can range from yes/no, to a lengthy list usually presented on a card. Most interview schedules contain both types of question. As a general rule, in nearly all commercial research together with most large-scale social research either pre-coded questions are used, or the interviewer classifies replies into pre-coded categories. In any case, it is true that in order to analyse answers to open-ended questions a researcher has to group or code the answers after the interview stage of the research. Answers to open-ended questions are, of course, very rich sources of people's experience and expression, and can be very effectively used to add colour to research reports – as a reading of, for example, the Newsons' work will reveal.

Questionnaires are really interviews expressed as form or pen-and-paper alternatives. They can contain open-ended questions but more typically have an emphasis on, or are exclusively, pre-coded. Most questionnaires are delivered to, and collected from, one specific individual by another. Normally they are completed by respondents on their own, though sometimes with an investigator present.

Interviews and questionnaires are by far the most commonly used methods in the research reported in this book. The only other basic method used is documents, which can be of two types. First, existing records and reports compiled or kept for purposes often far removed from research but useful for it. These are many and varied. Simple examples are educational and occupational applications and records, archives of public and social institutions, biographical dictionaries, membership lists, and so on. Similarly, previous research can provide data that are capable of being reworked or used in conjunction with ongoing research. Such data can also sometimes assist research into areas for which they were not necessarily designed or intended. Potentially rich and well-used fields here are the census and other governmental investigations. The second type is 'created' documents which normally result from a researcher asking respondents to keep a diary or record of particular events or behaviour over a period of time. For example, *Family Expenditure Survey* is based partly on a daily record book of expenditure kept for fourteen consecutive days.

Obviously, much greater detail can be obtained on the individual studies reported in this book by reference to the original. More comprehensive and extensive treatment of social science survey methods can be found, at an introductory level, in McNeil (1985) and Morison (1986); and more detailed accounts in Bulmer (1984), Marsh (1982) and Miller (1983). Readers who are unfamiliar with the methodology, scope and limitations of the census will find these succinctly covered by Benjamin (1970). Further useful references are: Cox (1976), who sets the census into a historical and comparative context within the discipline of demography; definitions used in the census are in *Definitions, Census 1981* (1982); comprehensive details of the GHS are to be found in the introductions and appendices to each report.

Households and heads

Social research is not only concerned with individuals. A major area of interest is the basic social institution of the family. However, for a number of fairly obvious reasons, many people do not live in families — by any standard definition of that word. Because of this, the difficulty of 'recognizing' a family and the demands of large-scale research, most work in this field is done on the basis of households rather than families.

Household Until 1980 the OPCS used the following definition of household:

> one person living alone or a group of people, who all live regularly at the address . . . and who are all catered for by the same person for at least one meal a day (Atkinson, 1971).

Thus members of a household need not be related by blood or marriage, though the term household includes families. From 1980 the OPCS definition changed to:

> one person or a group of people who have the accommoda-
> tion as their *only* or *main* residence and . . . who *either* share
> at least one meal a day *or* share the living accommodation
> (McCrossan, 1985)

The GHS is concerned with 'private households', therefore excluding institutional dwellings such as hotels, hospitals, boarding schools, barracks, prisons, etc. Once it has drawn a sample of households, the aim of its research is to discover information about these and/or the individuals who compose them.

Head of household Research using the household as its basic unit normally classifies these by the head of household and may so classify its members (for example, by social class). Heads of household are defined by OPCS by the relationship between one of its members and the household accommodation.

> He or she is the person or the husband of the person who
> owns the accommodation or who is legally responsible for
> its rent or has the accommodation as an emolument or
> perquisite or has it by virtue of some relationship with
> the owner who is not a member of the household. When
> two members have equal claim to be head, the following
> is applied: if they are of different sex the male is chosen;
> if they are of the same sex the elder is chosen (*GHS 1984*).

Obviously such a definition results in a clear preponderance of male heads of household. For example, the *GHS Introductory Report* (1973) found that four-fifths of heads were male, and that three-fifths of female heads were heads by virtue of being the only member of a household. *GHS 1985* revealed little change: 76 per cent of heads of household were male, and 65 per cent of female heads were the sole member of their household.

CHAPTER 3

The Distribution of Social Strata in Britain

> There can hardly be a town in the South of England
> where you could throw a brick without hitting the
> niece of a bishop.
>
> GEORGE ORWELL (1937)

This chapter provides a view of the distribution of social
strata in our society, together with some of the interrela-
tions between them. As such it provides a context within
which to review the data on social differences contained
in the following chapters.

SOCIAL CLASS

The only national figures relating social class to the
entire population of Great Britain are to be found in the
census. Theoretically it would be possible to allocate each
person enumerated in the 1981 census, some 55, 556, 911,
to a class. More meaningful is to view that part of the
population who have or have had an occupation, that is
those aged sixteen years or over who are economically
active – either in work or seeking it – retired or permanently sick. Of this part of the population some 31
million persons were classified by social class, 19 million
men and 12 million women. The main categories not
classified were members of the armed forces and those
whose occupations were inadequately described. Hence
Table 3.1 presents as accurate a picture as is available
of the national distribution of social class.

TABLE 3.1 Percentage distribution[1] of the social classes in Great Britain

| | Social class (RG 80) | | | | | | |
	I	II	IIIn	IIIm	IV	V	All
Males	5	22	12	36	18	7	100
Females	1	21	39	9	22	7	100
Both	4	22	22	26	19	7	100
As % of each class							
Males	90	63	33	87	57	62	63
Females	10	37	67	13	43	38	37

1. Of economically active, retired or permanently sick who were classified.

Calculated from table 16A, *Economic Activity*, *Census 1981*, *Great Britain* (1984).

The following subsections illustrate how other forms of social stratification are related to, and affect, the distribution of social class. They also review regional differences in class and the class composition of different industries.

Sex

As can be seen from the top section of Table 3.1, if both sexes are taken together the largest single social class is IIIm, which represents some 26 per cent of the population, followed by IIIn and II with 22 per cent each. Overall, 48 per cent are classified as non-manual and 52 per cent as manual. The difference between the social class distribution of the sexes is very marked, and clearly related to the fact that men and women follow different types of occupation. Only in classes II and V is there any close similarity in the proportions of males and females. In class I the proportion of males to females is some five to one, a situation reversed in the case of class IIIn, where the proportion is approximately one to three. Although a much higher proportion of women are classified as non-manual than men (61 compared to 39 per cent), the majority are to be found in IIIn, the routine, lower-skilled end of the range of occupations. This pattern is interestingly reflected in the manual classes. Here the proportion of men is larger than women (61 and 39 per cent), but men are more often to be found in IIIm, that is skilled occupations – 36 per cent of men, 9 per cent of women – and somewhat less often in partly skilled occupations (IV) – 18 compared with 22 per cent.

A parallel view of the same data is provided in the lower section of Table 3.1, the sex composition of each social class. Note that because of the way in which the population has been defined the overall representation of the sexes is 63 per cent men, 37 per cent women. This allows for comparison with each class, the split being reproduced in classes II and V. Basically the figures underline the fact that classes I and IIIm are predominantly male – about nine in every ten people in them are men – and that only class IIIn is predominantly female – some two-thirds of its members are women.

When looking at sex differences here, it should be borne in mind that it is typically male occupation which provides the basis of social class allocation in respect to married women, families, children and so on. Obviously, the major reason for this is methodological: a smaller proportion of women are employed, they are more often in part-time employment, their careers are less continuous (see pages 191–3). In any case it has been argued that male social class is the best single indicator of class for a whole variety of purposes, despite the clear implications of married couples with dissimilar occupations, and efforts to establish female-based class classifications (see pages 45–6 and 48–9).

Age

Since the occupational structure of our society changes over time, age and social class will be interrelated. This can be illustrated either by looking at the age

TABLE 3.2A Percentage[1] of males in each social class, by age group

	I	II	IIIn	IIIm	IV	V	All
			Social class (RG 80)				
16–24	8	7	19	17	18	20	15
25–34	28	22	21	21	17	15	21
35–44	23	22	15	19	14	13	18
45–54	18	19	14	17	16	15	17
55–64	13	16	15	14	18	17	16
65+	11	14	16	13	17	20	14
All ages			each class = 100				

TABLE 3.2B Percentage[1] of males in each age group, by social class

	I	II	IIIn	IIIm	IV	V	All
16–24	3	11	15	41	21	9	
25–34	7	24	12	37	15	5	
35–44	7	27	10	37	14	5	each
45–54	6	25	10	36	17	6	group
55–64	5	23	12	33	20	8	= 100
65+	4	21	13	31	21	9	
All	5	22	12	36	18	7	

1. Of economically active, retired or permanently sick who were classified.

Calculated from table 16A, *Economic Activity, Census 1981, Great Britain* (1984).

structures of the classes, or at the class compositions of age groups. The figures for men are in Tables 3.2A and B. Table A should be read vertically: each column displays the percentage of a social class in each age group. Table B should be read horizontally: each row shows the percentage of an age group in each social class. The tables reveal a clear pattern. At the extremes, for example, Table A shows that class I has a higher percentage of younger age groups (28 aged 25–34 and 23 aged 35–44) and a lower percentage of the older groups (13 aged 55–64, 11 aged 65 and over). Social class V is different, it has a 'U'-shaped age structure – with 20 per cent of its members aged both 16–24 and 65 and over, and only 13 per cent aged 35–44. Table B shows that 7 per cent of those aged 25–34 are in class I, compared with 5 per cent of 55–64 and 4 of 65-year-olds and over. The percentage of those aged between 25 and 54 in class V is much lower than that for people both older and younger, while the percentage of those in class IIIm declines up the age groups.

Fairly obviously, then, an immediate conclusion is that the social classes have different age structures. Such differences are crucial when comparing classes in terms of a whole set of factors, but particularly when those factors themselves are related to age – such as sickness and death (see Chapter 4).

Explanation of these differences is difficult because our knowledge of the factors involved is limited. In the case of social class I, the figures, just discussed, reflect the increased share of such jobs in the country's occupational structure, together with increases in opportunities to gain higher education and professional qualification, available to the age groups. On the other hand, the jump between the age groups 16–24 and 25–34 in the proportion in class II (mainly managerial) almost certainly reflects the movement of men into such jobs as they become older and more experienced. In the same way the differences in the percentages of those aged 16–24 and the older age groups in classes other than I and II are likely to be due

to inter-generational changes in job and training opportunities. However they also reflect changes in occupation
during working career, some of which amount to intra-
generational social mobility (see pages 207–18). The nature
and extent of these factors would be revealed only by

TABLE 3.3A Percentage[1] of females in each social class,
by age group

			Social class (RG 80)				
	I	II	IIIn	IIIm	IV	V	All
16–24	18	15	28	22	17	5	21
25–34	38	24	19	15	16	15	19
35–44	17	22	18	18	21	23	20
45–54	13	19	17	18	21	24	19
55–64	8	12	11	15	16	21	14
65+	7	9	6	12	9	11	8
All ages				each class = 100			

TABLE 3.3B Percentage[1] of females in each age group,
by social class

	I	II	IIIn	IIIm	IV	V	
							All
16–24	0.9	15	54	10	19	2	
25–34	2	27	40	7	19	6	
35–44	0.9	24	36	8	23	8	each
45–54	0.7	21	36	9	25	9	group
55–64	0.6	19	34	10	26	11	= 100
65+	0.9	23	28	14	25	10	
All	1	21	39	9	22	7	

1. Of economically active, retired or permanently sick, only those
classified.

Calculated from table 16A, *Economic Activity, Census 1981, Great Britain*
(1984).

longitudinal studies of people's careers, while here only a cross-sectional picture is presented. Likewise it is probable, but not demonstrated, that the rise in the percentage of the age groups in class V (from 5 per cent for the 25–34 group to 9 per cent among those aged 65 plus) is partly the result of some men moving to such jobs later in their working careers as a result of deteriorating health and/or ability to cope with, or get, other jobs.

The figures for women, in identical form, are presented in Tables 3.3A and B. In the case of women there are additional factors to those outlined above. Not only is the female labour market to a large degree separate and different from the male, but a large proportion of women break their employment for, or have it affected by, family reasons. The timing and extent of such interruptions almost certainly vary according to social class. See, for example, Chapter 7, which illustrates class variation in age at marriage, age of motherhood and size of family. What the tables here show reflects what was seen above in Table 3.1. Very few women are to be found in class I, and a very large proportion in IIIn – which includes occupations such as typist, secretary and shop assistant. Of the age group 16–24 more than half are in class IIIn, and 28 per cent of members of that class are of that age group. This proportion declines sharply, to 40 per cent of those aged 25–34, and the mid-30s per cent for older age groups – possibly reflecting job changes related to family formation and raising. What is clear is that the percentages of women in classes IV and V (semi- and unskilled manual) rise steeply with age. While 21 per cent of those aged 16–24 are to be found in these two classes, the percentage for ages 55–64 is 37, and for 65+, 35 per cent. This is due not only to differences in job, training and educational opportunities experienced by the age groups, but also probably to the fact that many women originally in skilled occupations return to work in differently classified jobs.

Ethnic group

As we saw in Chapter 2, problems surround the definition and operationalization of ethnic groups, and these impose limitations to identifying their social class location and distribution. The 1971 census included questions on country of birth both for each person and their parents, that of 1981 asked only for individuals' country of birth. While an analysis of the data by social class from the 1971 census was published in 1978, no such analysis for 1981 has yet appeared. Hence data concerning the population of Great Britain by ethnic group based on country of birth are now dated.

As can be seen from Table 3.4, the social class distribution of males born in various countries shows considerable variation, and their overall distribution is quite

TABLE 3.4 Males[1] born outside the UK, by social class (percentages[2])

| | Social class (RG 70) | | | | | |
	I	II	IIIn	IIIm	IV	V
Irish Republic	3	10	7	36	23	21
Old Commonwealth	15	29	15	22	14	4
New Commonwealth	6	11	10	34	25	14
America	1	4	4	46	27	17
India	10	14	12	29	23	12
Pakistan	4	6	5	24	36	24
Europe	3	12	14	44	19	8
Africa	10	20	20	25	20	6
Asia/Oceania	16	19	21	26	16	3
Foreign countries	8	20	10	32	22	8
All outside UK	7	14	10	33	23	14

1. Economically active and retired.
2. Of classified only.

Calculated from tables (a) to (f), (j), (l), (m) and (n), *Country of Birth*: Supplementary Tables, Part 2, *Census 1971, Great Britain* (1978).

different from that for all the economically active in Great Britain. For instance a greater percentage of those born outside the UK than inside were in the manual classes

TABLE 3.5   Social class of 'coloured'[1] citizens, by birthplace[2] (percentages[3])

	Social class (RG SEG 70)						
	1	2	3	4	5	6	
Males							
A[2]	1	2	8	45	27	17	
B	9	5	33	26	21	6	
C	10	6	15	32	24	13	each
D	3	4	5	25	38	25	row
E	–	–	18	35	31	16	=
F	8	15	22	35	15	5	100
Total Great Britain[4]	5	13	18	40	16	8	
Females							
A[2]	0.2	0.5	40	9	43	8	
B	1	1	55	10	29	3	
C	4	3	44	10	34	6	each
D	7	4	45	12	29	3	row
E	–	–	56	3	38	3	=
F	0.8	7	63	11	17	0.8	100
Total Great Britain[4]	1	5	50	9	27	8	

1. Defined as those born and/or whose parent(s) born in New Commonwealth (NC) countries.
2. A = Born NC America, one or both parents born NC
   B = Born NC Africa, one or both parents born NC
   C = Born India, one or both parents born NC
   D = Born Pakistan, one or both parents born NC
   E = Born UK, one or both parents born NC America
   F = Born UK, one or both parents born NC other than America
3. Of classified economically active and retired.
4. Entire population of GB as at note 3 above.

Devised from table 2.10, Lomas and Monck (1977).

99

(70 compared to 61), while that in class V was twice as high (14 and 7 respectively). Particularly marked are the differences between those born in the Irish Republic – 80 per cent manual, with 44 per cent in classes IV and V – and the Old Commonwealth – 59 per cent non-manual, and only 18 per cent in classes IV and V. Differences are also apparent among those from New Commonwealth countries: for example, the percentages in the non-manual classes range from 56 for Asia/Oceania, 50 for Africa, 36 for India, 15 for Pakistan and 9 for America.

A somewhat similar picture is given, separately by sex, of 'coloured citizens' in Table 3.5. As will be seen in the footnote, 'colour' has been defined by birthplace of subject and/or parent(s). The assumption that such persons are 'coloured' is not, of course, an entirely accurate one. In 1971 the number of persons so defined as 'coloured' in Britain was about 1½ million, some 40 per cent of whom had been born in Britain. The composition of those born in Britain was heavily biased towards the younger age groups; in contrast to the 700,000 of working age, all but 2 per cent were born overseas (Lomas and Monck, 1977). The bottom row to each section of the table gives the overall percentage in each class for the total population of Great Britain, thus allowing comparison. With the exception of groups B and C (for definition see footnote to table) all have higher percentages in the manual classes, particularly class 6, than has the overall population.

These variations are due to complicated and interrelated factors, for example date of entry into Britain and the operation of a quota system for immigration, both of which relate to the job opportunities available and to the ethnic and cultural heritages of the groups. It can be argued that the effect of quotas meant that later entrants were more likely than earlier to have qualifications and skills, which, though possibly thwarted by discrimination, might be expected to lead to occupations in the 'higher' social classes. At the same time later entrants were often dependants and may have been without special training or skill. In this respect it is interesting to note that the female distributions are more similar to the overall for Great Britain than are the male. This suggests that the women involved integrated more normally into the labour market than the men (though as we have seen, the sexes have different if not separate labour markets). Lomas and Monck suggest an interesting comparison between male West Indians born in Britain and outside it (rows E and A). Some 45 per cent of the latter were in class 4, and 3 per cent in classes 1 and 2. Of those born in Britain (who, obviously, have a lower age structure), while none was in classes 1 and 2, a higher proportion were in 3 (18 compared to 8 per cent). The authors comment: 'This suggests that the UK-born . . . are progressing up the ladder (if we accept that valuation).'

TABLE 3.6 Employees by ethnic group, sex and social class (percentages)

| | Social class (RG SEG 70) | | | | |
	1 & 2	3	4	5	6
Males					
White	19	23	42	13	3
West Indian	5	10	48	26	9
Asian	13	13	33	34	6
Indian	11	13	34	36	5
Pakistani	10	8	39	35	8
Bangladeshi	10	7	13	57	12
African Asian	22	21	31	22	3
Females					
White	7	55	5	21	11
West Indian	1	52	4	36	7
Asian	6	42	6	44	2
Indian	5	35	8	50	1
African Asian	7	52	3	36	3

Derived from tables 91 and 92, Brown (1984a).

The data in Table 3.6 are more satisfactory in that they are based on self-identified ethnicity (see pages 79–82), were collected more recently and relate only to those in employment. At the same time they are limited to three groups (with one subdivided) and based on a sample rather than the population. Looking at the figures for men shows that the percentage of the West Indian and Asian groups in the manual classes is higher than the White (83, 73 and 58 per cent), and markedly so for classes 5 and 6. The percentages in classes 1 and 2 range: White 19, Asian 13, and West Indian 5, while the proportion of White in class 3 is double that of the other two groups. There is considerable variation within the Asian group, for example the proportion of African Asians in classes 1 and 2 is higher than the White, and only 25 per cent are in classes 5 and 6 compared with nearly 70 per cent of Bangladeshi, and just over 40 per cent of Indian and Pakistani. Since the Pakistani and Bangladeshi groups are often combined for research purposes, it is important to note the difference in their class composition; for example, the percentages in classes 5 and 6 are 43 for the former and 69 for the latter.

The figures for women show not only an overall distribution different to that of the men (as we have come to expect), but also less marked differences between the ethnic groups. The proportion of Asian and West Indian women in the non-manual classes is lower than White, and while they have larger percentages in class 5, that for White is higher in class 6 (though this is largely because they were more often in full-time jobs). A further analysis of the data by level of qualification found these overall differences remained, though they were smaller among those with qualifications than those without. However, the holding of educational and vocational qualification is related to ethnic group (see Table 8.3 and pages 282–4).

Industry

The economic activities of a society can be seen as centred around particular production processes, trades or services, normally referred to as industries. Clearly those industries which are concerned with production as distinct from the provision of a service will differ from each

TABLE 3.7 Male and female social class profiles of certain industries (percentages[1])

| | | Social class (RG 80) | | | | | |
		I	II	IIIn	IIIm	IV	V
Agriculture, horticulture	M	0.4	49	0.6	5	45	0.5
and fishing	F	1	22	40	8	22	7
Banking, finance and	M	3	35	53	2	3	3
insurance	F	0.2	5	89	0.6	2	3
Chemicals	M	10	20	10	28	27	5
	F	2	11	40	9	32	7
Coal extraction[2]	M	2	5	3	63	27	0.5
	F	0.7	8	53	5	19	14
Construction	M	3	11	2	62	11	10
	F	0.4	11	74	5	5	5
Education	M	8	70	5	5	11	2
	F	1	52	11	5	15	17
Post and	M	2	9	13	37	37	2
telecommunications	F	0.1	6	51	3	34	6
Public administration,	M	9	28	39	10	10	4
defence and social	F	1	14	63	3	10	9
security							
Railways	M	3	7	12	54	13	11
	F	0.9	5	55	8	9	22
Retail distribution	M	2	44	21	22	8	3
	F	0.5	18	71	3	6	2
Textiles	M	2	16	5	45	24	9
	F	0.1	4	14	33	44	5

1. Of classified, usually resident population in employment, percentages over 1 rounded.
2. Includes manufacture of solid fuels.

Calculated from table 18A, *Economic Activity, Census 1981, Great Britain* (1984).

other in structure and in the nature of the occupations involved. Since social class is based on occupation, industries will have different proportions of each class within them. A selection of eleven industries is listed in Table 3.7, together with their class profile, by sex. Obviously some industries are predominantly non-manual, others manual. In banking, finance and insurance some 91 per cent of male and 94 per cent of female employees are in classes I, II and IIIn. In contrast 78 and 82 per cent of males and females in textiles are in the manual classes, just over 90 per cent of men are in coal extraction and 83 per cent of those in construction are in the manual classes, whereas the percentages for women are 38 and 15.

The table shows that even between rather similar industries, there are considerable differences in social class profiles. For example, both construction and coal extraction have high proportions of male manual workers, but the respective percentages for the unskilled (V) are 10 and 0.5. Again, as we saw above, there are clear, general sex differences. Overall, and in nearly all industries, women, in comparison with men, are underrepresented in class I (ranging from 0.1 to 2 per cent compared with 0.4 to 10 for males) and in the manual classes, while overrepresented in the other non-manual classes (particularly IIIn) and in class V (ranging from 2 to 22 per cent compared with 0.5 to 11 for males).

Geographical distribution

Regional The Registrar General divides Great Britain into ten regions, listed in Table 3.8 and displayed on the map (Figure 3.1). These regions are not equal in size, nor in terms of the proportion of the population of Great Britain living in them. In order to facilitate comparison between the regions, the figures in each row of Table 3.8 give the percentages of economically active men from each social class within each region.

TABLE 3.8 Social class of males[1] in each region of Great Britain (percentages[2])

			Social class (RG 80)				
	I	II	IIIn	IIIm	IV	V	All
Scotland	5	19	11	39	18	8	
Wales	5	21	10	38	18	8	
North	4	18	10	42	18	8	
Yorkshire and Humberside	4	20	10	40	18	7	each
North West	5	20	11	37	18	8	region
East Midlands	5	21	10	40	18	6	= 100
West Midlands	5	21	10	40	19	6	
East Anglia	5	24	11	36	18	6	
South East	7	27	14	32	15	5	
South West	6	25	12	35	17	5	
England/England and Wales/Great Britain	6	23	12	36	17	6	

1. Of economically active, classified males only.
2. Rounded.

Calculated from table 17, *Economic Activity*, *Census 1981*, *Great Britain* (1984).

As will be seen, the largest region in terms of population, the South East (which includes London), had the most distinctively different distribution of social classes. It had the highest percentage in each of the non-manual, and the lowest of manual classes. In consequence, as the map shows, it has the lowest manual-class percentage of any region, some 7 per cent less than the average for all regions. A similar, though less marked, pattern applied to the South West. Conversely, the North and the Yorkshire and Humberside regions had comparatively high percentages of manually occupied males (68 and 65 per cent, or 9 and 6 per cent more than the average for all regions), and correspondingly low percentages of non-manual occupations. There are also interesting differences between

FIGURE 3.1 Percentage of manual males and females in each region of Great Britain

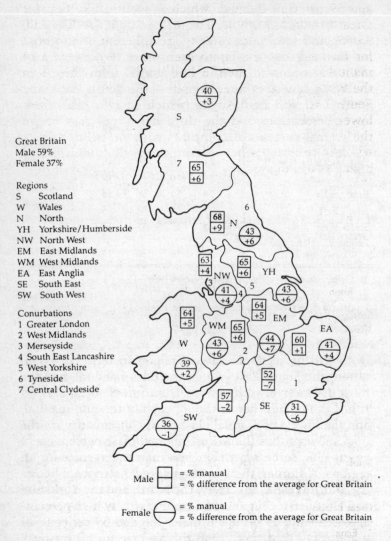

Great Britain
Male 59%
Female 37%

Regions
S   Scotland
W   Wales
N   North
YH   Yorkshire/Humberside
NW   North West
EM   East Midlands
WM   West Midlands
EA   East Anglia
SE   South East
SW   South West

Conurbations
1 Greater London
2 West Midlands
3 Merseyside
4 South East Lancashire
5 West Yorkshire
6 Tyneside
7 Central Clydeside

Male ▯ = % manual
     = % difference from the average for Great Britain

Female ◯ = % manual
      = % difference from the average for Great Britain

Devised from table 17 and map on p.xxc, *Economic Activity, Census 1981, Great Britain* (1984)

the countries involved. England, and England and Wales together have a distribution of 41 per cent non-manual and 59 per cent manual, which is identical to that for Great Britain as a whole. The distributions for Scotland, 35/65, and for Wales, 36/64, are different from those for England, but similar to each other. With regard to manually occupied men, a line drawn from Bristol to the Wash separates three regions – the South West, the South East and East Anglia (which in two cases have lower percentages and the third has 1 per cent above the average percentage, compared with Great Britain as a whole) – from the other seven regions, all of which have higher percentages.

TABLE 3.9 Social class of females[1] in each region of Great Britain (percentages[2])

| | Social class (RG 80) | | | | | | |
	I	II	IIIn	IIIm	IV	V	All
Scotland	1.1	21	38	9	22	9	
Wales	0.8	23	38	8	23	8	
North	0.7	19	39	9	24	10	
Yorkshire and Humberside	0.8	20	37	9	25	9	each
North West	0.9	20	39	9	25	7	region
East Midlands	0.7	19	36	12	25	7	= 100
West Midlands	0.8	19	38	10	25	8	
East Anglia	1.1	21	39	9	25	7	
South East	1.5	23	45	7	18	6	
South West	0.9	23	41	8	21	7	
England	1.1	21	41	9	22	7	
England and Wales	1.1	21	41	8	22	7	
Great Britain	1.1	21	40	8	22	7	

1. Economically active, classified females only.
2. Over 2, rounded.

Calculated from table 17, *Economic Activity*, *Census 1981*, *Great Britain* (1984).

A similar picture can be obtained from the figures relating to economically active women in Table 3.9. Although the figures are different for the sexes, the patterning is similar. The map shows that regions which have above- or below-average percentages of manual males have similar for females. Another detailed view of the regional distribution of the social classes in Great Britain is given in Table 3.10. Here, instead of the numbers in each social class in a region being expressed as a percentage of the total for each region (as above), they are expressed as a percentage of the total for each social class in Great Britain. For example, 8.6 per cent of all social class I people in Great Britain were in Scotland in 1981. The first column in the table discloses that the regional percentages of economically active social class I males range from 40.4 per cent in the South East to 3.2 per cent in East Anglia. The right-hand column of the table shows the percentage

TABLE 3.10 Percentage of males[1] in each social class, by region of Great Britain

| | Social class (RG 80) | | | | | | |
	I	II	IIIn	IIIm	IV	V	All
Scotland	8.6	7.9	8.3	9.8	10.0	11.4	9.3
Wales	4.1	4.6	4.2	5.2	5.0	6.1	4.9
North	4.4	4.5	4.8	6.6	6.1	7.5	5.7
Yorkshire and Humberside	6.6	8.0	7.8	9.8	9.6	9.6	8.9
North West	10.5	10.5	11.4	11.9	12.5	14.4	11.7
East Midlands	5.9	6.8	6.2	8.0	7.7	6.2	7.2
West Midlands	8.2	8.8	8.3	10.6	10.9	8.7	9.7
East Anglia	3.2	3.5	3.2	4.4	3.7	3.0	3.4
South East	40.4	37.0	38.0	27.5	27.1	26.6	31.5
South West	8.0	8.4	7.8	7.3	7.4	6.4	7.6
England	87.3	87.5	87.6	85.0	85.0	82.5	85.8
Great Britain	each class = 100						

1. Of economically active, classified males only.

Calculated from table 17, *Economic Activity, Census 1981, Great Britain* (1984).

of all social classes in each region, i.e. what percentage each region contains of the economically active male population of Great Britain. Approaching a third (31.5 per cent) of such males reside in the South East, and the figures range down to 3.4 per cent in East Anglia. If each social class was equally distributed throughout the regions, then the figures in the separate social class columns would correspond with the figure in the appropriate right-hand column. For example, one might expect to find about a third of the economically active males in each social class in the South East, since that proportion of all economically active males live there. In fact there is considerable variation. In the South East region the percentages in social classes I, II and IIIn are consistently higher than those for all social classes taken together, while those for classes IIIm, IV and V are all lower. Quite the opposite is true of Scotland, where the percentages for non-manual classes are all lower and those for manual all higher than the percentage for all social classes. Other regions display more complex patterns, as can be seen from the table.

Local The regions so far dealt with are large geographical areas of mixed social composition. It might be expected that the social class variations within them would be as great as, or greater than, the variations between them. Such an assumption would be confirmed on a common-sense level by anyone familiar with any town, city or district in Great Britain.

As well as the analysis of social class by region, the census includes one of the Metropolitan Counties, which are the major conurbations. For example, in the Yorkshire and Humberside region there are two such areas, that of South Yorkshire – centred on Sheffield – and West Yorkshire – centred on Bradford and Leeds. Table 3.11 allows comparison between the male social class composition of these two MCs and the remainder of the region, which includes the cities of Hull and York. As can be seen, South

TABLE 3.11 Male social class composition[1] of Yorkshire and Humberside region (percentages)

| | Social class (RG 80) | | | | | |
	I	II	IIIb	IIIm	IV	V
South Yorkshire Metropolitan County	4	16	9	45	20	6
West Yorkshire Metropolitan County	4	21	11	39	18	7
Remainder of Yorkshire & Humberside region	5	23	11	37	17	8

1. Of classified only.

Calculated from table 17, *Economic Activity, Census 1981, Great Britain* (1984).

and West Yorkshire MCs are distinguishable in terms of the proportion of non-manual classes (29 per cent and 36 per cent respectively), this difference being reflected mainly by the relatively high percentages of classes IIIm and IV in South Yorks and higher proportions of classes II and IIIn in West Yorks. In turn these differences indicate different male occupational structures of the two MCs based on the differing industrial structures of the two. Both the MCs have a lower percentage of non-manual classes than the remainder of the region (where it is 39 per cent) – though, of course, this may well reflect commuting patterns as well as differences in the occupational structures. A comparison of the figures for women reveals very few such differences between the three parts of the region. The proportion of non-manual females is the same in the two MCs and only 2 per cent higher in the remainder (57 and 59). South Yorks MC has a somewhat higher proportion of classes IV and V than does West Yorks MC and the remainder of the region (36 compared with 33) and 10 per cent of this is social class V.

Although they are not generally available, it is possible to obtain 'Small Area Statistics' on a ward or grid basis. For example, the Bradford Metropolitan District was divided into thirty wards for the 1981 census. Using these data it is possible to show the ecology of social class in Bradford. Figure 3.2 relates to the twenty-three wards which constitute what was the City of Bradford and two towns until the 1974 local government reorganization. The overall distribution of economically active males by social class (RG 80) in that area was: I, 4 per cent; II, 20 per cent; IIIn, 12 per cent; IIIm, 37 per cent; IV, 20 per cent; V, 8 per cent.

As the map reveals, these figures hide considerable variation between areas. The range in the case of social classes I and II together, for example, is from 8 per cent in Little Horton Ward to 55 per cent in Bingley Rural Ward, and in the case of classes IV and V from 13 per cent in Baildon to 54 per cent in University Ward. Looking at the map shows not only the class distinctiveness of wards, but also that those of similar structure tend to be grouped together by location. For example, compare those to the North East with those in the centre and to the South West. Further variation within the wards would be revealed by reference to census data on a grid basis if these were available. (Ward and grid data are obtainable only on request and payment from the Office of Population Censuses and Surveys. They may, however, be available from local libraries or local authorities.) It is interesting to note that the census uses some 18,000 wards, which in urban areas may contain up to 10,000 households. The smallest unit used is the enumerator district – literally, that area in which a single person collects census forms. There are 125,000 of these districts with an average population of 460 (ACORN, 1979).

Such regional, and particularly local, variations in the distribution of social classes are clearly indicative of some sort of residential segregation. Bradford may be accepted as a typical example. Although representatives of all the social classes are to be found in all the wards, some of the wards can be characterized by their predominant

FIGURE 3.2 **Social class distribution of economically active males in Bradford**

(a) Percentage of classified males aged 16 to 64 in social classes I and II (RG)

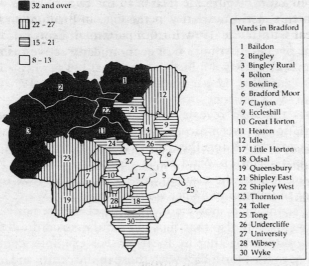

(b) Percentage of classified males aged 16 to 64 in social classes IV and V (RG)

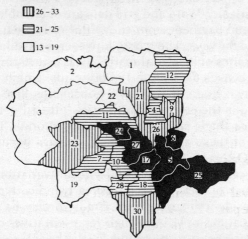

Devised and calculated from *Small Area Statistics, Census 1981, Great Britain.*

social class. Others are more mixed, with a distribution approximating to that of the district as a whole, the conurbation, region or nation. This phenomenon is of course well known to people like headteachers, social workers, doctors, local authority personnel and the police, who deal with clients drawn from particular areas.

SEX

The most fundamental aspect of the demography of the sexes is the biological fact that the sex ratio at birth is imbalanced in favour of males. In Western societies there are about 105–106 male births to each 100 female births, while worldwide higher variations have been observed – for example, in Korea the proportion has been 115.3 males (Novitski, 1977). It has been suggested that at fertilization the figures could be more disproportionate, at around 60 males to 40 females (Penrose, 1973). It seems likely that implantation and all subsequent stages of gestation display a higher wastage of male than female foetuses (Teitelbaum, 1972).

Despite this fact, women are the majority sex in our society. The figures in Table 3.12 reveal that, of the estimated 49,923,500 persons in England and Wales in 1985, 51.3 per cent were females and 48.7 per cent males – the difference amounting to an extra 1,263,500 females. A female majority has been the case historically, though an interesting change has taken place during the present century. Earlier this century there were more females than males in each of the age groups – reflecting the fact that, while more boy babies were born, their chances of survival and their expectation of life were poorer than girls' (see pages 125–9 and 160–2). By the 1931 census, as the result of improvements in medical and health care and consequent enhanced survival at birth, there was a higher percentage of boys than girls in the age group 0–14 years

TABLE 3.12 Percentage[1] of each sex in age groups, England and Wales, June 1985

Ages	% of population	Females	Males	Difference in 1000s	
All	100	51.3	48.7	1263.5	More females
0–9	12.2	48.7	51.3	160.5	
10–19	14.7	48.7	51.3	194.5	More males
20–29	15.6	49.4	50.6	96.2	
30–39	14.1	49.8	50.2	33.2	
40–49	11.7	49.7	50.3	38.9	
50–59	10.8	50.4	49.6	48.3	
60–69	10.1	53.3	46.7	33.6	More females
70–79	7.6	59.5	40.5	713.2	
80–89	2.9	70.4	29.6	583.0	
90+	0.4	80.0	20.0	106.3	

Ages	% of population	Females	% of all females	Males	% of all males
Under 16	20.5	48.7	19.5	51.3	21.6
16 to 44	42.1	49.4	40.6	50.6	43.7
45 to retirement age[2]	19.1	43.2	16.1	56.8	22.3
Over retirement age[2]	18.2	66.9	23.8	33.1	12.4

1. Estimated, 1981 census based.
2. 60 for females, 65 for males.

Calculated from table 1, *Mortality Statistics 1985a* (1987).

in England and Wales. This change has been maintained, so that by 1985 males were the majority in all age groups up to 40–49 years, while the older age groups displayed female majorities, increasing in size with age (see Table 3.12). It seems unlikely, however, that in the future males will become the majority sex in all age groups. Current projections of the figures suggest that the male majority will remain only up to the 50–59 age group for the next twenty-five years. Whereas the ratio of women over men in the 75 years and over age group is at present 2:1, by the year 2011 it will have fallen to 1.6:1 (Wells, 1987). Both these predictions are subject to changes in mortality, fertility and migration.

As the lower part of Table 3.12 displays, demographic differences, together with differing retirement ages for the sexes, means that almost twice the proportion of women compared to that of men were over the age of retirement (23.8 compared with 12.4 per cent). At the same time, 65.2 per cent of males and 60.1 per cent of females were under the age of 45 years. There are likely to be many social implications arising from the fact that women remain a majority only in the older age groups. It is of more than passing interest to note that the heightened interest in women's rights and position, together with the emergence of women's movements, have occurred at a point in history where for the first time those women most likely to be actively involved in such concerns are a sexual minority.

There is some geographical variation in the sexual composition of our society. This is mainly due to the higher male births and longer female lives, already mentioned, together with sex-selective migration. Consequently, the proportion of males is higher in areas with high birth rates and lower in areas with a high number of the elderly. Major contrasts are to be found only between or within individual settlements (*People in Britain*, 1980). Concentrations of men are scattered and are to be found in heavily industrialized areas – such as the West Midlands, South Yorkshire, Slough and Staines, Teesside, areas on coalfields, and some inner-city areas of the Midlands and the South. Some of these areas are likely to be affected by the presence of New Commonwealth immigrant groups, among whom men predominate. Male concentrations are also to be found in rural areas as a result of female migration out, in the face of inadequate employment opportunities. On the other hand, concentrations of women are most marked in coastal retirement areas – the coasts of Kent, Sussex, Dorset, Devon, North Wales and West Lancashire. Older urban areas, like West London, Liverpool, Newcastle and Scottish cities, also have higher proportions of women, possibly because of selective migration in by younger women and out by men, together with higher male mortality rates in deprived areas (though such concentrations are absent from cities in the Midlands).

ETHNIC GROUPS

The problems of definition and operationalization of ethnicity, discussed in Chapter 2, are not rehearsed here, but need to be borne in mind. The main source of data on the size, composition and distribution of ethnic groups in Great Britain is the annual *Labour Force Survey* (LFS), which includes a self-identification question (see page 81).

TABLE 3.13A Percentage[1] of each ethnic group in the metropolitan Counties and Great Britain, 1985

	Inner London	Outer London	Greater Man- chester	West Mid- lands	West York- shire	Other Metropolitan Counties	All	Great Britain (1000s)
White	4	7	5	4	4	7	31	51,222
West Indian/								
Guyanese	38	17	5	15	3	2	80	547
Indian	7	27	5	21	5	0.6	65	689
Pakistani	7	9	14	25	12	4	71	406
Bangladeshi	46	5	0	15	5	5	75	99
Chinese	22	11	6	2	3	8	51	122
African	45	15	2	4	2	3	71	102
Arab	31	15	2	7	5	7	68	61
Mixed	18	16	8	6	3	5	55	232
Other	28	21	0	4	0	3	56	117
All minorities	21	18	6	16	5	3	68	2,376
All population[2]	4	8	5	5	4	7	33	54,235

TABLE 3.13B Estimated population of Metropolitan Counties and Great Britain, by ethnic group, 1985 (percentages[3])

	Inner London	Outer London	Greater Man-chester	West Mid-lands	West York-shire	Other Metropolitan Counties	All	Great Britain
White	79.3	90.0	94.3	85.6	94.1	98.2	90.8	95.6
West Indian/ Guyanese	8.7	2.2	1.0	3.2	0.8	0.3	2.5	1.0
Indian	2.0	4.4	1.3	5.6	1.6	0.1	2.6	1.3
Pakistani	1.2	0.9	2.3	3.9	2.4	0.4	1.6	0.8
Bangladeshi	1.9	0.1	0	0.6	0.2	0.1	0.4	0.2
Chinese	1.1	0.3	0.3	0.1	0.2	0.3	0.4	0.2
African	1.9	0.4	0.1	0.2	0.1	0.1	0.4	0.2
Arab	0.8	0.2	[–][4]	0.2	0.1	0.1	0.2	0.1
Mixed	1.7	0.9	0.7	0.5	0.3	0.3	0.7	0.4
Other	1.4	0.6	0	0.2	0	0.1	0.4	0.2
All minorities	20.7	10.0	5.7	14.4	5.9	1.8	9.2	4.4

1. Those over 1 rounded, based on estimated population.
2. Includes 'not stated'.
3. Rounded to first decimal place; percentages exclude those 'not stated' (1.2% for GB).
4. Less than 0.1 per cent.

Calculated from table 5.3, *Labour Force Survey 1985* (1987).

Because the number of persons in ethnic minorities is relatively small and grouped geographically (see below), LFS yearly surveys are subject to relatively high sampling errors. Consequently, the most satisfactory estimates are obtained by averaging the results for several years. The estimated average size of the ethnic minority population of Great Britain 1984–6 was some 2.43 million persons, amounting to 4.5 per cent of the total population (Shaw, 1988). The largest single group of those surveyed by the LFS is Indian, some 31 per cent of all ethnic minorities, which together with Pakistani and Bangladeshi constituted 52 per cent. Some 26 per cent were West Indian (22) or African (4), 10 per cent were designated 'Mixed',

5 and 3 per cent were Chinese and Arab respectively and the remaining 5 per cent 'Other'. Details of the numbers in each of the ethnic groups identified by the LFS in 1985 and in Table 3.13A and the percentages these represent of the overall population of Great Britain are in Table 3.13B. As can be seen from the latter, the largest groups in percentage terms were Indian (1.3), West Indian/Guyanese (1) and Pakistani (0.8). Bangladeshi, Chinese and African were each 0.2 per cent, Arab 0.1, Mixed 0.4 and Other 0.2 per cent. Overall some 43 per cent of the minorities were born in the UK, varying from three-quarters of the Mixed group, more than half the West Indians, to just over one in ten of Arabs. The vast majority of those born outside the UK were born in the New Commonwealth/Pakistan, with the exceptions of the Arab (85 per cent born elsewhere, mainly Middle East), Chinese (26 per cent elsewhere, mainly China and Vietnam) and Other (34 per cent elsewhere).

Age and sex

In comparison with the majority, ethnic minorities have young age structures (see Table 3.14). Overall more than a third of the minorities were under the age of 16, and less than one in five over the age of 45, compared with the corresponding figures for the majority of one in five under 16 and two in five 45 and over. Only some 3 per cent of the ethnic minority population had reached retirement age. There are clear differences between the groups. Pakistani/Bangladeshi and Mixed have extremely young age structures, with around half aged under 16 years. Such differences are largely a reflection of the pattern of immigration from particular countries of origin.

With the exception of West Indian/African, the proportion of males to females in minority groups is somewhat higher than in the overall population, particularly for Pakistani/Bangladeshi (see right-hand column of table).

TABLE 3.14 Ethnic groups by age and sex (percentages[1])

		Under 16	16–29	30–44	45 and over	Males per 100 females
White	M	21	23	21	35	95
	F	19	21	20	41	
All minorities[2]	M	35	27	19	19	104
	F	34	30	20	16	
West Indian/African	M	27	31	16	26	94
	F	26	34	19	21	
Indian	M	32	25	24	19	102
	F	31	30	23	16	
Pakistani/Bangladeshi	M	45	21	16	18	117
	F	46	26	17	11	
Chinese	M	29	29	26	16	101
	F	28	26	32	16	
Mixed	M	52	28	11	9	103
	F	54	26	11	9	
All[3]	M	22	23	21	34	95
	F	19	21	20	39	

1. Average for 1984–6.
2. Includes 'other'.
3. Includes 'other' and 'not stated'.

Calculated from table 4, Shaw (1988).

Geographical distribution

Ethnic minorities are concentrated in the Metropolitan Counties, and particularly those of London, West Midlands, Greater Manchester and West Yorkshire, as is shown on Table 3.13A. Some 33 per cent of the population of Great Britain live in the MCs, 31 per cent of White compared with 68 per cent of ethnic minorities – ranging from 80 per cent for West Indian/Guyanese to 51 per cent for Chinese. A high proportion of most minorities live in London (for example, over half of West Indian/Guyanese, Bangladeshi, African and Other), and particularly in Inner London (for example, over 40 per cent of Bangladeshi and African). The Pakistani group was the most widespread and had its largest percentage (25) in the West Midlands, where 21 per cent of the Indian group also lived.

A different view based on the same data is provided in Table 3.13B which analyses the population of Metropolitan Counties and Great Britain by ethnic group. Overall the minorities amounted to some 9 per cent of those counties' populations, ranging from just over 20 per cent in Inner London to almost 6 per cent in Greater Manchester and West Yorkshire. Differences in the ethnic composition of the MCs is also apparent.

AGE

We have already viewed in this chapter several aspects of the age structure of our society. The basic demographics of age are in Table 3.12, together with sex differences (pages 113–5), social class (Tables 3.2 and 3.3) and ethnic differences (Table 3.13). Here we are concerned with the geographical and/or social distribution of the elderly and children.

The OPCS chooses to define the elderly as those over the age of retirement – 65 years for men and 60 for women (*Britain's Elderly Population*, 1984). The 1981 census identified some 9.7 million such persons amounting to 18 per cent of the population, a very significant increase from 1911 when the respective figures were 2.7 million and 6 per cent. Of each twenty elderly persons in 1981, fourteen were under 75, five between 75 and 84, one 85 or over. There were almost two women for each man aged 75 to 84 and four women aged 85 and over to every man of that age.

The southern regions of England all have slightly higher than average proportions of the elderly, while the Midlands and northern regions and Scotland are a little below, indicating a North/South divide. Counties with the highest proportions of elderly are East and West Sussex, Isle of Wight and Dorset; those with the lowest are Bedford, Buckinghamshire, Cleveland and Berkshire. The highest concentrations at district level are ten areas on the south coast where the elderly constitute over 30 per cent of the population (e.g. Rother and Worthing, 35; Eastbourne, 34), while the lowest are areas of rapid, planned growth, such as Redditch and Tamworth in the Midlands and Cumbernauld and Kilsyth in Scotland (all at around 10 per cent). However it has to be borne in mind that there are relatively few areas of high concentration and that the proportion of all elderly people who live in them is small. Small Area Statistics demonstrate finer detail; for example, those for Brighton and Hove (on the south coast) show that wards there vary in their elderly population from 10 to 40 per cent.

The 1981 census found that some 12.1 million, that is 22 per cent, of the population were aged under sixteen years, a significant decrease from 1911 when the respective figures were 13.4 million and 33 per cent. Concentrations of children are even less marked than those of the elderly. For example, if every district were to have the same proportion of children and the elderly about one child in twenty-seven would need to move from above- to below-average area, compared to one elderly person in fifteen (*Britain's Children*, 1985). Variations in the proportion of the population under the age of sixteen tend to mirror that of the elderly, so East Sussex has the lowest at 18 per cent, Cleveland the highest at 25. The regions show very little variation, from a low of 21 per cent in the South West to 23 per cent in the West Midlands. High proportions of children are to be found in growth areas, especially those planned and acting as dormitory suburbs. Highest in 1981 were Cumbernauld and Kilsyth and Milton Keynes (new towns at 29 per cent) and Tamworth (28 per cent). The lowest were all in London – Kensington and Chelsea and Westminster (13 per cent) and City of London (7 per cent).

CHAPTER 4

Life-Chances

Birth, and copulation, and death,
That's all the facts when you come down to brass
   tacks:
Birth, and copulation, and death.

T. S. ELIOT (1932)

Present social inequalities in health in a country
with substantial resources like Britain are unaccept-
able and deserve to be so declared by every section
of public opinion.

'The Black Report', Black (1980)

In this chapter we are concerned with the fundamental,
vital aspects of birth, health and death in contemporary
British society. We see how forms of social stratification
in our society affect, and are related to, life-chances from
before birth, through birth and life, to death. We also view
something of the roles of the health service, life-styles and
social institutions in affecting these life-chances.

Our topic has a long history of social class analysis.
The relationship between wealth and health was well
established and recognized by the turn of this century,
partly as a result of the work of those pioneers of the
social survey, Booth and Rowntree (for a short account
of their work see Abrams, 1951). Stevenson, the 'inven-
tor' of the Registrar General's social class classification of
1921, which is the basis of the present one, was particularly interested in the influence of wealth *and* culture on
mortality (death rates), natality (birth rates) and disease
(Stevenson, 1928). Prior to his interest, surveys had been
made of whole districts chosen to represent wealth and

poverty, hence he argued that there had been a neglect of culture as opposed to wealth. The criterion of wealth placed publicans, well known for their high death rates (they lived less long), above clergymen who had low death rates. Stevenson argued that this conflict showed that culture – in his case, habits of diet and hygiene – was also important in relation to health. Similarly, he recognized that wealthy districts also contained relatively poor people – servants and the like – while poor districts contained relatively wealthy ones, such as pawnbrokers and publicans. For these reasons he saw the need for a 'scale of social position (largely but by no means exclusively a matter of wealth or poverty, culture also having been taken into account)' based on occupation. This allowed for the classification of the whole population in terms of individual, as opposed to area, criteria. Indeed, he went on to argue that his social classes were meaningful because the mortality statistics fitted them: that is, the 'highest' social class had the lowest mortality, and there was a fairly regular increase class by class so that the 'lowest' class had the highest mortality. This type of distribution is commonly referred to as a gradient. As will be seen below, it remains a common and accurate characteristic of mortality and ill-health.

Similarly, and more obviously, sex and age have long been seen as important factors related to health and death. However, the complex interplay between all the forms of social stratification has not received as much attention as might be expected, at least in the manner which fits the concerns of this book. In particular, there are few data which deal, either specifically or within a general context, with ethnic groups' life-chances. Hence what follows is neither as comprehensive nor as systematic as is desirable. It presents, however, the currently available evidence from the main viewpoint of social class data, with relatively full reference to sex and age and, where available, ethnicity.

The nature of the topics we now consider disposes us to

the use of governmental statistics. While the purpose and manner in which such data were collected do not always coincide with our objectives, they are comprehensive in scope and in providing both the national and an historical picture. As we have recognized earlier, all data have limitations and have to be viewed from within these limits. These considerations, not rehearsed here, must be borne in mind when reading this chapter, along with some particular concerns. Most medical data come from the analyses of people seeking or receiving treatment or care and so obviously tell us little directly about the health of others. Left unrecorded are those health incidents and conditions that remain untreated, or self-treated via the chemist, or otherwise. Self-reported levels of health and ill-health are clearly subjective and cannot be categorized in a way which would allow direct comparison with medical data. The categories used in medical research are often discrete entities in which aspects of the public's health concern may be lost or disguised. For example, menstrual-cycle problems and forms of back pain are not recorded in a single category and do not appear in the list of the ten most frequent reasons for women consulting a doctor. If they were treated as a single category they would be among the five most frequent reasons (Wells, 1987). Again, official statistics have been accused of being male-biased and therefore relatively uninformative about women (see, for example, Macfarlane, 1980). What is clear is that until comparatively recently many studies of health have not directly addressed sex differences and that they continue to ignore ethnic ones. This situation is probably because the condition, rather than the patient and their culture, has traditionally been the centre of focus for much medical and governmental research. Even where social data, including class, are collected in respect to health, this is not always analysed or published. Some of these considerations are specifically illustrated below, but are raised here as a general issue.

BIRTH, INFANCY AND CHILDHOOD

Survival at birth and during the first years of life is clearly related to social stratification. Indeed, there is evidence of social class variation in the length of pregnancy – with the incidence of curtailed (28 to 37 weeks compared to mature, 38 to 41 weeks) rising from 7 per cent in social class 1 to 10 per cent in class 5 (RG SEG 50A) (Butler and Bonham, 1963). Deaths of babies at birth following curtailed pregnancies are about tcn times as high as those from mature ones. Not only does length of pregnancy affect birth weight – a major factor in survival (see below) – but follow-up studies have suggested that the length of pregnancy is an important factor in the subsequent development of children. Davie, Butler and Goldstein (1972) showed it related to various factors such as school performance (reading and social adjustment), clumsiness, handicaps, and ability to copy designs. These relationships are complicated by the fact that there are social class variations both in length of pregnancy and in other measured variables. However, to take as an example reading ability at age seven, the authors' write: 'the effect of length of pregnancy is relatively small, but nevertheless important ... After allowing for all other factors except birth weight the best readers were those born at the "expected" time (normal gestation), and the worst were those born more than two weeks early, the difference being equivalent to about three months of reading age.'

Table 4.1 shows the incidence of low birth weights (under 2500 grams), at which the death rate at birth is almost ten times higher than that for all babies (124 compared with 13 per thousand) and deaths during the first month of life are nine times higher (72 compared with 8 per thousand). The incidence of low birth weight rises across the social classes from 5.4 per cent for class I to 8.2 for class V, and there are some marked differences according to the birth place of mothers. Those born in

TABLE 4.1 Percentage of low-birthweight[1] babies, by father's social class and mother's country of birth,[2] England and Wales

			Social class (RG 80)			
I	II	IIIn	IIIm	IV	V	All
5.4	5.2	5.5	6.5	7.2	8.2	6.6

UK	Bangladesh/ India	West Indies	Pakistan	Irish Republic	Old Commonwealth
6.4	11.9	9.0	10.5	5.8	3.9

1. i.e. live births weighing under 2500 grams.
2. Social class data refer to 1980–2, country of birth to 1980.

Derived from table 5.2, McDowall (1985) and table A5.16, Macfarlane and Mugford (1984).

Bangladesh/India have rates in excess of 80 per cent higher, and those born in Pakistan a rate over 60 per cent higher, than those born in the UK. Those born in the West Indies have a rate in excess of 40 per cent higher, while those born in the Irish Republic and (markedly) the Old Commonwealth have lower rates than the UK.

Infant mortality refers to deaths of children between birth and the age of one year. Such deaths are normally recorded under three headings:

stillbirths are babies who display no life at birth;

neonatal deaths are those that occur between a live birth and the end of the first month following it;

postneonatal deaths are those that happen between one month and one year following a live birth.

Infant deaths are those occurring between a live birth and the age of one year.

Stillbirth rates rise steadily across the social classes, the rate for class I being only 56 per cent of that for social class V; they are slightly higher for males than females; and also higher for those whose mothers were born in the New Commonwealth (particularly those from Pakistan) in comparison with those from the UK, while being lower for the Irish Republic and Old Commonwealth (Table 4.2). Infant death rate patterns are similar to those for stillbirths in respect to social class and sex, but display variation according to mother's country of birth. Those from Pakistan again have the highest rate, followed by the West Indies, with Bangladesh/India and the Irish Republic with identical rates and only the Old Commonwealth having a lower rate than that for the UK.

TABLE 4.2 Stillbirths, neonatal, postneonatal and infant deaths,[1] by father's social class, sex and mother's country of birth, England and Wales[2]

| | Social class (RG 80) | | | | | | | | |
	I	II	IIIn	IIIm	IV	V	Male	Female	All
Stillbirths[3]	4.0	4.1	5.2	5.3	6.3	7.2	5.9	5.2	5.5
Neonatal deaths[4]	4.7	4.2	4.6	4.9	6.1	6.3	6.0	4.8	5.4
Postneonatal deaths[4]	2.4	2.8	2.6	3.2	4.0	5.2	4.5	3.5	4.0
Infant deaths[4]	7.0	7.1	7.1	8.1	10.1	11.4	10.4	8.2	9.4

	UK	Bangla-desh/India	West Indies	Pakistan	Irish Republic	Old Commonwealth
Stillbirths[3]	7.0	9.8	9.8	13.9	6.5	4.8
Neonatal deaths[4]	7.4	8.3	10.1	15.2	8.1	6.0
Postneonatal deaths[4]	4.2	4.4	5.4	6.8	4.7	3.6
Infant deaths[4]	11.6	12.8	15.4	22.0	12.8	9.6
No. of live births[5]	569	16.2	7.0	13.8	9.2	2.5

1. For definitions see text; legitimate births only.
2. Figures for class relate to 1985, those for mother's country of birth to 1980.
3. Rates per 1000 total births.
4. Rates per 1000 live births.
5. In thousands.

Derived from tables 1, 3, 4 and 5, *Mortality Statistics 1965b*, (1987), tables 13, 16 and 17 *Mortality Statistics 1985c* and table A5.17, Macfarlane and Mugford (1984).

Overall, then, the data show that babies born middle-class, female and to mothers born in the UK and Old Commonwealth have better chances of survival in birth and infancy than have their peers of different class, sex and mothering.

Data concerning deaths in childhood (ages 1–14 years) are to be found in Table 4.3. The standardized mortality ratios (SMR; for definition see footnote to table) display a distinct rise across the social classes for each sex. Note that because SMRs have been separately computed for the sexes, only the pattern, not the figures, can be compared. Hence the incidence of death in childhood is clearly related to class and, as the lower part of the table shows, also

TABLE 4.3 Child deaths: standardized mortality ratios[1] by social class, and death rates by sex, England and Wales

| | Social class (RG 80) | | | | | | |
	I	II	IIIn	IIIm	IV	V	All
Male SMR (1–14 years)	74	79	95	98	112	162	100
Female SMR (1–14 years)	89	84	93	93	120	156	100

| | Death rate per million | |
	Males	Females
Ages 1–4	498	408
Ages 5–14	255	184

1. SMRs are computed by means of the formula:

$$\frac{\text{observed deaths}}{\text{expected deaths}} \times 100$$

where expected deaths are those which would be found in a social class if the age-specific death rate for the whole population was replicated in the group in question. The SMR for any given population is 100; the figures relating to any group within it are expressed as a ratio (hence a ratio of 200 = twice, and of 50 = half the overall rate).

Devised from table 7.8, *Occupational Mortality* (1978) and table 4, *Mortality Statistics 1985d* (1987).

to sex and age. The rates for those aged 1–4 years are higher than those for ages 5–14 and higher for boys than girls. In fact, as will be seen, the sex difference increases with age: at ages 1–4 the boys' death rate is 22 per cent higher than that for girls, while at ages 10–14 years it is 39 per cent higher.

In general, childhood appears less hazardous for girls than for boys; for example, girls have lower rates of hospital admission, out-patient treatment and deaths because of accidents (Macfarlane, 1979). Finally, though fortunately the numbers are relatively low, more boys than girls start life with a malformation, the rates per 10,000 total births in 1980 being 226 for boys and 196 for girls (*Congenital Malformation Statistics*, 1983).

HEALTH, HEALTH BEHAVIOUR AND HEALTH SERVICES

There are two main types of data on the distribution of sickness, disease and conditions of ill-health – normally referred to as morbidity – which indirectly provide evidence concerning the state of health in our society. One is surveys of self-reported health and sickness, together with surveys of particular conditions, which is viewed here, the other is analyses of the causes of death, which is viewed later in the chapter (see pages 153–60 below).

Two aspects of health can be identified, which while related do not always coincide. The subjective – how people feel about, and react to, their health or its lack; and what might be seen as the objective – the diagnosis made, and treatment given, by doctors when consulted. Here we are mainly concerned with views of health, health behaviour and the use of health services gained from the general public and analysed in terms of social stratification.

Self-reported health

The *General Household Survey* (GHS), the research for which is continuous, provides a rich source of self-reported health and associated behaviours. Some of the topics covered are published for each year, while others feature, and are treated in greater depth, only from time to time. Hence the data here are not necessarily the most up-to-date, but have been chosen to provide a general idea of the health of the social strata in our society. Since no efforts were made to define medically or diagnose either conditions or their severity, what we view are subjective attitudes. In a real sense this enhances our understanding, in that people's attitudes to their health are at least as important as clinical symptoms in terms of their behaviour and its effects upon their lives.

The GHS draws a distinction between two types of sickness:

chronic – longstanding illness, disability or infirmity;

acute – that occurring in the fourteen days prior to interview and which restricted normal activities.

As can be seen in Table 4.4, the incidence of both types increases across the social classes, though more markedly for chronic than acute sickness. The first almost doubles from 20 per cent for class 1 to 38 for class 6, while the proportion of sufferers who see chronic sickness as limiting their activities in any way rises even more steeply, from 9 to 27 per cent. The sex differences are smaller, 31 per cent of women compared with 29 per cent of men report chronic sickness, a similar percentage difference (18 and 16) such sickness as limiting their normal activities.

Obviously, age is a significant factor in health and sickness. For example, the percentage of people reporting chronic sickness increases over the age groups from 10 to 63 per cent: 0–4 years, 10; 5–15, 16; 16–44, 22; 45–64, 43; 65–74, 56; 75 and over, 63 (Table 8.17, *GHS, 1985*). This age pattern is true for both sexes and for each of

TABLE 4.4 Self-reported health and health behaviour,[1] by social class and sex (percentages)

| | Social class (RG SEG 80) | | | | | | | | |
	1	2	3	4	5	6	Male	Female	All
Chronic sickness	20	27	28	31	35	38	29	31	30
Limiting chronic sickness	9	14	15	18	23	27	16	18	17
Acute sickness[2]	11	10	13	13	14	15	11	14	13
Number of restricted activity days[3]									
Men	13	17	19	22	23	25			20
Women	20	21	27	30	35	44			29
Consulted NHS GP[2]	11	12	13	14	16	18	11	16	14
Absent from work because of own sickness or injury[4]									
Men	—	3	—	5	5	4	3		4
Women	—	3	—	5	8	5	3		5
Taking prescription drugs[5]									
Men	27	28	29	29	34	30			
Women	37	35	34	42	43	47			

1. By persons aged 16 and over.
2. In 14 days prior to interview.
3. In a 12-month reference period.
4. Percentage of part- and full-time employees absent in the week prior to interview.
5. Excluding contraceptive pill.

Devised from tables 8.19, 8.20, 8.24 and 8.26, GHS 1985; table 7.5, GHS 1980; table 6.38, GHS 1984; and table 2.14, The Health and Lifestyle Survey (1987).

the social classes. However, in comparing the sexes some interesting differences can be observed. In childhood (0 to 15 years) males have higher rates of chronic and limiting chronic sickness than females (16 and 7 per cent, compared with 13 and 5), between the ages of 16 and 64 the rates are almost identical, but females have higher rates at ages 65 or over (60 and 44, compared with 56 and 40). This difference is at least partly due to longer life expectancy for females, so that elderly women are, on average, older than men in the same age group (see pages 160–2 below).

In the case of acute sickness in the fourteen days before interview the social class gradient of incidence is less dramatic than that for chronic sickness, from 11 to 15 per cent. However, the average number of days of restricted activity due to acute sickness almost doubles across the classes for males (13 to 25) and more than doubles for females (20 to 44), the overall average being 20 for males and 29 for females. Despite such differences, reported absence from work because of own sickness or injury in the week prior to interview does not show a social class pattern and the percentage of women at 5 is only one higher than that for men (rows 7 and 8, Table 4.4).

Consultation with an NHS doctor in the fourteen days prior to interview rises across the social classes from 11 per cent for class 1 to 18 per cent for class 6. This is not just a straightforward reflection of the need for GP consultation due to the rise in level of chronic sickness, seen above. Apart from need, sex and age differences, together with the willingness and necessity to make use of the services, also involved are differences in the physical-health demands made by types of occupation. There is some evidence which suggests that when standardized for age and sex the non-manual classes, on the basis of self-reported need, make greater use of health services than do the manual classes (see pages 146-52 below).

Sex difference in GP consultation is marked: the female percentage at 16 is nearly one and a half that for males, and particularly pronounced in the age group 16 to 44 years (women 17 per cent and men 7 per cent). This is partly accounted for by aspects of childbirth and family planning, which accounted for 12 per cent of consultations by this group in 1981 (*GHS 1981*), although, as we have seen, acute sickness is more prevalent among women than men. This prevalence is confirmed by the *Health and Lifestyle Survey* (1987) which asked its respondents to identify which of thirteen common symptoms they had experienced in the previous month. With the exceptions of painful joints, indigestion and cold/flu at ages 18 to 44 years, and ear problems and coughs at ages 45 to 84 years, a larger percentage of women than men reported they had experienced each symptom. Some 28 per cent of women, compared with 16 per cent of men, reported having suffered from four or more symptoms, the biggest differences occurring in the ages 40 to 59 years.

The *GHS 1980* invited respondents to rate their health in the previous year as good, fairly good or not good. Women were more likely than men to report their health as not good (15 compared with 11 per cent) and less likely to see it as good (54 and 64 per cent). Such sex differences were found among both those reporting and those not reporting chronic sickness and in all age groups. Women appear generally more inclined towards seeing their health as only fair or not good. The *Health and Lifestyle Survey* asked for self-assessment as excellent, good, fair or poor 'compared with someone of your own age'. Blaxter (1987) found such assessments to be very strongly related to socioeconomic circumstance. For example, of men over the age of fifty three times as many in the lowest as in the highest income group saw their health as fair or poor. Explanation of these differences is not simply a question of the incidence of health problems. Apart from the possible variation in the seriousness of conditions, it seems probable that the variation also reflects differences in attitudes towards health between the social strata. For example, that there are different concepts of good health, that some strata may be less, and others more willing to admit problems, or to be concerned about them, that occupational and social demands for, and of health vary, together with interrelationships between these and the provision of health services. Interestingly, Blaxter (1987) found that both women and men tended to identify a male when asked to think of someone who is 'really healthy', hence it could be that healthiness is less readily seen as a female characteristic. At the same time it does appear that some common problems apply particularly to women.

The final aspect of health behaviour in Table 4.4 is the taking of prescription drugs (other than contraceptive pill). The social class gradient is less marked and regular for men than for women, and a higher percentage of women in each class and overall were taking such drugs. Drug-taking also increased through the age groups, even when those with a chronic condition were excluded.

Sight, hearing and teeth

Table 4.5 summarizes data on self-reported aspects of sight, hearing and dental health of persons aged over sixteen years. The percentage of those with sight difficulties rises across the social classes, almost doubling from class 1 to 6 (10 to 19 per cent) and is higher among women than men. Similarly, about two-thirds of women wear glasses and/or contact lenses, compared with 57 per cent of men. While women of all ages are slightly more likely to wear glasses, the most marked sex difference is among those aged 16 to 44 years (41 compared with 29 per cent). Difficulty with sight even when wearing glasses is also more common among women at all ages, and rises for both sexes across the social classes. As will be seen the table reveals little pattern to the class distribution of the wearing of glasses; however, the overall rate hides a sex difference. Among men it is the non-manual classes which have higher rates than the manual – overall 64 and 55 per cent. In contrast, among women the opposite is true – 66 and 69 per cent (devised from data in GHS 1982).

There are no social class data on the most serious sight problems, but the majority (over 60 per cent) of the

TABLE 4.5 Sight, hearing and teeth, by social class and sex[1] (percentages)

| | Social class (RG SEG 80) | | | | | | | | |
	1	2	3	4	5	6	Male	Female	All
Sight									
Wears glasses[2]	67	67	64	60	65	69	57	67	62
Has difficulty[3]	10	12	13	14	18	19	12	16	14
Hearing									
Wears hearing aid, or has difficulty	7	12	11	13	16	21	15	12	13
Teeth									
No natural teeth	6	17	18	25	34	39	20	27	23
Regular check-up with dentist[4]	68	62	58	41	39	30	42	58	50

1. Persons aged over 16 years.
2. Includes contact lenses.
3. Includes those who wear and do not wear glasses.
4. Percentage of those with some natural teeth.

Devised from tables 8.35 and 8.37, *GHS 1982*; tables 7.19 and 7.20, *GHS 1979*; and tables 8.34, 8.35, 8.38 and 8.39, *GHS 1985*.

registered blind and partially sighted persons in our society are women. Many of the causes of these conditions are mainly prevalent amongst the elderly and around 60 per cent of people with them are aged 75 years and over. Hence these sex differences are explained in terms of the greater expectation of life for females. However, the majority of blind and partially sighted children (0–15 years) are boys and a male majority exists among adults up to the age group of 50–64 years (*Registered Blind and Partially Sighted Persons*, 1987).

Both the wearing of hearing aids and difficulty with hearing rise across the social classes, with a very marked difference, three times greater, at the extremes – the two together being reported by 7 per cent of class 1 and 21 per cent of class 6. In contrast to sight, more men than women have difficulty with their hearing; 15 compared to 12 per cent. A fairly common form of hearing problem is tinnitus – the subjective sensation of noise (typically ringing, hissing or booming) in the ears or head without any relevant auditory stimulus – the severity and duration of which varies very widely. The *GHS 1981* found that 15 per cent of those interviewed had experienced it, and there were clear class and age gradients; from 10 per cent in class 1 to 19 in class 6; and from 12 per cent of those aged 16–44 to 20 per cent aged 65 and over. In each group and social class more women than men had experienced it.

As Table 4.5 shows, while the percentage of those without any natural teeth rises from 6 in class 1 to 39 in class 6, that for those with some natural teeth who have regular dental check-ups falls from 68 to 30 per cent. The overall percentage of women without any natural teeth is markedly higher at 27 per cent than men at 20 per cent, though the differences are only marked at ages over 34 years. Interestingly enough, among those with some natural teeth women were more likely to have regular dental check-ups than men (58 compared with 42 per cent). As the GHS remarks the reasons why those with higher rates of total tooth loss are more likely to go to the dentist are not fully known. The common view that childbearing affects women's dental condition is not generally supported by dental research and there is no evidence that women are more willing to accept dentures than are men.

Fewer people are losing all their natural teeth now than in the past. The decline has been somewhat more marked for men than women and for the non-manual than the manual classes. Between 1968 and 1983 the percentage of men without natural teeth fell from 33 to 20 per cent and that of women from 40 to 30 per cent (falls of 36 and 25 per cent respectively). By 1985 while the female percentage had fallen to 27, that for men had remained the same. The social class figures for total tooth loss in 1968 ranged from 15 per cent in class I (RG 66) to 47 per cent in class V (Gray, Todd, Slack and Bulman, 1970). While not directly comparable with the data here, it suggests a drop of the order of 60 per cent in total tooth loss in class I, but of only 17 per cent for class V. Such class differences may well reflect differing attitudes towards dental health and use of dental services. Beal and Dickson (1974) explored these differences among the mothers of five-year-olds attending dental examinations at school. Those from classes I and II had markedly more favourable attitudes than those from classes IV and V. They were more likely to favour filling teeth, to have children who regularly brushed teeth and spent less on sweets, and were more likely to take themselves and their children regularly to the dentist. It appears, then, that the classes that behaved in the manner which makes dental problems less likely were also those who made most use of dental services. However, the authors point out, such mothers may have been more aware of the 'right' answers and/or more inclined to give them. They also record that the area in which most of the mothers from classes I and II lived had a larger number of dentists than the others. Obviously the use and effectiveness of health services are related to their provision and quality – a concern taken up below (pages 146–52). A more recent study confirmed class differences in children's dental attendance, but also an independent relationship with mother's attendance pattern (Todd and Dodd, 1985). The dental attendance of children from non-manual homes was markedly better than those from manual homes. However the attendance of children from both classes whose mothers were themselves regular attenders was much closer.

Mental health

While all forms of health and sickness have social dimensions and vagaries – subjective dimensions and problems of definition and diagnosis – nowhere are these better

137

illustrated than in respect to mental health. So, what follows is not only a view of a substantive area of health but also a reflection on some of the general difficulties and limitations of surveying health and its social concomitants.

Women apparently suffer more from mental illness and disorders than do men. This is revealed by the analysis of self-reported symptoms (*Health and Lifestyle Survey*, 1987); its incidence in GP consultations – in the course of a year one woman in every twenty compared with one in fifty men aged between 25 and 75 seeks a consultation which is diagnosed as depression or anxiety (*Morbidity Statistics from General Practice 1981–82*, 1986); and analyses of hospital admissions, incapacity for work and causes of death (*Health and Personal Social Services Statistics 1986, Social Security Statistics 1986, In-Patient Statistics from the Mental Health Inquiry 1982, Mortality Statistics 1985*). A specific view of sex differences in the incidence and diagnosis of mental illness has been provided by Grimes (1978). By relating all first admissions to mental hospitals and units in 1975 to the estimated populations of each sex, allowing for deaths, it was calculated that about 10 per cent of the entire population would be admitted during their lifetime. The sex differences were quite stark, at roughly one in twelve (8.6 per cent) for men and one in eight (12.4 per cent) for women. Only at ages lower than seventeen years was the male probability of admission higher than the female. The only diagnostic group having a higher male than female rate was alcoholism and alcoholic psychoses – the rates being very similar for schizophrenia, drug dependency and personality disorders – while all other diagnoses including depressive and other psychoses, senile and pre-senile dementia and psychoneuroses, had higher female than male rates.

This and similar studies of other aspects of ill-health, based as they are on the recorded incidence at specific places, highlight the limits of our knowledge. It is, then, appropriate to examine the recognized limitations of such studies. Their data are only of presented and diagnosed conditions, so that the extent to which they provide a straightforward view of the incidence of ill-health in the population is questionable. To be sure that they did would require knowledge about those not in contact with health services, any social difference in willingness to use services, and whether there was social bias in diagnosis, treatment and admission. For example, Macfarlane (1980) has raised the question of whether there is more likelihood that a mentally sick man would be cared for at home than a woman, and whether women run more risk of having their problems diagnosed as mental. Brown and Harris (1979) in a study of women showed there is considerable depressive illness among women who have never consulted a doctor about it. Explanations for the differing rates of mental ill-health of the sexes have been offered in terms of constitutional (biological and reproductive) differences between the sexes. However, current reviews of the evidence reject these in favour of differences in the social environment, social roles, socialization patterns and tendencies to express emotional difficulties, of women and men (Jenkins, 1985; Jenkins and Clare, 1985).

Such evidence as exists suggests that, in terms of their own social class, mental patients are more likely to be from the manual than the non-manual classes. However, analysis of patients' father's class has revealed no such variation, it being similar to the general population. A clinical study of schizophrenics traced occupation decline in patients' careers, indicating that the complaint was not the result of their class but rather its cause (Goldberg and Morrison, 1963). Similar findings have been reported in respect to psychiatric patients – including sufferers from neurosis, manic depression and personality disorders (Hare, Price and Slater, 1972). It seems extremely likely that 'social drift' (downward social mobility) is a feature of many forms of chronic and progressive illness.

Hospital use

Admission into hospital can be taken as a general indicator of more serious ill-health than those we have viewed so far. Hospital admission covers a wide range of conditions and is subject to variation on factors such as availability of beds, referral practices, circumstances of the would-be patient and, indeed, choice. Our view is limited to NHS hospitals, though the availability and use of private ones affects the situation (see pages 152–3 and table 4.10 below).

Until recently the survey for the *Scottish Hospital In-Patients Statistics* (published annually) collected occupational data, which enabled social class analysis of all NHS patients (excluding maternity and mental cases). Table 4.6 contains two age-standardized measures, one relating to use and the other to length of use of hospital beds. As can be seen, for both measures and both sexes there is a fairly steady rise across the classes I to V. In particular, the rates for classes IV and V are much higher than for I to III. It is necessary to appreciate that differences in admission to, and length of stay in, hospital do not reflect only differences in rates of illness and disease, in the classes and sexes, though clearly these do exist. Differences in physical and social environment are relevant. For example, poor housing, lack of amenities or privacy and overcrowding are likely to limit the possibility of home care and treatment. This could well lead to more frequent admission and longer stays in hospital, particularly for those in class V, where such provisions are most limited (see Chapter 5). Similarly there are likely to be sex differences in respect to the role demands made upon, and home care available to, discharged patients — probably, in general, balanced in favour of men.

Hospital admission rates for all causes other than maternities are highest, and markedly so, for ages 0 to 4 and 65 years and over, for both sexes. Males have higher rates than females in childhood (0–14 years), lower rates

TABLE 4.6 Standardized discharge ratios[1] and mean-stay ratios[2] of hospital in-patients, by social class and sex, Scotland

| | Social class (RG 60) | | | | | |
	I	II	III	IV	V	All
Male						
Discharge ratio	93	84	92	105	149	100
Mean-stay ratio	78	88	99	103	112	100
Female[3]						
Discharge ratio	99	95	92	100	156	100
Mean-stay ratio	88	93	99	103	107	100

1. The standardized discharge ratio is the result of comparing the actual rates of discharge for each class with that expected if the age structure of each class were the same as that for the population. The actual rate is expressed as a rounded percentage of the expected, hence the overall figure for each sex is 100.
2. The standardized mean-stay ratio is calculated as above.
3. Married women classified by husband's occupation.

Derived from table 2, Carstairs (1966).

between the ages of 15 and 54, and higher rates from 55 years and upwards. The average length of stay in hospital also displays a sex difference, being nine days for males and twelve for females (*Hospital In-Patient Inquiry 1983*). Sex differences in length of stay are pronounced at ages 65 and over. Women's average stay rises from three days longer than men at 65 to 69, to eight days longer at 75 to 79 and eleven days at 85 to 89; with 69 per cent of female beds and 53 per cent of male beds being occupied by those over the age of 65. Length of stay is very similar for both sexes among children up to the age of 15, while between the ages of 16 and 64 the average male stay is slightly longer than the female.

Life-style and health

There is growing evidence that certain social habits are related to health, or are hazards to health. In other words that life-style may well be the key to health and morbidity patterns. Being overweight, cigarette smoking, high alcohol consumption, unhealthy diet and lack of exercise, have been so associated and display evidence of variation along social stratification lines. However, health, or its lack, is the result of the interplay of many factors, the complexity of which is not as yet fully understood, rather than of one in isolation.

The Health and Lifestyle Survey (1987) used a 'Body Mass Index' to derive a measure of obesity, separately formulated for each sex (for definition see footnote to Table 4.7) (Cox, 1987; see also James, 1979, and Knight, 1984). The percentage of adults who were obese rises across the social classes – from 5 in class 1 to 13 in class 6 for men and from 6 to 19 for women. The percentage of obese women is almost twice that of men – 15 compared with 8. While the percentage of both sexes who were obese rose from the age group 18 to 29 (women 7, men 4 per cent) to that of 50 to 59 (women 22, men 12 per cent), the percentage of obese men over this age declined, while that for women stayed at about the same level. Interestingly enough, the study also showed that women had better eating habits than men – more fruit and salads (the consumption of which declined across the classes, especially for men) and less fried food and chips (consumption of which increased across the classes) – and that about a quarter of both sexes thought they ate too much. However, food is not the only factor in obesity.

While regular, energetic physical leisure activity is a minority pursuit, there is clear evidence that those who undertake it have lower resting pulse rates and blood pressures, better respiratory functioning and fewer weight problems than those who do not (Fenner, 1987). In addition, exercise is associated with protection from, and

TABLE 4.7 Obese adults,[1] by sex and social class of houschold (percentages)

| | Social class (RG SEG 80) | | | | | | |
	1	2	3	4	5	6	All
Men	5	10	6	9	7	13	8
Women	6	13	12	18	17	19	15

1. Based on Body Mass Index (BMI) derived from weight (kilos) over height (mctrcs) squared; and defined, for men BMI = 30.0 and over, for women BMI =28.6 and over.

Calculated from table 4.7, *The Health and Lifestyle Survey* (1987).

prevention of, a variety of forms of ill-health, including mental, and with independence in old agc (Wells, 1987; Fenner, 1987). Women are less likely than men to take part in active leisure pursuits. For cxamplc, *GHS 1983* found 24 per cent of women compared to 39 per cent of men had indulged in at least one outdoor activity in the four weeks prior to interview, while excluding walking the percentages were 10 and 25 respectively. Participation in sports, games and physical activities declines across the social classes – see Tables 10.10 and 10.11 and pages 382–3. However, the critical factors in exercise are its frequency, length and intensity. *The Health and Lifestyle Survey* measured these and divided the reported activity of its respondents in the two preceding weeks into three groups – none, some, a lot. The percentage in 'a lot' was higher among the employed in non-manuel than manual classes and that in 'non' lower. This might be expected because of assumed differences in physical activity involved in work. However, Fenner reports that respondents' perceptions of the amount of physical effort in their work suggest such assumptions are inaccurate. Sex differences are clear: for example, of those aged 18 to 39 years, the percentage of women in 'none' was 45, and that in 'a lot' 17, while the corresponding percentages for men were 37 and 32.

Cigarette smoking is probably the best recognized health hazard and is regularly surveyed in the GHS. Table 4.8 contains the results for 1984. As will be seen, the percentage of smokers rises sharply across the social classes, from 16 in 1 to 42 in 6. It is also clear that the percentage of ex-regular smokers and those who have never smoked shows a generally class-related pattern, though the average number of cigarettes smoked per week does not. Women are less likely to be smokers than men (32 compared with 36 per cent), much more likely never to have smoked, or only occasionally to smoke, and, if smokers, to use fewer cigarettes. It is of interest to note, however, that in the face of a general decline in smoking, the sex difference has narrowed. Between 1972 and 1984 the percentage of men who smoked fell from 52 to 36 while the percentage of women decreased from 41 to 32 – only around half the proportion. The average consumption of cigarettes per week of male smokers decreased from 120 to 115 and that of the female increased from

TABLE 4.8 Cigarette smoking,[1] by social class and sex

| | Social class (RG SEG 80) | | | | | | | | |
	1	2	3	4	5	6	Men	Women	All
Percentages									
Current smokers	16	29	29	39	40	42	36	32	34
Ex-regular smokers	28	29	21	26	21	18	30	17	23
Never/only occasional smokers	56	42	50	36	39	40	34	51	44
Average number of cigarettes smoked per week per smoker									
Men	108	121	108	121	108	114	–	–	115
Women	78	93	93	101	99	96	–	–	96

1. By persons aged over 16 years.
Devised from tables 10.6 and 10.7, *GHS 1984*.

87 to 96. Also, and in contrast to male smokers, females in every social class smoked more cigarettes in 1984 than in 1972. Sex differences in the percentage of smokers are small in the non-manual classes and really marked only in classes 5 and 6 (males 45 and 49 per cent respectively, compared with females 37 and 36). Women are more likely to smoke low tar cigarettes and less likely to roll their own cigarettes than are men (*GHS 1984*).

The Royal College of Psychiatrists (1986) has estimated that alcohol is responsible for some 4000 deaths and 5000 first admissions to psychiatric hospitals each year. While in the past the major concern has been with men, who have higher levels of consumption than women, evidence is growing which suggests that women may be at higher risk of physical harm than men to a given quantity of alcohol. Accurate data on the population's drinking is, of course, very difficult to collect. The data from the GHS in Table 4.9 shows that percentages of the extremes of drink-

TABLE 4.9 Adult alcohol-drinking habits, by social class and sex (percentages)

| | Social class (RG SEG 80) | | | | | | | | |
	1	2	3	4	5	6	Men	Women	All
Heavy[1]	5	6	7	14	11	12	20	2	10
Moderate[2]	8	9	8	10	9	8	14	4	9
Light[3]	73	70	64	50	46	41	50	61	56
Occasional[4]	8	10	14	16	19	20	9	20	15
Abstainer	7	6	8	9	14	18	7	13	10

1. Drinks 7 or more units (e.g. $\frac{1}{2}$ pint beer/measure of spirit/glass of wine) between once a week and most days.
2. Drinks 7 or more units once/twice a month or 5–6 units between once a week and most days.
3. Drinks 1 in 4 units between once a month and most days.
4. Drinks 1 or more units between once a year and twice in 6 months.

Note. Since drinking was based on type of drink most regularly used it may underestimate drinking of those who use more than one type.

Calculated from table 11.4, *GHS 1984*.

ing – 'heavy' and 'abstainer' (for definitions see footnote to table) – rise across the social classes (from 5 to 12 per cent and from 7 to 18 per cent). A similar percentage of each class are 'moderate' drinkers; the non-manual classes are more likely to be 'light' drinkers than the manual, who have a higher proportion of 'occasional' ones. Women were twice as likely to report being 'abstainers' or only 'occasional' drinkers than men, while the latter were ten times more likely to be heavy drinkers (2 compared with 20 per cent) and three and a half times more likely to be 'moderate' drinkers than women. The definitions of levels of drinking used are very wide (see footnote to table) and reported drinking has been consistently lower than would be expected from alcohol sales figures! (GHS 1984).

Use and role of the NHS

Our considerations so far have shown something of the very real social inequalities in health and these are further and dramatically illustrated in respect of mortality (pages 153–60). Such inequalities raise a number of questions about the use and role of the NHS in this situation. The government's intentions at the inception of the NHS were very clear, it

> want[ed] to ensure that in future every man and woman and child can rely on getting all the advice and treatment and care which they may need in matters of personal health, that what they get shall be the best medical and other facilities available: that their getting these shall not depend on whether they can pay for them, or on any other factor irrelevant to the real need (A National Health Service, 1944).

The essential elements, then, were that need should be sole criterion of use and quality of service and that service should be free at point of use. Since there has been no formal reformulation of the NHS it is appropriate to ask the question whether or not it functions in the way it was designed. We concentrate on the first criteria

– need and quality, though in passing it should be noted that some charges were introduced early on and that their scope and level have increased since, particularly over the past decade. The deterrent effect of charges on the use of health services, balanced as they are to an extent by exemptions, is extremely difficult to assess.

At a straightforward level, the use of health services would be expected to vary directly according to the ill-health or needs of an individual or group. As we have seen, there is evidence that the manual classes (especially the semi- and unskilled) make greater use of the health service than the others, and this is also true of women in comparison with men. The question now is the extent to which that use accurately reflects the differences in need based on the incidence of ill-health or, put differently, whether other factors intervene. Obviously, measuring the need for, let alone the quality received of, health services is a difficult area to research.

In some ways sex differences in the use of health services are more straightforward than social class ones. Quite apart from the differing age structures of the sexes, a major factor is the conditions surrounding, and related to, reproduction. The exclusion of pregnancy and childbirth together with associated complications removes much of the reported higher female usage (see pages 132–3 and 140 above and Reid, 1989). What cannot be discovered, as yet, is the extent to which the long-term effects of childnearing and, indeed, contraception (particularly the 'pill') affect the health of women and hence their use of health services. For a discussion of the need for a new definition of reproductive mortality, see Beral (1979). Nor, for that matter, can we tell the difference between that and the effects of particular occupations on men and for some women the combination of the two. Beral (1985) analysed the causes of death of 1.2 million women aged between 45 and 74 years and found that those who had given birth were more likely to have died from diabetes mellitus and gall bladder disease and certain circulatory diseases than those who had not. However, as yet, the available data do not allow for the identification of which aspects of pregnancy are most strongly related (Weells, 1987). For a review of some of the various issues which surround the health of women, including reproduction and the training of medical personnel, see Roberts (1981).

Given the differences in the sexes' use of the health services, it is not surprising that the average annual cost to the NHS per female is higher than that per male – £272 compared with £234 in 1984 (*Social Trends 17*). This difference is almost completely accounted for by the much greater cost per female aged 75 years and over (£1159 compared to £945), since from ages 0 to 24 and 45 to 74 average male costs are higher, and for ages 25 to 44 the female cost amounts to only £6 more.

In respect to social class use of health services, there is the added factor of private medicine, which, as shown below (Table 4.10), is mainly the prerogative of the non-manual classes, especially 1 and 2. This situation might be seen as enhancing the health care opportunities of the manual classes, since it relieves the NHS of certain of its patients. That this is not demonstrated adds an extra dimension to inequalities in health care and the functioning of the NHS. A further point of note is that, perhaps surprisingly given its importance, research in the area of the social aspects of health care provision and use tends to be somewhat piecemeal, and well removed from the consistent monitoring of overall aspects of the NHS.

In his now classic survey of welfare in our society Titmuss (1968) wrote,

> We have learnt ... that the higher-income groups know how to make better use of the service [i.e. NHS]; they tend to receive more specialist attention; occupy more of the beds in better equipped hospitals; receive more elective surgery; have better maternal care, and are more likely to get psychiatric help and pyschotherapy than the low-income groups – especially the unskilled.

TABLE 4.10 Private medical insurance and hospital use, by social class, sex and age[1] (percentages)

| | Social class (RG SEG 80) | | | | | | Age | | | |
	1	2	3	4	5	6	16–44	45–64	65+	All
Private medical insurance										
Males	21	23	9	3	2	2	8	9	4	8
Females	24	21	7	2	1	1	7	8	3	7
Private in-patient stays	13	16	7	2	1	nil				5
Private out-patient visits	5	4	2	1	2	[–][2]				2

1. Persons over the age of 16, during previous 12 months.
2. Less than 0.5 per cent.

Derived from table 7.33, *Social Trends 17* (1987) and tables 9.21 and 9.24, *GHS 1983*.

Hart (1971), in a paper 'The inverse care law', claimed that there existed 'massive but mostly non-statistical evidence in favour of Titmuss's generalizations'. Brotherston (1976) has accurately pointed out that the NHS is a 'self-help' system, which reacts to individual demands, rather than seeking out those in most need. Consequently, it is likely that knowledge of the system and ability to use it – which he sees as related to intelligence and education (and which can be suspected of social class distribution) – affect the dispensation of both preventive and curative services.

In an extremely interesting analysis of GHS data, Le Grand (1978) produced evidence of social class differences in expenditure related to need; see Table 4.11. The data in the first row are similar to those in Table 4.4, but expressed here as a class profile of self-reported sickness; the second row is the same data standardized for age and sex. By computing the unit cost of GP consultation, hospital in-patient stay and out-patient visit (dividing total costings by total numbers for the NHS), Le Grand was able to show what proportion of NHS expenditure was received by each social class on the basis of self-reported use in the GHS – rows 3 and 4. If expenditure were simply on the basis of need, then the figures in rows 3 and 4 would match those in rows 1 and 2, which they do approximately in respect of classes 3 and 4. However, in the case of classes 1 and 2 the expenditure is higher and for that of classes 5 and 6 it is lower, than percentage reporting sickness. Finally, rows 5 and 6 show the ratio of expenditure per sick person in each class to that for classes 5 and 6. This reveals that sick persons in classes 1 and 2 received something in the order of 40 per cent more expenditure than those in classes 4, 5 and 6, while those in class 3 received 17 per cent more.

TABLE 4.11 Expenditure on NHS health care, by social class

| | | Social class (RG SEG 70) | | | |
		1 & 2	3	4	5 & 6
% reporting chronic or acute sickness	Actual	13.9	19.7	34.5	31.9
	Standardized[1]	14.8	19.4	36.7	29.1
% of health care expenditure	Actual	16.8	22.5	33.4	27.3
	Standardized[1]	18.8	20.5	34.6	26.2
Ratio of expenditure per sick person to that for classes 5 & 6	Actual	1.41	1.33	1.13	1.0
	Standardized[1]	1.41	1.17	1.05	1.0

1. For age and sex.

Derived from table 2, Le Grand (1978).

In fact, it is quite possible that these figures underestimate the differential expenditure to the extent that it has been assumed that each unit of use had equal cost. Some studies have shown that GPs tend to spend more time in consultations with middle-class than with working-class patients – from an average of over six minutes for class I to four and a half for class V (Buchan and Richardson, 1973; Cartwright and O'Brien, 1976). The latter study found:

> General practitioners knew more about the domestic situation of their middle-class patients, although working-class patients had been with them longer. Middle-class patients discussed more problems and spent longer in conversation with the doctor. They may also ask more questions and get more information.

Using unpublished GHS data, Le Grand concludes that the incidence of type of complaint does not vary much within the classes – in contrast to the rates. Hence he sees the differences between them as caused by class variation in the rate at which those reporting a condition use the health service. A similar study by Forster (1976) drew the same conclusion. Le Grand (1982), in reviewing the evidence, identifies three further factors affecting the lower use of health services by classes 5 and 6. First is their greater need for sickness absence certificates, which does not necessarily lead to subsequent contact and may artificially 'inflate' their use. Second, the costs involved in use – for example travelling and time off work – are relatively higher for the working classes, who also appear to have less favourable perceptions of the benefits from health care. The *GHS 1981* also showed that these groups made fewer consultations on the basis of indicators of need.

Other aspects of the NHS – including mass radiography, cervical screening, pregnancy and infant care, dental treatment, breast operations and hospital referrals – have been shown, in relation to need, to be used most by classes I and II and least by IV and V. Alderson (1971) concluded that classes I and II were 'a group . . . who are aware of the provisions of the health service and who also attain a higher proportion of the resources ... than would be expected by chance, and a much higher proportion in relation to their needs when compared with others'. This conclusion was supported by Cartwright and O'Brien (1976), who added, 'There is also evidence to suggest that the middle class may, in relation to a number of services, receive better care.'

While recognizing the limitations of the research and the absence of later evidence to the contrary, the conclusions of the Working Party on Inequalities in Health submitted to the Secretary of State in 1980 ('The Black Report', see Townsend and Davidson, 1982), commented:

> The lack of improvement, and in some respects deterioration, of the health experience of ... [classes IV and V], relative to class I, throughout the 1960s and early 1970s is striking.
>
> Inequalities exist also in the utilization of health services, particularly and most worryingly of the preventive services. Here, severe under-utilization by the working classes is a complex result of under-provision in working-class areas and of costs (financial and psychological) of attendance which are not, in this case, outweighed by disruption of normal activities by sickness.

Private medicine

Like private schooling, private medicine has co-existed with the welfare state provision since its establishment. The growth of occupation-based health insurance schemes, with 'free' or discounted premiums for employees, together with perceived and actual concerns over NHS provision, has led to substantial growth in the private health services sector in recent years. Apart from the question of choice, the ability to pay for, and/or the opportunity to participate in schemes of private health services is likely to be limited to some parts of society. Table 4.10, above, illustrates how the incidence of private medical insurance is strongly related to social class, sex and age. For both sexes it is common only in classes 1 and 2 (over 20 per cent) and rare in classes 5 and 6 (2 per cent for males and 1 per cent for females). Overall, 1 per cent more males than females are covered (8 compared with 7); only in class 1 is the female percentage higher. People of 65 years and over are less likely to be covered than those between 16 and 64. This is likely to reflect the changes and opportunities outlined above, as well as the fact that the elderly can be excluded from such schemes or be charged very high subscriptions. The lower section of the table shows that some 5 per cent of hospital in-patient stays and 2 per cent of out-patient visits were private, again with a sharply marked class pattern.

MORTALITY

Interestingly, much of our knowledge about the incidence of particular diseases and medical conditions among the British population (morbidity) stems from our knowledge of the causes of death (mortality). This is partly because the registration of death, as required by law, includes cause of death and the deceased's last occupation and therefore provides a ready data base. There are, of course, many small-scale clinical studies of particular conditions, and the careful analysis of GP consultations (*Morbidity Statistics from General Practice 1981–82*) and hospital admissions (*Hospital In-patient Inquiry 1983*), but the latter are limited in social stratification analysis to sex and age (for a review, see Reid, 1989). Because of our concern and the limitations of space, our main view of the causes of death is via the Registrar General's decennial supplement which combines death data with population data from the census to produce mortality tables. Since the analyses contained in the most recent of these are not as extensive as the previous one we make use of both (*Occupational Mortality*, 1978; 1986).

Many problems arise in compiling data of this nature.

For example, the simple recording of the incidence of death by cause and by social class would be rather meaningless, mainly because age is an obvious factor in death, and as we saw in Chapter 3 the age structures of the classes, and indeed the sexes, vary. In order to make comparisons more meaningful standardized mortality ratios (SMRs) are used (for definition see footnote to Table 4.3). It is also fairly obvious that while death rates have traditionally been used as indicators of levels of health, they do not tell us very much directly about the living members' society. Social change and medical advance can, and do, affect the life-chances of succeeding generations. As the Registrar General pointed out in 1971, many of the then currently registered deaths 'reflect damage caused by infections in the pre-antibiotic era,

TABLE 4.12 Standardized mortality ratios[1] for selected, grouped causes, by social class and sex

| | Social class (RG 80) | | | | | |
	I	II	IIIn	IIIm	IV	V
Men (aged 20–64)						
Infectious/parasitic diseases[2]	65	62	93	89	117	215
Cancers / other neoplasms	69	77	89	115	117	154
Endocrine/nutritional/ metabolic diseases[3]	72	76	110	99	118	156
Diseases of the blood	86	79	122	105	98	114
Mental disorders	35	48	55	84	97	342
Diseases of nervous system	69	61	100	80	109	185
Diseases of circulatory system[4]	69	80	102	108	113	151
Diseases of respiratory system[5]	36	50	83	102	129	210
Diseases of digestive system[6]	67	79	91	92	112	204
Injury and poisoning	67	70	78	93	121	226
ALL causes of death[7]	66	76	94	106	116	165

154

TABLE 4.12 (contd)

	I	II	IIIn	IIIm	IV	V
			Social class (RG 80)			

Women[8] (aged 20–59)

	I	II	IIIn	IIIm	IV	V
Infectious/parasitic diseases[2]	66	80	77	102	111	153
Cancers/other neoplasms	87	92	95	105	107	117
Endocrine/nutritional/ metabolic diseases[3]	46	54	86	100	116	186
Diseases of the blood	71	75	107	104	102	125
Mental disorders	50	57	82	67	83	144
Diseases of nervous system	76	68	89	86	96	99
Diseases of circulatory system[4]	50	63	78	110	122	158
Diseases of respiratory system[5]	37	53	70	94	115	160
Diseases of digestive system[6]	58	74	76	93	96	148
Injury and poisoning	65	79	93	62	93	121
ALL causes of death[7]	69	78	87	100	110	134

1. Based on deaths in 1979–80, 1982–3 and population in 1981, Great Britain. See footnote to Table 4.3 for definition. Overall SMR for each cause is 100.
2. Includes respiratory tuberculosis.
3. Includes diabetes and nutritional deficiency.
4. Includes heart disease, embolisms and thrombosis.
5. Includes influenza, pneumonia, bronchitis and pneumoconiosis.
6. Includes ulcers and cirrhosis of the liver.
7. Includes causes not specified here.
8. Classified by own or husband's occupation.

Derived from microfiche tables GD28 and GD34, *Occupational Mortality* (1986).

and mirror the social class differences known to exist in those decades' (*Occupational Mortality*, 1971).

As can be seen in Table 4.12, there is a positive gradient to SMRs for both men and women in nearly every listed cause and for all causes of death – they rise from class I to V and there are marked differences between classes I and

II and IV and V, the first pair being consistently considerably lower than the second. The table presents selected grouped causes, but even the definitive list contains very few instances of other patterns – such as negative gradients, irregular relationships with, or independence from, social class. The figures relating to infant and child deaths are at Tables 4.2 and 4.3 above.

A similar overall pattern is clear from Table 4.13 in respect to the mean annual death rates, standardized for age. Notice that the male rate is both higher overall than the female rates and rises more steeply over the classes. Although some of this difference is due to the difference in the age groups used for the sexes (males 20 to 64, females 20 to 59), males do have higher death rates and on average live less long than females, and average length of life declines through the classes from I to V (see pages 160–2 below). The table shows that married women have lower death rates than do single women, both overall and in each class (note that the married are classified by husband's occupation).

TABLE 4.13 Age-standardized, mean annual death rates,[1] by social class and sex, Great Britain, 1979–80/1982–3

	Social class (RG 80)						
	I	II	IIIn	IIIm	IV	V	All[2]
Men (aged 20–64)	375	425	529	597	651	944	557
Women (aged 20–59)							
Married[3]	140	122	143	196	188	221	143
Single	162	180	201	240	270	350	223

1. Per 100,000 population.
2. Includes unclassified.
3. Classified by husband's occupation.

Derived from microfiche tables GD16, GD20 and GD24, *Occupational Mortality* (1986).

The interpretation of these strong general patterns of relationship between social class and mortality rates is far from straightforward. It has been argued that there are two major aspects of class involved:

(1) life-style – wealth, personal habits, diet, home environment, physical exercise and mental stress (the last two are partly general occupational factors);

(2) specific occupational hazards.

Obviously these are not the only factors, nor are they really separable. In the past it has been argued that occupational hazards might be isolated by comparing the death rates of men and married women (classified by husband's occupation), since the women would share only the first aspect. However, the usefulness of such comparisons has always been limited by our lack of knowledge concerning the proportion of married women at work and their own occupation – in contemporary times, with a large proportion of women in the workforce it is probably of even less utility. In any case there are further substantive factors. Mortality differences may well indicate differences in the availability, quality and/or use of medical care. There is likely to be selection in and out of occupations on the basis of health (as we have seen on page 139, health may be a cause of social class as well as class being a factor in health). Finally, there are questions concerning the diagnoses of cause of death – not always a straightforward affair – and as to whether these may have a class bias, as well as a sex one.

Not only does the overall SMR, that for all causes of death, display the now familiar social class gradient, but it has a considerable history, well beyond that recorded in Table 4.14. Perhaps surprisingly given the social changes and medical advances in the present century, the *Royal Commission on the National Health Service* (1979) stated:

> Nor does the evidence suggest that social inequalities in health have decreased since the establishment of the NHS. The position of those in social classes IV and V appears to have worsened relative to those in classes I

and II, though it should be remembered that all social classes are healthier now than they were thirty years ago (para 3.10).

While the exact extent of inequality in health and mortality between the classes remains debatable – because of changes in the classification, collection, processing and publication of data – the trend has been established (see also Townsend, 1974; Townsend and Davidson, 1982).

TABLE 4.14 Male standardized mortality ratios,[1] by social class, since 1921–3

| | Social class (RG various) | | | | | |
	I	II	III	IV	V	All[2]
1921–3	82	94	95	101	125	100
1930–2	90	94	97	102	111	100
1949–53	86	92	101	104	118	100
1959–63	76	81	100	103	143	100
1970–2	77	81	104	113	137	100
			n m			
1979–80/82–3	66	76	94 106	116	165	100

For definition of SMR see note to Table 4.3.
1. Rows 4 and 5 for ages 15 to 64, the others for ages 20 to 64; rows 1 to 5 are for England and Wales, row 6 for Great Britain.
2. Includes unclassified.

Derived from table 8.1, Brotherston (1976) and appendix IV, *Occupational Mortality* (1986).

There is extremely little direct data on morbidity or mortality for ethnic groups in Britain, mainly because of the factors outlined in Chapter 3 (though for that on birth and infant deaths see Tables 4.1 and 4.2). Table 4.15 contains male SMRs by country of birth and social class and allows us to address two questions: Do immigrants display similar class gradients of mortality to those born in England and Wales? To what extent is any difference in their mortality due to their different distribution within the classes? Note that because of differences in the data bases comparisons between this table and others in this chapter are not valid. As will be seen, males of different countries of birth display patterns quite separate from the familiar class gradient. Those from Europe and Poland show no gradient from class I to IV, and while V is higher it is lower than that for 'all countries'. Those from the Indian subcontinent have a gradient in the non-manual but not in the manual classes, while those from the Caribbean display almost the opposite gradient to that for 'all countries', with the highest SMR for class I and non-manual higher than manual. Those from the African Commonwealth have high SMRs at both extremes, classes I and V. Only those from all Ireland have the familiar gradient across the classes, but the SMRs involved are all much higher than those for 'all countries'.

TABLE 4.15 Male standardized mortality ratios[1] from all causes, by country of birth and social class

| | Social class (RG 80) | | | | | | |
	I	II	IIIn	IIIm	IV	V	All
All Ireland	96	99	108	122	129	157	122
Indian subcontinent	90	101	114	105	109	107	101
Caribbean Commonwealth	199	128	60	87	82	109	90
African Commonwealth	128	115	111	91	119	268	108
Europe[2]	94	87	95	85	91	109	88
Poland	85	90	101	92	98	128	95
All countries[3]	77	81	99	106	114	137	100

1. Of those aged 15 to 64; for definition of SMR see footnote to Table 4.3.
2. Includes USSR.
3. Includes those born in England and Wales.

Derived from table 3.4, *Immigrant Mortality in England and Wales 1970–78* (1984).

Explanation of such mortality differences between migrants is extremely complex and awaits proper investigation. Among the important factors are influences of country of birth and of 'new' country, selection of who migrates and the process of migration and adjustment. What is clear is that ethnicity appears to influence mortality independent of social class (in much the same way as mortality varies by geographical region within England and Wales) and/or that class may be a less reliable predictor/determinant in this case than elsewhere. While obvious, it should be noted that the above provides no insights into the mortality of those members of ethnic groups born in Britain.

LIFE EXPECTANCY

It is evident from the differences in the age structure and death rates of the social strata that they also enjoy different average lengths of life. The Registrar General, using the actual deaths and the estimated population, periodically computes life expectancy figures as displayed in Table 4.16. Somewhat similar figures are used by insurance companies for fixing the rates for life insurance. It should be appreciated, however, that the life expectancies given here do not refer directly to the lives of the current population, since they are based on previously recorded lives and deaths which have been affected by conditions that may now be changed. With this limitation, however, they remain as accurate a view of life expectancy as is available. The top section of the table shows a rise in the expectation of life for males aged 15 and 45 across the social classes. At the extremes and on average, then, a 15-year-old male in class I could expect to live till 72.2 years while in class V to 68.5 a difference of almost four years. From the age of 45 years the pattern is maintained though the difference has closed to 2.3 years. Building in data for ages 0 to 14 and assuming rates for those 65 and over allowed the Registrar General to suggest that life expectancy from birth ranges from 72.2 years for males in social class I to 65 for class V. Hence a male subject from birth to the SMR of class I could then be expected to live 7.2 years longer than one subjected to that of class V (*Occupational Mortality*, 1978).

TABLE 4.16 Life expectancy tables, by social class for males and by sex

			Social class (RG 70)						
	At age	I	II	IIIn	IIIm	IV	V	All[1]
Male expectation of life[2] in years	15	57.2	57.0	56.0	55.7	55.1	53.5	55.6
	45	28.5	28.3	27.5	27.2	27.0	26.2	27.4

		Female	Male
Expectation of life[2] in years	0	77.0	71.0
	10	68.0	62.2
	20	58.1	52.5
	30	48.3	42.9
	40	38.7	33.3
	50	29.4	24.3
	60	20.9	16.4
	65	NA	13.0
	70	13.4	10.1

1. Includes unclassified.
2. From age specified, rounded to first decimal place, based on deaths and estimated population for 1970–2/1980–2.

Derived from table 8a, *Occupational Mortality* (1978) and table V, *English Life Tables 14* (1987).

The lower section of the table shows that a girl at birth would, on average, be expected to live some six years longer than a boy, the expectations of life being 71 for males and 77 for females. This difference remains at just over five years, though dropping marginally through the age groups to 60 years, where it is 4.5, and to 70, where it is only 3.3 years. Notice that the age given should be added to the expectancy, so that at the age of 70 men would, on average, expect to live to 80.1 and women to 83.4 years.

During the present century there has been a fairly dramatic increase in life expectancy, though with marked sex differences, women benefiting more than men. Between 1910–12 and 1980–2 expectation at birth increased by 19.5 years for boys and 22 years for girls. Much of this change is due to the reduction of infant mortality, though at the age of 20 years life expectancy over the period has increased by just over 7 years for men and just over 10 for women. At older ages the proportional improvement in expectation is even greater for women, whose expectation at age 60 displays an increase over the period of 5.5 years compared with only 2.3 years for men. As a consequence of this and differing retirement ages, expectation of life in pensionable age is almost 21 years for women (from the age of 60) but only 13 years for men (from the age of 65). And, in any case, women are more likely to survive to pensionable age than men.

OVERVIEW

This chapter has been concerned with social differences and inequalities in the vital aspects of life – birth, health and death. In broad terms we have seen that the non-manual in comparison to the manual classes are more likely to survive birth and childhood, enjoy better health and a longer life and receive, on the basis of need, more health care. These class differences are particularly stark at the extremes of the professional and unskilled manual classes. Not only have such class differences in health a considerable history, but they have persisted through several decades of NHS provision. We have also reviewed life-chance differences between the sexes, where despite their higher rates of ill-health females have better survival rates and longer average life expectancy than males. The illustration of these social differences, at least within the limitations of the data, has been relatively straightforward. Their explanation is much more problematic, as are their implications.

Explanations for social differences in health and survival are, and have been, sought across a broad spectrum. In respect to sex, at one end are biological factors, such as reproduction, constitutional and hormonal differences, at the other social factors, such as differences in social environment, roles and behaviour. Many of these provide evidence of association rather than causal relationship. What remains clear, then, is that health and its lack is affected by a complex interrelationship of factors which are also dynamic. Currently attention is focused on lifestyle and behavioural habits as key factors to health and morbidity (Wells, 1987). Hence it is still appropriate to conclude with Morris (1975),

> Prenatally and during infancy major biological causes are postulated for feminine superiority. Thereafter ways of living may be very different – in occupation, for example, . . . in the behaviour that culture expects. How much is biological, what social, is a continuing debate.

Biological factors are not appropriate to social class life-chances. Here social and economic factors – including income, work and specific occupational health hazards, housing and environment, attitudes about health, lifestyle, and the provision, nature and use of health services – appear to be the basic ingredients within the interrelationship of which lies explanation. Clearly, our knowledge and understanding at present is limited and what is required is considerable and extensive new research which directly addresses social differences in health.

CHAPTER 5

Wealth, Poverty and Expenditure

> What thoughtful rich people call the problem of
> poverty, thoughtful poor people call with equal
> justice the problem of riches.   R. H. TAWNEY (1913)

A large proportion of the social differences dealt with
in this book can be seen to have an economic basis.
Many reflect existing economic inequalities, others are
the results of long-term or past inequality. At a straightforward level the ownership of goods and the use of
services to some extent depend on ability to pay for
them. Of course, the relationship is not simple or direct,
for motivation or desire to own or use something is important and can be overriding. Clearly, though, choice and
even motivation are affected by economic circumstance.

In our society earnings and, particularly, accumulated
wealth are very much private affairs. The census, unlike
those in some other countries, contains no questions
about them. Industrial disputes over pay are often characterized by a lack, or confusion, of information about
scales and earnings. In social research, as in real life, it
is almost impossible to obtain an accurate and comprehensive picture of people's access to and possession of
wealth in its variety of forms. What is available are some
limited, separate views of aspects of wealth. The most
common and important form of wealth for most adults
in our society is earnings from an occupation, and it is
here we begin.

164

EARNINGS

The Department of Employment regularly publishes very detailed statistics concerning the earnings of people in employment in Great Britain, based on a random survey of employees 'in all categories, in all occupations, in all types and sizes of business, in all industries'. Unfortunately, these data are only published by industry group and for manual and non-manual workers. Thus in this section it is necessary to use the crude dichotomy of social class, which wherever possible has been avoided.

As might be expected, non-manual workers earned more than manual workers and this was true of both sexes (see Table 5.1). On average, male non-manual workers' gross weekly earnings were 43 per cent more than those of male manual workers (their pay being 143 per cent

TABLE 5.1 Average gross weekly earnings,[1] hourly earnings[2] and weekly hours for manual and non-manual employees,[3] April 1987

| | Social class (DE) | | | |
| | Full-time males | | Full-time females | |
	Non-manual	Manual	Non-manual	Manual
Average gross weekly earnings[1]	266	186	157	115
Average hourly earnings[2]				
Including overtime	680	417	418	292
Excluding overtime	679	404	416	287
Average weekly hours				
Normal basic	37.2	39.1	36.2	38.0
Overtime	1.5	5.5	0.6	1.6
Total	38.7	44.6	36.8	39.7

1. In £s rounded.
2. In pence, rounded.
3. On adult rates and whose pay was not affected by absence.

Derived from tables 86 and 87, *New Earnings Survey 1987* (1988).

of the manual average), while the difference for female workers was 37 per cent. These differences have grown: in 1979 the comparable percentages were 22 and 20 (*New Earnings Survey 1979*). Men earn about two-thirds more than women; the difference between male and female non-manual workers is 69 per cent, and that between manual workers 62 per cent. This difference has closed somewhat: in 1973 men earned nearly twice as much as women – non-manual 95, manual 93 per cent more. A further illustration of such differences is that in 1987 22 per cent of female workers (manual 40 and non-manual 17 per cent) compared with 4 per cent of males (manual 6 and non-manual 3 per cent) earned less than £100 per week (Tables 92 and 93, *New Earnings Survey 1987*).

It is also clear from the table that the differences in the actual rates of pay for manual and non-manual workers are greater, since normal hours worked and overtime are both higher for the former. Hence in terms of earnings per hour (second section of Table 5.1), male non-manual workers earned 163 per cent of the male manual rate with overtime included, and 168 per cent with overtime excluded. For women the differences were smaller, at 143 and 145 per cent respectively. On an hourly basis, partly because women in full-time employment work fewer hours than men, the earning differences between the sexes are somewhat smaller than for weekly earnings, especially for manual workers. Non-manual male workers earned 163 per cent of the hourly rate for non-manual women, and manual men 143 per cent of the female manual hourly rate. Working hours are examined in further detail below on pages 192–3 and Table 6.1.

A dated, but more detailed social class analysis is provided in Table 5.2. While inflation has affected the 'reality' of the figures, there are few grounds on which to suspect the pattern displayed of change. For men in general, average pay declines across the classes as a percentage of all earnings, but the eightfold classification (see pages 57–8 for details) reveals some interesting variation

TABLE 5.2 Men's average pay in each social class as a percentage of the average for all men, and that of women as a percentage of men's, 1978

| | Social class (RG/B) | | | | | | | | |
	1A	1B	2B	3	4	5	6	7	All
Men's average pay (as % of all men)	159	104	154	71	90	83	73	65	100
Women's average pay (as % of men's)	81	72	63	74	69	52	62	67	68

Devised from tables 2.28 and 2.30, Routh (1980).

among the non-manual workers. Managers and administrators (2B) earned more than lower professionals (1B), and clerical workers (3) earned less than all others, save for the unskilled (7). The second row of the table shows an uneven class pattern in the percentage of men's earnings earned by women. Overall, women in 1978 earned some 68 per cent of men's earnings, ranging from but 52 per cent in the case of skilled manual workers to 81 per cent for higher professionals. This last figure reflects the need for higher educational qualifications for such occupations and the fact that the relationship between educational qualifications and income is more marked in respect to women than men (see Table 8.4).

Of course, average earnings cover a wide range, as is illustrated in Table 5.3. Together with yearly averages for males and females are their median weekly earnings and an indication of the extremes involved. Note that the median is the figure in the middle of the earnings range, exactly half the earnings for each class are above the figure shown and half below it. The range of earning is illustrated by the lowest and highest decile (that is, tenth) of each class and by the highest percentile (1 per cent). Hence the table clearly demonstrates not only the expected income differences between the classes, but also considerable variation within them. Most of the general observations made about incomes from Tables 5.1 and 5.2 can be repeated in respect to Table 5.3. Differences in earnings between the sexes is marked on all the measures and in all classes. The median weekly earnings of all women was below that earned by the lowest decile of all men, and differences can be seen even among higher professionals. Each of the measures also displays a difference between non-manual and manual workers. The first, with the exception of class 3 (clerical workers), earned above the overall figure and the latter below. With this same

TABLE 5.3 Average and median earnings, by social class and sex, 1978

| | | | | | Social class (RG/B) | | | | |
	1A	1B	2B	3	4	5	6	7	All
Males									
Average yearly earnings[1]	8.3	5.4	8.1	3.7	4.7	4.4	3.8	3.4	4.8
Median weekly earnings[2]	109	96	98	68	86	79	73	66	82
Lowest decile (£ p.w.)	73	64	60	50	62	57	50	47	55
Highest decile (£ p.w.)	167	142	172	97	124	144	107	97	129
Highest percentile (£ p.w.)	256	211	324	140	182	168	154	143	220
Females									
Average yearly earnings[1]	6.7	3.9	5.1	2.7	3.2	2.3	2.4	2.3	2.7
Median weekly earnings[2]	85	69	71	51	59	46	45	43	52
Lowest decile (£ p.w.)	45	43	40	37	42	32	32	31	36
Highest decile (£ p.w)	137	106	104	69	85	68	64	62	84
Highest percentile (£ p.w.)	208	142	162	94	109	96	90	87	125

1. In £1000s, rounded to one decimal point.
2. Rounded to nearest pound; for definition of median see text.

Derived from tables 6.8 and 6.9, *Royal Commission on the Distribution of Wealth and Income*, Report No. 8 (1979).

exception there is a decline in earnings across the classes from 1 to 7.

The method of the payment of earnings also varies. Two-thirds of non-manual workers are paid monthly and over half have their wages paid directly into an account, whereas three-quarters of manual workers are paid weekly and just over half are paid in cash (Table 6.17, *Social Trends 16*, 1986).

Table 5.4 provides a view of median earnings, by ethnic group as well as social class and sex. As will be seen, median White male earnings were some £20 more than West Indian and about £18 higher than Asian. The figures for women are less marked and different, White female earnings were just over £4 higher than Asian and £3 lower than West Indian, and this reflects the smaller differences in job levels and pay among women than men. While part of the difference in male earnings is accounted for by ethnic differences in job levels, it is clear from the upper section of the table that these

TABLE 5.4 Median[1] gross weekly earnings[2] of full-time employees, by social class, ethnic group and sex, 1982

| | Social class (RG SEG 70) | | | | |
	1 & 2	3	4	5	6
White males	184.7	135.8	121.7	111.2	[99.9][3]
Asian and West Indian males	151.8	130.4	112.2	101.0	97.8

Men			Women		
White	West Indian	Asian	White	West Indian	Asian
129.0	109.2	110.7	77.5	81.2	73.0

1. For definition see p.167.
2. In £ and p, rounded to nearest 10p.
3. Based on small numbers.

Derived from tables 109 and 111, Brown (1984a).

differences are sustained within the social classes. In each class the White median is higher than the Asian and West Indian, and are closest for classes 3 and 6. While it is reasonable to conclude that such evidence indicates clear inequality of earnings between the ethnic groups, the factors involved are complex (for full details, see Brown, 1984b). For example, while differences remain within all classes among those aged 25 to 54 the gap in class 6 is wider and that in 1 is less. Brown concludes that the differences he reports have shown no overall change from 1974; the gap between ethnic majority and minorities has not closed in percentage terms. The same source reveals male median earnings differences within the Asian group, while in round figures those for Indian and African Asian, at £115 and £114, were similar to each other and above the overall figure, those of Pakistani and Bangladeshi were lower, at £106 and £89.

There are frequent claims and discussion about the closing of differentials of incomes between social groups – sometimes amounting to the suggestion that we shall all soon earn the same! *The Royal Commission on the Distribution of Income and Wealth* (1979) surveyed the dispersion of earnings over time and concluded:

> The evidence, therefore, suggests that changes in occupational structure have tended to widen the dispersion of earnings. This may seem surprising given the apparent contraction in the differences in earnings between occupational classes. However, the summary figures show that although the dispersion of earnings for the higher paid occupational classes has declined over time it is still greater than that for the lower paid occupational groups. Hence the movement from lower to higher paid occupations has widened the overall dispersion of earnings (para. G.25).

Earnings are, of course, subject to taxation and this in turn affects distribution of income. The net effect of changes in income tax and national insurance contributions between 1979 and 1985 was to widen weekly real take-home pay, as is illustrated in a governmental reply to a Parliamentary question (*Hansard*, 17 July 1986, quoted in Townsend, Corrigan and Kowarzik, 1987).

Bottom fifth of earners	−£2.33	or	−2.9 per cent
Middle earners	+£2.61	or	+2.3 per cent
Top fifth of earners	+£20.41	or	+ 11.6 per cent

Taking into account increases in indirect taxation and rates together with further cuts in income tax meant that over the period 1978/79 to 1988/89 the proportion of earnings paid in taxes by married men with children *increased* for those on or below average earnings and *decreased* for those above. The tax paid by a married man with two children on average earnings (estimated at £254 per week in 1988/89) increased from 35.1 to 37.3 per cent of his gross earnings, while for one on half the average the increase was from 2.5 to 7.1 per cent, over the period. On the other hand the tax paid by a married man with two children earning five times the average earnings decreased from 48.8 to 34.2 per cent of his gross earnings, and that for one on twenty times the average (just over £5000 per week) from 74.3 to 38.5 per cent (Treasury answer to Parliamentary question – *Hansard*, 10 January 1989, quoted in the *Guardian*, 16 January).

There are two further aspects, tax avoidance and fringe benefits from employment, which are largely unrevealed in official data. Opportunities for the first exist at most levels, though they vary widely according to source of income, being greatest in the case of self-employment (Playford and Pond, 1983). Fringe benefits are largest and most common among the better paid and their full value is not taxed. Hence they represent a further dimension of earnings differentials. Among directors surveyed in 1981 by the British Institute of Management almost 98 per cent had company cars (one in eight additionally had prime use of a chauffeur-driven company car), over 80 per cent had travel accident and life insurance, over half private medical insurance (see also Table 4.10 and pages 152–3) and more than one in five had free telephone or allowance and low interest loans. Further benefits, such as profit-sharing, share deals and private school fees, were part of the reward for smaller proportions.

Household income

Since the majority of people live with others in households (for definition, see pages 89–90) individual income is only part of the picture. The *Family Expenditure Survey 1986 (Revised)* (1988) showed that for households with heads who were employees the normal weekly disposable income declined across the social classes (FES): 1, £316.0; 2, £307.9; 3, £226.5; 4, £185.2; 5, £157.9. However, these data do not identify either the composition of the household or the number of incomes it contains. Households with more than one economically active member are clearly likely to have a higher per capita income than those with one or none. The two main situations of this kind are families in which both spouses and/or children are economically active and non-family households. The first are relatively common: *GHS 1985* found that in 55 per cent of married couples under retirement age both husband and wife were working. Table 5.5 demonstrates the social class variation in the distribution of households with given numbers of economically active members. There is no clear class pattern, but some distinct differences. At the extremes class I has by far the lowest proportion of households with none and three or more, while class V has the lowest with two and the highest without any. Overall almost half the households had two or more economically active members. Since most of those without are retired person households more useful figures in respect to income can be gained by omitting them (see second section to table). Almost three in five households with economically active member(s) have two or more, 15 per cent three or more. In the latter case there is a clear class pattern, with the middle classes below and working classes above the overall figure. In the case of households with a single economically active member, only class IIIm is below the average, and I, IIIn and V above.

The figures in Table 5.5 are based on the social class of head of household and therefore give no indication of the occupation of other members. A complete picture of the occupations of each member together with that of the head, which would be valuable, is not available. A view of the social class of married couples in which the wife is economically active can be found in Table 7.7.

TABLE 5.5 Percentage of households[1] in each class with given number of economically active members, England and Wales, 1981

| | Social class (RG 80)[2] | | | | | | |
	I	II	IIIn	IIIm	IV	V	All
All households							
None	9	13	17	13	18	19	15
One	43	38	39	35	36	39	37
Two	40	38	34	37	32	28	36
Three or more	9	11	10	15	14	14	13
Households with economically active member(s)							
One	47	43	47	40	44	48	43
Two	44	44	41	42	39	35	42
Three or more	9	13	12	18	17	17	15

1. With economically active and retired heads.
2. Of head or household, classified only.
Calculated from table 8, *Household and Family Composition* (1985).

Income and wealth are not easily separated. For our purposes, the latter can be identified as assets which have a marketable value which belong to an individual or household, both physical – property and land, consumer durables, and other possessions – and financial – money, rent and investments (accounts, stocks and shares). Obviously, many forms of wealth provide income, in the form of interest or dividends, but the importance of wealth is very wide-reaching. As Atkinson (1980) points out, it also provides 'security, freedom of manoeuvre and economic and political power. Moreover, wealth is very much more concentrated than income and has a major influence on the overall degree of inequality.'

Unlike social class differences in the ownership of wealth for which there are no data, the concentration of personal wealth is readily illustrated, see Table 5.6. These data are estimated by combining the distribution of wealth as disclosed by deceased people's estates with estimates by the Central Statistical Office based on personal sector balance sheets. What they show is that 1 per cent of the adult population (around 400,000 people) owned 20 per cent of marketable wealth in 1983, 10 per cent owned over half, and the most wealthy half of the population owned 96 per cent, leaving the other half of society to share but 4 per cent of the wealth. Put boldly, 1 per cent owned five times the wealth owned by half the population: inequality in wealth is extremely marked and blatant. Indeed, it may be difficult to appreciate. Pond (1983) provides a useful illustration based on the figures for 1979. If wealth had been equally shared, each adult would have had £12,000; in reality the lower half had on average £1200, the higher £23,000 (which is some twenty times higher), the top 1 per cent had almost a third of a £million. Of course, there is also a considerable range of wealth to be found within each grouping.

TABLE 5.6 The distribution of wealth in the UK, 1983

	Marketable wealth	Marketable wealth plus occupational and state pension rights
Percentage of wealth owned by:		
Most wealthy 1% of population[1]	20	12
Most wealthy 2% of population	27	16
Most wealthy 5% of population	40	25
Most wealthy 10% of population	54	35
Most wealthy 25% of population	78	57–60
Most wealthy 50% of population	96	80–84
Total wealth in £billions[2]	745	–

1. Aged 18 and over.
2. Estimates vary according to assumptions.
Derived from table 5.22, *Social Trends 16* (1986).

The addition of the projected value of pensions (see second column of Table 5.6) reduces the figures while sustaining the pattern of very high concentration. The inclusion of pensions has been questioned. Pond (1983) asks why if future pensions are counted as wealth, are not future inheritance and earnings? Burghes (1979) has pointed out that only about a third of the population has an occupational pension and that the value of all pensions depends on reaching, and length of life beyond retirement age – all of which are social class related (see pages 113–6 and 160–2).

There are two further aspects of wealth that need to be considered. First, its concentration has a history (see, for example, *Royal Commission on the Distribution of Incomes and Wealth*, 1979; Atkinson and Harrison, 1978). Wealth has remained similarly distributed throughout this century, and appears not seriously affected by changes in government. During the

Conservative period 1970–4 the richest's share of wealth fell somewhat, mainly due to the fall in stock market prices of 1970 – hence there was no comparable gain for the poor. During the Labour government of 1974–9, committed to 'a redistribution of wealth and power in favour of working people', the earlier loss was partly regained (Pond, 1983). It is difficult to see that dramatic reductions to the top rates of income tax, changes in other forms of taxation and to the economic climate by the Conservative governments of the 1980s will not be to the benefit of the already rich. Second, inheritance plays a substantial role both in its accumulation and its continued concentration. Harbury and McMahon (1980) found that two-thirds of those who left £100,000 or more in 1965 had had fathers who had left at least £25,000. They comment, 'This illustrates the importance of having a moderately wealthy father. If there were no connection between wealth of fathers and sons, one would expect less than 1 per cent of the population of sons to have had fathers with this size fortune.'

While it is not possible to demonstrate by data a relationship between personal wealth and social class, one may be safely assumed. Such wealth is the result of inheritance, creation, saving or accumulation, the legal opportunities for which are clearly related to class. Some relatively minor aspects of wealth are dealt with elsewhere – home-ownership and consumer durables at Tables 7.25 and 7.28, motor cars at Table 10.9. The ownership of stocks and shares and the use of financial services are in Tables 5.7 and 5.8. The first shows that despite governmental efforts to democratize or widen share-ownership through privatization the proportion of shares held by the middle classes (particularly AB) is very substantially greater than the working classes. On the other hand, the proportions owned by males and females, and the age groups other than 16 to 24 are much more similar than might have been expected. Table 5.8 provides a more detailed view by class. Of those surveyed some 15 per cent claimed ownership of stocks/shares, the percentage in class AB being twice the overall and three times higher than class D. The figures for unit trusts are lower and have a somewhat sharper class pattern. As might be expected, the rest of the table shows that the use of various financial services is greater in the middle classes than working classes and declines across the classes. The only areas in which class E has particularly high comparative use – making a will and life assurance – almost certainly reflect age rather than class, since state pensioners form a major part of this class. Ownership of cheque cards, like credit cards, shows noticeable class variation, as do bank overdrafts and loans – perhaps indicating that money makes money or, in this case, credit. Hire purchase, the more expensive form of credit, is more common in the working than middle classes. Car and house insurance, like mortgages, obviously reflect class differences in ownership (see Table 10.9) and home tenure (see Table 7.25).

Though it may not disturb the overall picture, it should be realized that quite small quantities of wealth may make for dramatic differences between units of similar income – for example, the inheritance of a home or the availability of assets at time of crisis. The effect of these may be proportionately most pronounced among the less

TABLE 5.7 Percentage of shares owned, by social class, sex and age

	Social class (MR)					
AB	C1	C2	DE	All	Male	Female
42	29	19	10	100	55	45

	Age				
16–24	25–39	40–54	55–64		65+
7	24	27	21		21

Derived from table 5.21, *Social Trends 17* (1987).

TABLE 5.8 Percentage of each class using various financial services

	Social class (MR)					
	AB	C1	C2	D	E	All
BANK ACCOUNT	91	88	81	73	56	79
Current	89	84	74	64	47	73
Deposit/saving	39	36	36	33	29	35
Cheque card	77	67	51	37	23	53
LIFE ASSURANCE						
Death only	44	47	53	54	52	50
Policy maturity/death	48	48	52	45	25	44
INSURANCE						
House/flat	70	63	56	44	30	53
Home contents	72	71	68	60	50	65
Comprehensive car	79	62	49	32	15	48
Any car	89	77	73	55	26	64
Private health	27	15	8	6	3	12
Paid for by employer	11	6	3	3	[–]	4
SAVINGS						
Building society	72	64	56	49	34	56
Unit trust	11	5	3	3	3	5
Stocks and shares	30	20	13	10	8	15
Premium bonds	47	41	30	24	22	33
CREDIT						
Credit card	63	49	35	25	15	35
Hire purchase	5	7	11	11	6	8
Bank overdraft/loan	14	14	12	10	2	11
Mortgage	52	46	42	27	9	37
HAVE MADE WILL	41	29	17	15	23	24
BELONG TO A PENSION SCHEME	47	42	40	31	10	36

Derived from pages 3, 25, 51, 73, 95, 106, 112, 130, 136, 142, 174, 182, 192, 202, 218, 238, 252, 262, 266 and 272 of BMRB's *Target Group Index 1987*, vol. 32.

well-off. Obviously again, not all middle-class people can be seen as wealthy.

Our consideration of wealth is neatly summed up by Pond (1983):

> Britain is a deeply divided society, and the deepest division of all is the equality in the ownership of wealth. That the inequalities have persisted so for so long helps in itself to legitimate them, to make them more acceptable. . . . And the extremities of wealth inequalities somehow deprive the statistics of credibility or meaning. Yet the truth is that inequality feeds on itself. Wealth begets income and opportunity, status and power; and from each of these springs wealth. The inequalities are circular and self-perpetuating.

POVERTY

A good deal of debate surrounds the definition of poverty, both in real life and social research. Broadly speaking there are two approaches: the absolute, in which a minimal level of income is defined as the poverty line; and the relative, in which reference is made to a standard of living, rather than survival or subsistence. At least for most people the concept of abject poverty has given way to those which involve some measure of standard of living relative to that enjoyed by the majority of members in society. However, it is not difficult to find those who see poverty in very basic terms. Sir Keith Joseph, who became the Conservative Secretary of State for Education, wrote:

> An absolute standard means one defined by reference to the actual needs of the poor and not by reference to the expenditure of those who are not poor. A family is poor if it cannot afford to eat. It is not poor if it cannot afford endless smokes and it does not become poor by the mere fact that other people can afford them. A person who

enjoys a standard of living equal to that of a medieval baron cannot be described as poor for the sole reason that he has chanced to be born into a society where the great majority can live like medieval kings (Joseph and Sumption, 1979).

Probably the best-known study of poverty is that of Townsend (1979) which identifies an 'official' level of poverty as that income at which state supplementary benefit (since 1988 called income support) is payable together with the cost of housing (for a definition, see footnote to Table 5.9B). By this standard, poverty is shown to be more widespread and frequent than might be expected. Townsend calculated that some 6 per cent of the population (3.3 out of 55.5 million persons) was in poverty and a further 22 per cent (11.9 million persons) on its margins, see Table 5.9A. These figures increased to 9 and 30 per cent in respect to a relative income standard – a net disposable income of less than 50 per cent, or between 50 and 79 per cent, of mean of household income for its type.

As can be seen from Table 5.9A, poverty was much more frequent in class 8 (at 15 per cent) than in the other classes, though its incidence is uneven across the classes. The percentage on the margin of poverty increases steadily over the classes from 6 per cent in class 1 to 32 per cent in class 8. Taken together, the two measures display a similar pattern, rising from just less than one in ten in class 1 to nearly half in class 8. When viewing these figures, bear in mind that the classification includes the retired and dependants of working people. Townsend comments, 'The correlation between occupational class and poverty is more striking if the retired are excluded.' On the other hand the table also reveals that the percentage of those enjoying an income 200 per cent or more above the supplementary standard, plus housing cost, declined sharply across the classes from 76 of class 1 to 20 of class 8.

Proportionately more children and elderly than young

TABLE 5.9A Percentage of each class in households with net disposable incomes in previous year of given percentages of supplementary benefit plus housing cost[1,2]

| | Social class (HG/B) | | | | | | | | |
	1	2	3	4	5	6	7	8	All
Less than 100	3	1	4	7	1	6	5	15	6
100–139	6	9	10	18	22	25	29	32	22
140–199	15	24	33	35	35	37	34	32	33
200 and over	76	67	52	40	42	31	32	20	39

TABLE 5.9B Percentage of each sex and age group in, or on margins of, poverty[2]

| | | Age | | | | |
		0–14	15–29	30–44	45–64	65 and over
Less than 100	Male	8	2	3	3	14
	Female	7	4	4	5	17
100–139	Male	25	13	21	11	37
	Female	29	16	20	16	43

1. Income at which state supplementary benefit was payable, plus rent including rates or mortgage and insurance but not repairs.
2. Less than 100 per cent of 1. defined as poverty; 100–139 per cent defined as on margins of poverty.

Devised from tables 7.10 and 7.13, Townsend (1979).

and middle-aged people were found in, or on the margin of, poverty (see Table 5.9B). The percentage of women in poverty was higher than men at all ages over 15, and also in respect to being on the margin, save for those aged 30 to 44. The survey shows that the factors associated with poverty were unskilled manual occupation, old age, disability, childhood, one-parent families, lack of education and unemployment. The social groupings running the highest 'risk' of poverty were: households composed of a man, woman and three or more children, unskilled manual status (89 per cent in, or on margin of, poverty); those aged 80 or over (86 per cent); those retired, living alone aged 60 or over (82 per cent); those aged 0 to 14, with parents of unskilled manual status (76 per cent); those with appreciable or severe disability and of retirement age (73 per cent). The only group to escape risk completely was professional or managerial status living alone or with spouse only, aged under 60.

Obviously a major factor in poverty is low income. *Social Trends* regularly surveys low-income families, which it defines by reference to a fixed point in the total income distribution – the 20 per cent of families with the lowest net incomes in the UK (adjusted for size and composition). Between 1971 and 1982 the composition of this group changed, mainly due to increases in the number of unemployed and one-parent families. The percentages of composition were (figures in brackets are for 1971): single people of working age, 34 (19); pensioners, 27 (52); working-age couples with children, 23 (17); working-age couples without children, 9 (7); one-parent families, 7 (5). Around 68 per cent of these families' gross income in 1982 came from social security benefits. For pensioners the percentage of income from this source was 88; for one-parent families, 84; working-age single, 65; working-age couples with children, 45, and those without, 59 (Tables 5.17 and 5.18, *Social Trends 16*, 1986).

Among the elderly, poverty is very strongly related to social class, based on occupation prior to retirement, as is shown in Table 5.10. The proportion of those in classes 5 and 6 whose income was at or below the level qualifying for supplementary pension was thirty times higher than in classes 1 and 2, and incomes at or below 140 per cent of the SP rate over six times higher. This clearly reflects not only the fact that occupational pensions are class-related, but that so too is their value together with unearned income and, hence, median gross income. When

TABLE 5.10 Income and poverty among the elderly,[1] by social class (percentages)

| | Social class (RG SEG 70) | | | |
	1 & 2	3	4	5 & 6
Income at or below supplementary pension level	1	8	15	30
Income at or below 140% of SP level	6	20	34	38
% with unearned income	63	55	34	34
Value[2] (per week)	6.3	3.0	1.7	0.3
% with occupational pension	66	37	29	20
Value[2] (median[3] per week)	34.0	26.8	15.5	12.3
Gross median[3] weekly income	73.4	36.9	30.7	28.0

1. Those aged 65 and over.
2. In £s and p, rounded to nearest 10p.
3. For definition see p.167.

Devised from tables 9.3, 9.4, 9.9 and 9.10, Victor (1987), based on unpublished *GHS 1980* data.

looking at these incomes it is worth bearing in mind that in the same year the average male weekly wage was £110. The source also reveals that even among the elderly, age continues to be a factor in poverty: 7 per cent of those aged 65 to 69 had incomes at or below the SP level compared with 28 per cent of those over 80 (for a most thorough and extensive review of data, see Victor, 1987). It would appear that despite the introduction of state pensions the same groups now as in history run the most risk of poverty in old age: the very old, women, the disabled and those who had manual occupations.

A survey of what the public in the 1980s regards as necessities provides a further view of poverty (Mack and Lansley, 1985). It reveals that most people see a wide range of goods and activities as necessities and that the concept of a minimum standard of living is based on social rather than survival or subsistence criteria. Respondents were presented with a list of thirty-five items and asked to choose (a) those that they thought necessary and which all adults should be able to afford and which they should not have to do without, (b) those that may be desirable but are not necessary. More than nine people in every ten placed the following in (a): heating, indoor toilet (not shared), damp-free home, a bath (not shared), and beds for everyone. More than two-thirds also included: enough money for public transport, warm waterproof coat, three meals a day for children, self-contained accommodation, two pairs of all-weather shoes, a bedroom for every child over ten of different sex, a refrigerator, toys for children, carpets, celebrations on special occasions such as Christmas, roast joint or equivalent once a week, and a washing machine. There was considerable agreement across the different social groups in the sample about the concept of 'socially perceived necessities'. The authors argue that poverty amounts to the enforced lack of three or more necessities (caused by low pay, rather than choice). Multiplying the number in their sample by the population leads them to suggest that one person in every seven is in poverty – some 5 million adults and 2.5 million children. They identify five particular groups which to some extent overlap – the unemployed, single parents, the sick and disabled, pensioners and the low-paid.

A somewhat similar, comprehensive approach is reported by Townsend, Corrigan and Kowarzik (1987). They have developed an 'objective' index of seventy-seven indicators of deprivation, based on indicators of conditions, relationships and behaviour, covering both material and social aspects and grouped as follows:

Material deprivation: dietary, clothing, housing, home facilities, environment, location, work (paid and unpaid).

Social deprivation: rights to employment, family activities, integration into community, formal participation in social institutions, recreation, education.

Table 5.11 provides an interesting view of people's attitudes towards state benefits and anti-poverty measures.
An overall majority see pensions and supplementary benefit as being too low, the percentage rising only slightly
across the social classes, in contrast to the steep rises for
unemployment benefit (doubles from AB to D and E) and
child benefit (almost three times greater for E than AB).
Men are somewhat more inclined than women to agree

TABLE 5.11 Attitudes towards benefits and anti-
poverty measures, by social class and sex (percentages)

| | Social class (MR) | | | | | | | |
	AB	C1	C2	D	E	Male	Female	All
AGREE TOO LOW								
State pension	53	58	59	62	60	63	54	59
Unemployment								
benefit	26	27	40	53	52	46	35	40
Child benefit	12	16	29	26	34	26	23	24
Supplementary								
benefit[1]	52	54	67	54	62	57	61	59
AGREE								
Differences in pay between highest and lowest too great	59	65	83	83	81	75	76	76
Government should increase taxes for rich	40	56	69	71	70	66	60	63
Gap between rich and poor today is too great	51	64	83	81	83	74	74	74
Government should introduce minimum wage for all workers	58	65	66	75	66	68	65	66

1. Respondents were told that those not working received £59.2 a week,
   excluding rent, for family with two young children.

Devised from tables 9.6, 7.7 and 9.7, Mack and Lansley (1985).

that benefits are too low. A fairly high degree of consensus over, and support for, anti-poverty measures can be seen. The least popular and that which shows the greatest class variation is increased taxes for the rich: only 40 per cent of class 1 compared to 70 per cent of D and E agreed.

EXPENDITURE

As we have seen, there is substantial evidence of differences in income and wealth between the social classes; in general the 'higher' the class, the higher the income and wealth. Obviously a similar relationship would be expected in the case of expenditure. The most comprehensive figures available are provided by the Department of Employment in their regular surveys of the expenditure of a sample of households in the UK (*Family Expenditure Survey 1986 [Revised]*, 1988). Note that the data in Tables 5.12 to 5.14 is that of households, many of which have more than one earner (see above), and that the classification of social class, although based on the RG, is unique, 1 and 2 being non-manual, 3, 4 and 5 manual (for details, see page 65).

The bottom two rows of Table 5.12 show that expenditure, both per household and per person, declines across the classes 1 to 5, the overall average dividing the non-manual and manual. This pattern is repeated in respect to each type of expenditure listed, with the exceptions of tobacco, which rises across the classes, and clothing and footwear, food and alcohol, together with services, where expenditure is higher in class 2 than 1. In Table 5.13 the data have been recast and expressed as a percentage of each class's overall expenditure. This shows a somewhat less regular pattern, but with some clear similarities. The percentages of expenditure directed to the necessities of fuel, light and power and food both rise across the classes. Differences in housing cost percentages are uneven and

TABLE 5.12 Average weekly household expenditure,[1] by social class,[2] 1986

| | Social class (FES) | | | | | |
	1	2	3	4	5	All[3]
Housing (gross)	50.47	43.78	30.15	29.59	27.92	36.19
(net)	50.19	43.46	29.23	27.25	23.69	35.07
Fuel, light and power	12.21	11.76	10.23	10.19	9.77	10.79
Food	46.32	48.08	40.53	36.44	33.40	41.04
Alcoholic drink	11.36	12.99	11.22	9.16	9.01	10.71
Tobacco	3.02	4.82	6.41	6.38	6.65	5.20
Clothing and footwear	21.92	22.96	15.50	13.74	13.35	17.28
Durable household goods	24.65	18.65	16.32	13.49	11.14	17.84
Other goods	21.54	20.82	15.65	13.73	11.63	16.92
Transport and vehicles	46.66	40.27	34.12	26.18	21.51	34.65
Services	39.22	42.33	21.99	18.66	18.19	28.52
Total expenditure[4]						
per person	96.95	89.92	64.26	61.03	60.05	74.96
per household	278.24	267.70	202.11	176.00	158.83	219.04

1. In £s and p.
2. Of head of household.
3. Includes unclassified.
4. Includes miscellaneous.

Derived from table 15, *Family Expenditure Survey 1986 (Revised)* (1988).

perhaps surprisingly close – the difference between gross and net housing cost reflects the working of the Housing Benefit Scheme. In percentage terms, expenditure on both alcohol and tobacco rises across the classes.

Since there is social class variation in the average number of persons in households, however, it could be argued that per-person expenditure reveals more satisfactory figures to look at; these are in Table 5.14. Note that 'person' here includes children, and no allowance is being made for class variation in the proportion of children in households (or their ages) even though this affects expenditure. The general picture is much the

TABLE 5.13 Average weekly itemized expenditure as a percentage of total household expenditure, by social class,[1] 1986

| | Social class (FES) | | | | | |
	1	2	3	4	5	All[2]
Housing (gross)	18.1	16.4	14.9	16.8	17.6	16.5
(net)	18.0	16.2	14.5	15.5	14.9	16.0
Fuel, light and power	4.4	4.4	5.1	5.8	6.2	4.9
Food	16.6	18.0	20.1	20.7	21.0	18.7
Alcoholic drink	4.1	4.9	5.6	5.2	5.7	4.9
Tobacco	1.1	1.8	3.2	3.6	4.2	2.4
Clothing and footwear	7.9	8.6	7.7	7.8	8.4	7.9
Durable household goods	8.9	7.0	8.1	7.7	7.0	8.1
Other goods	7.7	7.8	7.7	7.8	7.3	7.7
Transport and vehicles	16.8	15.0	16.9	14.9	13.5	15.8
Services	14.1	15.8	10.9	10.6	11.5	13.0
Miscellaneous	0.4	0.6	0.4	0.4	0.3	0.5

1. Of head of household.
2. Includes unclassified.
Calculated from table 15, *Family Expenditure Survey 1986 (Revised)* (1988).

same as in the other tables. There is a clear divide on each item between non-manual and manual expenditure, while tobacco is the only item to rise across the classes (note that this, like alcohol, is per adult). There are very few other exceptions: class 2 has somewhat higher per-person expenditure than class 1 on alcohol and clothing and footwear; classes 4 and 5 spend more on fuel, light and power than class 3. The consistent class differences in expenditure on tobacco reflect the differing proportions of cigarette smokers in the classes – see Table 4.8.

TABLE 5.14 Average weekly household expenditure[1] per person,[2] by social class,[3] 1986

| | Social class (FES) | | | | | |
	1	2	3	4	5	All[4]
Housing (gross)	17.58	14.70	9.58	10.26	10.55	12.38
(net)	17.48	14.59	9.29	9.44	8.95	12.00
Fuel, light and power	4.25	3.95	3.25	3.53	3.69	3.69
Food	16.13	16.15	12.88	12.63	12.62	14.04
Alcoholic drink[2]	5.66	6.10	5.19	4.57	4.70	5.23
Tobacco[2]	1.50	2.26	2.97	3.18	3.47	2.54
Clothing and footwear	7.63	7.71	4.92	4.76	5.04	5.91
Durable household goods	8.58	6.26	5.18	4.67	4.21	6.10
Other goods	7.50	6.99	4.97	4.76	4.39	5.79
Transport and vehicles	16.25	13.52	10.84	9.07	8.13	11.85
Services	13.66	13.21	6.99	6.47	6.87	9.76
Total expenditure[5]	96.95	89.92	64.26	61.03	60.05	74.96

1. In £s and p.
2. Adults only for alcoholic drink and tobacco.
3. Of head of household.
4. Includes unclassified.
5. Includes miscellaneous.

Calculated from table 15, *Family Expenditure Survey 1986 (Revised)* (1988).

OVERVIEW

This chapter has demonstrated the extent and strength of the relationship of inequalities of wealth and poverty with the social strata in Britain. Such differences may have been anticipated by readers, but are still likely to have an impact when straightforwardly presented. Severe divisions of economic well-being are not those terms in which many choose to see our society. Indeed, it may be argued that it is such a disinclination that limits not only discussion but also the extent and nature of research in the field. Certainly, as we have seen, knowledge is limited and somewhat piecemeal. In particular, and perhaps not surprisingly, the very rich and their circumstances are well shielded from public gaze and better protected from, and by, economic change. We have also seen that despite some apparent efforts towards redistribution, the realities of wealth differentials in our society appear stubbornly tied to those of our history.

CHAPTER 6

Work, Unemployment and Social Mobility

Each in his place, by right, not grace,
Shall rule his heritage –
The men who simply do the work
For which they draw the wage.

RUDYARD KIPLING (1902)

WORK

Work covers a wide range of activities and has a number of connotations. Our concern here is almost exclusively with paid work, since most of the data reviewed apply to those in full-time employment. This is not, of course, to deny the importance of unpaid work, the bulk of which is undertaken by women. Likewise it is important to appreciate that there are differences between the sexes in terms of their involvement in the labour market (for a full review see Webb, 1989). In comparison with men, women are less likely to be economically active or self-employed and more likely to work part-time. It is estimated that in 1985 some 80 per cent of the population of Great Britain aged 20 to 59 was economically active, 94 per cent of men, 65 per cent of married women and 75 per cent of non-married women (calculated from Table 4.4, *LFS 1985*). Women are more likely than men to work part-time. Of those aged 16 and over in employment, 96 per cent of men worked full-time compared with 76 per cent of non-married women and 45 per cent of married women. Twice as many men as women were self-employed (15 compared with 7 per cent, overall 12 per cent). The

191

aspects of work which follow need to be viewed within this context.

Hours at work

In the previous chapter we noted that there were differences in both average earnings and hours worked between manual and non-manual classes. Here, in Table 6.1, we take a more detailed view of working hours by occupation and sex. Just over 60 per cent of those surveyed worked more than 36 but no more than 40 hours a week in 1987. Non-manual employees worked longer than did manual ones, men longer than women. Of male non-manual

TABLE 6.1 Percentage[1] of non-manual and manual, male and female employees[2] with certain total weekly working hours,[3] April 1987

| | Social class (DE) | | | |
| | Full-time males | | Full-time females | |
Hours	Non-manual	Manual	Non-manual	Manual
Less than 30	3	0	5	0
30–36	21	2	28	16
36–40	57	43	59	61
40–44	9	16	5	11
44–48	5	15	2	6
48–54	3	13	0.7	4
54 and over	2	12[4]	0.4	2

1. Over 1 rounded.
2. On adult rates and whose pay was not affected by absence.
3. Range of hours '30–36' means over 30 but not over 36.
4. Includes 5 per cent working over 60 hours.

Derived from tables 155 and 156, *New Earnings Survey 1987*.

workers, 81 per cent had a working week of up to 40 hours compared to 45 per cent of manual workers, the majority of whom worked more hours. While a quarter of male manual workers worked more than 48 hours a week, this was the case for only one in twenty of the non-manual. The extremes are particularly marked: 3 per cent of male non-manual but no manual employees worked a week of less than 30 hours. Only 2 per cent of non-manual compared to 12 per cent manual workers had a 54 or more working hour week, the latter group having 5 per cent who worked in excess of 60 hours.

Overall, women worked considerably shorter hours than men, around 60 per cent of both non-manual and manual working between 36 and 40 hours. Indeed, the differences between the two groups of women workers were less marked than for the men, 92 per cent of non-manual and 77 per cent of manual female workers having a working week of up to 40 hours. Again, however, the extremes are dissimilar; 5 per cent of non-manual but no manual women worked less than 30 hours a week, while 6 per cent manual and 1 per cent non-manual worked more than 48 hours. The clear difference in overtime hours (male manual 5.5, non-manual 1.5; female manual 1.6, non-manual 0.6) obviously accounts for some, but by no means all, the differences in hours worked and, indeed, earnings (see pages 163–9 above).

Holidays

A further aspect of hours at work, and consequently of hourly pay, is the number of weeks worked in a year. Quite apart from such considerations, holiday entitlement is an important condition and attraction of employment. The range of holiday entitlements, not including the eight Bank Holidays, of full-time, manual and non-manual employees, by sex is in Table 6.2. As can be seen, overall non-manual employees enjoy the longest holidays, men faring somewhat better than women –

TABLE 6.2 Percentage of full-time employees[1] with given number of weeks holiday,[2] by social class and sex

	2 or less	2+ to 3	3+ to 4	Weeks[3] 4+ to less than 5	5 to less than 6	6 to less than 8	8 or more
Males	3	4	20	24	39	8	3
Manual	3	5	19	28	40	5	0.3
Non-manual	4	3	20	19	38	10	5
Females	4	4	25	25	31	4	6
Manual	5	6	22	31	30	7	0.6
Non-manual	4	4	26	24	31	4	8

1. On adult rates of pay.
2. Not including the eight bank holidays, but including holiday for long service.
3. E.g. 2+ to 3 means more than 2 weeks, no more than 3 weeks, etc.

Devised from tables 193 and 194, *New Earnings Survey 1987*.

though this difference may be affected by differences in extra holidays given for long service, which are included but not identifiable.

In terms of overall male holiday entitlement, five weeks equally divides the range: half receive up to five weeks, half receive five weeks or more; and this provides a measure for comparison with other groups. Hence the percentage of employees entitled to five or more weeks ranges: male non-manual 53 per cent (of whom 15 per cent have six or more); male manual 45 per cent; female non-manual 43 per cent (12 per cent six or more); female manual 37 per cent. The higher proportion of female than male non-manual employees with eight or more weeks' holiday (eight compared with five) is accounted for by the sexual imbalance in such occupations as teaching.

Occupational pension schemes

Until 1988 there were two main forms of pension provision, that of the National Insurance Scheme (NIS) and the pensions provided by some employers, many of which were mandatory and involved opting out of the earnings-related part of NIS. Presently, employees may choose to opt out of both these forms of pension into private schemes. At the time of writing, the most up-to-date data on participation in employers' schemes are that in Table 6.3. For both sexes the proportion in schemes decreases across the classes from 1 to 6, though in each class that for men is higher than women (overall 66 compared with 55 per cent). These class differences are mainly explained by differences in employers' provision of a scheme (see second and fourth rows to table). For example, almost a third of men in class 6 compared to 8 per cent of those in class 1 had an employer who did not run a pension scheme. In all classes women's employers were less likely to run a scheme than those of the men. Just over 40 per cent of both sexes aged 18 to 24 years were part of an employer's pension scheme, rising to some two-thirds for those aged 25 to 34. For women there was

TABLE 6.3 Percentage of full-time employees who were members of employer's pension scheme, by social class and sex

| | Social class (RG SEG 80) | | | | | | |
	1	2	3	4	5	6	All
Males	84	74	81	60	55	51	66
Employer has no scheme	8	18	10	27	29	32	22
Females	[–][1]	59	62	35	37	[–]	55
Employer has no scheme	[–]	30	17	41	39	[–]	24

1. Number of cases too small for analysis.
Devised from table 7.46, *GHS 1983*.

only a slight increase in the older age groups, but 77 per cent of men aged 45 to 54 years were members of pension schemes.

Conditions at work

The topics dealt with so far in this section are aspects of the conditions of work. A more general view of this, on a full social class basis, is provided by Townsend (1979). He uses the term 'work deprivation' to describe the factors listed in Table 6.4. Certainly many, but not all, can be seen as undesirable. As might be expected, the incidence of unusual hours of work, poor conditions and amenities, lack of job security and welfare/fringe benefits increases across the social classes. In each case there is a marked difference between non-manual classes (classes 1 to 5) and manual, and within the latter between skilled, semi- and unskilled workers. The most interesting differences between classes, for our purpose, are those between the routine non-manual (class 5) and the skilled manual (class 6). The latter had more than twice the former's percentage of those working before 8 a.m. or at night, and of those who did not receive sick pay (which was also more likely to be less than usual earnings). There were also differences between these classes with respect to poor working conditions, length of notice, variation in pay, length of paid holiday and pension cover. Variations on these factors between other classes may also be observed in the table.

Job satisfaction

Our views of work so far have been from the outside and tell us little of how the people involved feel or think about the work they do. A common question asked in surveys concerns people's satisfaction with their work. Such questions can be seen as problematic because of the variation of meaning and expectations that we can

TABLE 6.4 Percentage of men[1] in each class employed in jobs with certain characteristics

| | Social class (HG/B) | | | | | | | |
	1	2	3	4	5	6	7	8
Work mainly outdoors	6	8	16	12	20	37	30	63
All working time spent standing or walking about	2	16	27	28	32	69	79	89
At work before 8 am or at night	15	19	15	20	19	46	50	55
Working conditions very poor or poor	2	12	6	10	11	29	27	40
Subject to 1 week's notice	5	2	12	23	33	52	56	77
Pay varies	26	35	34	36	48	62	64	60
No pay during sickness	3	6	11	14	22	47	50	63
Sick pay less than usual	7	8	5	8	12	44	50	41
No occupational pension	10	2	18	21	36	54	49	76
No meals paid/subsidized by employer	47	49	73	74	84	82	77	81
Value of fringe benefits in previous year (£s)	451	303	209	225	107	65	56	38

1. Aged 16 and over and working more than 10 hours per week.

Derived from tables 10.11 and 12.2, Townsend (1979).

assume surround such an idea. However, the GHS has regularly asked, 'Which of the statements on this card comes nearest on the whole to what you think about your present job?' The card has printed on it 'Very satisfied, Fairly satisfied, Neither satisfied nor dissatisfied, Rather dissatisfied, Very dissatisfied'. Perhaps surprisingly, Table 6.5 indicates a very high level of satisfaction; overall, some 79 per cent were 'very' or 'fairly' satisfied. Social class 2

TABLE 6.5 Percentage of men[1] in each class satisfied and dissatisfied with job

| | Social class (RG SEG 70) | | | | | | |
	1	2	3	4	5	6	All
Very/fairly satisfied	83	85	78	81	78	75	79
Rather/very dissatisfied	12	12	16	15	17	18	16
Neither	2	3	5	5	6	6	5

1. Aged 16 and over and working more than 10 hours per week.
Devised from table 4.8, GHS 1977.

contains the most satisfied, followed by class 1, with the other classes not far behind. Dissatisfaction rose from around one in eight in class 1 to approaching one in five in class 6. In fact social class differences are far from dramatic, and other variables have been shown as significant. For example, women tend to be 'very satisfied' more than men (50 per cent as compared to 34 per cent), married persons more than single (43 as compared to 38 per cent), and part-time more than full-time workers (56 as compared to 39 per cent) (GHS 1977).

Absence from work

The GHS regularly surveys absence from work in the week prior to interview. As Table 6.6 displays, some 7 per cent of all workers had been so absent, and the main reason was their own illness or injury. For both sexes, absence for this reason was somewhat higher in the manual than in the non-manual classes, though the pattern is far from a regular gradient. Women had slightly higher sickness absence rates than men and the difference is more pronounced if only full-time workers are considered (the figures in the table include full- and part-time),

TABLE 6.6 Percentage of employees absent from work,[1] by social class and sex

| | Social class (RG SEG 80) | | | | | |
	1 & 2	3	4	5	6	All
Due to own illness/injury						
Men	2	3	5	4	5	4
Women	5	4	7	6	6	5
Men and women						
Strike/short time/lay off	[–][2]	[–]	1	2	[–]	1
Personal and other reasons	2	2	2	2	2	2
All absence	5	5	8	8	8	7

1. In week prior to interview.
2. Less than 0.5 per cent.
Devised from tables 7.32 and 7.37, *GHS 1983*.

since absence is higher for full- than for part-time female employees (*GHS 1981, 1983;* EOC, 1983).

As can be seen in the second section of the table, there are no class differences in absence for personal and other reasons, and only class 5 has a higher than average absence rate for industrial reasons. Hence, the pattern for all absence is similar to that for own sickness or injury – around one in twenty of all non-manual and one in twelve of all manual workers having been absent in the given week. Rates of absence do not appear to be related to the presence of dependent children for either sex, but not surprisingly the age of child does affect women's absence. Women with children under the age of five had an absence rate for personal and other reasons (including on account of children) of 7 per cent, compared with 2 per cent of those with older children and 1 per cent with none. The absence rate of men with children under five for personal and other reasons was 2 per cent.

Trade union membership

The percentages of full-time employees who were members of trade unions, or staff associations, are to be found in Table 6.7. Men are more likely to belong than women, 58 compared to 50 per cent (which is in some contrast to membership of other types of organization, see Chapter 10). Although the pattern is uneven, the classes with the highest proportion of members of both sexes were 4 and 5, while 3 and 6 were only somewhat lower, and 1 and 2 were the lowest. Public sector employees were more likely than those in the private sector to be members: 85 compared to 43 per cent of men, over three-quarters compared with a third of women. This difference reflects the fact that whereas 95 per cent of employees in the public sector said there was a trade union at work, this was true of only 58 per cent of those in the private sector. Within the private sector membership was much higher in larger establishments than in smaller ones. The table also shows that the membership is related to age. Of

TABLE 6.7 Percentage of full-time employees who were members of a trade union, by social class, sex and age

| | Social class (RG SEG 80) | | | | | | |
	1	2	3	4	5	6	All
Males	46	35	59	66	63	55	58
Females	[–][1]	40	49	61	53	[–]	50

| | Age | | | | |
	16–24	25–34	35–44	45–54	55–64
Males	21	47	56	59	67
Females	24	45	52	56	58

1. Small numbers: class 1, 8 out of 24; class 6, 23 out of 39.

Devised from tables 7E and 7.51, GHS 1983.

males and females aged between 16 and 24, 21 and 24 per cent respectively were members, about half the percentage of those in the ages 25 to 34 (47 and 45). The proportion in membership climbs steeply to retirement age for men, and much less steeply for women. Not surprisingly, of women working part-time only a third were members.

The PSI survey found a higher percentage of West Indian and Asian than White employees were trade union members (men, 64, 59 and 57 respectively; women, 57, 38 and 34). These differences were again mainly due to differences in the type, level and place of work (Brown, 1984a).

Changing jobs

An indication of the mobility of the workforce is gained from the *LFS 1985*. Among the currently employed, 90 per cent of men were with the same employer as they had been twelve months previously (of whom 3 per cent were doing different jobs), 3 per cent had the same job with a different employer and 6 per cent had changed both job and employer. The comparable percentages for women were: 88, 3, 2, and 8. Mobility was somewhat higher among the young. Of those aged 16 to 29 only 83 per cent of males and 81 per cent of females had remained with the same employer.

UNEMPLOYMENT

There are several definitions of unemployment used in social research. The official recording of unemployment has been affected by a series of nineteen changes in definition made by the Conservative governments of the 1980s. Nearly all of these changes resulted in a reduction of the officially recorded unemployed (Unemployment

Unit, 1986). So the level of unemployment depends upon both how it is defined and how data are collected. What is clear is that unemployment in our society has risen dramatically in the last decade and a half. For example, from 4 per cent of the economically active (for definition see page 91) in the census of 1971 to 9 per cent in that of 1981. By the mid-1980s the official figure was 11.8 per cent (see page 205). Because of these complexities it is necessary to take several views of unemployment. However, as will be seen, despite changes in extent and differences in definition, general patterns prevail.

The census defines unemployment as those people who state that they are 'seeking work', and in 1981 the percentages were: men, 10; women, 7; overall, 9. Table 6.8 shows that the percentage of men unemployed rose tenfold across the classes; from 2 per cent in class I to 21 in class V. The figures for women are similar for the non-manual classes, but are much lower in the manual (with an uneven pattern). This difference may well reflect that 'some women . . . do not regard themselves as seeking work if there is little chance of getting a job' (Britain's Workforce, 1985). The census also showed that unemployment varied according to country of birth, though this may be partly or wholly due to differences in the

TABLE 6.8 Percentage of unemployed[1] in each social class and sex, Great Britain, 1981

			Social class (RG 80)				
	I	II	IIIn	IIIm	IV	V	All[2]
Males	2	3	5	9	11	21	8
Females	3	2	4	5	6	3	4
Both	2	3	4	9	9	14	6

1. Unemployed classified by last occupation; based on economically active persons.
2. Classified only.

Devised from table 4, Britain's Workforce (1985).

class structures of the groups identified. The percentage of unemployed ranged: Old Commonwealth, 8; Republic of Ireland, 11; New Commonwealth and Pakistan, 14.

The *LFS 1985* provided a comprehensive view of unemployment, other than in respect to social class. It defined unemployment as those who in the week prior to interview had not had a paid job and had actively sought work (or had not sought it because they were waiting to start a new job, or the results of an interview, were sick or on holiday). Full-time students were included if they met the definition, unless unavailable for work within two weeks, as were people on TOPS courses who said they were looking for work.

The survey revealed an overall rate for the UK of 11 per cent of the economically active, with marked regional variations from 16 per cent in Northern Ireland to 7 per cent in the South East outside Greater London. Scotland and Wales, together with the regions north of a line between the Bristol Channel and the Wash, had rates higher than the average, those to the south lower. The survey also showed that 45 per cent of the unemployed had been seeking paid work for more than a year, 20 per cent for three or more years.

Table 6.9 shows the unemployment rates by sex, age and ethnic group. While the rates for men and women were similar (11 and 10 per cent), unemployment was higher for non-married women at 14 compared with 8 per cent for married. Those aged between 16 and 19 years had markedly higher rates than those older, but whereas for men and married women the percentage declined through the age groups, among non-married women the rate was almost constant for ages 20 to 59. For both sexes unemployment is almost twice as common among ethnic minorities than overall. It is particularly high for the West Indian and Pakistani/Bangladeshi groups. The final section of the table shows unemployment among those with and without qualifications (for definition, see Appendix B). In general, rates of unemployment for those with qualifications, particularly higher ones, are lower than those without. However, ethnic minority men with higher qualifications have a much higher rate than the overall one (10 compared to 3 per cent – and see Chapter 8).

Official statistics of unemployment are based on people claiming benefit (unemployment/supplementary/national insurance credits) at Unemployment Benefit Offices

TABLE 6.9 Percentage of economically active unemployed, by age, sex, ethnicity and qualification, Great Britain, 1985

| | Age | | | | | | | |
	16–19	20–24	25–34	35–49	50–59	60–64	65+	All
Men	20	17	11	8	8	9	7	11
Married women	18	16	12	6	5	4	0	8
Non-married women	18	12	12	13	11	7	8	14

| | Ethnic origin | | | | | |
	White	Non-White	West Indian	Indian	Pakistani/ Bangladeshi	Other[1]	All[2]
Men	11	21	23	18	28	17	11
Women	10	19	19	15	44	18	10

| | Qualifications[3] | | | |
	Higher	Other	None	All
All men	3	9	17	11
Ethnic minority men	10	22	29	21
All women	5	10	13	10
Ethnic minority women	6	22	23	19

1. Includes mixed.
2. Includes ethnic origin not stated.
3. For definition see Appendix B below.

Devised from tables 4.22, 4.17 and 4.24, *Labour Force Survey 1985* (1987).

on the day of the monthly count, who on that day were unemployed and able and willing to do any suitable work (excluding students claiming during a vacation). These are published monthly in the *Employment Gazette*. On this basis, the annual average percentage of the unemployed in the UK for 1985 and 1986 was 11.8, for men 13.7 and for women 9.1. Until September 1982 the DOE produced figures for unemployment and notified job vacancies at unemployment offices broken down into non-manual and manual, allowing for useful comparisons. For example, Table 6.10 shows a clear imbalance between the non-manual/manual divide of the unemployed and the workforce. Non-manual males represented 40 per cent of the workforce but only 20 per cent of the unemployed; in contrast the respective figures for manual classes are 60 and 80. Female unemployment is split more evenly – 58 per cent non-manual, 42 manual – reflecting more closely their proportions in the workforce (63 and 37 per cent). Since the passing of equal opportunity legislation, vacancies cannot be presented by sex. Overall, however, it is clear that non-manual vacancies (46 per cent) are more abundant in proportion to the unemployed (31 per cent) than are manual vacancies.

TABLE 6.10 Percentage of non-manual and manual unemployed persons[1] and notified vacancies, UK, September 1982

| | Social class (DE) | | |
	Non-manual	Manual	Total in 1000s
Males unemployed	20	80	2,123
Females unemployed	58	42	831
Male and female unemployed	31	69	2,954
Notified vacancies	46	54	115

1. People claiming unemployment/supplementary benefit/National Insurance Credit, excluding students during vacation.

Devised from tables 2.11 and 3.4, *Employment Gazette*, November 1982.

There are some reservations to be made to these figures. Not all unemployed persons register as such; for example, a major motivation for registration is gaining social security benefits, but not all the unemployed qualify or are entitled to these. This applies particularly to women, who consequently are more likely than men to be excluded from the official figures. Contrary to what is sometimes suggested, Brown (1984b) found that the rate of unregistered unemployment was not more frequent among ethnic minorities. Further, it is estimated that notified vacancies at employment offices may be only about a third of those existing in the economy. It should also be borne in mind that wide variations are to be found in unemployment and vacancies in different parts of the country. However, there are clear and general indications that unemployment among manual workers, particularly men, is both more common and less likely to be alleviated, than among non-manual workers. A number of other studies support this finding. For example, Smith (1980) suggests that the risk of unemployment is six times higher for an unskilled manual worker than for a non-manual one. McKay and Reid (1972) showed that the mean length of unemployment for unskilled workers was 20.5 weeks, for semi-skilled 12.6, and for skilled 9.7 weeks. Smee and Stern (1978) suggest that higher unemployment rates for the less skilled are due to more frequent job-changing, higher probability of unemployment between jobs, and longer spells when unemployed.

In Table 6.11 a further view of unemployment is provided by the *GHS 1983*. Again there is a difference in definition and application. Unemployed are those looking for work (or who would be but for temporary sickness) and those waiting to take up a job already obtained, whether or not they are registered or claiming benefit. The percentages, unlike the DOE's, are those of the total population, including self-employed, economically inactive and members of the armed forces. The view is of unemployment during twelve months, rather

TABLE 6.11 Male unemployment in past twelve months,[1] by social class, marital status and age (percentages)

| | Social class (RG SEG 80) | | | | | |
	1 & 2	3	4	5 & 6	Married	Single
None	94	89	83	68	87	70
1 spell	5	9	15	28	12	25
2 spells	1	1	2	4	1	4

| | Age | | | |
	18–24	25–39	40–59	60–64
None	65	84	88	83
1 spell	28	14	11	16
2 spells	7	2	1	1

1. Prior to interview.
Derived from table 7D, *GHS 1983*.

than current as in the surveys above. The table shows, as might be expected, that the incidence of unemployment rises across the classes and is markedly more frequent in the manual, both for one and two spells. It also reveals that the young and unmarried experienced it most.

From the *Northern Ireland Census 1981*, Religion Report, it can be calculated that while the overall rate of those 'out of employment' in 1981 was 19 per cent, rates among those declaring their religious denomination varied as follows: Roman Catholic, 30; Church of Ireland, 15; Presbyterian, 11; Methodist, 10; Other, 12.

SOCIAL MOBILITY

People change jobs, and sometimes this change entails a change of social class. Sociologists refer to this as intra-generational mobility, that is, upward or downward movement between social classes during a person's working life. The other form of social mobility referred to by sociologists is inter-generational, that is, the change in social class between two generations, the data being typically but not always limited to males (that is, father and son).

The classic British study of male, inter-generational mobility, carried out in 1949, is that by Glass (1954), data from which appeared in the first edition of this book, and it provides an interesting comparison with the most recent study on a similar scale (Goldthorpe, Llewellyn and Payne, 1980 and 1987). The authors argue that because of the nature of the social class scale they used (pages 68–72 for details) the seven classes do not form a consistent hierarchy. Consequently, they define upward and downward mobility only as movement into and out of classes I and II (the service class) regardless of origin or destination. Their basic data are contained in Tables 6.12A and B. Both tables use the social class of the respondents at time of interview and that of their fathers when the respondents were aged fourteen years. The first table (A) is an 'inflow' view, showing the social class origins of the respondents by their class in 1972. Hence the left-hand column of figures shows that 25 per cent of those in class I originated in that class, 13 per cent were from class II, and so on down the column. The second table (B) is an 'outflow' view, showing the social class achieved by respondents from different class origins. Hence the top row of figures shows that of respondents with class I fathers, 46 per cent were themselves in that class, 19 per cent in class II, and so on across the row.

There are a number of ways in which these data can be viewed, and for a full discussion within the theory and literature of social mobility see Chapter 2 of Goldthorpe *et al.* (1980). What is fairly obvious is that all classes are composed of men from the whole range of class origins, though the proportion whose class is the same or similar to that of their origins is much higher than

TABLE 6.12A Social class composition by father's[1] class when respondents were aged fourteen (percentages)

Father's social class (HG)	Respondent's social class 1972 (HG)							
	I	II	III	IV	V	VI	VII	All
I	25	12	10	7	3	2	2	8
II	13	12	8	5	5	3	3	6
III	10	10	11	7	9	6	6	8
IV	10	12	10	27	9	7	8	10
V	13	14	13	12	17	12	10	13
VI	16	22	26	24	31	42	35	30
VII	12	17	23	18	27	28	37	25
	Each column = 100							
All	14	12	10	8	12	22	22	100

TABLE 6.12B Social class distribution of respondents by father's[1] class, when respondents were aged fourteen (percentages)

Father's social class (HG)	Respondent's social class 1972 (HG)								All
	I	II	III	IV	V	VI	VII		
I	46	19	12	7	5	5	7		7
II	29	23	12	6	10	11	9		6
III	19	16	13	7	13	16	16	Each	8
IV	14	14	9	21	10	15	16	row	10
V	14	14	10	8	16	21	17	=	13
VI	8	9	8	6	12	31	26	100	30
VII	7	9	9	6	13	25	32		25
All	14	12	10	8	12	22	22		100

1. Or other head of household.

Derived from tables 2.1 and 2.2, Goldthorpe *et al.* (1980).

would be expected if 'perfect' mobility existed – that is, if the social class system were completely open and social origin had no bearing on, or did not affect, one's achieved social class. If that were the case, it would be expected that the overall figures in Table 6.12A would be the same, or approximately so, as those across the social classes. So, since 8 per cent of those surveyed had fathers from class I, they should themselves constitute that percentage of class I. In fact they are 25 per cent (three times higher) of that class, while at the other extreme only 12 per cent of those in class I had fathers from class VII (the class that provided 25 per cent of those surveyed). The opposite pattern can be seen in respect of those in the working classes (VI and VII); for example, in the latter case, 37 per cent had origins in that class compared to 2 per cent from class I. The only class that gets very close to the idea of 'perfect' mobility is V (row 5), where the percentages in classes I and II are 13 and 14, matching their overall figure of 13 per cent. Clearly, the general picture is one far from that of 'perfect' mobility, there being a strong relationship between origin and destination. This is further illustrated by the different view given in Table 6.12B. Here can be seen the social class distributions of sons from different class backgrounds – giving an indication of the chances of men from certain backgrounds of achieving each class. For example, of those from class I 65 per cent were in the service class (46 per cent in I and 19 in II), the percentages for class II being 52, 29 and 23 respectively. Of those from the working class 57 per cent stayed in that class. Social mobility, as defined by the authors (see above), was then of the order of 12 per cent of class I and 20 per cent of class II who entered the working-class and around 16 per cent of those from classes VI and VII who moved from working to service class.

A conclusion drawn by the authors is that social mobility may be easier upwards than downwards. In other words, in the face of general upward mobility in society the service class appears to be fairly stable – its members remain in that class. This is interestingly related to intra-generational mobility as illustrated by movement from class of origin to first job and then to

TABLE 6.13 Social class origins, first job[1] and job in 1972 of men aged thirty-five and over (percentages)

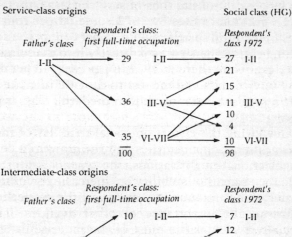

Service-class origins   Social class (HG)

Father's class	Respondent's class: first full-time occupation	Respondent's class 1972
I-II	29 I-II	27 I-II
		21
		15
	36 III-V	11 III-V
		10
		4
	35 VI-VII	10 VI-VII
	100	98

Intermediate-class origins

Father's class	Respondent's class: first full-time occupation	Respondent's class 1972
	10 I-II	7 I-II
		12
		11
III-V	31 III-V	13 III-V
		22
		6
	59 VI-VII	26 VI-VII
	100	97

Working-class origins

Father's class	Respondent's class: first full-time occupation	Respondent's class 1972
	4 I-II	3 I-II
		6
		8
	20 III-V	8 III-V
		20
		6
VI-VII	76 VI-VII	48 VI-VII
	100	99

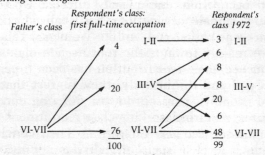

1. First job following full-time education (i.e. that not interrupted for more than two years except by National Service). Excludes holiday jobs or jobs held while waiting to take up an apprenticeship; trainees, etc., classified as belonging to occupations which they were training for.

Derived from figure 2.1 and note 33, p.66, Goldthorpe, Llewellyn and Payne (1980).

211

current class/occupation of men aged thirty-five years and over. The first section of Table 6.13 shows that while only 29 per cent of the sons of service-class fathers went directly into that class, by 1972 some 63 per cent were there. In the third section, while 76 per cent of the sons of working class fathers entered directly into that class only 48 per cent were there in 1972, 8 per cent having moved to the service class and the rest to the intermediate class, while 6 per cent had moved from the latter class into the working class.

In reviewing the effects on social mobility of increasing educational opportunities and the growth in demand for educational qualifications, the writers suggest that, while the chances of mobility are increasingly influenced by educational attainment, there is little evidence of a decline in the importance of other avenues. This is especially evident since most of the increase in upward mobility they traced occurred before the expansion of higher education in the 1960s.

Obviously, social mobility is related to the job opportunities available to sons and the differences between those and those available to their fathers. Goldthorpe, Llewellyn and Payne observe that the decline in the proportion of manual occupations has mainly affected women. The structure of male occupations has changed only since the inter-war period and, unlike women's, this change was not mainly towards the routine non-manual. As a consequence, male redistribution has been from manual to classes I and II. Similarly, they suggest that part of upward mobility may be due to differing social class birth rates, requiring working-class recruitment into the middle classes (see also Chapter 7). Their conclusion is that a high level of social mobility is not incongruent with stability in the higher classes, both of which are trends demonstrated in their data. Indeed, Goldthorpe *et al.* (1978, 1980) show that upward mobility increased over time – younger men had better chances of gaining service-class jobs and a lower risk of downward mobility.

However, this was not seen as indicating that Britain had become a more open society, since the increase is mainly accounted for by changes in the economic structure over the period considered. The *relative* chances of men from different classes display little change and the conclusion reached is:

> even in the presumably very favourable context of a period of sustained economic growth and of major change in the form of the occupational structure, the general underlying processes of inter-generational class mobility – or immobility – have apparently been little altered and indeed have, if anything, tended in certain respects to generate still greater inequalities in class chances.

Much the same conclusion is reached in a similar study of social mobility between 1972 and 1983 (Goldthorpe *et al.*, 1987). Despite the change from one economic era to another, the relative chances of mobility remained much the same as they had been for most of the century. In the period there was a heightening both of opportunities created by structural changes *and* risks from the return of large-scale, long-term unemployment (though as we have seen above, this was greatest in the manual classes). The combination of a deterioration of economic climate with a government since 1979 which explicitly rejected greater social equality is seen to have widened differences especially, but not only, through the emergence of a highly disadvantaged underclass. Goldthorpe supposes that in the long run tendencies towards greater inequality will widen the already marked inequalities of opportunity.

One of the few British studies to provide views of female social mobility based on their own employment is that of Abbott and Sapsford (1987). Since it differs in a number of important respects from Goldthorpe *et al.* – it was conducted in 1980–4 as compared with 1972, covered the UK, not just England and Wales, used a quota as opposed to random sampling and MR rather than HG social class, and had fewer respondents – direct comparisons are

TABLE 6.14A Social class composition of employed women, by father's class (percentages)

| Father's class (MR) | Respondent's social class (MR) | | | | | |
	A	B	C1	C2	D	All
A	50	17	13	5	2	11
B	24	35	23	12	4	20
C1	15	17	21	13	13	17
C2	9	23	33	56	54	38
D	3	7	10	14	27	14
			Each column = 100			
All	2	23	37	13	25	100

TABLE 6.14B Social class composition of employed women, by father's class (percentages)

| Father's class (MR) | Respondent's social class (MR) | | | | | |
	A	B	C1	C2	D	All
A	8	38	44	6	4	Each	11
B	2	41	44	8	5	row	20
C1	2	24	46	10	19	=	17
C2	[–][1]	14	32	19	35	100	38
D	[–]	12	27	13	48		14
All	2	23	37	13	25		100

1. Under 1 per cent.

Derived from tables 19 and 20, Abbott and Sapsford (1987).

limited. Tables 6.14A and B are inflow and outflow views of female social mobility similar to those for males (6.12A and B).

As can be seen from Table 6.14A, there is considerable heterogeneity in classes A and B (though less than in the case of men), while the manual classes are more homogeneous. Of those with class D occupations, 27 per cent had origins in that class and 81 per cent came from manual backgrounds, with only 6 per cent from A/B. For those in C2 the respective percentages were 56, 70 and 17. For those in class A, 50 per cent had the same background, a further 24 per cent were from B and only 12 per cent from manual origins. A greater variety of origins was found among women in class B.

Table 6.14B shows that only 8 per cent of women who originated in class A stayed in that class, while 48 per cent of those from class D had remained in that class. Movement between the extremes was limited: less than 1 per cent from D to A and 12 to B, and 10 per cent from A to C2/D. Overall 39 per cent of women had crossed the non-manual/manual divide, 44 per cent from manual to non-manual (though 31 per cent went to C1) and 56 per cent were downwardly mobile from classes A or B, 44 per cent to C2 and 12 to manual classes.

The authors conclude, 'There is considerable female inter-generational mobility ... downward mobility occurs more frequently for women ... women of whatever origin are more likely than men to end up in routine non-manual jobs.' They also report that separate analyses of part- and full-time, married and single employees, all revealed similar patterns. They took this to indicate that sex rather than marital status or part-time employment is the key factor in labour market segregation.

Evidence suggests differences between the sexes in terms of intra-generational mobility. Chapman (1984), in a replication of the Goldthorpe, Llewellyn and Payne study, which included women, found that men experienced more upward mobility than women and that women were less likely to be countermobile (see pages 210–2 above). Similar findings are reported by Greenhalgh and Stewart (1982), who found that single and full-time females experienced less disadvantage than those married, divorced or working part-time. Martin and Roberts (1984), in a detailed and large-scale study of women's lifetime work histories, provide a valuable insight into the effects on women's employment of leaving to have children. They found that some 51 per cent of women returning to work changed social class, 37 per cent 'down' and 14 per cent 'up'. Part-time returnees were more likely to be downwardly mobile (45 compared with 19 per cent) than were the full-timers. Subsequently, 60 per cent of returnees stayed in the class they entered, 23 moved 'up' and 17 'down'. Mobility was affected by movement between part- and full-time work: moving to the first was more likely to lead to downward mobility, the second to upward. Clearly, then, interruption in work history and part-time employment, related to women's domestic responsibilities, are important factors affecting female intra-generational mobility.

Abbott and Sapsford (1987) also address a further aspect of female social mobility, that of the relationship between class of father and that of husband, or marital mobility. Apart from being an aspect of women's intra-generational mobility it is also a measure of the openness of the class structure (see also pages 233–5 which look at the social class of spouses). Table 6.15 reveals that while there is fluidity, most of it is short-range. Overall 70 per cent of women married men from the same side of the manual/non-manual divide, 19 per cent with manual origins married men from non-manual classes, and 11 per cent with non-manual origins married men from the manual class. In general the pattern of female marital mobility

TABLE 6.15 Women's marital mobility (percentages)

Father's class (MR)	Husband's social class (MR)						All
	A	B	C1	C2	D		
A	33	45	7	14	1		10
B	21	52	13	10	3	Each	19
C1	10	33	21	25	12	row	18
C2	5	24	12	47	12	=	37
D	4	14	10	44	28	100	15
All	12	32	13	32	11		100

Derived from table 11, Abbott and Sapsford (1987).

is similar to that of male intra-generational mobility, though there is more downward mobility for women through marriage than for men through occupation.

At the same time it is clear that marital mobility at the extremes is limited: a large majority of women from classes A/B and C2/D married men of similar class to their fathers'. Some 78 per cent of women of class A origin, and 73 per cent of class B, married men of either A or B; only 15 and 13 per cent respectively married men from the manual classes. Of class D daughters, 72 per cent had husbands from the manual classes, only 18 per cent those from A and B, while the respective percentages for those from class C2 were 59 and 29. Not surprisingly, the most assortive mating occurred in class C1. Left unanswered by this and other studies is the exact nature and mechanism of this mobility. The data relate father's and husband's class, but fail to illuminate the role women's own class plays at the time of marriage, and the effects of intra-generational mobility of spouses.

Of course, in all forms of social mobility its incidence is dependent upon the number of social classes used to measure it. For example, Townsend (1979) demonstrates the difference between using the simple non-manual/manual dichotomy compared to an eightfold classification (HJ/B). With the first measure 19 per cent of the men in his survey had been upwardly and 14 per cent downwardly mobile in comparison with their fathers, and the respective figures for women were 20 and 13 per cent. In other words, around two-thirds of both sexes had not been mobile. Using the eight social classes and treating movement between them as equal gave the result of only 31 per cent of men being in the same class as their fathers, 41 per cent having been upwardly and 29 per cent downwardly mobile – with the figures for women being only marginally different from those for the men at 29, 42 and 29 per cent. A similar critical factor is the age and career stage at which father and child's occupations are compared in order to identify social mobility. In Tables 6.13 and 6.15 it was seen that sons and daughters had been involved in a considerable amount of intra-generational mobility, and fathers are likely to have been similarly involved. Ideally one would compare like with like – the occupation each held for the majority of their working lives or both at an age when further change is unlikely. Similarly, full work histories of both would greatly illuminate the changes in, and relationship between, intra- and inter-generational mobility. However, such data collection poses fairly severe problems for large-scale research.

Useful illustration of British people's views is provided by Harrop (1980), whose research was based partly on market research data. Perhaps surprisingly, the public has an accurate view of the amount of social mobility and of the proportion (two-thirds) of those who 'inherit' their class from parents, which accords closely with the data of Goldthorpe *et al.* When presented with ability, education and social background as factors for mobility, the public overwhelmingly chose ability as the most important (79 per cent of middle-class respondents and 62 per cent of working-class); education was a poor second at 15 and 25 per cent respectively. Even among those who chose education as the most important, almost 70 per cent saw the quality of education being dependent upon individual ability rather than social background. Hence the public have a very individualistic, or meritocratic, view of mobility in some contrast to that of most social scientists. The public's view, Harrop argues, allows it to have an optimistic view about the openness of society while recognizing the extent of parent–child class determination. The compatibility of these views is sustained because of the level of residential segregation of the classes and the way in which it obscures the class bias in the distribution of opportunity. Within-class interaction and comparison is much more common than across classes, with the result that differences in achievement are typically viewed as resulting from differences between individuals rather than as a product of the social structure.

CHAPTER 7

Family, Marriage and Home

The rich man at his castle,
The poor man at his gate,
God made them, high or lowly,
And order'd their estate.

Mrs C. F. Alexander 'All Things Bright and Beautiful'
(Hymn 573, *Hymns Ancient and Modern*, 1950)

THE FAMILY

The family is almost certainly the oldest, the most basic and the most common of human institutions. Almost every society, throughout history and across the world, contains families. While dictionary definitions of the family are straightforward – 'a primary social group consisting of parents and their offspring, the principal function of which is provision for its members' (Hanks, 1979) – the actual form and nature of families in our society have a considerable range and have been and are subject to change (for a review of these and their implications see OPCS, 1987). Some of these aspects are explored in what follows, but initially we use the traditional and what is the majority concept and experience of the family, that based on marriage.

In our society the family through marriage has a legal status for all and a religious (or symbolic) significance for many. The latter is witnessed by the relative stability and popularity of church or religious weddings, despite a marked decline in church attendance. Of those marriages which were the first for both partners in Great Britain during 1985 69 per cent had a religious, and 31 per cent a civil, ceremony (*Social Trends 17*, 1987). The

219

comparable percentages for weddings which were remarriages for either or both partners were 21 and 79.

The legal and formal importance of the family and marriage is brought out by the fact that marital status, along with one's sex, age and occupation, is one of the pieces of information most commonly required for official and other purposes by a whole host of agencies. Family relationships lie at the basis of inheritance law and that surrounding responsibility for child care and education. Social and governmental agencies and research regard marital condition as a vital statistic and analyse and classify a whole series of other factors by it – sex, age, health, mortality, economic activity, the population and so on. Unfortunately for our purposes, not all such research cross-tabulates marital status and family data directly with social class. This is curious to the extent that the evidence is collected, particularly for example in the census, but is not published. At marriage the occupation of bride and groom and of their parents must be recorded, and at birth that of the father. Similarly, court proceedings, including divorce, usually contain reference to a party's occupation. This information is not, however, presented in the statistical returns. But, as Leete (1979) has pointed out, while the registration of births and deaths is subject to official returns, those of marriage are not and therefore there is likely to be greater variation in accuracy.

Marriage

Other than the family and school, marriage is the commonest institution in our society, being experienced by all but a minority of people. By the age of forty only about 5 per cent of women and 9 per cent of men in our society have not been married (*Marriage and Divorce Statistics 1985*). Of each 100 persons in the population of England and Wales over the age of sixteen in 1985, 61 were married, 26 single, 9 widowed and 5 divorced. While the same percentage of each sex was divorced, men were more likely than women to be single (29 per cent compared with 24) and married (63 per cent compared with 58) and much less likely to be widowed (4 per cent compared with 14). These sex differences are mainly accounted for by three facts: women tend to marry at an earlier age than men; men are somewhat less likely to marry at all (to some extent related to the fact that there are more men than women under the age of fifty and that people of that age currently account for around nine in ten of all marriages); and women, who live longer, are more likely to outlive their spouses.

Sex differences in age at marriage can be illustrated in a number of ways. For example, of those aged between sixteen and nineteen years in 1985 it is estimated that 36 in each 1000 women but only 7 per 1000 men were married – a dramatic change from 1975 when the corresponding figures were 101 and 22 respectively. Both average and median age at marriage are markedly lower for women than for men. Leete (1979) identified a growing surplus of single men at the younger marriageable ages, due to the unequal sex:birth ratio, as well as to the fact that men tend to marry women from younger age groups than their own, which had been affected by declining birth rates. In turn, this widens the gap between the marriage rates of the sexes and leads to more men marrying women older than themselves. In the long term, it seems likely that the proportion of men who never marry will be larger than the proportion of women, reversing the pattern established between the wars. The gap between the number of bachelors and spinsters has grown quite dramatically – from 107 bachelors per 100 spinsters in 1961 to 123 per 100 in 1985.

Unfortunately for our purposes, marriage and marital status statistics are not regularly published or analysed by social class and hence there is little direct or extensive evidence about class variation in the incidence of marriage (or, for that matter, for divorce – see below).

An interesting analysis of a sample of marriages in 1979 (Haskey, 1983) includes the calculated percentages of men and women marrying by given ages, shown in the upper section of Table 7.1. These are based on the age-specific marriage rates for 1979 and are therefore hypothetical to the same extent as life expectancy figures (see Table

TABLE 7.1 Cumulative percentages[1] of men and women[2] ever marrying, by age, and married couples[3] and men under twenty years as a percentage of all, by social class and sex

	Social class (RG 80/70)						
Age	I	II	IIIn	IIIm	IV	V	All[4]
Men							
20	0	3	5	4	10	8	6
25	65	47	44	46	44	52	46
30	84	73	71	74	68	67	72
40	93	89	84	86	81	74	85
Women							
20	0	17	19	21	25	23	20
25	35	65	66	69	65	79	66
30	62	87	81	86	71	98	82
40	[–][5]	93	87	94	86	[-]	91
Married couples under 20	0.3	0.4	0.5	0.8	0.8	1.2	0.7
Married men under 20	0.03	0.07	0.2	0.3	0.3	0.6	0.3

1. E.g. right-hand column = 6 per cent married by age 20, 46 by 25, etc.
2. Social class of men and women in their own right.
3. Based on husband's class.
4. Cumulative percentages based on national statistics.
5. Not available.

Derived from table 6, Haskey (1983) and calculated from table 47, *Household Composition Tables (10% Sample), Census 1971* (1975).

4.16 above). For men and women the proportion married by the age of twenty years rises across the classes. For men aged twenty-five and over the married proportion is highest in class I; and with some variation, in general the non-manual classes are above, the manual below the overall figure. For women (whose class is based here on their own occupation) of the same ages, the pattern is almost the reverse of that of the men. In particular the percentage married in class I is lower than the overall figure and that for class V higher.

The figures also indicate class and sex differences in age at marriage. Members of the manual classes and particularly women marry at an earlier age, as has been illustrated by a number of studies over time (for example, Pierce, 1963; Gavron, 1966; Gorer, 1971). An extensive, different set of figures can be calculated from the census (see lower section of Table 7.1). These are based on married couples' ages and the husband's social class. The top row shows that the percentage of married couples both of whom are under the age of twenty increases fourfold, from 0.3 in class I to 1.2 in class V. While there is a difference between the non-manual and manual classes, the largest difference is for class V, where the percentage is some four times higher than for class I, half as high again as for class IV and nearly twice the overall figure. The second row to the table displays a similar, but even more marked pattern to the percentage of married men under the age of twenty, by social class. As only male social class has been used the data do not allow for the analysis of figures for women, although as we have seen above these would be higher overall. Dunnell (1979) explored women's attitudes concerning the best age for marriage. While the most popular age for all classes was twenty to twenty-four, the percentage favouring the teens rose dramatically from 3 for class I to 12 for both class IV and V. Conversely, those favouring marriage at twenty-five years or over declined from almost two-fifths of class I to less than a quarter for all the manual classes.

There are some very clear differences in the incidence of marriage in ethnic groups, as illustrated in Table 7.2 Note that these figures relate to those currently married. The proportion married in the Indian and Pakistani/Bangladeshi groups is for both sexes markedly higher than the other ethnic groups. At ages 16 to 29 40 and 45 per cent of men and well over 60 per cent of the women in these two groups were married compared to 29 and 45 per cent of White men and women. At ages 30 to 44 nearly all of the Indian and Pakistani/Bangladeshi groups were married. In contrast the West Indian/African group had generally a lower proportion married than all other groups. This difference is particularly pronounced in the age group 16 to 29, where the proportion for both sexes is about half that for all groups.

TABLE 7.2 Percentage of population currently married, by ethnic group, age and sex, Great Britain, 1984–6[1]

	White	West Indian/ African	Indian	Pakistani/ Bangladeshi	Other	All minorities	All[2]
Males							
16–29	29	15	40	45	27	30	29
30–44	84	82	94	95	87	90	84
45+	81	77	90	97	83	86	81
All 16+	67	51	73	76	58	64	67
Females							
16–29	45	23	63	76	42	48	45
30–44	88	69	94	97	87	86	87
45+	61	67	69	88	68	71	61
All 16+	63	47	75	85	63	65	63

1. Results of three years LFS averaged.
2. Includes 'not stated'.

Derived from table 5, Shaw (1988).

Cohabitation

Living together as husband and wife without being legally married can be viewed in two ways: as a current condition, or as a pre-marital one. Both have considerably increased in the period since the GHS began to survey them regularly, by questioning women aged 18 to 49. Between 1979 and 1985 the percentage of all women cohabiting increased from 2.7 to 5, and that for non-married women from just under 11 to just under 16 (*GHS 1985*). Cohabitation was most common among those in their early twenties – 9 per cent in 1984/5 – followed by those aged 18 to 19, at 7, and those 25 to 29 at 6 per cent. Divorced women had the highest rate – 21 per cent of those surveyed – with separated at 18, single 13 and widowed at 7 per cent.

Cohabitation prior to marriage which was the first for both partners and at which the wife was under thirty-five increased from 7 per cent of marriages in 1970–4 to 26 per cent of those in 1980–4. The respective percentages for marriages which were not the first for one or both partners were 12 and 37. In both types of marriage, couples where the bride was twenty-five or older were more likely to have cohabited than in those where she was younger.

Kiernan (1980) suggests that pre-marital cohabitation may be more common among more educated and 'higher' social class couples. A further analysis revealed that the percentage of married women who had cohabited ranged from 18 for those who stayed at school beyond the statutory leaving age to 10 who left at that age, and from 13 for those married to non-manual husbands to 11 for those with manual (Brown and Kiernan, 1981). Some 32 per cent of a sample of couples who married between 1978 and 1981 either gave the same address in their marriage entry or reported having cohabited prior to marriage (Haskey and Coleman, 1986). This study, which analysed the full range of classes (RG SEG, based on husband's occupation), revealed very little appreciable variation in the rates between the social classes.

Divorce

Divorce is the most obvious and dramatic indication of marriage breakdown, but by no means the only or necessarily the most common one. In 1985 the divorce rate (persons divorcing per 1000 married people) was 13.4, which was more than double the rate in 1971 (*Social Trends 17*, 1987). Of the divorces in 1985 23 per cent were where one or both partners had been previously divorced.

National figures on divorce by occupation of the husband were published yearly, in 'Civil Judicial Statistics', until 1921, and research in the early part of this century suggested that only some 29 per cent of all divorces were working-class (as defined by husband's occupation at marriage: McGregor, 1957). Data on divorces in the 1960s, based on husband's occupation at time of divorce, displayed a quite different picture (*Statistical Review of England and Wales 1967*, 1971; Gibson, 1974). The calculated divorce rate was lowest in class I, followed by classes II and IV, higher in III (and markedly higher for IIIn than IIIm) and highest in class V – twice that for classes I, II and IV.

Social and legislative change obviously affect both the incidence and distribution of divorce; however, the figures in Table 7.3, based on a sample of divorces in 1979, display a pattern similar to that of the 1960s. Except for class IIIn, the standardized divorce ratios (for definition see footnote to table) and rates rise across the social classes. The range from class I to V is more than four to one. A number of class-related factors affect divorce rates. For example, marriages at younger ages, particularly the teens, are higher risks for divorce than later ones. As we saw above, teenage marriage is more prevalent in classes IV and V than in others, especially I and II. A similar

TABLE 7.3 Divorce rates[1] and standardized divorce
ratios[2] for the social classes

			Social class (RG 80)				
	I	II	IIIn	IIIm	IV	V	All[3]
Divorce rate	7	12	16	14	15	30	15
Standardized divorce ratio	47	83	108	97	111	220	100

1. Per 1000 husbands aged 16 to 59.
2. The number of actual divorces expressed as a percentage multiple of the
   expected number (calculated for ages 16 to 59 by multiplying estimated
   number of married men in each class by national divorce rate).
3. Includes others.

Devised from tables 3 and 5, Haskey (1984).

situation is to be found in respect to married couples with
pre-maritally conceived child(ren) (see below). However,
such factors do not remove the clear influence of social
class on divorce rates. As Haskey (1984) concludes, 'It is
possible that social class is a good predictor of divorce
differentials because it distinguishes different patterns of
social norms, behaviour and expectations in the crucial
period before marriage.'

Wives are more likely than husbands to be granted
a divorce: of divorces in 1985, 72 per cent were granted
to wives, 28 per cent to husbands and hardly any (0.4
per cent) to both (*Marriage and Divorce Statistics 1985*).
There is a similar sexual bias in the petitions for divorce,
though a majority were filed by husbands in the period
1901–5 and during and immediately following both world
wars. Differences exist between the sexes over which of
the five 'facts' for 'the irretrievable breakdown of marriage' (the sole grounds for divorce since the Divorce
Reform Act 1969) were used in divorce proceedings.
While nearly half of the divorces granted to women
cited husband's unreasonable behaviour, 44 per cent of
those granted to men cited wife's adultery.

Social class differences in the grounds for divorce are illustrated in Table 7.4. The percentage of decrees for adultery granted to husbands is higher than to wives (42 compared with 24) and in both cases is somewhat more common in the middle than the working classes. Decrees for unreasonable behaviour are much rarer grounds for husbands than for wives (6 compared with 42 per cent) and rise across the classes. Wives with husbands in class V were two and a half times more likely to win their divorce on this ground than those with husbands in classes I or II. The class differences in adultery and unreasonable behaviour decrees might be seen to mirror commonly held views of class-based marital misbehaviour, but are just as likely to reflect differing class attitudes towards the acceptability of grounds

TABLE 7.4 Distribution in each social class[1] of divorces, by class of decree[2] and party (percentages)

| | Social class (RG 80) | | | | | | |
	I	II	IIIn	IIIm	IV	V	All[3]
To husband							
Adultery	46	40	45	46	39	32	42
Behaviour	0	4	10	6	7	11	6
Separation	46	54	45	45	45	50	47
To wife							
Adultery	25	37	30	25	22	15	24
Behaviour	25	27	40	41	43	67	42
Separation	47	33	27	31	30	17	30
Decrees granted to wife	57	65	68	70	71	81	71

1. Of husband.
2. Rows do not add to 100 because decrees of nullity and divorce for desertion are not shown.
3. Includes others.

Devised from table 3, Haskey (1986b).

for divorce. Decrees for separation are more commonly granted to husbands than to wives, and whereas in the case of husbands there is no class pattern, for wives there is a decline across the classes. Wives of husbands in classes I and II were more than twice as likely as those with husbands in class V to win their divorce on this ground. This difference may be related to the relative ease with which separate accommodation can be afforded or arranged in the 'higher' classes. The final row of the table shows that while the majority of decrees in all social classes is given to wives, this increases from 57 to 81 per cent from I to V.

Of course, as Haskey (1986b) points out, the record-ed ground for divorce cannot be taken as the root or actual cause of marital breakdown − 'whatever the cli-ent's reason for wanting divorce, the lawyer's function is to discover grounds' (Chester and Streather, 1972). The likelihood of success and/or the speed of divorce, together with the implications for children, finance and accommo-dation, are likely to affect choice of grounds and, indeed, which spouse pursues them.

Remarriage

Marriages are formally broken either by divorce or by the death of one partner, and, obviously, those divorced and widowed are eligible for remarriage. Consequently, marriage opportunities and rates are related not only to the basic demographics of the sexes and to differences in their length of life (see Chapter 4), but also to the incidence of divorce and changing cultural factors sur-rounding marriage, divorce and second and subsequent marriages. In 1985 only 64 per cent of all marriages were the first for both parties; 20 per cent were the first for one party only (of the other parties 94 per cent were divorced and 6 per cent widowed); and 16 per cent were second marriages for both parties − of which 76 per cent were both divorced, 10 per cent were both widowed, and

15 per cent were mixed (*Marriage and Divorce Statistics 1985*).

Haskey (1987) provides a detailed view of the remarriage in the two and a half years following divorce by a sample of couples who divorced in 1979. While overall almost identical proportions of divorced husbands and wives remarried (34 and 33 per cent), Table 7.5 reveals marked social class differences. In the non-manual classes husbands were more likely than wives to have remarried (overall, 41 and 27 per cent), while in the manual classes the situation was the opposite, with wives more likely, at 35 compared with 31 per cent. Hence, remarriage of non-manual, divorced husbands is almost a third higher than those from the manual classes, and the reverse is true for their wives. The highest proportions of husbands and wives remarrying were found in classes IIIn and IIIm. While there is no clear pattern to remarriage of both partners, generally the rate for husbands alone declines, and that for wives alone increases, across the classes. Interestingly enough, the social class pattern of remarriage was similar for partners with and without children.

TABLE 7.5 Percentage of divorced partners in each social class[1] remarrying within two and a half years of divorce

| | Social class (RG 80) | | | | | | |
	I	II	IIIn	IIIm	IV	V	All[2]
Both	12	6	17	13	7	4	10
Husband only	32	32	29	20	22	25	24
Wife only	16	17	17	27	25	16	23
Neither	40	45	37	40	47	55	43
Husbands[3]	44	38	45	33	28	29	34
Wives[3]	28	23	34	40	31	20	33

1. Based on husband's occupation at time of divorce.
2. Includes unclassified.
3. Irrespective of spouse.

Derived from table 2, Haskey (1987).

In comparing his results with those of a study in 1973 (Leete and Anthony, 1979) Haskey finds remarriage within two and a half years of divorce to have fallen appreciably. This suggests that there may be either a trend away from remarriage or a change in its tempo. He concludes, 'It is virtually certain that cohabitation – whose prevalence increased substantially during the 1970s, particularly amongst divorced and separated women,' (Brown and Kiernan, 1981) 'played an important role in such changes.'

The remarriage rate of divorced and widowed men is nearly three times higher than that for women. This is mainly due to differences in the sizes of the eligible populations. There are many more widows and divorced women, especially in the older sections of the population, than widowers and divorced men (*Social Trends 17*). Overall, the ratio of divorced men to women in 1985 was 78 per 100, and was due almost entirely to higher remarriage rates for male divorcees aged over twenty-five (Sparks, 1986). Leete and Anthony's (1979) study of divorced couples, suggested the fact that women generally have care of children after the divorce, does not explain why they have lower rates of remarriage than men.

One-parent families

While some are formed on purpose, many one-parent families are the result of broken marriages due to divorce, separation or death. Haskey (1986a) estimated there were some 940,000 one-parent families in Great Britain in 1984. *GHS 1985* data suggests that by 1985 one-parent families amounted to 14 per cent (over one in eight) of all families with dependent children in our society – an increase from 8 per cent in 1971. Between 1971 and 1985 the percentage of all families with dependent children headed by a lone father remained fairly stable at around 1 to 2 per cent, while those headed by a lone mother rose from 7 to 12 per cent. In the early to mid-1980s some 91 per cent of heads of one-parent families were women. Between the early 1970s and 1980s, the proportion of one-parent families headed by men fell from around one in seven to one in eleven. Among lone mothers there was a marked increase in the proportion both of those who were divorced (25 to 40 per cent) and those who were single (15 to 21 per cent). The first rise is accounted for by the general increase of divorce over the period and the accompanying decline in remarriage rates. The second rise is due in part to an overall rise in the number of illegitimate births and to an increasing proportion of mothers bringing up children on their own. A decline in the proportion of lone parents of both sexes who were widowed or separated is largely due to increasing numbers in the other categories. There are no data on the distribution of one-parent families by social class, though these would reflect the class differences in the related aspects – such as divorce, illegitimate birth rates and mortality rates, which have been reviewed above.

The PSI survey found lone parenthood much more frequent in West Indian households than in Asian and White. Some 18 per cent of West Indian households were composed of a lone parent and a child(ren) under sixteen, compared with 4 and just over 3 for Asian and White, and such households formed the following percentages of all households with children: 31, 5 and 10 respectively (Table 17, Brown, 1984a). This situation reflects differences in patterns of marriage and childbearing. It is not uncommon for West Indian women to have children prior to establishing a marital or cohabiting household. This does not mean however that such lone parents are mainly young – four-fifths of those surveyed were aged twenty-five or over. The percentage of male lone-parent households was also higher among West Indians (2 per cent), than Asian (1 per cent) and White (0.5 per cent).

Class endogamy

Considering the evidence given elsewhere in this book concerning the relative segregation of people in different social classes in, for example, housing, employment, education, interests, leisure activities and so on, it is perhaps quite reasonable to anticipate that there would be some relationship between the social class origins, or class, of marriage partners (see also pages 216–7 above). An intriguing though now dated study is that of Berent (1954), which classified the social origins of the partners in some 5100 marriages into four classes. In 45 per cent of marriages the spouses shared the same class origin. Clearly such a relationship is very much higher than would be expected to happen by chance – if choice of partner was unrelated to class. Combining social origin with educational level revealed that 83 per cent of the marriages showed correspondence on one or other of the measures, 71 per cent on at least education, 45 on at least social origin; only 7 per cent had no correspondence on either. The higher accord on education than on origin is of interest given the relationship between the two (see Chapter 8).

Similar findings are reported in the *Statistical Review of England and Wales 1967* (1971) and led the Registrar General to comment, 'It is of interest to note that despite trends to increased social mobility and more open social structure, there is a marked persistence of homogamy by couples in the sample.' More recent studies have used partners' social class at time of marriage, rather than their origins (Leete, 1979; Haskey, 1983). Data from the latter study are at Table 7.6, expressed as the ratio of the observed number of marriages with partners of the same class to the expected (calculated on the assumption that choice is independent). As can be seen, there is a distinct tendency for brides and grooms to be of similar social class at marriage. The ratios have a 'U' shape, indicating that endogamy is most pronounced at the extremes and highest in class V.

TABLE 7.6 Ratio of observed to expected marriages[1] in which bride and groom were in the same social class[2]

| | Social class (RG 80) | | | | | |
	I	II	IIIn	IIIm	IV	V
Bachelor/spinster	3.2	2.5	1.4	1.1	1.4	7.9
All	5.0	2.1	1.4	1.1	1.5	6.3

1. On assumption of independence of spouses' class, a ratio of over 1 indicates an association between them – the larger, the stronger.
2. Based on bride's and groom's own class.

Derived from table 2, Haskey (1983).

A further view of this relationship can be gained from the census, by analysing the class of married couples in which both spouses were economically active: see Table 7.7. The clear trend is for the occupations of spouses to fall into the same class (the cells in bold type) or adjacent ones and this is particularly so for classes 1, 2 and 6. The relative infrequency of one spouse with a non-manual and the other with a manual job is shown by the value of the cells (in italic type) at the top right and bottom left, all of which are less than 1. The differences which occur between the social classes of husband and wife have some obvious implications for social research, given the fairly consistent use of male social class to characterize families and children. For example, educational research typically relates children's progress to father's class. In some cases this measure could lead to unwarranted assumptions about home background. Two families where the fathers were of the same class, but where mothers' class differs widely, could be providing very different home environments, which might affect children's educational experience and achievements (see also Chapter 8), and such families may have widely varying incomes and patterns of expenditure.

TABLE 7.7 Social class of spouses[1] where both are economically active (ratios[2])

Husband's social class (RG SEG 80)	Wife's social class (RG SEG 80)[1]					
	1	2	3	4	5	6
1	8.0	1.0	1.3	0.5	0.4	0.3
2	0.8	8.2	1.1	0.7	0.6	0.5
3	1.0	0.8	1.3	0.6	0.6	0.7
4	0.2	0.6	0.8	1.5	1.5	0.3
5	0.1	0.6	0.9	1.1	0.9	3.3
6	0.1	0.3	0.6	1.0	1.6	4.0

1. Based on own occupation of each.
2. Ratio of observed figures to that expected (see footnote to Table 7.6 above).

Calculated from unpublished table DT 4061U, *Census 1981*.

CHILDREN

Up to the Second World War social class was inversely related to family size: the smallest families were those of the 'highest' classes, and family size increased across the classes, the 'lowest' having the largest families (*Demographic Review 1977*, 1979). The popularization of efficient birth-control methods, particularly the 'pill' in the early 1960s, affected the traditional pattern of family size (see also next sub-section). By 1961 social class II had replaced I as that with the smallest families; by 1971 it was class IIIn and the absolute differences in mean family size were small, though relative differentials remained. The most dependable national view of social class variation in family size comes from the 1971 census (there were no questions concerning fertility in 1981) and is provided in Table 7.8. The figures show a 'U'-shaped pattern, with the lowest number of children

TABLE 7.8 Mean family size of women married for twenty-five to thirty years, by social class,[1] England and Wales, 1971

			Social class (RG 70)				
	I	II	IIIn	IIIm	IV	V	All[2]
Mean family size	2.04	1.99	1.86	2.20	2.24	2.47	2.14
% difference from national average	−4.7	−7.0	−13.1	+2.8	+4.7	+15.4	

1. Of husband.
2. Includes unclassified.

Derived from table 4.33, *Demographic Review 1984* (1987).

in class IIIn and the averages rising in both directions to class I and V (though the latter is considerably higher than the former). The non-manual classes are below and the manual above the overall mean, and the second row to the table shows the differences in percentage terms – ranging from −13 for class IIIn to +15 for V.

The PSI survey found that a higher proportion of West Indian and Asian households than White contained children – 57, 73 and 31 per cent respectively. This at least partly reflects differences in age and household structure, since in comparing only those with children the average number of children per household was almost identical for Whites and West Indians (1.6 and 1.7), but considerably higher for Asians at 2.6. Approaching a third of all Asian households had more than two children, compared with 12 per cent of West Indian and 5 per cent of White (Brown, 1984a).

A rather similar social class pattern is found for general fertility. Werner (1984), by combining legitimate and illegitimate births, calculates the average number of children born to women by the age of twenty-five in the social classes (RG; based on the chief economic supporter of the household) to be: 1, 0.24, II, 0.4; and IV, 0.79; V, 0.96. The percentage of women who became mothers by the age of twenty-five rose across the classes from 19 in I to 55 in V.

This considerable variation by class in the age of motherhood is shown in detail in Table 7.9. The proportion of first-time mothers aged under twenty rises dramatically across the classes, while that for those aged thirty and over declines. In 1984 a quarter of first-time mothers in classes I and II were aged up to twenty-five, and three-quarters over that age; in contrast, in classes IV and V, the proportions were two-thirds and one-third. It is also clear that some fairly big changes have taken place between 1971 and 1984. In classes I and II the percentage of first-time mothers aged thirty or over has doubled, and

TABLE 7.9 Distribution of mother's[1] age at birth of first child, by social class,[2] England and Wales, 1971 and 1984 (percentages[3])

| | Social class (RG 70/80) | | | |
	I & II	IIIn	IIIm	IV & V
1971				
Under 20	5	10	20	31
20–24	39	45	53	48
25–29	42	36	21	16
30 and over	14	10	7	6
1984				
Under 20	2	5	9	17
20–24	23	34	45	50
25–29	46	43	34	25
30 and over	29	19	12	8

1. Married women.
2. Of husband.
3. Of births in calendar year.

Calculated from table 4.40, *Demographic Review 1984* (1987).

that of those under twenty halved. Similar differences are to be seen for classes IIIn and IIIm; only IV and V diverge from the pattern. In these latter classes, although the proportion of teenage first-births has declined, it remains much higher than for the rest, and in contrast there was a small rise in those aged 20 to 24.

Differences in the mean age at birth of first child are provided in Table 7.10, and further illustrate the point just made. Since the data in Tables 7.9 and 7.10 are for married women, it is obvious that age of marriage, which as we saw is class-related, affects the situation. So too does the interval between marriage and first-birth, the median time of which declines from 37 to 18 months from classes I and II to IV and V (second row to Table 7.10). Werner (1988) records that the difference between the median interval for these two classes increased from 16 to 23 months between 1972 and 1978 and then fell back again during the 1980s. The differences in intervals between first and second/second and third births are very much smaller and have no consistent class pattern.

TABLE 7.10 Mother's age at birth of first child[1] and median interval[2] between marriage and birth of first child[3] in each class[4]

| | Social class (RG 80) | | | | |
	I & II	IIIn	IIIm	IV & V	All[5]
Mean age at birth of first child	28	26.5	25.2	24	26
Median interval between marriage and first birth	37	33	26	18	28

1. Legitimate.
2. In months; for definition of median see p.167.
3. In first marriage.
4. Of husband.
5. Includes others.

Derived from tables S12 and S11, *Birth Statistics 1985* (1986).

Not all babies are conceived in marriage or born into families. Children born outside marriage are categorized as illegitimate – though they may, subsequently, become legitimate. In 1984 some 17 per cent of the 637,000 live births in England and Wales were classified as illegitimate – an increase since 1974 of 96 per cent, largest for women aged 20 to 24 (134 per cent) and lowest for teenagers (59 per cent). Analysis by social class is only possible when such births are jointly registered by both parents, which happened in 61 per cent of illegitimate registrations in 1984 – compared with 48 per cent in 1974 (*Birth Statistics 1984*). Table 7.11 shows that the percentage of births conceived within marriage declines across the classes from 91 in classes I and II to 75 in IV and V, whereas the percentage for those conceived prior to, but born in marriage increases from 5 to 9, as does that for jointly registered illegitimate births, from 5 to 16. In all classes and age groups the proportion of births conceived in marriage was lower in 1983 than in 1973 – 4 per cent overall, composed of a 2 per cent decrease in pre-marital

TABLE 7.11 Percentage[1] of births conceived inside and outside marriage, by social class, England and Wales, 1983

| | Social class (RG 80) | | | | |
	I & II	IIIn	IIIm	IV & V	All
Conceived in marriage[2]	91	89	81	75	83
Conceived before marriage[3]	5	5	8	9	7
Illegitimate, jointly registered by both parents	5	6	12	16	10

1. Of total live births with details of father.
2. Marriage to birth interval 8 or more months.
3. Marriage to birth interval 0 to 7 months.

Derived from table 9, Werner (1985).

conceptions and a 6 per cent increase in jointly registered illegitimate. In both cases the change in the non-manual classes was lower, and that in the manual classes higher, than the overall figure. Werner (1985) reports that a survey of a sample of records shows that the majority of parents jointly registering illegitimate births in 1983/4 were resident at the same address. It seems likely therefore that such parents had a stable relationship and were taking joint responsibility for their child.

Family planning

One factor commonly assumed to be related to family size and spacing is the use of contraception. This is not an entirely straightforward factor, since some families were limited before effective contraception was available, and not all methods of contraception are reliable means of avoiding pregnancy. At a simple level it can be said that the use of contraceptives lessens the likelihood of unwanted pregnancies and is more likely to result in families of planned size (assuming, of course, that 'planned' means limited and/or spaced births).

As can be seen from Table 7.12, contraceptive use has changed rapidly from 1970 onwards. Not only did overall use by ever-married women increase, but there were distinct changes in the popularity of methods. The 'pill' replaced condoms as the most popular non-surgical method, the use of unreliable methods of withdrawal and safe period declined together with abstinence and 'cap', while the use of IUDs (the coil) doubled and sterilization increased sixfold (see below).

The same trends are observable in respect to social class use. In 1970, of married women not planning to become pregnant, over 90 per cent of those in the non-manual classes were using mechanical or chemical contraceptives, compared to just over two-thirds of those in classes IV and V (Bone, 1973). Some clear differences existed in the type of contraceptive used – the non-manual made

TABLE 7.12 Changes in the use of contraceptives
(percentages)

Contraceptive use by ever-married women aged 16 to 39/40[1]

	1970[2]	1976[2]	1983[2]
Pill	19	32	29
IUD (coil)	4	8	9
Condom	28	16	15
Cap	4	2	2
Withdrawal	14	5	4
Safe period	5	1	1
Abstinence	3	[−][3]	1
Sterilization	4	15	24
None	25	23	19

Percentage of recent mothers[4] taking the contraceptive pill

	Social class (RG 60/80)						
	I	II	IIIn	IIIm	IV	V	All
1967–8	32	18	24	18	17	13	20
1984	34	33	41	46	40	61	43

1. Data for 1970 are for those aged 16 to 40, England and Wales; for
   1976 and 1983, for those aged 16 to 39, Great Britain.
2. Columns do not add to 100 due to rounding and use of more than one
   method.
3. Less than 1 per cent.
4. Legitimate births for 1967/8, all births for 1984.

Derived from table 5.5, GHS 1983, and tables 4 and 8, Cartwright (1987).

more use of the 'pill' and 'cap' and less of 'withdrawal'
than the manual, there was little variation in the use of
condoms and IUDs. By 1975, Bone (1978) records greater
similarity between the classes – especially in respect to
the 'pill' which was then used by 42 per cent overall. The
growth in the use of the 'pill' and IUD was matched by
a decline in the least effective methods, withdrawal and
safe period, though the former remained more prevalent

in the manual classes. These changes may be seen as due to the considerable increase in the use of family planning services, related to a growth in their provision at this time. This growth in use was greatest in the manual classes, so that while use still declined across the classes in 1975, it was less marked than in 1970.

A similar pattern emerged in the use of contraception by unmarried women who did not reject pre-marital intercourse (Bone, 1973). The percentages using any method in 1970 ranged from 48 in the non-manual classes to 40 in class IIIm and 33 in IV and V. Dunnell (1979) showed that pre-marital intercourse with husband-to-be was slightly less frequently reported by women in classes IV and V – just under half compared to just over half in the other classes. However such intercourse without contraception was more common in the manual classes: 14 per cent in IIIm and 20 in IV and V compared with 8 per cent in the non-manual.

A different view of contraceptive use, by mothers some months after birth, further illustrates marked changes in methods. The lower section of Table 7.12 shows that the percentage of recent mothers using the 'pill' more than doubled between 1967/8 and 1984. In the first year mothers in social class I were the most likely to be using it, and use declined across the classes to V (32 to 13 per cent). This pattern was reversed in 1984, when class V mothers used it most – three in five. While all classes' use had increased, the increase in class I was marginal, that in V dramatic and that in the rest substantial. In 1975 there were no class variations in the use of IUDs by recent mothers (Cartwright, 1978), their use increased only in classes I and II by 1984, to 13 per cent, compared to all other classes, at 8 per cent (Cartwright, 1987). Condoms were used by a higher percentage of the non-manual than the manual classes in 1984, 29 compared with 22 per cent.

Sterilization had by the mid-1980s become a very popular method of contraception, second only to the 'pill'. Some 21 per cent of all women aged 18 to 44 in the *GHS 1984*, or their partners, were sterilized, ranging from 1 per cent of those who had not had a live birth to 48 of those who had had three or more, and 9 per cent of those aged 25 to 29, to 41 of those aged 40 to 44. The percentage among married or cohabiting women or their partners was 27, with a member of manual-class couples somewhat more likely to have been sterilized than non-manual – 28 compared to 25 per cent. Overall male sterilization was more common than female – 14 per cent compared with 12 – and was accounted for by the differences among non-manual couples – where 15 per cent of men and 10 per cent of women were sterilized – as there were no differences between the sexes in the manual classes.

A further aspect of family planning which has grown in importance since the Act of 1967 is abortion. The *Report of the Committee on the Working of the Abortion Act* (1974) contained a social class analysis of abortions in 1970 and 1971, though since there are no available figures for pregnancy by class it is not possible to estimate any differences in termination rates. The estimated abortion ratio percentage of live births (for married women only) was highest for (RG) class II (6.9), followed by I (5.2), with III, IV and V almost the same at 4.5/6. The estimated abortion rate per 1000 women aged 15 to 44 years was somewhat different – II (8.3); III and V (6.2/1); I (5.5); and IV (4.7). As might be expected the percentage of NHS as opposed to private abortions increased across the classes from 61 in class I to 86 in class V, though class II had the lowest, at 59.

Adoption and fostering

On the other hand there are families who are unable to produce children of their own, some of whom seek to adopt or foster children. (Of course, it is also true that some parents with children of their own adopt or foster other children, and not all fostering and adoption is done by families.) Research suggests that adopters and fosterers have different social class profiles, as do the backgrounds of the children involved. Grey (1971) in a study of 3400 adoption application files found classes I and II provided a third of prospective adopters from 20 per cent of the population but less than 10 per cent of the natural mothers offering children for adoption. In contrast, the comparable percentages for classes IV and V were, respectively, 14, just over 20, and almost 30. Some caution is necessary in respect to the figures relating to natural mothers since for 30 per cent class data were not available. However, the overrepresentation of the upper non-manual classes among adopting parents is confirmed by data from the National Child Development Study (see next section), in which very definite social class differences were found between adoptive homes, those of the whole cohort and the population as a whole. The proportion of adopted children in class I homes was twice as large as that for the other two groups; and they were more likely to be in non-manual homes and less likely to be in manual homes than the other groups (Seglow, Pringle and Wedge, 1972). The NCDS also found that the proportion of adopted children living in non-manual homes at ages seven and eleven was some five times higher than for illegitimate children and much higher than for legitimate children (Lambert and Streather, 1980).

In contrast to adoption, both foster parents and natural parents of fostered children have been found to come predominantly from the manual classes, particularly classes IV and V. Holman's (1975) study of foster children found 60 per cent of natural, and 38 per cent of foster, parents were semi- or unskilled (see also George, 1970). Hence, the evidence clearly suggests a marked social class divide between adoption and fostering.

Bringing up children

Social differences in the rearing and care of babies and
young children have received detailed attention in social
research since the Second World War. Three large national cohorts of children – all those born in Great Britain in
a single week of 1946 (National Survey of Health and
Development – NSHD), 1958 (National Child Development Study – NCDS), and 1970 (Child Health and
Education Study – CHES) – have been and are being followed through life. A further source is the smaller- scale
but more detailed study conducted by a husband-and-wife
team on overlapping samples of mothers and children in
Nottingham (Newson and Newson, 1963, 1968, 1976,
1977).

It is important to bear in mind that most of the
evidence from these studies presented below is based
on mothers' answers to questions in interviews. Doubts
may be raised about the accuracy of such reports (see,
for example, Yarrow, Campbell and Burton, 1964; Davie,
Butler and Goldstein, 1972). Respondents from different
social classes [may vary in their awareness of what is
a socially acceptable answer] and in their familiarity
with current professional opinion and literature about
childrearing and (in their anxiety about giving what
they consider to be socially acceptable responses.) A
further point is that, given the purpose of this book,
and the nature and extent of the material to hand, the
data have been selected to emphasize social, particularly
class, differences. It should be remembered that in many
areas of child care and rearing social differences are very
small or non-existent.

Infant feeding Breastfeeding of babies displays considerable change over time and distinct social class differences.
In the 1930s the majority of babies were breastfed. Interest
in infant feeding methods arose when it was discovered,
in 1946, following the introduction and popularization

of modified cow's milk, that only 45 per cent of babies were breastfed at the age of two months (Douglas, 1948). The social class variations recorded then were also found by Davie, Butler and Goldstein (1972) for children born in 1958. At that time, while over two-thirds of babies were initially breastfed, only 43 per cent were so fed at the end of their first month. Initial breastfeeding declined from 78 per cent in class I to 64 in class V, but more marked was difference in the length of breastfeeding: of mothers in class I who did it initially, 25 per cent stopped within a month compared to 44 per cent of mothers in class V. A study in England and Wales in 1975 (Martin, 1978) showed that breastfeeding had dropped from 68 to 51 per cent overall and that the social class differences had increased. While over three-quarters of class I babies were breastfed and of these nearly a quarter were still so fed at six months, less than two-fifths of those in classes IV and V were initially breastfed and only 10 per cent of those were so fed at six months.

The latest data to hand at the time of writing suggest that the popularity of breastfeeding rose again by 1980 to an overall percentage of 65 (Martin and Monk, 1982), see Table 7.13. In comparison with 1975 its incidence has risen in all social classes, but particularly in IIIn, and there is now a clear divide between the non-manual and manual classes. Length of breastfeeding has also risen: in 1975, of those mothers who started, 46 per cent were still doing it at six weeks and 26 per cent at four months, the comparable percentages for 1980 being 63 and 40. There are clear social class differences: the 'higher' the class, the more likely the baby is to be breastfed and the longer the time of such feeding. However despite these increases only 26 per cent of all mothers in Great Britain breastfed their children for as long as the four months recommended by the DHSS working party of 1974, and this figure declines from 58 for class I to 11 for classes IV and V.

TABLE 7.13 Incidence and duration of breastfeeding of babies in each social class,[1] Great Britain, 1980 (percentages)

| | Social class (RG 80) | | | | | |
	I	II	IIIn	IIIm	IV & V	All[2]
Initially breastfed	87	78	77	59	52	65
Initially breastfed and still so fed at:						
1 week	94	91	85	86	83	88
6 weeks	85	74	62	56	52	63
4 months	67	53	39	32	22	40
6 months	57	46	34	27	15	34
9 months	36	22	18	13	11	18

1. Of father.
2. Includes unclassified.
Devised from tables 3.3, 4.7 and 4.8, Martin and Monk (1982).

Use of medical services Local authorities provide under statute a number of clinics and services for babies and children. The use of these is general and widespread: for example, some 77 per cent of all mothers reported having been to an infant welfare clinic, and some 93 per cent of all children were immunized against diphtheria, see Table 7.14. There are small but real social class differences in the use of clinics, particularly in regularity of attendance. In Table 7.14, for example, it is noticeable that while there is little variation from the average for all social classes in 'some attendance' (77 per cent), it is social classes IIIn and IIIm who are most likely to report having been regular attenders. In relation to infant welfare clinics, 66 and 60 per cent respectively reported regular attendance compared with 54 per cent of each of the other social classes, except for social class V for which the figure was 48 per cent. For both types of clinic, social class V had the smallest percentage of mothers who

TABLE 7.14 Mothers reporting use of (a) infant welfare clinics, (b) toddlers' clinics, (c) immunization and dental services, by social class (percentages)

| | Social class (RG 60) | | | | | | |
	I	II	IIIn	IIIm	IV	V	All
(a)							
No	26	25	17	21	25	25	23
Regularly	54	54	66	60	54	48	57
Occasionally	19	20	17	18	20	26	20
(b)							
No	46	44	36	43	46	52	44
Regularly	17	19	23	20	18	14	19
Occasionally	35	35	40	36	35	31	35
(c)							
Smallpox	93	85	83	73	68	64	75
Diphtheria	99	97	96	94	91	87	93
Attended dentist	83	80	81	76	72	68	76

Derived from tables A71, A74, A76, A80 and A82, Davie *et al.* (1972).

were regular attenders, though these mothers used infant welfare clinics marginally more 'occasionally' than social classes I, II and III.

A much more straightforward picture emerges in relation to immunization and dental care. In each case there is a linear decline in percentage from social class I to V. The figures for the middle classes are above the average for all social classes, and those for working classes are below.

Talking and social adjustment There is very little systematic evidence on any scale about social class differences in the way in which children are taught, or learn, to talk. The medical examination of children in the NCDS included a speech test and an intelligibility of speech report, which gives an indication of how successfully children learnt to talk. The test required children to repeat a series of short sentences designed to cover English letter sounds and most of the combinations of sounds used in normal speech. The stricture on the nature and conduct of the test mentioned in the footnote to Table 7.15 should be noted (though this would not account for the overall better performance of girls than boys). As can be seen, almost two-thirds of the children from social class I (65 per cent) made no mistake in the speech test, compared with rather more than one-third in social class V (36 per cent) – figures which vary quite markedly from the average for all social classes (49 per cent). There is an increase in the percentage of children making errors from social class I to social class V, particularly noticeable in the group making ten or more errors. Here the percentage for social class I is only a sixth of that for social class V.

One assumed objective of the socialization of the children in the family is to prepare them for life in other groups. In our society the first other group universally entered into is the school class. The NCDS gives Bristol

TABLE 7.15 Children's speech test scores and intelligibility,[1] by social class and sex (percentages)

| | Social class (RG 60) | | | | | | | | |
	I	II	IIIn	IIIm	IV	V	Boys	Girls	All
Speech test errors									
0	65	58	56	46	44	36	45	52	49
1 to 9	34	40	42	51	52	58	51	46	48
More than 10	1	2	2	3	4	6	4	2	3
% fully intelligible[1]	94	92	90	85	82	78	83	89	86

1. The authors argue that these differences may, in part, be due to the preference of the doctors involved for 'middle-class' speech.

Derived from tables A147 and A149, Davie *et al.* (1972).

Social Adjustment Guide (BSAG) scores (Stott, 1963) for the children in the study. In this test teachers choose from a series of behaviour descriptions those which best fit the child in question. A score is given such that the higher the score, the more deviant the behaviour, producing three groups: 'stable', 'unsettled' and 'maladjusted'. It should be noted that these are not clinical terms, but merely an indication of behaviour, and that while many of the behaviour deviations noted in the BSAG are abnormal by any standard, a proportion of them reflect school and teacher norms which are likely to be middle-class. As Table 7.16 shows, there is an increasing percentage of 'unsettled' and 'maladjusted' children from social class I through to social class V. What is very noticeable, however, is that while there is little real difference in the percentages for the middle classes, a marked difference occurs in each case between IIIn and IIIm, the latter being similar to social class IV. However, there is again a markedly higher percentage in social class V. Boys, as might be expected, are more often seen by their teachers as being 'unsettled' or 'maladjusted' than are girls.

An analysis from CHES defined three groups of children:

Difficult – destroys belongings, fights other children, is irritable, steals, is disobedient, tells lies, bullies.

Troubled – often worried, often solitary, miserable or tearful, fearful or afraid, fussy or overparticular.

Hyperactive – very restless, squirmy or fidgety, cannot settle.

Boys were more likely than girls to exhibit the characteristics of the difficult and the hyperactive child, but there was little sex difference in those associated with the troubled child (Butler and Golding, 1986). There were strong social class associations with the behavioural content of the descriptions; an increasing prevalence across the classes from I to V. The percentage of children whose

TABLE 7.16 Percentage of stable, unsettled and maladjusted children according to BSAG scores, by social class and sex

| | Social class (RG 60) | | | | | | | | |
	I	II	IIIn	IIIm	IV	V	Boys	Girls	All
Stable (0–9)	77	73	73	63	59	51	58	71	64
Unsettled (10–19)	17	19	19	23	24	27	25	19	22
Maladjusted (20+)	6	9	8	14	16	22	17	10	14

Derived from table A232, Davie *et al.* (1972).

mothers reported that they had temper tantrums at least once a week increased markedly across the classes from 6 for class I to 23 for class V.

Sex and modesty Children early become aware of their own bodies, and conscious of their bodily functions; later they are curious about other bodies in the family. The parents, and more especially the mother, have the power to some extent to control, ignore or encourage such interest. Evidence suggests that mothers from different social classes behave differently in this respect. Most children display an early and often continuing interest in their own genitals. Table 7.17 shows that non-manual-class mothers are markedly more tolerant of this than are manual-class mothers, especially at an early age. While 75 per cent of social classes I and II compared with only 7 per cent of social class V did not discourage genital play at age one, by age four it was discouraged or punished by a clear majority of all mothers of all social classes. There is a difference, however, in the manner in which it was discouraged, with the manual classes, particularly social class V, much more likely to punish or to threaten the child (social class I, 5 per cent; social class V, 48 per cent). To some extent this difference reflects a social-class-linked preference for punishment (see Tables 7.19 and 7.20 below).

TABLE 7.17 Mothers' attitudes towards children's genital play, seeing parents unclothed and being given the facts of life, by social class (percentages)

| | Social class (RG 60) | | | | | |
	I & II	IIIn	IIIm	IV	V	All
Genital play						
Age 1, discouraged[1]	25	50	57	69	93	–
Age 4,						
ignored/permitted	17	11	10	5	10	10
discouraged	78	71	54	54	42	59
punished/threat of	5	18	36	41	48	31
Seeing parents unclothed						
May see both	59	45	27	24	15	32
May see same sex only	22	23	22	22	17	22
May see neither	19	32	51	54	68	46
Knowledge of facts of life						
Child knows at age 4	44	26	15	14	15	20
Mother would tell if asked	44	47	30	39	10	34
Mother would not tell yet	12	27	55	47	75	46
% of whom would give falsehood	8	19	41	40	66	35

1. Actual cases only (i.e. excluding cases where information is not available because child has not been observed in genital play).

Derived from tables 36, 39, 40 and 41, Newson and Newson (1968).

The Newsons (1968) suggest that, if a child is allowed to see his parents unclothed, this 'may be considered a stage further on in permissiveness' from viewing other children naked. Certainly the social class differences here are more marked, as is shown in the middle section of

Table 7.17 – so much so that the majority attitude of social classes I and II with regard to seeing both parents naked was the minority attitude for the population as a whole. Interestingly enough, the second row in the section displays a very similar set of figures – around 22 per cent for all social classes. The top row shows the clear 'permissiveness' of the non-manual classes, while the 'modesty' of the manual classes is displayed in the third row. A further and similar aspect of this area concerns the basic knowledge of reproduction which at age four amounts to 'a baby comes from mummy's tummy'. As shown, there exist social class differences both in the extent of children's present knowledge, in the likelihood of their being given the facts, and in the likelihood of being given a false explanation. In each case the 'higher' the social class, the more likely the child is to have been favoured with accurate knowledge. As the Newsons write, in lighthearted vein, 'It has been suggested to us that attitudes towards sexual modesty might be a better index of social class affiliation than the more conventional occupation of father.'

Discipline and obedience According to mothers' reports, children from different social classes vary in their degree of obedience and disobedience at the age of seven; see Table 7.18. Perhaps surprisingly, overall some 40 per cent of children were seen as never being disobedient, girls more than boys, with a range from 45 per cent in social class I to 36 per cent in class V. The class V children were more likely to be seen as frequently disobedient (5 per cent as compared with 2 per cent in class I). Given that these figures are based on mothers' reports, and that the study lacked a definition of 'disobedience' (whose meaning can vary widely), too much weight should perhaps not be put on them. The same report does, however, contain references to specific kinds of behaviour – 'fighting' and 'destroying belongings' – which show similar social class disturbances (Tables A225 and A217, Davie *et al.*, 1972).

TABLE 7.18 Mothers' reported frequency of child's disobedience, by social class and sex of child (percentages)

| | Social class (RG 60) | | | | | | | | |
	I	II	IIIn	IIIm	IV	V	Boys	Girls	All
Frequently	2	3	3	4	4	5	5	3	4
Sometimes	52	54	55	55	57	58	59	51	55
Never	45	43	42	41	38	36	36	45	41

Derived from table A227, Davie *et al.* (1972).

Similar findings are reported by Bone (1977) of children aged one to four years. Mothers were questioned on a range of areas of behaviour – eating, toilet training success, ease of control and relationships with other children – and their replies assessed on degree of difficulty as perceived by the mother. Overall, 'difficult' children were identified as 10 per cent of the sample, with a rise across the classes from 7 for class I to 12 for classes IV and V. Interestingly enough, the clearest relationship was between 'difficult' children and the mother's age at the child's birth. Younger mothers were more likely both to have 'difficult' children and to be wives of manual workers.

Mothers' attitudes towards methods of discipline and punishment are summarized with respect to four-year-olds in Table 7.19. A first observation from the top section of the table is that smacking is a very common practice among mothers of four-year-olds, and that a sizeable proportion of those who disapprove of it actually indulged (compare the first row of the table with the second and third added together). The main social class difference in this part of the table is that mothers in classes I and II are overrepresented in the 'smack less than once a week' category – 33 per cent as compared with the overall average of 22 per cent – and in class V underrepresented at 11 per

TABLE 7.19 Mothers' attitudes towards, and use of, punishment for child aged four, by social class (percentages)

| | Social class (RG 60) | | | | | |
	I & II	IIIn	IIIm	IV	V	All
Smacking						
Disapproves of	20	14	16	16	22	17
Uses less than once a week[1]	33	23	20	24	11	22
Uses once a week to once a day[1]	61	68	70	66	79	68
Other punishments						
Threat of authority figure	10	23	29	29	46	27
Threat to send away or leave	10	34	29	27	30	27

1. Mothers reporting smacking never, or once a day, are small in number (3 and 7 per cent) and show no class variation.

Derived from tables 44, 45, 48 and 49, Newson and Newson (1968).

cent. The latter are overrepresented in the more frequent smacking category – 79 per cent compared with the overall average of 68 per cent. According to the Newsons, classes I and II are more likely to use punishments other than smacking, usually verbal methods, both in general and for specific reasons. In the second section of Table 7.19 there is a clear social class difference in the use of threats. In the case of threats involving authority figures there is a steady increase in their use across the classes from 10 per cent in classes I and II to 46 per cent in V. There is an interesting variation in the otherwise similar pattern for threats to send away or to leave the child: their most common use occurs in social class IIIn, and they are less often used in IV.

By the time children reach the age of seven years, physical punishment appears to be less generally used,

TABLE 7.20 Mothers' scores on corporal punishment index,[1] by social class and sex of child at age seven years (percentages)

| | Social class (RG 60) | | | | | | | |
	I & II	IIIn	IIIm	IV	V	Boys	Girls	All
High (5 or more)	21	27	34	31	40	40	30	31
Medium (3 and 4)	30	33	29	32	33	37	23	31
Low (0 to 2)	49	40	37	37	27	23	47	38

1. Based on mothers' replies to questions concerning: physical punishment used when – child is very slow, refuses to do something, is rude, has picked up bad language (1 point each); frequency of smacking (1+ per day = 3, 1+ per week = 2, 1+ per month = 1); 2 points if implement used, 1 for threat of implement/trousers taken down or skirt up. Maximum total = 10.

Devised from tables 42 and 43, Newson and Newson (1976).

though social class differences remain. Table 7.20 displays mothers' scores on an index of corporal punishment (for details, see footnote). The scores have been divided into three nearly equal levels. High scores rise over the classes, the proportion in class V being nearly twice that

TABLE 7.21 Mothers' level of bamboozlement of child scores,[1] by social class (percentages)

| | Social class (RG 66) | | | | | |
	I & II	IIIn	IIIm	IV	V	All
High (2 or more)	11	20	32	39	39	29
Medium (1)	21	32	34	31	40	32
Low (0)	68	48	34	30	21	39

1. Based on mothers' reporting: concealing her ignorance from child; not carrying out threats following warning; threatening child with policeman/leaving child/send away from home/won't love if naughty. Maximum total = 10.

Devised from tables 50 and 51, Newson and Newson (1976).

in classes I and II. Mothers' use physical punishment considerably more for boys than for girls. The Newsons report that its use is particularly marked in class V, where girls are much more likely to receive such punishment than in other classes.

A further interesting and related aspect of mother–child interaction is what mothers do when their child asks a question to which they do not know the answer. As can be seen in Table 7.21, willingness to 'bamboozle' the child by concealing ignorance, bluffing or duping varies considerably by social class. More than two-thirds of mothers in classes I and II, but only a fifth of those in V, report avoiding it completely. High scores vary from 11 per cent in classes I and II to 39 per cent in IV and V. Unlike the use of physical punishment, this behaviour does not display differences based on the sex of the child.

Child-centredness The Newsons (1976) analysed mothers' answers to ten of their questions (see Table 7.22) as an index of child-centredness which they claim gives 'a

TABLE 7.22 Mothers' scores on index of child-centredness,[1] by social class and sex of child (percentages)

| | Social class (RG 66) | | | | | | | |
	I & II	IIIn	IIIm	IV	V	Boys	Girls	All
High (7 to 10)	60	43	25	28	16	29	35	32
Medium (5 & 6)	30	37	38	29	27	32	37	34
Low (0 to 4)	10	20	37	43	57	39	28	34

1. Based on mothers' replies to questions concerning: child has special place to keep things; friends come and play; sympathetic to child not wanting to go to school; keeps child's drawings; child shares something of special interest with mother; child has some say in holidays; mother rebukes child's rudeness or ignores; mother feels sorry for being cross with child. Maximum total = 10.

Devised from tables 34 and 35, Newson and Newson (1976).

meaningful indication of mothers' underlying attitudes'. Overall, the index was used to divide the mothers into three similar-sized groups scoring high, medium and low. The social class differences are stark. About half of the non-manual-class but only a quarter of the manual-class mothers scored 'high'. At the extremes, while 60 per cent of classes I and II had 'high' and 10 per cent 'low' scores, the equivalent figures for class V were 16 and 57. Mothers of boys and those with large families were found to be less child-centred than others. Again this appears to be partly a further function of class, since both large families and low scores on the index were clearly related only in the working class.

Father's role A major difference between the social classes in childrearing appears in the degree of involvement of the father. As might be expected, this also varies with the age of the child. Table 7.23 shows that, while the father's participation does increase with the age of the child between one and four years, the social class differences remain. Generally speaking, the figures show a larger percentage of participating fathers as one moves up the social classes, together with an increase in the percentage of such fathers between the child's first and fourth birthdays. This increase is most marked for high participation in social class V (from 36 to 49 per cent), and is reversed in the case of social class IV, where the percentage drops from 55 to 44. In the case of fathers with 'little' or 'no' participation, it is interesting to note that when the child is one year old the percentage in social classes I and II (19 per cent) is much larger than IIIn, and similar to that in IV. At age seven the measure of father's participation was less demanding in terms of practical services, centring instead on common interests and involvement with the child. A more modest, though consistent, social class trend is discernible, which is almost entirely due to fathers and sons, since there was no significant class trend with respect to daughters. Middle-class fathers of sons were the most

TABLE 7.23 Extent of father's participation in child care and comparative parental strictness,[1] by social class (percentages)

| | Social class (RG 66) | | | | | | |
	I & II	IIIn	IIIm	IV	V	Boys	Girls
Father's participation							
At age 1							
High	57	61	51	55	36		
Little/none	19	6	16	18	36		
At age 4							
High	64	59	48	44	49		
Little/none	4	5	10	14	10		
At age 7						Boys	Girls
High	47	43	40	36	34	50	31
Low	20	24	27	25	32	23	28
Parental strictness							
Husband stricter	22	31	46	35	52		
Wife stricter	23	22	22	27	28		
Agree on strictness	55	47	32	38	20		

1. As reported by mother at interview.

Devised from table XXXI, Newson and Newson (1963); tables 53 and 54, Newson and Newson (1968); and table 31, Newson and Newson (1976).

participant, probably reflecting, according to the authors, the development of increasingly sex-based interests and activities. Mothers were also asked how their husbands compared with themselves in strictness with the child. Mothers in the 'higher' social classes were less likely to think their husbands stricter than themselves, and this is because they agree on strictness (in social classes I and II disagreement was 45 per cent; in social class V, 80 per cent). Finally it was found that the level of participation by the father was related to the wife's agreement of strictness. Where the father is high on participation, 43 per cent of all mothers said that they agreed with their husbands on strictness, compared with 31 per cent where fathers participated at a moderate or low level.

Variation in the help mothers received from fathers is also illustrated in CHES (Osborne, Butler and Morris, 1984). In this particular study a composite 'social index' measure was used to define five groups from most advantaged to most disadvantaged; these had a strong relationship with RG's social classes (over 80 per cent of the two extreme groupings were class I or class V). Comparing the most advantaged with the most disadvantaged families it was found that fathers in the first group were more likely to help with housework and shopping, taking the child to school and putting the child to bed, than the second, but there was little or no social variation in respect to day or evening baby-sitting.

THE HOME

While the majority of our society live in homes that house traditional families composed of married couples with or without children, it is fairly obvious that many people do not. Some people live alone, by choice or circumstance, live with others who do not constitute a family, or live temporarily or permanently in institutions. For this reason and the demands of large-scale research, the main unit of study for homes and home circumstances is the household (for definition see pages 89–90).

The *GHS 1985* surveyed 9993 households which had a mean size of 2.56 persons and composed of: married couple with dependent children, 28 per cent; married couple without dependent children, 35 per cent; lone-parent family, 8 per cent; one person, 24 per cent; other (including two or more unrelated adults or families), 5 per cent. All save one-person households may also have contained other non-family members. These types of household contained the following percentages of the people surveyed: 45, 32, 9, 10 and 4. The mean household size has decreased from 2.91 persons in 1971 mainly due to an increase of one-person households (17 to 24 per cent) and a decrease in those with five or more members (14 to 8 per cent).

Type and tenure of dwelling

The GHS regularly surveys household's accommodation. In 1985 four out of five households in Britain lived in houses, the other fifth in flats, maisonettes, rooms and shared premises. Some 62 per cent of dwellings were owned or being purchased by their occupants (24 and 38 per cent respectively), 28 per cent were rented from a local authority and 11 per cent were privately rented.

Tables 7.24 and 7.25 show that while households of all social classes live in all types of dwellings and use all types of tenure, there are distinct class patterns to both. Just over nine out of ten households in class 1 occupy

TABLE 7.24 Type of home accommodation, by social class[1] (percentages)

| | Social class (RG SEG 80) | | | | | | |
	1	2	3	4	5	6	All[2]
House	91	87	80	87	81	75	80
Detached	41	39	20	15	9	4	19
Semi-detached	34	30	33	37	34	29	32
Terraced	16	18	27	35	38	42	29
Flat/maisonette	9	13	21	14	20	25	20
Purpose-built	5	6	13	10	15	20	15
Converted/rooms	4	4	8	3	4	4	4
With business/ other	[–][3]	3	[–]	1	1	1	1

1. Classified heads of household only.
2. Includes economically inactive heads of household.
3. Less than 1 per cent.

Devised from table 5.19, GHS 1985.

houses compared to three-quarters of those in class 6, and while similar proportions of all classes inhabit semi-detached houses, the percentage in detached declines across the classes 1 to 6 from 41 to 4 and that for terraced houses increases from 16 to 42. Of course, given the differences in income of the classes (see Chapter 5) and range in costs of accommodation, there will be big variations in the size, condition and location of dwellings within these types. Private rents and mortgage repayments have been shown to decline markedly across the classes (*GHS 1977*).

While owner-occupancy drops from nearly nine in every ten class 1 households to a third of those in class 6, council renting rises much more steeply across the classes from 2 to 57 per cent. Other renting displays little social class variation and no pattern. This tenure pattern is not simply the result of differences in income, since owner-occupancy is higher in non-manual than manual classes even when incomes are matched. Table 7.25 includes household tenure by ethnic group. While overall the proportion of owner-occupiers in all ethnic minorities was only somewhat lower than for the ethnic majority (54 compared with 59 per cent), considerable differences between them can be seen. For example, some three in four Indian and Pakistani households were owner-occupied, in contrast to the majority of Bangladeshi households which were rented – partly a reflection of the accommodation available in the areas where this group has chosen to live (*LFS 1985*). Similarly the majority of West Indian/Guyanese, African and Arab households lived in rented dwellings. However, whereas the majority of the first two groups rented from local authorities (as did the Bangladeshi), the majority of the latter privately rented their homes.

The pattern of household tenure changed quite considerably between 1977 and 1985. The proportion of owner-occupied homes grew by 10 per cent, while local authority and other renting declined by 6 and 3 per cent. These changes are at least partly due to the sales of coun-

TABLE 7.25 Type of home tenure, by social class and ethnic group (percentages)[1]

		Social class (RG SEG 80)						
		1	2	3	4	5	6	All[2]
(1)	Owner-occupied	88	87	74	66	46	33	62
(2)	Local authority rented	2	5	14	28	41	57	28
(3)	Other rented[3]	9	8	11	6	13	11	11

	White	West Indian/ Guyanese	Indian	Pakistani	Bangladeshi	Chinese	African	Arab	Other ethnic
(1)	59	39	77	74	35	47	26	35	42
(2)	28	47	11	16	45	24	40	19	30
(3)	12	13	11	9	19	27	33	45	27

1. Class data are for 1985, ethnic are average for 1983–5.
2. Includes economically inactive heads of household.
3. Furnished/unfurnished, private/housing association/with job or business.

Devised from table 5.13, *GHS 1985*, and table 5.11, *Labour Force Survey 1985* (1987).

cil housing (especially to tenants exercising their 'right to buy' under the 1980 Housing Act) and the continuing decline in the stock of private rented accommodation (in 1971 20 per cent of households so rented their homes – *GHS Introductory Report*, 1973). While all the social classes have followed these general trends, the largest percentage increase in owner-occupancy in the manual classes was in class 4 and the lowest in 6.

It should be remembered that the social classes vary in size (see Chapter 3) and that no conclusions concerning the proportions of each type of dwelling in Britain can be made. The *GHS* makes no breakdown other than for the types shown. A now-dated study showed that caravan households were predominantly skilled and other manual – the non-manual, especially the professional, being underrepresented in relation to the general population (Consumer Council, 1967).

Accommodation and amenities

While a number of criteria might be used to assess the adequacy of a household's accommodation, the common one is the bedroom standard, which relates the number and type of people in a household to available bedrooms, according to the following rules:

A bedroom for

(a) each married couple

(b) each other person over twenty-one years

(c) each pair of same-sex persons aged ten to twenty

(d) each other person aged ten to twenty with children under ten of same sex (otherwise given bedroom on own)

(e) each pair of children under ten (remainder given bedroom on own)

(Gray and Russell, 1962).

There is clear evidence that the general level of housing accommodation has significantly risen in the past three decades. In 1960 in England and Wales, 6 per cent of owner-occupiers, 14 per cent of council tenants and 15 per cent of other renters had accommodation below the bedroom standard (GHS 1972). Between 1971 and 1977 the overall percentage of households below the bedroom standard fell from 7 to 4 per cent, and occurred in all social classes other than 1 (in the order of 2 per cent for classes 2 and 3, 3 per cent for classes 4 and 5, and 4 per cent for class 6) (GHS Introductory Report, 1973; GHS 1977).

The overall situation in 1982 is shown in Table 7.26: 4 per cent of households have homes below the bedroom standard and the proportion rises fourfold from classes 1 and 2 to 6. Since the standard may be regarded

TABLE 7.26 Percentage[1] of households in each social class with accommodation below/equal/above the bedroom standard[2]

| | Social class (RG SEG 80) | | | | | | |
	1	2	3	4	5	6	All
Below standard	1.5	1.4	3	4	5	6	4
Matched standard	16	22	30	34	38	41	31
Above standard	83	76	67	61	57	53	66
1 above	38	41	39	41	39	40	41
2 or more above	45	35	28	20	18	13	25

1. Those over 2 rounded.
2. For definition see text above.

Devised from unpublished data from GHS 1982, supplied by OPCS.

as minimal (especially in respect to sharing by persons aged ten to twenty-one) the proportion above it may be regarded as a better indicator. In this case the percentage declines from class 1 at 83 per cent overall (45 per cent two or more, and 10 per cent three or more) to class 6 at 53 per cent (13 per cent two or more, and nil three or more). These are, of course, overall figures which cover all types of household. Predictably, small adult households are most likely to have accommodation above the bedroom standard (48 per cent, two or more), large family households are most likely to fall below it (18 per cent) (GHS 1977).

Although there is a whole range of amenities which could be regarded as basic or necessary for households in our society, the most common ones in social research are baths/showers, WCs, hot-water and central-heating systems. The provision of these amenities has increased considerably in the past few decades. In 1971 one in eight households lacked the sole use of bath/shower and WC, and almost half lacked central heating. In both cases the lack increased across the social classes (1 to 6), the first

TABLE 7.27 Percentage of households[1] living in accommodation with certain characteristics, by social class and ethnic group

(A)	Social class (RG SEG 80)						
	1	2	3	4	5	6	All
No central heating	9	14	25	31	38	46	30

(B)	White	West Indian/ Guyanese	Indian/ Pakistani/ Bangladeshi	Other[4]
No sole use of fixed bath	2	5	3	8
WC inside building	3	5	5	9
Below bedroom standard[2]	3	14	25	7

(C)	White	West Indian	African[3]	Indian/ Pakistani/ Bangladeshi	Other[4]
Property built pre-1919	27	47	59	62	40
Shared dwelling	3	10	28	15	13
Below bedroom standard	4	18	16	30	12

(D)	White	West Indian	Asian	Indian	Pakistani	Bangladeshi	African Asian
No sole use of basic amenities	5	5	7	5	7	18	5
No central heating	43	38	44	37	66	56	27
More than 1.5 persons per room	1	3	12	7	17	32	7
No garden	11	32	21	15	21	56	18
No washing machine	22	37	44	38	61	78	22

1. Classified by head of household.
2. For definition see text above.
3. Based on 29 households.
4. Includes other stated and mixed origins.

Devised from (A) table 5.23, GHS 1985; (B) table 8.8, Social Trends 17 (1987); (C) table 8, National Dwelling and Housing Survey (1979); (D) tables 41 and 43, Brown (1984a).

from 4 to 11 per cent, the second from 18 to 72 (*GHS Introductory Report*, 1973). By 1985 only 2 per cent of households lacked sole use of bath/shower and WC and there was virtually no class variation. While central heating was to be found by then in seven out of every ten households, this provision declined from 91 per cent of social class 1 households to 54 per cent of class 6 (see upper section to Table 7.27). The rest of the table illustrates the considerable variation in the household accommodation of ethnic groups. It is clear that ethnic minority households are more likely than the majority to lack basic amenities, live in older property, to share the dwelling and to be overcrowded in terms both of the number of persons per room and bedroom standard. West Indian households have less space and fewer amenities than White, and Asian have the least. Within the Asian group, Pakistani and particularly Bangladeshi households are noticeably less well accommodated.

Other groups in society have been shown to display variations from the general picture above. For example, Bone (1977) surveyed the homes of some 2500 children under the age of five and found that 14 per cent were one or more bedrooms below standard, 7 per cent had no separate, unshared bathroom, 3 per cent shared toilets with other households and 5 per cent had no permanent hot-water system. All but 3 per cent of social class I had no inadequacies whereas the figure for classes IV and V was ten times higher at 30 per cent and included 3 per cent with all four inadequacies. The rise in the incidence of inadequacies was steady across the classes, with the non-manual below and manual above the overall average. Townsend (1979) found that of the housing of those in poverty (for definition see pages 179–80), 13 per cent were below the bedroom standard, 19 per cent had no sole use of an inside toilet and 56 per cent had only one room heated in winter.

Domestic amenities and consumer durables

There is evidence mainly from market research sources to show social class differences in the ownership of domestic amenities and consumer durables; see Table 7.28 (for motor cars see Table 10.9). As might be expected, the general pattern reveals that the 'higher' the class, the

TABLE 7.28 Percentage of households in each social class owning certain consumer/household durables and with garden and/or allotment

| | Social class (MR) | | | | | |
	AB	C1	C2	D	E	All
Telelphone	97	94	89	79	69	87
2 or more	45	30	22	15	10	25
Television	98	97	98	97	96	98
Vacuum cleaner	92	88	85	81	72	84
Washing machine	87	80	83	78	62	78
Continental quilt	77	74	71	65	48	67
Net curtains	57	62	67	68	61	63
Secondary glazing	30	22	16	11	7	17
Refrigerator[1]	93	91	90	87	81	88
Fitted kitchen units	79	68	63	50	37	60
Electric toaster	69	58	49	42	35	51
Electric food-mixer	62	57	52	44	33	50
Electric underblanket	43	37	33	31	32	35
Electric coffee maker (filter)	43	34	28	20	11	27
Microwave oven	32	28	30	21	11	25
Electric dishwasher	19	7	4	2	1	6
Garden	92	87	85	81	78	85
Allotment	2.9	3.1	3.4	3.7	2.2	3.1

1. A refrigerator or a fridge-freezer or both.

Derived from page 280 of BMRB's *Target Group Index* (1987) vol. 29; page 120, vol. 30; pages 27, 31, 43, 47, 71, 145, 161, 189, 237, 252, 309, 329, 337 and 341, vol. 33, and page 94, vol. 30 (1988).

higher the frequency of ownership. Overall, this tendency is such as to suggest that ownership is merely the result of being able to afford to purchase or rent the amenity or durable. However, it is easy to see in the list some which nearly all households have – such as televisions, telephones and refrigerators. Some show little class variation, like TVs, and others are clearly class-related – electric dishwashers, secondary glazing. Such differences suggest that factors other than finance are also involved, such as perceived needs and values, together with exposure to advertising, availability, and so on. Parallel data on ownership by different age and income groups are indicative of the general importance of money since the lower parts of both groups have lower levels of ownership of most domestic amenities.

As might be anticipated from social class differences in types of household accommodation, the percentage with gardens declines from class AB to E (lower section, Table 7.28; see also 7.24). With the exception of class E, the class similarity in the proportion of households with allotments suggests that there are reasons for 'ownership' other than lacking a garden.

Moving home

Evidence that we live in a mobile society is provided in Table 7.29. Overall just less than a third of households surveyed in 1982 had moved within the previous five years. The percentage declined across the classes 1 to 6 from 44 to 25. It is evident that class 1 is the most mobile since the percentage who had moved twice or three or more times (9 and 11 per cent) was much greater than the other classes whose percentages were close to the overall of 6 and 5 per cent. The lower section of the table similarly shows that among those who had had or were contemplating a move, class 1 stands out from the rest. Of course, it has to be remembered that these figures relate to all types of household, varying in

269

TABLE 7.29 Household moves, potential[1] and frustrated[2] movers, by social class (percentages[3])

| | Social class (RG SEG 80/70) | | | | | | |
	1	2	3	4	5	6	All
Moves in last 5 years[4]							
0	56	66	64	69	72	75	68
1	24	24	22	22	20	17	21
2	9	5	6	5	5	5	6
3 or more	11	5	8	4	4	3	5
Moved in last year[5]	10	6	9	6	6	6	7
Potential movers[1]	25	16	13	15	16	14	17
Frustrated movers[2]	11	8	8	7	6	3	7

1. Currently thinking about moving at time of interview.
2. Not currently thinking of, but have seriously in previous two years.
3. Of households in each class.
4. Data collected in 1982.
5. Data collected in 1980.

Devised from unpublished data from *GHS 1982*, supplied by OPCS and calculated from table 3.40, *GHS 1980*.

size, composition and age – factors related both to moving and reasons for moving. The most popular general reasons for considering moving were: insufficient accommodation, dissatisfaction with present environment, reasons connected with employment or education. The main reasons for not moving having considered it were: cost of, or inability to find, suitable housing; job-related problems; personal reasons – health/marital factors/bereavement.

Other studies have shown that moving home within, as opposed to beyond, the local area is class-related, and that it is likely to be due to different reasons. For example, Davie, Butler and Goldstein (1972) found that of families with children who had moved, the percentage which moved out of the local area declined from 63 per cent in class I (RG) to 27 per cent in class V. It can be conjectured, on the basis of social class differences in home tenure and accommodation, family size and formation, and employment and income, that the middle classes move more frequently for work-related reasons and the working classes because homes are or become unsuitable.

CHAPTER 8

Education

Education is only the image of and reflection of society. It imitates and reproduces the latter in an abbreviated form, it does not create it.

EMILE DURKHEIM (1952)

The hereditary curse upon English education is its organization upon lines of social class.

R. H. TAWNEY (1931)

School was not invented just for the little people to become the same as the big people . . .

Thirteen-year-old girl, quoted by EDWARD BLISHEN (1969)

Education has been fairly extensively analysed in terms of social class. The origins of interest in the relationship between social class and education are clearly both historical and political. The development of the British education system, from the point where education was wholly the preserve of the rich, through forms of voluntary education for the poor, to compulsory education for all, has been characterized by concern about social class and about equality. The introduction of universal education following the Forster Act of 1870 had produced, by the late nineteenth century, 'two distinct educational systems – elementary for the working class and secondary for middle-class children' (Silver, 1973). Vestiges of this situation remain today, notably in the continuance of independent and 'public' schools alongside those provided by local education authorities (LEAs). It seems likely that the Education Reform Act of 1988 which included provision for schools to 'opt out' of LEA

272

control, together with the development of City Technological Colleges (CTCs) and the present growth in the
independent sector (see pages 206–13) will lead to growing
segregation in education.

Empirical research into the relationship of social class
with education was initially systematized in the inter-
war period, mainly through the interest of psychologists,
notably Burt (1937; 1943), in relating intelligence and
educational performance to social background and class.
After the Second World War the field blossomed, and
between the mid-1950s and 1960s became a veritable
industry, with a wealth of government and academic
social science research into a host of topics, and using
a variety of approaches.

Two factors coincided to promote this flourishing interest in social class and education. The first was a continuing concern about social equality in education among
some educationalists, the public and politicians. In the
1950s and 1960s this focused particularly on how the
1944 Education Act (which in abolishing the payment
of fees in secondary schools was seen as removing an
obvious source of social inequality) actually worked out
in practice. The ensuing empirical research revealed,
briefly, that many working-class children were still being
kept out of grammar schools, but by 'academic' rather
than financial criteria, and that those who did get in
progressed less well than expected. This led to suspicions
that academic selection involved social selection, and
that equal educational opportunity did not necessarily
result in equality of achievement. The debate caused
by this research culminated in calls for the abolition
of selection, the introduction of comprehensive schools,
and more subtle educational reforms of the curriculum
and of teaching methods.

The second important influence was the emergence
and development of sociology and in particular of the
sociology of education. Whether the discipline merely
heightened existing interest or actually created the new

research developments is open to debate. It seems probable, however, that sociology did more than just provide a body of empirically minded researchers who thought social class an important concept for explaining how society worked. It also needed to be recognized that the theoretical emphasis in the application of sociology to education was, at least to the end of the 1960s, very clearly that of structural functionalism. (Simply, structural functionalism is a particular sociological perspective according to which society is viewed as a set of inter-related social systems or parts.) As Banks (1968, 1971) has written: 'One of the major strengths of the structural functionalist approach to education is the placing of educational institutions firmly in their relationship with the wider social structure. . . . Consequently . . . the sociology of education has developed as a largely macrocosmic study . . .' Certainly during the late 1950s and the 1960s researchers tried to explain classroom performance, and the functioning of schools and of the educational system, in terms of their relationships with other parts of society. Most important among these were family and social background, of which a commonly considered aspect was social class. This interest resulted in a fairly substantial body of data which described reasonably well the relationship between parental social class and children's educational achievement. Explaining the results was harder, however, particularly when it came to demonstrating how social class affected children's educational performance – and this situation remains true today (for a review, see Reid, 1978a and 1986a).

Since then changes have occurred that have resulted in a dearth of large-scale studies of social class and education. The sociology of education has incorporated an interpretative perspective – attempting to view social reality more through the eyes of the participants – and this has given rise to in-depth, small-scale research (though social class has remained a prominent factor). LEA secondary schooling has been transformed, albeit incompletely and in varied form, into a comprehensive system. Although the debates that have raged over comprehensive schools clearly demanded a basis of fact from research, few substantial data on social class have emerged – perhaps because both sides have had too much at risk to undertake it. Governmental interest, which had been expressed in a number of commissions and reports together with questions on education in the census, subsided. The single, notable exception is in Scotland where the Centre for Educational Sociology has been monitoring school leavers since 1977 (see Table 8.6 below, and McPherson and Willms, 1987; 1988). The net result is that for some aspects of our interest here, only dated material is available.

While interest in social class and education has declined, research into other aspects of stratification has grown in the last two decades. On the one hand the educational attainments of young immigrants from New Commonwealth countries, and later their children, was identified as a cause of concern. This led, in the late 1970s, to the setting up of a governmental Committee of Inquiry into the Education of Children from Ethnic Minority Groups, which produced two reports: *West Indian Children in Our Schools* (1981) and *Education for All* (1985). On the other hand, there was a growth of interest in the educational performance of the sexes, or perhaps more accurately in what was seen in the underperformance of females. Such interest coincided with the development of feminism, legislation on sexual equality and the establishment of the EOC. Hence the change in emphasis can be seen as the product of significant social change in Britain, bringing to the forefront other aspects of inequality. It was certainly not caused by a solution of social class inequality. As we shall see, the changes led to the neglect not only of class in itself, but also of class within ethnicity and sex. Ignoring problems does not make them disappear and in this case may seriously detract from a proper understanding of related areas (Reid, 1986b). One implication for our review here is that in large measure the forms of stratification have to be viewed separately. Having looked at some aspects of the social context within which the research took place, we can now turn to the findings, first in respect to adults and then to children.

ADULTS AND EDUCATION

Everybody accepts that some occupations are open only to those with particular educational qualifications – especially, for example, the professions – having learned in school that qualifications are importantly related to occupation. Hence they might well expect a relationship between adults' education and social class. The most useful source of data here would be the census – questions on schooling and education were included in 1961 (*Education Tables (10% Sample)*, 1966) and 1966 and 1971 – but data from 1961 are now too old, those of 1966 were not published by social class and those of 1971 not published at all. The questions were dropped from the 1981 census, perhaps because of the more comprehensive, though sample-based, data from the GHS, which is used here.

There are two alternative ways in which the relationship between adult social class and education can be seen. Either one can look at the educational composition of the classes, or at the social class of those holding differing levels of qualifications. The first is to be found in Table 8.1A, and by sex in 8.1B. Looking down the columns in A shows overall that the 'higher' the social class, the smaller the percentage without formal qualification and the larger that with higher qualifications. The extremes are fairly dramatically marked – over 80 per cent of class 1 have gained higher educational qualification, while in class 6 the same proportion gained no qualification. Less than 1 per cent of class 6 had degrees compared with two-thirds of class 1. There is a fairly clear divide between the non-manual classes, in which the majority (between 58 and 92 per cent) had at least GCE O level or equivalent, and the manual classes, in which at least half (50 to 83 per cent) had no qualification. While there are very clear differences in the qualifications of the social classes, it should also be noted that each level of qualification is represented in each class. Perhaps surprisingly, some 2 per cent of class 1 were without qualification, and 1 per cent of classes 4 and 5 had degrees or equivalents.

Table 8.1B reveals that within the same pattern there are clear differences between the sexes both in terms of social class (see lower section of table) and qualifications (see left-hand column). Women are underrepresented in classes 1, 2 and 4, and overrepresented in the others, particularly 3 (see also pages 92–3). Women were less likely than men to be graduates (6 compared to 11 per cent) and more likely to have no qualification (45 compared to 39 per cent). Despite the fact that proportionally fewer women had gained educational qualification, a larger proportion of women than men continued full-time education beyond school (25 compared with 20 per cent). This is almost certainly due to more men gaining qualifications through part-time study. In turn this reflects differing opportunities for gaining qualifications while working. For example, several predominantly male professions (such as engineering, accountancy and law) make such provision, and earlier data showed that 6 per cent of men compared with 1 per cent of women had gained higher educational qualification by part-time study (*GHS 1978*).

The second view is in Table 8.2, in which the same data are recast to show the social class distribution of both the holders of various levels of educational qualifications and of those whose last full-time education was school, polytechnic/college or university. Here it can be seen that higher education is extremely strongly associated with non-manual occupation, lack of qualification with

TABLE 8.1A Highest educational qualifications[1] of persons,[2] by social class, Great Britain, 1984/5[3] (percentages)

| | Social class (RG SEG 80) | | | | | | |
	1[4]	2	3	4	5	6	All
Degree or equivalent	65	14	11	1	1	[–][5]	9
Higher education below degree	16	17	18	5	2	1	11
GCE A level or equivalent	7	12	8	9	3	1	8
GCE O level/CSE higher grades or equivalent	4	19	21	15	10	5	16
GCE/CSE other grades/commercial/ apprenticeship	2	9	12	18	10	8	12
Foreign or other	3	4	3	3	4	1	3
No qualifications	2	25	27	50	70	83	42

TABLE 8.1B Highest educational qualifications[1] of men and women,[2] by social class, Great Britain, 1984/5[3] (percentages)

| | Social class (RG SEG 80) | | | | | | |
	1[4]	2	3	4	5	6	All
Men							
Degree or equivalent	63	14	18	1	1	1	11
Higher education below degree	18	17	18	5	2	1	10
GCE A level or equivalent	7	13	14	9	4	2	10
GCE O level/CSE higher grades or equivalent	4	18	19	15	9	5	14
GCE/CSE other grades/commercial/ apprenticeship	2	8	5	18	11	9	12

TABLE 8.1B (contd)

	1^4	2	Social class (RG SEG 80) 3	4	5	6	All
Foreign or other	4	5	4	3	4	1	4
No qualifications	2	24	21	49	69	82	39
Women							
Degree or equivalent	80^4	11	8	2	$[-]^5$	nil	6
Higher education below degree	5	17	17	3	2	1	11
GCE A level or equivalent	6	8	6	5	2	1	5
GCE O level/CSE higher grades or equivalent	2	21	22	16	11	5	17
GCE/CSE other grades/commercial/ apprenticeship	3	10	15	14	10	7	13
Foreign or other	2	3	3	5	3	2	3
No qualifications	2	30	29	56	71	84	45
Social class of sample							
Men	7	21	17	38	14	4	100
Women	1	9	51	8	23	8	100
All	5	16	31	25	17	5	100

1. For definitions, see Appendix B below.
2. Aged 25 to 69 and economically active (for definition, see page 91 above); excludes those in full-time education.
3. Data for the two years combined.
4. The figures for females in this column are small, 98 overall.
5. Less than 1 per cent.
Devised from table 7.10 (a), *GHS 1985*.

manual occupation. Overall 95 per cent of those with degrees and 74 per cent of those with other higher education were in non-manual classes; 70 per cent without qualification were in manual classes. All but 6 per cent of those who finished their full-time education at university and 21 per cent of those at polytechnic or college were

TABLE 8.2A Social class distribution of persons[1] with given educational qualifications[2] and last type of educational establishment[3] attended, Great Britain, 1984–5[4] (percentages)

	Social class (RG SEG 80)					
	1	2	3	4	5	6
Degree or equivalent	34	24	37	3	1	[–][5]
Higher education below degree	7	26	51	11	4	[–]
GCE A level or equivalent	4	24	34	29	7	1
GCE O level/CSE higher grades or equivalent	1	19	43	24	11	2
GCE/CSE other grades/commercial/ apprenticeship	1	12	31	38	15	4
Foreign or other	5	21	30	23	19	2
No qualifications	[–]	10	20	30	29	11
Last attended[3]						
School	2	15	26	30	21	7
Polytechnic/college	8	19	52	12	8	1
University	34	25	34	4	2	[–]

TABLE 8.2B Social class distribution of men and women[1] with given educational qualifications[2] and last type of educational establishment[3] attended, Great Britain, 1984–5[4] (percentages)

	Social class (RG SEG 80)					
	1	2	3	4	5	6
Men						
Degree or equivalent	41	27	27	4	1	[–][5]
Higher education below degree	13	35	31	18	3	[–]
GCE A level or equivalent	6	27	24	37	6	1
GCE O level/CSE higher grades or equivalent	2	27	23	39	8	1
GCE/CSE other grades/commercial/ apprenticeship	1	15	7	61	13	3

TABLE 8.2B (contd)

	Social class (RG SEG 80)						
	1[4]	2	3	4	5	6	All
Foreign or other	7	29	20	29	15	1	
No qualifications	[–]	13	9	47	24	8	
Last attended[3]							
School	3	20	74	43	16	4	
Polytechnic/college	15	26	30	22	6	1	
University	41	28	25	5	2	[–]	
Women							
Degree or equivalent	17[6]	16	63	2	2	nil	
Higher education below degree	1	14	78	2	5	[–]	
GCE A level or equivalent	2	15	63	8	10	2	
GCE O level/CSE higher grades or equivalent	[–]	11	65	8	15	2	
GCE/CSE other grades/commercial/ apprenticeship	[–]	7	63	9	17	5	
Foreign or other	1	9	46	13	26	4	
No qualifications	[–]	6	33	10	36	15	
Last attended[3]							
School	[–]	7	44	9	28	10	
Polytechnic/college	2	13	71	4	9	1	
University	18	18	59	3	2	[–]	

1. Aged 20 to 69 and economically active (for definition see p.91); excludes those in full-time education.
2. For defintions, see Appendix B below.
3. Full-time.
4. Data for the two years combined.
5. Less than 1 per cent.
6. The numbers for females in this column are small, 98 over all.

Devised from tables 7, 9 (b) and 7.10 (b), *GHS 1985*.

not in the non-manual classes, whereas the majority who finished at school (58 per cent) were in the manual classes and only 2 and 15 per cent respectively were in classes 1 and 2. There are very marked sex differences in this pattern (see Table 8.2B), mainly due to the sexes' distinctive occupational structures (evident too in the lower section of Table 8.1B), but also reflecting sex differences in the age and career pattern of the economically active in the sample. For example, a much higher percentage of women with degrees and other higher education are to be found in class 3 (63 and 78 per cent respectively, compared with 27 and 31 per cent for men). This follows from the inclusion in that class of such predominantly female occupations as primary school teaching, social work and paramedical jobs.

It should be noted that the data in Tables 8.1 and 8.2 cover persons aged 25 to 69 years and therefore reflect a considerable period of educational history. In particular, over the period the educational differences between the sexes have closed – see Table 8.10 and pages 296–7 below. This is also illustrated by age group differences in GHS samples. For example, the percentages of those with qualifications in 1981/2 aged 25 to 29 were men 68, women 69, whereas for men aged 60 to 69 it was 38 and for women aged 50 to 69, 30 (*GHS 1982*).

As suggested above, the relationship between adult's social class and educational qualifications and experience, and that between education and class, can be explained fairly straightforwardly. As we have seen, however, these relationships are not exact: not all people with higher education are to be found in the non-manual classes, nor are these classes made up exclusively of people with higher education. It may be assumed that this is due not only to changes in the occupational structure of society together with changing educational entry demands over time, but also to changes in educational opportunities and achievements of successive generations, as well as the importance of factors other than education in both getting a job and furthering a career.

A somewhat comparable set of data on the qualifications of persons aged between 25 and 44 by ethnic group is at Table 8.3. Note that academic and vocational/pro-

TABLE 8.3 Percentage of adults[1] by highest educational and vocational qualifications,[2] by ethnic group and sex

	Men			Women		
	White	West Indian	Asian	White	West Indian	Asian
Degree or higher degree	10	3	6	4	1	4
GCE A level, HND/HNC, or above (not degree)	12	5	11	10	5	7
GCE O level/OND/ONC	18	13	15	21	18	12
CSE and others below O level	4	8	7	5	12	6
No academic, but vocational/professional qualification	15	6	5	10	10	1
Professional/clerical qualification	18	4	9	26	28	6
Apprenticeship	20	11	2	2	[−][3]	Nil
City and Guilds	7	7	2	2	1	[−]
No vocational/ professional, but academic qualification	18	14	31	21	17	23
No qualification	38	64	56	50	54	71

1. Aged 25 to 44.
2. For definitions, see Appendix B below.
3. Less than 1 per cent.
Derived from table 75, Brown (1984a).

fessional qualifications are shown separately, since Brown (1984a) argues appropriately enough that a single hierarchy is problematic (for details and definitions see Appendix B). The percentage without either type of qualification ranged from 38 and 50 for White men and women to 64 for West Indian men and 71 for Asian women, the other groups being in the 50s. There are marked differences between the sexes for each type and level of qualification and in each ethnic group. Over all men are more often and more highly qualified than women. In terms of qualification, White men were somewhat more highly qualified in academic and much higher in vocational/professional terms than Asian men, and much higher in both than West Indian men. The proportion of White and West Indian women with either type of qualification is similar, though in academic ones the level of the Whites' is somewhat higher. Asian women are less likely than other women to have either type of qualification, though the percentage with GCE A level (or equivalent) and degrees, at 11 per cent, approaches that of the Whites (14) and is much higher than West Indians (6). This reflects the fact that the gulf between the well and poorly educated is greater among the Asian group than the other two. It should be borne in mind that a high proportion of the ethnic minority adults surveyed here received their schooling, education and/or vocational training abroad in a variety of systems of education. This factor is obviously related to the differences in qualifications.

Education, earnings and unemployment

A further aspect of the relationship between education and social class is the connection between education and income. Table 8.4 shows the median earnings (for definition see page 167) in 1985 of holders of various educational qualifications by sex. The table reveals that the higher the educational qualifications, the higher the earnings. Male degree-holders earned 70 per cent more than males without qualifications, while the figure for females was 91 per cent. Overall, there is a strong relationship between qualifications and earnings, though not a complete one – not all holders of educational qualifications earned more than those without, nor were all high income earners holders of qualifications. The table also

TABLE 8.4 Median weekly earnings[1] of holders, of given educational qualifications[3] by sex

	Males	As % of all females	Females[4]	As % of all females	Female as % of male
Degree or equivalent	240	145	174	156	73
High education below degree	200	121	150	134	75
GCE A level or equivalent	176	107	119	106	67
GCE O level/CSE higher grades or equivalent	167	101	110	99	66
GCE/CSE other grades/commerical/ apprenticeship	151	91	100	90	67
No qualification	141	86	91	81	64
All[5]	165	100	112	100	68

1. In £s; for definition of median, see p167 above.
2. Persons aged 20 to 69, in full-time employment (31 or more hours per week – 26 or more for teachers or lecturers – including paid overtime). Full-time students in work in reference week excluded.
3. For definitions see Appendix B below.
4. Females were younger on average than males (37 compared with 40) and worked fewer hours per week than men (39 compares with 43).
5. Includes foreign and other qualification.

Derived from table 7.13, *GHS 1985*.

reveals distinct differences between the sexes. At each educational level women earned less than men. Overall, women's median earnings were 68 per cent of men's, although women with higher educational qualifications had earnings somewhat closer, at 73 and 75 per cent (see right-hand column). Only part of the overall sex earnings difference is explained by the fact that women worked fewer hours and were slightly younger (see footnote to table). More of the difference is accounted for by the varying occupations (with different levels of income) followed by the sexes – what amounts to sex segregation in employment (see pages 92–3, and 165–7 and Webb, 1989).

The differing age structure and deployment of men and women in the same occupation produces earning differences despite equal pay. In schoolteaching, for example, the average earnings of male teachers in maintained schools in 1984/5 was £10,776 and for females £9,418 (*Education Statistics for the United Kingdom 1986*). This difference reflects the male predominance in secondary as opposed to primary schools (the former having more and better paid posts of responsibility) and among head and deputy head teachers.

Education can be shown to be related not only to occupational class and income but also to unemployment. A survey of Scottish school leavers entering the employment market in 1980 (Main and Raffe, 1983) showed that the best qualified were most likely to secure employment (79 per cent), while less than half (45 per cent) of those without qualifications were employed. While graduate and professional unemployment has received a good deal of media attention, their rates compared favourably with the less well qualified. The *Labour Force Survey 1983* revealed that proportionally more of the unemployed were without educational qualifications (52 compared with 41 per cent of the employed) and fewer had any form of higher education (6 compared with 15 per cent). Among those aged 16 to 19 years in the labour force, educational qualifications were even more starkly related – 44 per cent of the unemployed and 24 per cent of the employed were without qualifications. It appears, then, that educational qualifications provide a buffer against unemployment, a relationship which appeared unaffected by YOP and YTS schemes in the early 1980s, since employers sponsoring them used similar recruitment criteria to those used for permanent jobs (Barry and O'Connor, 1983).

Social class

Unfortunately for our purposes, available research findings preclude a comprehensive review of social stratification and education based on the same data. The following discussion is therefore somewhat segmented (for its implications see page 324). The main weight of research has been with parental social class and children's terminal educational qualifications (O and A level GCE/further and higher education). It is possible, however, to trace social differences in participation and performance throughout the educational system even if in places this requires the use of research from the past two decades or so. Some of the earlier data from this period are dated in that together with general educational change, LEA secondary education has been reorganized and higher education considerably expanded. The extent to which these and other changes have affected the relationships outlined below is, without specific empirical evidence, open to some debate.

While the statutory age for entry into the educational system in Britain is five, provision is made for younger children. LEAs provide places in nursery schools and day nurseries – the latter open for longer hours and terms than do the former, which are similar to infant schools – together with nursery classes in infant schools. The most dramatic growth in such provision has been in private voluntary playgroups, which are self-supporting and often initiated by parents. Table 8.5 suggests that in the 1970s, the middle classes were better catered for by, or took greater advantage of, pre-school education than the working classes. These figures are based on children aged 0 to 5, while pre-school education is normally associated with the age of three and over. On the assumption that the proportion of children over three is the same in each social class, the percentage attending nursery

287

TABLE 8.5 Percentage of children under five in each social class receiving pre-school education

| | Social class (RG SEG 70) | | | | | | |
	1	2	3	4	5	6	All
1972							
Day nursery/ playgroup	18	26	18	12	9	7	14
Nursery school[1]	14	12	9	7	8	7	8
Not yet started	68	62	73	81	84	85	78
1976–7[2]							
Day nursery/ playgroup	25	25	24	18	14	14	20
Nursery school/class	16	14	12	13	15	14	14
Not yet started	59	61	64	69	72	72	67

1. Includes primary and independent schools for under-fives.
2. Data for two years combined.

Devised from table 4.1, *GHS 1972* and table 5.1, *GHS 1977*.

school shows a steady decline across the social classes. The percentage for social class 1 (14 per cent) was twice that for classes 4 and 6 (7 per cent). For day nurseries and playgroups the differences were more marked, though not as regular, although the divide between working and middle class was greater than for nursery schools. This may indicate middle-class 'self-help' – that is, voluntary playgroups. In both forms of pre-school education the middle classes were above, and the working classes below, the average.

The data suggest a fairly dramatic change following governmental calls for expansion in the White Paper, *Education: a Framework for Expansion* (1972), though the proposed level of provision was still not achieved by the end of the 1980s. The overall percentage of children in either form of provision increased from 22 to 34 per cent between 1972 and 1976/7. In particular, the percentage of working-class children in nursery schools or classes just about doubled, from around 7 to 14 per cent, and day nursery and playgroup provision changed similarly. The latter type of provision continued to decline across the classes, from 25 per cent for classes 1 and 2 to 14 per cent for classes 5 and 6. On the other hand, nursery schooling shows little social class variation. Even so it may be argued that in terms of need, assumed by the White Paper to be greater among the 'disadvantaged', the resulting change amounts to little more than a numerical equality of provision. Most of the increase was in part-time provision (*Statistics of Education 1979*), and the change took place during a period of sharp decline in the number of children in this age group. Data on this aspect of education is no longer collected by the GHS.

Whether, and how, such experience affects subsequent performance at school is not clearly indicated by research. What can be shown, however, is that by the age of seven, the differences in performance of the social classes in infant or first schools in the essentials of reading and arithmetic are marked. The data in Table 8.6 are based on the test scores of some 15,000 seven-year-olds from the NCDS. In the case of reading, it shows that social class V children were six times as likely to be 'poor' readers as those from social class I (48 per cent compared with 8). The study also points out that the lower level at which a 'poor reader' is defined, the more marked is the imbalance in terms of social class. Hence a social class V child was some fifteen times more likely to be a *non*-reader at the age of seven than a child from social class I.

The table also shows that the gradients across the social classes for the percentage gaining marks for reading and arithmetic in the lowest 29 per cent of the whole sample (top row of each section of the table) are not regular. The percentages for classes II and IIIn are very close for reading and identical for arithmetic. What is very noticeable, however, is the clear division between the middle classes and the working classes. For example,

289

TABLE 8.6 Reading and arithmetic attainment test scores of seven-year-old children, by father's social class (percentages)

	I	II	IIIn	IIIm	IV	V	All[1]
			Social class (RG SEG 60)				
Grouped Southgate reading test scores							
0–20	8	15	14	30	37	48	29
21–28	37	39	43	41	38	34	39
29–30	54	47	43	29	25	17	32
Grouped problem arithmetic test scores							
0–3	12	19	19	30	34	41	29
4–6	38	39	43	42	42	37	41
7–10	50	42	38	28	24	22	31

1. Includes those without father or social class information.

Devised from tables A165 and A168, Davie *et al.* (1972).

while the average of poor readers was some 13 per cent for the former and 34 per cent for the latter, social class IIIn had 14 per cent and IIIm 30 per cent. Class I is distinguished from the other middle classes by having a lower percentage of poor readers and a higher percentage of the best readers. Conversely, class V stands out from the other working classes by having markedly poorer scores. These early class differences increase with further schooling. Commenting later on the same children, Fogelman and Goldstein (1976) wrote,

> For a given 7-year score the children whose fathers were in non-manual occupations are, at the age of 11, about 1.0 years ahead of social classes III manual and IV, who in turn are about 0.4 years ahead of social class V. This, of course, is additional to the existing differences at the age of 7, which were respectively 0.9 years and 0.7 years. Thus the overall differences at 11 have increased to 1.9 years and 1.11 years respectively.

Douglas (1964), in the NSHD longitudinal study, using a battery of standardized tests including intelligence, reading and school attainment, showed that between the ages of seven and eleven middle-class children's scores increased, whereas working-class children's scores declined, so that the difference between them widened. Both these longitudinal studies found that the divergence of attainment test scores between the social classes observed at ages seven and eleven continued through secondary school. So the overall picture is one of a widening gap between children from different social classes, which is greatest at ages fifteen and sixteen. Fogelman *et al.* (1978) comment that their figures imply that at sixteen years only about 15 per cent of children in social class V could be expected to score above the mean of non-manual children. These findings are perhaps surprising. It could be held that schools ought to operate so that initial differences are at least not heightened, while it might be argued that their purpose should be to equalize differences by improving the performance of weaker pupils.

The most crucial stage of schooling is clearly the leaving examinations. Table 8.7 provides a dramatic view of the relationship between social class and secondary school examination achievement among Scottish school leavers. At each level of achievement the percentage passing declines across the social classes from I to V, and this can be compared with the overall percentage (the dotted line) which neatly divides the non-manual from the manual classes. As can be seen, at the extremes 95 per cent of children from social class I left school with at least some qualification and 58 per cent had three or more higher SCE passes, compared to only 45 and 4 per cent respectively of those children from class V.

Such differences have been noted in a variety of surveys over the past four decades (for a review, see Reid, 1981). Few of these surveys have held constant other factors which can be seen to affect educational achievement. Consequently, although the data in Table 8.8 are

TABLE 8.7 School examination performance of all
Scottish leavers, 1975/76 (cumulative percentages)

Father's social class (RG 70)

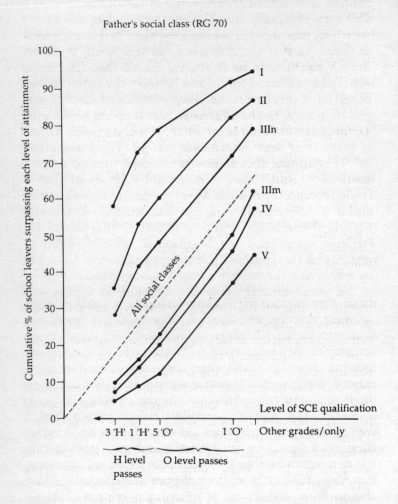

1. For definition, see Appendix B.

Devised from figure 1, Burnhill, (1981).

TABLE 8.8 Academic achievement by pupils[1] at LEA grammar schools, by grouped IQ scores at age eleven and social class of father, England and Wales[2] (percentages)

| IQ score | Achievement | Social class (RG 60) | |
		Non-manual	Manual
130+	Degree course	37	18
	At least 2 GCE A levels	43	30
	At least 5 GCE O levels	73	75
115–129	Degree course	17	8
	At least 2 GCE A levels	23	14
	At least 5 GCE O levels	56	45
100–114	Degree course	6	2
	At least 2 GCE A levels	9	6
	At least 5 GCE O levels	37	22

1. Born 1940–1.
2. Figures for degree course are for Great Britain.

Derived from table 5, appendix 1, part 2, *Higher Education* (1963).

dated they remain particularly valuable since they hold constant the type of school attended and the measured IQ ranges of the children studied. The table shows that, other than for children of the highest IQ range (130 or more) at the GCE O level stage, differences in achievement existed between middle- and working-class children in distinct favour of the former. In the middle IQ range (115–129) a quarter more middle-class children gained five or more O levels than did the working class, two-thirds more gained two A levels, and more than twice the number entered degree-level courses. Note, however, that these are not measures of pure achievement. They also involved staying on at school and using educational qualifications to enter higher education rather than employment. Hence part of the difference in A level success between the classes was due to differences in entry to sixth forms. Even at the highest IQ range the percentage of those who actually gained two A levels and subsequently went on to degree courses was 86 per cent for the middle class and 60 per cent for the working class. Very similar results were obtained in a study some six years later (*Statistics of Education 1961*, Supplement) which held constant the type of school and the grade of 11+ secondary school selection examination. Here, although the overall achievements at O level were higher, the social class differences remained. They were again revealed in the NSHD cohort study mentioned above, in which ability measured at the age of fifteen was held constant but not the type of school attended (Douglas *et al.*, 1968). It showed that the percentage of the top-ability group (16 per cent) who had gained five or more O levels (including at least three from English language, mathematics, science and a foreign language) varied from 77 per cent for the upper-middle-class children across the classes to 37 per cent for lower-working-class children. These findings were again broadly supported by Rutter *et al.* (1979) who, having controlled for verbal reasoning, found parental occupation to be related to the examination performance of children in their sample of London schools. The relationship was particularly strong among children in the middle band of ability and slightly less so for those in the higher ability band.

The most up-to-date data at the time of writing are in Table 8.9, and show the highest educational qualification held by a large sample of adults related to the social class of their fathers. The 'expected' pattern – the 'higher' the class, the larger the proportion with qualifications – is clear, as are the differences between the sexes. Some 52 per cent of men with fathers in class I had degrees compared to 24 per cent of women, while only 7 and 8 per cent respectively had no qualifications. Of those with fathers from class 6, 54 per cent of men and 68 per cent of women had no qualifications, and only 6 and 1 per cent respectively had degrees. Notice too how clear at every level of qualification is the divide between the

TABLE 8.9 Highest educational qualification[1] attained by persons[2] aged twenty-five to forty-nine, by father's social class, Great Britain, 1984–5[3] (percentages)

| | Social class (RG SEG 80) | | | | | | |
	1	2	3	4	5	6	All
Men							
Degree or equivalent	52	21	20	7	4	6	12
Higher education below degree	15	16	16	10	7	6	11
GCE A level or equivalent	11	15	15	12	10	9	12
GCE O level/CSE higher grades or equivalent	11	18	21	16	16	12	17
GCE/CSE other grades/commercial/ apprenticeship	2	7	8	12	12	11	10
Foreign or other	1	5	4	3	3	2	4
No qualifications	7	19	15	40	48	54	34
Women							
Degree or equivalent	24	11	7	3	2	1	6
Higher education below degree	23	16	18	7	6	3	10
GCE A level or equivalent	14	10	7	4	3	3	6
GCE O level/CSE higher grades or equivalent	20	26	27	18	15	11	20
GCE/CSE other grades/commercial/ apprenticeship	7	12	12	14	13	12	13
Foreign or other	4	4	4	3	2	2	3
No qualifications	8	20	21	50	58	68	42

1. For definitions, see Appendix B below.
2. Not in full-time education.
3. Data for the two years combined.

Derived from table 7.6 (a), *GHS 1985*.

TABLE 8.10 Percentage of male and female UK school leavers, by highest educational qualifications,[1] 1965/6 to 1985/6

	1965/6		1975/6[2]		1985/6	
	Males	Females	Males	Females	Males	Females
2 or more GCE A levels/3 or more SCE H levels	12.9	9.1	14.4	12.3	14.9	14.3
1 or more GCE A/ SCE H level	16.1	12.2	18.0	16.3	18.5	18.5
5 or more GCE/SCE O levels/CSE higher grades only	7.0	8.8	7.3	9.5	9.9	11.9
1 to 4 GCE/SCE O levels/CSE higher grades	14.5	15.9	23.9	27.0	24.3	28.8
GCE/SCE O levels/ CSE other grades	62.7	63.1	51.1	47.5	34.0	30.9
No qualifications					13.3	10.1

1. For definitions, see Appendix B below.
2. Raising the school leaving age in 1972/3 affected the numbers of pupils taking CSE/GCE/SCE examinations.

Calculated from table 29, *Education Statistics for the United Kingdom 1987* (1988).

attainments of the non-manual and manual classes.

As was recognized above, such data based on adults hide change, older adults being less likely to have qualifications than younger ones. In fact, sex differences in educational achievement have narrowed considerably in the past few decades, as is shown in Table 8.10 for UK school leavers and page 321 in respect to higher education. In 1965/6 girls were somewhat more likely than boys to leave school without a qualification and much more likely to leave without GCE A levels or their equivalents. By 1985/6 they were less likely to be without qualification (10.1 compared to 13.3 per cent), just as likely to have one or more A level and only 0.6 per cent less likely to have two or more, and this despite the fact that more females than males continued to leave with five or more O levels only. Overall, girls are more successful than boys at 16+ examinations and the gap at 18+ is closing – the only remaining, marked difference being passing three or more A levels (the percentages for England and Wales in 1985/6 were males 10.2 and females 8.8). This change is reflected in the fact that recently a higher proportion of girls than boys have stayed on into sixth forms. In England and Wales in 1983, 33 per cent of girls and 30 per cent of boys stayed for a year and 20 per cent of both for two years. In Scotland, girls were more likely to have stayed both for one (49 compared with 40) and for two years (22 compared with 19 per cent) (*Social Trends 15*, 1985).

Despite these and other changes the sexes remain differentiated in terms of achievement in particular subjects at 16+ examinations. For example, more boys than girls gain higher grade passes in science and mathematics, while more girls pass in English and foreign languages, while more extreme differences occur in respect to craft, design and technology compared with home economics. These differences can be seen to disadvantage women in the labour market (see, for example, Skeggs, 1989), though in educational terms boys can be seen as missing out as well. And, as is shown below (page 321), while females are more likely than males to continue their education on leaving school, fewer enter degree courses.

Areal class

So far our review has taken social class as an individual characteristic. However, as we have seen (page 105), it can also be used to characterize areas. Schooling is presently administered by LEAs, which display a wide range in the percentage of pupils living in households whose heads have non-manual occupations; from 50 per cent in Surrey to 11 per cent in Knowsley as compared to the average for all English LEAs which is 28 per cent. The DES *Statistical*

Bulletin 13/84 (1984) related these differences to the proportion of age groups gaining GCE and CSE qualifications and found a very strong relationship. For example, the percentage of pupils gaining one or more A level GCEs in Surrey was 22, in Knowsley 8 and overall 15. The comparable percentages for five or more O level GCE higher grades or equivalent were 33, 12 and 23 respectively. The survey included a number of other socioeconomic factors – measures of population density, household amenities and overcrowding, non-white children, unemployment, supplementary benefit payments, infant mortality and family size – which all to varying degrees displayed a relationship with educational achievement, though none matched the statistical significance of the social class measure in respect to attainment at A and higher grade O level GCEs. Several educational and resource variables, together with overall expenditure, were also associated with attainment but were 'of small degree' and much lower than the socioeconomic variables. As the Bulletin clearly indicates, any comparison of the educational attainment of LEAs 'would be seriously misleading if the socioeconomic background of pupils were not taken into account'. Of course, it has to be recognized that the LEAs are large and diverse, displaying considerable intra-area variation (see pages 109–12). However, as it is, this type of research reinforces that on individual class in identifying class as an important and fundamental variable in educational achievement.

There is a certain crudeness in the normal use of father's occupation as the single criterion of a child's social class. Not only has mothers' social class been shown to be related to educational performance (see pages 314–5), but we can suspect that fathers and mothers are important in combination. Moreover, it is obvious that aspects of social class beyond occupation have important effects, or are related to such performance. Particularly important here, and as has been demonstrated in research, is the educational level of parents. Certainly adult social class and occupation are related to education level (see pages 276–82). Studies with more information about their subjects reveal interesting insights. One of my own (Reid, 1969), for example, identified some sixteen 'family characteristics' related to both educational success and to 'middle-classness'. Detailed analysis revealed a small number of 'working-class' children (defined by father's occupation) who had *more* of these characteristics than many of the 'middle-class' children. They had, for example, middle-class, educated mothers and grandparents and came from educationally responsive and supportive, materially well-off, small families. These children were among the most successful in the whole sample and were the most successful working-class part of it. The reverse was also true; some 'middle-class' children had few of the 'family characteristics' and were not successful. The use of the simple occupational definition of class could be seen to misplace some success and failure. What is being argued, therefore, is that the class chances in education, as outlined above, may in fact be more blatant than they appear. More sophisticated criteria of social class than fathers' occupation might well reveal greater differences in educational performance between the classes.

Ethnicity

Research in this area has been limited both in scope and to the relatively unhelpful categories of West Indian and Asian (see pages 75–82). The collection of official educational data in respect to ethnic minorities ceased in 1972, and while restarted in 1983, none has yet been published.

The general picture to emerge from research is that Asian children perform similarly to, or somewhat better than, their White classmates, while West Indians perform less well, in both primary and secondary schools. Little (1981) surveyed performance in ILEA schools at the point of transfer from primary to secondary. He found New Commonwealth immigrant children a year below the age norm in reading, and underrepresented by about half in the top 25 per cent of the ability range in verbal reasoning, English and mathematics. In comparing Asians and West Indians who had received all their education in Britain, it was found that Asians performed similarly to Whites in mathematics and verbal reasoning, and only slightly less well in English, while West Indians performed markedly less well on all three measures. In fact, West Indian children have been shown to 'underperform' in comparison with socially disadvantaged White children in ILEA education priority area infant and primary schools (Barnes, 1975; see also Mabey, 1981).

Taylor (1976) found Asian boys doing better than Whites in 16+ examinations in Newcastle, and similar achievements for the two groups have been recorded in Leicester (Brooks and Singh, 1978) and the Midlands (Driver and Ballard, 1979). The most extensive surveys of this stage of education are those undertaken for the Rampton and Swann Committees (*West Indian Children in our Schools*, 1981, and *Education for All*, 1985). The main findings are presented in Table 8.11, which shows West Indian GCE O level/CSE performance to be markedly lower than that of Asians and Others in five LEAs. Note that the overall performance in these LEAs is lower than that for the whole of England (compare columns 4 and 5). While Asian achievement of higher grade passes in mathematics matched that of Others, in English it was lower (21 compared with 29 per cent) and in A level attainment, the West Indian score was the lowest. The data, however, reveal significant increases in West Indian attainments between 1978/9 (figures in brackets) and 1981/2; the percentage gaining five or more higher grade GCE O level/CSE passes doubled and that for A levels increased two and a half times. It is interesting to note that the percentage failing to gain any graded examination results is identical for all groups and that at 19 per cent it is greatly in excess of the 11 per cent for all England. Essen and Ghodsian (1979) presented similar

TABLE 8.11 Educational attainment[1] of ethnic groups in five English LEAs, 1981/2[2] (percentages)

	Asian	West Indian	Others	5 LEAs	All England
1 or more GCE A level	13(12)	5(2)	13(12)	12(10)	14(13)
5 or more higher grade GCE					
O level/CSE	17	6(3)	19(16)	18(15)	23(21)
1–4 GCE O level/CSE	64	75	62	63	66
No graded results	19	19	19	19	11
English GCE O level/CSE					
Higher grade	21(22)	15(9)	29	26	36(34)
Other grade	51(47)	60	46(41)	48	47
Maths GCE O level/CSE					
Higher grade	21	8(5)	21	20	26(23)
Other grade	46(41)	47	47(42)	46	47
Destination on leaving school					
Degree course	5	1[–][3]	5(4)	5(4)	6
Any full-time education course (includes degrees)	34(21)	27(16)	17(12)	21(13)	26(19)

1. For definitions, see Appendix B below.
2. Figures in brackets refer to 1978/9 and are shown only where markedly different from 1981/2.
3. Less than 0.5 per cent.

Devised from tables 3, 4, 5 and 7 Annex B, *Education for All* (1985).

findings from the NCDS study. Standardized test scores in mathematics and reading of 'first generation immigrants' were lower than white children's, but among 'second generation immigrants', only West Indians scored lower. A survey of sixteen schools in an Outer London borough found Afro-Caribbean pupils performing less well than others at sixteen and eighteen-plus (Craft and Craft, 1983).

This overall picture is well supported in general terms. Tomlinson (1980) has reviewed some thirty-three studies of ethnic performance in our schools, of which twenty-six showed West Indians scoring lower than Whites on individual or group tests, overrepresented in the ESN (educationally subnormal) category, or underrepresented in the higher streams of school. This general view of low West Indian performance is challenged, however, by Driver (1980). In the five multi-racial schools he researched, West Indian children did better overall in 16+ examinations than did Whites. The largest difference was between the two sets of girls. Among West Indians, girls did better than boys; among Whites, the boys did better than girls. He suggests that the explanation may lie in cultural differences, namely the female focus of Jamaican/West Indian life and English working-class attitudes towards the education of girls.

His research, like most in the field, has received a good deal of criticism (for example, see Troyna, 1984). Many of the studies are dated and limited, and there is considerable variation in the type and size of sample used. While some of these criticisms can be made in general terms about much educational research, certain criticisms are particularly important in this field. The most serious limitation is that most studies ignore social class as a factor. Failing to hold class-constant raises the question as to whose performance is being compared with that of ethnic minorities. Because of the residential segregation of social classes and ethnic minorities in our society the comparison will often be with White children from semi- and unskilled manual backgrounds. Hence the often-quoted similar performance of Asian children might well be limited to a similarity with White children of particular social classes.

Roberts *et al.* (1983) have claimed that Black under-achievement might be attributable to the fact that they reside in districts and attend schools where the attainment of all pupils is below average. An analysis of 16+ examination results in Bradford schools from 1983 to 1987 has led to the preliminary conclusion that social class rather than ethnic origin is the main source of variation (Archer, 1988). Ethnic groups are known to have different occupational/social class structures (see pages 98–102) which also vary in different parts of the country. Some ethnic group differences in educational achievement may be attributable to class or class in combination with ethnicity. Some ethnic minorities are overrepresented in semi- and unskilled employment, and suffer higher unemployment, lower incomes and poorer housing than Whites (see pages 169–70, 203–4, 262–7 above and Brown, 1984a), but such differences have not been taken into account in research. Craft and Craft compared Asian, West Indian and White middle- and working-class educational performance and found that the class differences at 16+ were similar within each ethnic group. The lower performance of West Indians in both social classes begs the question as to whether their location within the classes was the same as that of other groups. Further analysis, including sex, was thwarted by the fact that only 9 per cent (257) of their sample were West Indian – of whom only thirty-one were middle-class.

Failure to analyse ethnic educational performance by social class and to use scales sensitive enough to locate accurately ethnic minorities is likely to lead to a confusion between ethnicity and class. Before assuming ethnicity to be the central variable it would be prudent to examine the role of class, not only for our understanding but also since otherwise educational policy and strategies designed to combat the problem may prove inappropriate or inadequate (Reid, 1986b). As is the case with class, the definitions of ethnic groups used in research disguise or ignore important cultural variations, including values relating to education, concepts of sex roles, occupational and familial aspirations and the like, all of which are probably related to educational performance. Thus, the lack of full and proper social class and cultural identification in the research in this area means that our view and understanding of the relationships between ethnic group membership and educational performance and achievement is not as clear as it might, or should be.

Data are not generally available on ethnic minority participation in further and higher education, but as in the case of other forms of social stratification, degree course entry appears the sharpest differentiation. As Table 8.11 indicates, the *Education for All* survey found 5 per cent of Asian and 1 per cent of West Indian pupils compared with 6 per cent of all leavers in England bound for degree courses. In some contrast, both West Indian and Asian pupils are more likely to stay at school beyond the age of sixteen and to enter full-time post-school education (see also page 321 below and Craft and Craft, 1983). In the latter case the overall rate in the five LEAs was 20 per cent, with West Indian, Asian and Others at 28, 33 and 17 per cent respectively. Differing levels of school achievement and opportunities to enter employment are probably involved, as well as cultural factors.

Notwithstanding the reservations about research outlined here, it is clear on the evidence to date that ethnic group, like sex and social class, is clearly related to educational experience, attainment and outcome.

Age

In many ways age is the least straightforward form of social stratification to relate to education. As we have seen (page 282), the educational qualifications of adults vary according to age, reflecting educational and social change. More generally, we can recognize that society sees education as being firmly associated with childhood and early adulthood. This is clearly reflected in the comparatively less than generous provision for adult and continuing education, despite the development of such institutions as the Open University. More fundamentally, age forms the basis of school organization and is an important criterion of performance. Children progress from class to class on the basis of their age and are judged according to age-based standards or the average performance of their peers. Thus O level GCE, CSE and GCSE are 16+ examinations; passing them at other ages has implications concerning the person's ability. The new national assessments of children at age seven, eleven and fourteen of the Education Reform Act, 1988, have similar assumptions and implications. This emphasis on age and stage in schooling reflects, or contributes to, the competitive nature of our educational system, which has relatively less provision for those who might take longer to achieve given levels. A movement of children at critical stages because of age – from infant to junior school, for instance – may in some instances (for example, for those who have not mastered reading) have long-term implications for their subsequent achievements. The development of open-entry sixth forms indicates that some pupils whose performance at sixteen was not good may achieve well given an extra year – a fact recognized by some 'public' schools which arrange for their pupils to take three rather than two years over A level GCE courses.

There is also evidence to suggest that children born in autumn perform better in school than those born in spring and summer, mainly because the former are likely to receive longer schooling in infant or first school (up to two terms more), and remain the eldest in their school classes throughout their careers. Evidence from the NCDS indicates that the length of schooling is the crucial factor, since all the children surveyed were born in the same week of a year, yet roughly equal proportions started school before the age of five and after it. 'Early starters' were more likely to be middle-class and attend small schools – nevertheless, after holding constant these and other variables, test results in general ability, reading and mathematics at age eleven showed that 'early' performed better than 'late' starters (Fogelman and Gorbach, 1978). While such factors can easily be seen as advantageous in the early years of schooling, it is perhaps surprising that

305

they have been found to operate throughout the school career (Thompson, 1971; Barker Lunn, 1970, 1972). ESN pupils have been shown to include an overrepresentation of younger children in each age group (Pumfrey, 1975).

No relationship between season of birth and social class or ethnic group has been established, and there probably is none. The importance of ages and stages in schooling may, however, be indirectly related to differing performance along social stratification lines. Such a system is to the advantage of those best equipped, able and willing to tackle schooling as presented, and to the disadvantage of others. From our considerations so far, and those below, it is easy to align such differences with class and ethnic groups.

Type of secondary school

The empirical research interest in the secondary schooling of the social classes in Britain really stems from the 1944 Education Act. After this Act secondary schools were either selective, offering chances of public examination, or non-selective, normally leading to termination of schooling at the minimum school-leaving age. A document published at the height of this period of concern, 15–18 (1960) – often referred to as the Crowther Report – revealed sharp social class differences in secondary schooling.

The social class compositions of selective and non-selective schools were quite different: the former had a much higher percentage of social class 1 (RG SEG 50B) (18 compared to 4) and a lower percentage of social class 4 (10 compared to 23) than the latter. Male children from different social classes had very different school experiences. Whereas in social class I (RG 50) only about a quarter attended non-selective schools, while nearly half went to selective schools and 22 per cent to independent schools, in social classes IV and V over 80 per cent went to non-selective, less than 20 per cent to selective, and virtually none to independent schools.

Since this research, two main changes have taken place in secondary schools. First, before the raising of the statutory minimum school-leaving age to sixteen years in 1973, many of the non-selective schools introduced opportunities for education beyond the minimum leaving age, and for sitting public examinations. Secondly, most but not all areas introduced comprehensive secondary education. There is, however, wide variety in the comprehensive schemes existing in different areas of Britain. For example, the DES identified fourteen types of comprehensive school (including sixth-form but not tertiary colleges) just on the criterion of age of the children attending them (*Comprehensive Education*, 1978). In the mid- to late 1970s some areas had not introduced such schemes, and some of those introduced were at varying stages of development. These changes need to be borne in mind when looking at Table 8.12, which

TABLE 8.12 Type of secondary school[1] attended by children aged eleven to fifteen, by social class[2] (percentages)[3]

| | Social class (RG SEG 70) | | | | | | |
	1	2	3	4	5	6	All
Secondary modern	7	11	14	24	26	33	20
Comprehensive	39	55	60	63	60	52	59
Middle	6	3	6	5	4	3	5
Grammar	17	10	10	5	4	3	7
Independent	30	18	8	1	1	1	7
Other schools	2	2	3	2	4	7	3

1. Includes equivalent Scottish school types; part comprehensive/part selective shools included with comprehensive; independent includes direct grant; and 'other' includes special schools.
2. Of father or head of household.
3. Data for 1975 and 1976 combined.

Derived from table 7.1, *GHS 1976*.

shows the percentage of each social class (based on fathers) of eleven- to fifteen-year-old children attending types of secondary schools. Caution is necessary, since the type of school attended was identified by the parent involved. Given the state of flux in school organization at that time, some schools were probably misidentified (for example, some might still have been known by their old names, while others might have been in the process of changing).

The data can be construed in a number of ways. Perhaps the fairest way is to compare the percentage of each social class in each type of school with the overall figure (right-hand column). In this way one can see that the middle classes had a higher percentage in the remaining selective schools – that is, grammar and independent – and a lower percentage in secondary modern schools, the opposite being true of the working classes. The social classes other than class I all had remarkably similar percentages in comprehensive/middle schools – around the average for all social classes of 64 per cent for the two types together.

Some general observations can be made about the effects of secondary school reorganization. If the secondary modern and comprehensive schools are accepted, by definition, as non-selective, then the proportion of working-class children in such schools rose slightly from around, or over, 80 per cent to more than 90 per cent, and that of class I children rose sharply from 24 to 52 per cent between the late 1950s and mid-1970s. This does not necessarily mean that any particular school was better balanced in terms of the social class backgrounds of its pupils than before. Many comprehensive schools are neighbourhood schools – they cater for children from a limited area surrounding the school – and as was shown in Chapter 3, many such areas are occupied predominantly by one social class or another. Hence some comprehensives could be described as working-class, and others as middle-class. Given local variations in the development and organization of comprehensive schools, together with the lack of recent research, it is not possible either to substantiate or to refute the suggestion that comprehensivization has brought together the educational experience of the social classes.

What is clear is that the existence of independent, fee-paying schools as an alternative to those provided by LEAs has and continues to segregate education along class lines. The term 'independent' refers to independence from the LEA system and not, as many suppose, to financial independence. While parents pay fees, it has been estimated that various forms of state subsidy for such schools in 1979 amounted to between £350 and £500 millions – comparable to the sums received by either British Leyland or British Steel (Rogers, 1980). And this was prior to the Conservative government's introduction of the assisted places scheme.

In the UK in 1983 some 5.9 per cent of children of all ages attended independent schools; in Northern Ireland the percentage was more than double, while in Scotland it was much lower than the national figure. Just over 1 per cent more male than female children attended them (7.6 compared with 6.4: *Education Statistics for the UK, 1984*). We shall concentrate on independent secondary schools, attended by 8.5 per cent of UK secondary pupils in 1983 (*Social Trends 15*). These are clearly middle-class institutions. The first section of Table 8.13 shows the percentage of each social class (based on father's occupation when respondent was aged fourteen years) of privately educated men aged twenty to sixty in 1972. As can be seen, a third of social class I attended private primary school and the percentage declined dramatically across the classes to only 0.3 per cent of class VIII – a pattern repeated with slightly higher percentages for private secondary schools (36 to 1 per cent respectively). Notice that the only exception to the pattern of decline across the classes is class IV (small proprietors/self-employed artisans/own-account workers other than professionals)

TABLE 8.13 Attendance at private primary and secondary schools, by social class and sex (percentages)

	I	II	III	Social class (HG/A) IV	V	VI	VII	VIII	All
Males only[1]									
Private primary	33	14	7	10	2	1	0.9	0.3	5.8
Private secondary	36	16	7	11	3	2	0.9	1	6.5

	1	2	Social class (MR) 3	4	5	6	All
Males and females[2]							
Independent primary	15	11	5	2	[–][3]	[–]	5
Independent secondary	26	12	6	1	1	1	5

1. Aged 20 to 60 years in 1972; percentages over 1 rounded; private secondary schools are HMC, direct grant and independent non-HMC; class of fathers when respondents were aged 14.
2. Children in GHS samples 1976 and 1977; class is of head of household where father was not member of household.
3. Less than 1 per cent.

Devised from table 4.3, Halsey, Heath and Ridge (1980) and table 5.1, GHS 1977.

which had higher percentages than class III (routine non-manual).

A view of the situation in 1976–7, including both sexes, is to be found in the second section to the table. These data are based on parents' answers and may underestimate independent schools to the extent that not all parents may have appreciated that 'direct grant' schools (other than Catholic ones) had become independent by the time of the inquiry. Here again there are strong class differences: the proportion of class 1 attending independent primary schools is more than fifteen times greater than that of classes 5 and 6, and that for independent secondary schools twenty-six times greater. Notice also

310

the very marked differences between the non-manual and manual classes, and within the former between classes 1 and 2 and 2 and 3.

Most research has been on public schools, defined by the *Public Schools Commission* (1968) as those independent schools in membership of HMC, GBA and GBSA. While difficult to define or characterize accurately, they are the longer-established, most prestigious independent schools and are mainly boys' and boarding schools. In 1984 4.4 per cent of males aged fourteen attended HMC schools compared with only 0.5 per cent of females (based on information supplied by ISIS). Hence such schools are almost exclusively male and middle-class; the Commission reported that only 1 per cent of pupils were from the working classes while 85 per cent were from classes I and II, which comprised but 18 per cent of the male population at the time. It would be difficult, then, to disagree with the Commission's finding that public schools are 'socially divisive', in that they recruit and segregate a very particular group of children from the majority. Similarly, Halsey, Heath and Ridge (1980) conclude from their survey of male education: 'The private schools represent a bastion of class privilege compared with the relatively egalitarian state sector.' The significance of 'public' schools lies not only with their almost exclusively middle-class intakes but also with the destinations of their output. Public school products are remarkably successful in securing elite jobs in our society. This is clearly demonstrated in Table 8.14. When looking at the proportion of public school-educated holders of these positions, it should be remembered that only 2.5 per cent of the school population aged fourteen years were so educated. Of particular note is the very high proportion of MPs who have served the DES whose own education was at HMC school.

The table also indicates the strong relationship between attendance at Oxford and Cambridge universities and elite positions in our society, and suggests a powerful

311

TABLE 8.14 Percentage[1] of public school[2] and Oxbridge educated holders of various elite positions in the 1980s[3]

	Public school	Oxbridge
THE ESTABLISHMENT		
Civil Service (under-secretary and above)	50	61
High Court and Appeal judges	83	83
Law lords	89	89
Church of England bishops	59	71
Ambassadors	69	82
COMMERCE AND INDUSTRY		
Directors of major life insurance companies	92	50
Directors of clearing banks	70	47
Chairmen of clearing banks	83	67
Directors of Bank of England	78	89
Chairmen of merchant banks	88	59
Directors of 40 major industrial firms	66	40
POLITICS		
Conservative MPs	70	48
Labour MPs	14	15
Alliance MPs	52	30
Parliamentarians serving DES 1964–84[4]		
Conservative	79	63
Labour	31	34

1. Of total of group whose education was known.
2. In membership of HMC, GBA and GBSA, generally excluding other independents.
3. Dates: for establishment, 1984; for commerce, 1981; for industry, 1971; for politics, 1983.
4. In addition, a further 3 per cent Labour and 4 per cent Conservative attended other independent schools.

Compiled and devised from *Who's Who* (1984), *Whitaker's Almanac* (1984), Sampson (1982), Whitely (1974), Butler and Kavanagh (1984) and *The Times House of Commons* (1964–84).

TABLE 8.15 Percentage[1] of fourteen- and seventeen-year-olds and university entrants educated at LEA, independent and HMC schools

	LEA schools	Independent schools[2]	HMC schools
14-year-olds	93	7	2.5
17-year-olds	82	18	9.5
University entrants	75	25	na
Oxbridge entrants[3]	48	52	na

1. Percentages other than HMC rounded.
2. Includes HMC schools.
3. LEA figure includes FE; Oxbridge figures are for 1984/5.

Devised from table 12, *Education Statistics for the UK 1984*, table G9, UCCA (1984), information provided by ISIS, *Cambridge University Reporter* (1985) and *Oxford University Gazette* (1984).

relationship between attendance of independent school and Oxbridge. This is spelt out in Table 8.15, which shows that the independent school minority constitutes over half those admitted to Oxbridge. The Education Reform Act of 1988 which allows for schools to opt out of LEA control and be directly financed from central government, together with the institution of CTCs, will, in effect, expand the independent sector of schooling. While open to speculation, it seems unlikely that this expansion will seriously affect the social class composition of independent schools.

Higher and further education

The most comprehensive, though now dated, research in this area is *Higher Education* (1963, often referred to as the Robbins Report). Table 8.16 shows how very sharply separate were the social classes, based on fathers' occupation at the time the sample left school, in terms of entry to higher and further education. At each level of

TABLE 8.16 Highest level of education[1] attained by children born in 1940/1, by father's social class (percentages)

		Social class (RG 60)				
	I	II	IIIn	IIIm	IV & V	All
Higher education						
Degree level full-time	33	11	6	2	1	4
Other full-time	12	8	4	2	1	3
Part-time	7	6	3	3	2	4
A level/SLC	16	7	7	2	1	3
Other post-school course, or O level	25	48	51	42	30	40
No post-school course or O level/SLC	7	20	29	49	65	47

1. For definition, see Appendix B below.

Derived from table 2, appendix 1, part 2 section 2, *Higher Education* 1963).

education the percentage entering declines across the social classes. Some 33 per cent of class I undertook degree courses compared to only 1 per cent of classes IV and V. Put another way, the chances of a child from social class I entering degree-level education were thirty-three times greater than those of a child from classes IV and V. At the other extreme, while almost two-thirds (65 per cent) of classes IV and V neither gained qualifications nor entered post-school education, this was true of only 7 per cent of class I and 20 per cent of class II.

One interesting aspect of this research was that it related children's educational achievement to mothers' occupation before marriage. Table 8.17 allows for comparison, in terms of a simple non-manual/manual dichotomy, of both parents' social class with their children's level of education and presents a very similar picture. Note that the mothers and fathers were not matched with each other. The sample's educational attainment related nearly as closely to mothers' social

TABLE 8.17 Highest level of education,[1] by social class[2] of father and mother, of children born in 1940/1 (percentages)

| | Social class (RG 60) | | | |
| | Non-manual | | Manual | |
	Fathers	Mothers	Fathers	Mothers
Higher education				
Degree level full-time	12.0	14.8	1.5	1.9
Other full-time	7.5	8.3	1.7	2.4
Part-time	5.5	4.8	3.0	3.6
A level/SLC	7.9	9.3	1.7	2.0
Other post-school course, or O level	46.0	44.3	37.5	39.0
No post-school course or O level/SLC	21	18.2	54.5	51.0

1. For definition, see Appendix B below.
2. Based on father's occupation at school-leaving age and mother's occupation before marriage.

Devised from tables 1 and 3, appendix 1, part 2, section 2, *Higher Education* (1963).

class, defined by occupation before marriage, as it did to that of fathers at their children's school-leaving age. *Higher Education* suggests that a mother's occupation is an indirect measure of her education, and comments, 'But his [the father's] occupation ... presumably affects his family's income and children's education directly, whereas in the case of the mother the effect of her education, rather than that of her occupation before marriage, is presumably the more direct.'

Given the relative social class chances outlined above, the composition of the groups of students in Table 8.18 holds few surprises. Comparing the base line with the rest of the table reveals that in each type of higher and further education, social classes I and II were overrepresented, while the proportions of social class IIIn in each were rather similar. In contrast, the working classes, particularly classes IV and V, were

TABLE 8.18 Social class profile[1] of higher and further education students

	I	II	IIIn	IIIm	IV	V	% of 19-year-olds
			Social class (RG 60)				
Postgraduate	10	37	14	25	7	2	–
Undergraduate	18	41	12	18	6	1	3.3
3-year teacher training	7	33	14	29	9	2	1.7
Full-time further education	12	32	14	28	8	2	0.9
Part-time day	6	20	16	39	12	4	0.7
Part-time evening	5	22	14	39	12	3	0.1
Economically active males[2]	4	11	17	39	18	8	

Note rows do not add to 100 since not known are not shown.
1. Of father.
2. RG SEG 60.

Devised from tables 5, 65, 81, 102 and 135, appendix 2(B), part 1; table 3, appendix 2(A), *Higher Education* (1963), and table 1, *Socio-Economic Group Tables* (1966).

underrepresented in each type. The skilled manual class, IIIm, was also underrepresented, except in part-time further education, where the percentage was identical with that of economically active males. The social class composition of undergraduates, 71 per cent middle-class and 25 per cent working-class, was somewhat different from that of teacher trainees, where the percentages were 54 and 40 per cent respectively, and from further education, particularly part-time, where the working classes were in the majority. Although the social composition of postgraduates is somewhat similar to that of undergraduates, comparison between the two reveals a difference. The percentage of postgraduates in social classes I and II is lower than that of undergraduates, whereas in all the other social classes it is higher. At this educational level,

TABLE 8.19 Social class profile[1] of university graduates

| | Social class (RG 60) | | | | | | |
	I	II	IIIn	IIIm	IV	V	Unknown
Male	12	34	14	19	6	1	14
Female	15	39	13	14	5	–	12
Economically active males[2]	4	11	17	39	18	8	3

1. Of fathers at time of graduates' entry to university.
2. RG SEG 60.

Devised from table 1, Kelsall, Poole and Kuhn (1972) and table 1, *Socio-Economic Group Tables* (1966).

then, there may be some advantage for the working class. It is also interesting to note here that, in spite of the vastly differing social class chances of university entry, performance once at university is apparently not affected by social class. Certainly research in this field has failed to show any consistent relationship between social class and class of degree (Brockington and Stein, 1963; Kelsall, 1963; chapters by Newfield and Dale in Halmos, 1963).

A study of a large percentage of university graduates in 1960 (Kelsall, Poole and Kuhn, 1972, aptly subtitled *The Sociology of an Elite*) demonstrated their social class composition by sex. Table 8.19 again displays in both sexes that the majority of graduates came from the middle classes, which are a minority of society at large. As a group, the female graduates came more frequently from the 'higher' social classes than did the males. While 26 per cent of male graduates came from the working classes, this was true of only 19 per cent of the females, a higher proportion of whom came from classes I and II (54 compared to 46 per cent).

The situation did not change with the expansion of universities and other forms of higher education following the recommendations of *Higher Education*. The data

TABLE 8.20 Social class profile[1] and number[2] of university entrants, age groups and age participation rates[3]

| | Social class (UCCA)[1] | | | | |
	1	2	3	4	All
1970					
Profile of age group	9	7	21	63	100
Number in age group[2]	65.4	50.6	158	470	744
Profile of university entrants	30	14	28	28	100
Number of entrants[2]	18.8	8.8	17.5	17.5	62.5
Age participation rate[3]	29	17	11	4	8
1977					
Profile of age group	10	9	21	61	100
Number in age group[2]	84.8	70.6	171	505	831
Profile of university entrants	36	16	24	24	100
Number of entrants[2]	28.0	12.4	18.7	18.7	77.8
Age participation rate[3]	33	18	11	4	9

1. Note that class 4 includes *all* manual.
2. In 1000s.
3. Percentage that the entrants in each class constitute of the age group in that class.

Devised from table 6, Edwards and Roberts (1980).

contained in Table 8.20 are based on UCCA statistics (see footnote and pages 65–6 above for details of social class classification). As can be seen, despite a growth in the number of entrants to universities between 1970 and 1977 (from 62.5 to 77.8 thousand), the percentage of class 1 rose from 30 to 36 per cent while that of class 4 fell from 28 to 24 per cent. On the more sophisticated age participation rate (the percentage of the age group in each class who were entrants), class 1 rose from 29 to 33 per cent, while classes 3 and 4 stayed constant at 11 and 4 per cent respectively. In fact the extremes differ even more. Edwards and Roberts (1980) calculated that males in class I (RG) had in 1976 a 58 per cent chance of entering university and an 85 per cent chance of some form of higher education, while for females the respective percentages were 38 and 56. At the other extreme, males from class V had only a 1.4 per cent chance of university and a 2.1 per cent chance of any form of higher education; females of that class had the lowest chances of all at 0.8 and 1.2 per cent respectively. Much the same picture emerges from Halsey, Heath and Ridge's (1980, Table 10.8) comparison of different male age cohorts' university attendance. Of those born between 1913 and 1922, 7.2 per cent of classes I and II (HG/A) and 0.9 per cent of the working classes went to university, while of those born between 1943 and 1952, 26.4 per cent of classes I and II and 3.1 per cent of the working classes went. The increase over this considerable period of time for both groups of classes is of the order of three and a half times, which almost matches the overall participation rate increase from 1.8 to 8.5 per cent. As a consequence, the difference between the two sets of classes remained constant – some eight times higher for I and II than for the working classes. The greatest absolute increments of opportunity throughout that period of expansion went to classes I and II.

The most up-to-date view of the social class composition of candidates for, and admissions to, university comes from the yearly review by UCCA. The now familiar pattern is clear from Table 8.21. Social class I, which makes up 5 per cent of the population, presents 18 per cent of the candidates and gains 20 per cent of acceptances. This pattern, but with lower proportions, is followed by classes II and IIIn. The opposite is true for the manual classes; for example, class IIIm, which is 36 per cent of the population, provides only 14 per cent of candidates and secures 13 per cent of acceptances, and this disproportion increases through class IV to class V where 7 per cent of the population make only just over 1 per cent of both candidates and those accepted. There are

TABLE 8.21 Social class profiles[1] of university candidates and accepted candidates (percentages[2])

| | Social class (RG 80) | | | | | |
	I	II	IIIn	IIIm	IV	V
Candidates	18	47	12	14	8	1.3
Accepted candidates	20	48	11	13	7	1.1
Economically active/ retired males, 1981	5	22	12	36	18	7

1. Of classified only.
2. Those over 2 rounded.

Devised from tabulation on p. 6, UCCA (1988), and table 16A, *Economic Activity, Census 1981, Great Britain* (1984).

also differences in the social class composition of candidates and those accepted (compare rows 1 and 2): classes I and II have a slightly larger proportion of acceptances than they do of candidates, while the other classes have a lower proportion of acceptances than of candidates.

These differences can be defended from the implication that they reflect a social bias in selection by the universities, inasmuch as the classes also vary in terms of pre-entry examination performance. The average GCE A level scores of both candidates and those accepted decline somewhat across the social classes (a range of 1.5 for candidates and 0.9 for those accepted – see Table 8.22 which has a footnote explaining the scoring). Overall, 59 per cent of candidates are accepted, the percentage declining from 64 to 52 between classes I and V. UCCA comments, 'From the evidence ... it seems almost certain that there is a correlation between social class and examination qualifications.'

As was suggested above, more female school leavers than male, and more ethnic minority than majority, continue with their education. There is, however, considerable variation in the type of further or higher

TABLE 8.22 Average A level scores[1] of university candidates[2] and accepted candidates, by social class

	I	II	Social class (RG 80) IIIn	IIIm	IV	V	All
Candidates	9.7	9.2	8.8	8.5	8.5	8.2	9.1
Accepted candidates	11.4	11.0	10.7	10.6	10.5	10.5	10.9
Accepted as % of candidates	64	60	56	55	55	52	59

1. Based on two or best three passes, grades scored A = 5, B = 4, C = 3, D = 2, E = 1 and added, hence range is 2 to 15 (assumes same numerical value between each grade/same grades in different subjects are equal/grades from different exam boards are equal).
2. Home candidates.

Devised from tables E7, E8 and E9, UCCA (1988).

education undertaken and subjects studied. Vocational courses such as teaching, catering and nursing are predominantly female. Fewer women than men enter degree courses, around 7 compared with 9 per cent (*Statistics of Education, 1982*). The sexual composition of university undergraduates has changed: in 1971 it was male 68, female 32 per cent; by 1988, 57 and 43. Women are overrepresented in arts, language and education degrees and underrepresented in science and particularly engineering (UGC, 1987). Women constitute a small minority (17 per cent) of academic staff of universities and only 3 per cent of professors. Women are slightly more likely to enter polytechnics and twice as likely to enter other institutions of higher education to read for degrees, than men. The ethnic minorities, particularly West Indians, are less likely to enter degree courses (see Table 8.11) and are markedly underrepresented on postgraduate teacher education courses (Searle and Stibbs, 1985).

A number of studies of individual universities have displayed considerable differences in the social origins of their students. This could indicate social class differences in choice of, or opportunity to enter, particular universities. In 1960–1 the average proportion of undergraduates from the manual classes for all universities was 25 per cent (*Higher Education*, 1963). At one extreme 13 per cent of male and 6 per cent of female undergraduates were from the manual classes in Oxford and Cambridge (Kelsall, Poole and Kuhn, 1972, Table 22). This matches the figures of 10 and 12 per cent for both sexes in two Cambridge colleges (anonymous) reported elsewhere (Hatch and Reich, 1970). At the other extreme, Musgrove *et al.* (1967) showed that 41 per cent of the entrants to Bradford University, then a newly emerging technological university, came from manual backgrounds.

Of particular interest here is the Open University, which had as one of its aims the provision of higher educational opportunities for those who had 'missed out' on the conventional ones. The top row of Table 8.23 shows that its first intake was, in terms of the students' own social class, even more heavily biased towards the middle classes than that of a conventional university. Indeed some 93 per cent came from social classes I, II and IIIn, the vast majority, 62 per cent, coming from class II. In fact most of the entrants had already been successful in the educational system. Many were, for example, non-graduate teachers (hence the very large proportion of social class II). However, as the second row of the table shows, just over half the students' fathers (51

TABLE 8.23 Open University students, by own and father's social class (percentages)

| | Social class (RG 60) | | | | | |
	I	II	IIIn	IIIm	IV	V
Students	20	62	11	5	1	0
Fathers	8	26	13	34	13	4

Derived from table 4, McIntosh and Woodley (1974).

per cent) were from the working classes. Since this latter measure is the one used in the earlier tables, it is perhaps the most appropriate here. Clearly, in the early 1970s, the majority of the Open University students had been inter-generationally socially mobile (see pages 207–18). Since then, figures relating to applicants as opposed to entrants to the Open University suggest some change (Ashby, 1988). The sexual composition of applicants was two-thirds male in 1972 and virtually 50:50 in 1988. The largest occupational group in 1972 was teachers, 30 per cent; by 1988 this had declined to 6.2. Groups which had increased over the same period include housewives (11 to 18), retired/not in work (3 to 13), clerical and office staff (9 to 13), and shopkeepers/services/fire/police (4 to 7). The percentage in manual occupations rose from 6.7 in 1972 to 11 in 1980 (Open University, 1979) and appears to have settled at just less than 10.

A major area of expansion in higher education over the last two decades or so has been the polytechnics. Social class analysis of students at polytechnics has produced the familiar clear middle-class bias of students' backgrounds, particularly with respect to those on degree courses (64 per cent; working class 26; unclassified 11), though non-degree courses were only slightly lower (57 per cent; working class 30; unclassified 14). However the representation of classes I and II (46 per cent) is lower than at universities – compare with the data above (Whitburn, Mealing and Cox, 1976). The proportion of working-class students on non-degree courses was higher than for degree courses – 30 compared to 26 per cent – and was particularly high at just over 40 per cent on non-degree courses in engineering, technology and science. There was also considerable variation in the social class compositions of individual polytechnics; the middle-class proportion varied from 41 to 70 per cent. This finding is supported by other single-institution studies, for example Donaldson (1971), who found 85 per cent middle and 15 per cent working class, and Hatch and Reich (1970), who reported figures of 67 and 33 per cent respectively.

OVERVIEW

This chapter has demonstrated that, contrary to much popular belief that educational achievement is solely or mainly dependent on individual ability, there are extremely important social aspects. Educational experience and achievement are clearly related to each form of social stratification. One of three views can be adopted. Either our present systems of schooling and education are better equipped to cater for certain social groups, or those groups are variously equipped to take advantage of what the systems offer, or there is an interplay between systems and groups. All the views have strong implications for the educational system.

The evidence reviewed has also reflected the tendency of research to treat forms of social stratification as if they were separate entities. In fact, as has been indicated, the forms act in combination to produce cumulative educational advantage or disadvantage. This was illustrated in the case of class and sex in respect to higher educational chances (pages 318–9). It seems more than likely that further research would enable ethnicity to be incorporated and the analysis to be extended to cover other chances and achievements. Such considerations further underline the importance of recognizing social stratification as a single, composite phenomenon. Failure to do so not only detracts from explanations, in this case of educational achievement, but is also likely to flaw policies designed to alleviate inequality. Tackling educational inequality in any form of stratification in isolation is extremely unlikely to relieve inequality in others and may merely result in its redistribution. What is called for is more detailed, extensive and protracted research, for which at present there seems to be little enthusiasm and even less political will and resources.

CHAPTER 9

Religion, Law, Politics and Opinion

Laws grind the poor, and rich men rule the law.
OLIVER GOLDSMITH (1770)

Class is the basis of British party politics, all else is embellishment and detail.   P. G. J. PULZER (1968)

This chapter deals with topics which at first glance seem rather diverse and perhaps unrelated. Politics and religion are areas of life which are typically seen as more personal and intimate than many of the others reviewed in this book. This is because they involve belief and feeling, and are surrounded by social values. For example, there exists a profound social acceptance of an individual's right to his or her own views, and also the right to secrecy, in voting and in relationship with God. It is not surprising, therefore, that these areas are often emotionally charged: they arouse passion and enthusiasm, particularly when like-minded people gather, or attempt to bring new recruits into the fold.

Probably most of us who are involved in a social organization centring on politics, religion or leisure (see Chapter 10) are aware to some degree of social class exclusiveness or emphasis. Certainly many of the organizations themselves exhibit such an awareness. Sometimes this is explicit and assertive as in the case of some golf clubs, working men's clubs, trade unions, chambers of commerce, professional associations, and so on. More typically the awareness is expressed defensively, and exclusive social class labels or associations are deliberately avoided. Political parties and churches are in general careful to avoid, or to reject, such labels (for example, the working-class label of the Labour Party, or the middle-class/aristocratic/establishment image of the Conservative Party and the Church of England). An alternative tack is to emphasize the existence of minority social groups within the organization – be they based on class, ethnicity or sex – and sometimes then claiming that this proves their openness.

Such factors as individuals' desire for privacy of beliefs and feelings, and the concern of institutions with their public image, may partly explain why empirical research in these fields tends to be limited, both in scope and depth, in some contrast to some other areas. A further explanation for the comparative paucity of empirical research in this area is that there are recognized methodological problems associated with the investigation of opinion and attitudes. This is particularly true of large-scale research, the concern of this book, since private and deep-seated factors can perhaps only really be explored by using long in-depth interviews, which are not a feature of social surveys. Finally, the institutions involved are often not particularly research-minded. This reflects in some cases the nature of their organization and in others a resistance to inquiry combined with the power to sustain it. A prime example of the latter are the Freemasons.

A good case in point are the churches, whose information about the numbers of their members and attenders is often based only on rather dubious estimates. Gaine (1975), in reviewing the literature on religious practice and belief, concludes: 'It must be strongly emphasized that the above conclusions are highly tentative and cannot be made more definite due to the absence of agreed statistics and scientific study of the factors involved. In particular, the effects of social class, education, and locality need to be studied.'

RELIGION

As Matthijsen (1959) has pointed out, 'It is one of the idiosyncrasies of the English people to regard inquiries into a person's religion as something unheard of.' This idiosyncrasy may go some way towards explaining the relative lack and limited scope of empirical research in this field in Britain. For example, it was only in the 1851 census that attendance at religious worship was investigated, and then only on a voluntary basis. This is in marked contrast to the Northern Ireland census, which has always produced a volume of Religion Tables (*Northern Ireland Census 1981*, 1984), analysed by social class until the 1971 census. Such extensive and systematic data do not exist for the rest of Britain, even for a particular denomination. Consequently reliance has to be placed on smaller-scale researches.

Religious groups in Britain use a variety of methods to arrive at their membership numbers, ranging from the careful annual recording of those holding membership cards by the Methodists, to counts of those attending services by others. These and various estimates are brought together in the *UK Christian Handbook* (Brierley, 1982) to provide an overview. This suggested that in 1980 about 17 per cent of UK adults were church members, ranging from 13 per cent in England, 23 in Wales, 37 in Scotland and 80 per cent in Northern Ireland. While membership of Christian churches declined by half a million between 1983 and 1977/8, Muslims, Sikhs, Hindus and Buddhists increased, so that Muslims outnumber Methodists and Baptists together. The majority of Christian church members are either young or old people, and women outnumber men (Thompson, 1988). The percentage of the population having a looser affiliation than membership is very much higher. It has been argued that the religious communities encompass about 41 million, or 74 per cent, of the UK population (Brierley, 1982). A percentage breakdown of this is: Church of England and other Episcopal, 66; Baptist/Methodist/Presbyterian, 9; Roman Catholic, 13; other Trinitarian, 3; Jews, 1; non-Trinitarian, 3; Hindus/Sikhs/Muslims, 4.

A number of social surveys have shown that the general public are quite willing to associate themselves with religious, mainly Christian, denominations. For example, Table 9.1 provides the results of a Gallup Poll in which over 90 per cent said they had an affiliation, 60 per cent saw themselves as being Church of England, and there was little variation between the social classes in this or other affiliations. Where class differences are noticeable is in church attendance, which is analysed in the second half of the table. Here, with respect to regular attendance

TABLE 9.1 Self-reported religious denomination and church attendance, by social class (percentages)

| | Social class (MR) | | | | |
	AB	C1	C2	DE	All
Denomination					
Church of England	59	58	61	61	60
Church of Scotland	7	8	7	8	7
Free Church	11	12	7	10	10
Roman Catholic	11	9	11	13	11
Other	2	6	5	4	4
None	10	8	9	5	8
Attendance					
Once a week or more	20	14	9	11	12
Up to once a month	11	12	5	5	7
Just now and again	25	17	18	22	20
Christmas/Easter only	2	4	8	1	4
Special occasions only	19	27	34	32	30
Never	22	26	28	29	27

Devised from data supplied by Social Surveys (Gallup Polls) Ltd, from a survey conducted 21–29 March 1979.

(first two rows of that section) there is a decline across the classes, AB rates being in the order of twice those for DE, with non-manual rates above and manual below the overall figure. Clearly, very regular attendance is a minority habit – at around 12 per cent – and it would appear to be in decline since a poll in 1972 showed 15 per cent claiming attendance at least once a week (NOP, 1972). Certainly the separate view of young people (fifteen- to twenty-one-year-olds) given in Table 9.2 suggests lower proportions claiming affiliation and attendance. In particular, notice that some two-thirds replied that they never attended compared to just over a quarter in the general survey. A lack of a social class pattern to affiliation but a clear one for attendance is, however, observable in both sets of data. The young people's survey also included a question about the importance of religious belief of the respondents. A look at the extremes – 'very important' and 'not at all important' – reveals a decline across the classes for the first and a rise for the second, with the usual manual/non-manual divide with respect to the overall figure.

Sex differences in religious behaviour and beliefs have long been recognized. Table 9.2 reveals that just over twice the proportion of young males than females saw themselves as atheists or agnostics, and males were more likely than females to see religious beliefs as not very, or not at all, important (73 compared with 59 per cent). Sex, together with age differences are also displayed in Table 9.3. Overall seven in ten of those interviewed stated that they believed in God or a supreme being; the proportion being higher for females than males, and rising across the age groups. Of believers, half said they never attended religious services nowadays and only about one in five that they attended weekly or more often. Working-class respondents were somewhat more likely to be frequent attenders than middle-class ones, females more than males, and those over thirty-five years more than those younger. The survey also inquired about attendance ten

TABLE 9.2 Young people's[1] religious affiliation, attendance and belief, by social class and sex (percentages)[2]

| | Social class (MR) | | | | | | |
	AB	C1	C2	DE	Male	Female	All
Affiliation							
Church of England	58	44	52	50			51
Church of Scotland	6	7	6	7			7
Nonconformist	6	6	5	4			5
Roman Catholic	8	13	12	14			12
Other Christian	2	2	2	3			2
Non-Christian	4	3	2	3			3
Atheist/agnostic	11	17	11	11	17	8	13
Attendance							
Once a week or more	17	11	8	9	7	13	10
Once a month or more but less than once a week	9	6	5	2	3	6	5
Less than once a month	20	20	16	18	16	20	18
Never	54	64	72	71	74	61	67
Importance of Religious Belief							
Very important	14	12	6	8	8	10	9
Quite important	29	26	19	20	16	28	22
Not very important	34	35	38	35	35	37	36
Not at all important	23	27	33	34	38	22	30

1. Aged 15 to 21.
2. Columns do not = 100 because NAs and don't knows are not shown.

Devised from unpublished tables 90, 92 and 94, National Opinion Polls (1978).

TABLE 9.3 Percentages believing in God, and attendance at religious services, by social class, sex and age

	Social class (MR)					Age			
	ABC1	C2	DE	Male	Female	18–34	35–54	55+	All
Believe in God/ supreme being	71	68	75	65	77	59	71	86	71
Attend Now									
Once a week or more	17	19	20	15	22	15	22	20	19
Once a month or more but less than once a week	10	9	6	8	9	10	7	9	8
Less than once a month	30	20	17	21	25	22	24	23	23
Never	42	51	57	57	44	53	47	49	50
Attended Ten Years Ago									
Once a week or more	25	30	31	25	30	27	26	30	28
Once a month or more but less than once a week	12	11	9	10	11	10	10	12	11
Less than once a month	25	17	15	17	27	14	20	23	20
Never	37	39	42	43	36	45	41	33	39

Devised from data supplied by National Opinion Polls Market Research Ltd, from a survey conducted 17–19 October 1985.

years ago. As the lower section of the table shows, a higher proportion of current believers attended then – overall 28 compared with 19 per cent weekly and 39 compared with 50 per cent never. This decline can be seen along all the lines of stratification. The data suggest both that a sizeable proportion of those who believe have never been attenders and that many past attenders have ceased to attend.

A more detailed view of religious beliefs is provided in Table 9.4 (the questions asked are in the footnotes).

TABLE 9.4 Religious beliefs, by social class, sex and age (percentages)

| | Social class (MR) | | | | | | Age | | | |
	AB	C1	C2	DE	Men	Women	16–34	35–64	65+	All
(1) GOD										
There is a personal God	33	30	25	38	23	39	30	29	36	31
There is some sort of spirit/life force	48	46	41	35	45	38	40	43	40	41
I do not really think there is any God/spirit/ life force	14	14	19	16	21	12	15	19	12	16
I do not know what to think	5	10	14	11	11	11	14	8	11	11
(2) CHRIST										
Son of God	47	48	42	56	37	58	44	50	53	48
Just a man	35	33	34	29	41	24	37	30	28	32
Just a story	6	8	11	7	10	7	7	10	10	8
(3) BELIEVE IN										
God	71	70	59	73	58	76	62	68	76	68
Devil	22	25	17	23	22	20	24	21	19	21
Heaven	49	55	44	59	41	61	46	53	58	52
Hell	20	25	17	24	21	21	22	20	20	21
Reincarnation	23	27	24	25	20	30	23	26	26	25
(4) BELIEVE THAT										
Bible is essential	63	65	63	62	60	65	62	59	72	63
Church will survive	31	26	30	30	31	28	23	34	20	29
(5) OLD TESTAMENT										
Divine authority	6	7	7	17	8	12	7	10	13	10
Needs interpretation	40	44	37	34	33	43	38	39	36	38
Stories/fables	51	39	50	40	52	38	48	45	37	45
(5) NEW TESTAMENT										
Divine authority	9	13	9	20	11	15	13	12	18	13
Needs interpretation	46	45	36	34	34	44	37	40	40	39
Stories/fables	42	33	45	35	46	32	41	40	30	39

Answers to questions:
(1) Which of these statements comes closest to your belief? (As above)
(2) Do you believe Jesus Christ was the Son of God or just a main or just a story?
(3) Which of the following do you believe in? (As above)
(4) Do you think that the Bible is essential to the Christian Church or would the Church survive even if the idea that the Bible is of divine authority were to be rejected?
(5) Which of these comes nearest to expressing your views about the Old/New Testament? It is of divine authority and its commands should be followed without question. It is mostly of divine authority but some of it needs interpretation. It is mostly a collection of stories and tables.
Columns do not add to 100 because don't knows and no answer are not shown.

Devised from data supplied by Social Surveys (Gallup Polls) Ltd. from a survey conducted 10–14 July 1986.

Some 16 per cent of respondents, one in five men and one in eight women, rejected belief in a personal God or spirit/life force and a further 11 per cent did not know what to think. Of the seven out of ten who had a belief, three subscribed to a personal God and four to a spirit/life force. Belief in God is higher among women than among men (39 compared with 23 per cent), higher among those aged over sixty-five, and declines from class AB to C2 but is highest for DE (probably reflecting both its age and sex composition). Belief in a spirit/life force declines across the classes, is higher for men than women but shows very little relationship with age. Perhaps surprisingly, almost half of those interviewed believed Christ to be the Son of God. It is also interesting that, while 52 per cent believed in heaven, only half as many accepted reincarnation and even fewer believed in hell or the devil. The Bible was seen as essential to the survival of the church by the majority, though 45 per cent viewed the Old, and 39 per cent the New Testament, as stories or fables. Comparison of data from a parallel survey in 1979 (Gallup Polls, 1979) suggests that there may be a lessening of traditional Christian beliefs. The overall percentage believing in a personal God was lower by 4, that in Christ as the Son of God by 7 and in heaven by 5, while those believing the Old and New Testament to be stories/fables had grown by 12 and 9 per cent. Only small minorities saw the Testaments as having divine authority – 10 and 13 per cent respectively. However, it still seems reasonable, in view of the data, to conclude that the population in general, while rejecting institutionalized religion, to a considerable degree maintains acceptance of some of its beliefs.

Similar findings are gained from more intensive surveys such as that reported by Gerard (1985). Three-quarters of those surveyed reported a belief in God, three-fifths saw themselves as 'religious persons' and half regularly felt the need for prayer, meditation or contemplation. Only 4 per cent identified themselves as convinced atheists, but since about half of these also claimed denominational attachment or expressed some form of Christian belief in answering other questions, the true figure is probably nearer 2. The study used a scale of religious commitment based on a series of questions on two dimensions, religious disposition and institutional attachment. Overall 19 per cent of respondents had high scores, males 15 per cent and females, working 20, non-working 26 per cent. Age groups had more marked differences than social classes; the relevant percentages of high scorers were 18 to 24 years, 9; 25 to 44, 14; 45 to 64, 27; 65 and over, 28; class (MR) AB, 20; C1, 21; C2, 17; DE, 21. A range of other social factors was analysed, but when age was held constant other differences tended to disappear.

Obviously there is quite a difference between claiming an allegiance to a denomination and actual involvement in religious affairs. Less direct questioning in the context of inquiries into other areas, notably leisure, has produced what might well be more valuable evidence of religious involvement. Table 9.5 has data from a study of leisure which asked questions about club membership, including that of religious organizations. Sex differences were quite marked, females being more likely than males to be members of religious organizations (11 compared to 7 per cent). Membership for both sexes declined across the classes and was highest in the middle classes (here 1, 2 and 4).

TABLE 9.5 Membership of religious organizations, by social class and sex (percentages)

| | Social class (RG SEG 60/A) | | | | | |
	1	2	3	4	5	All[1]
Females	14	14	9	15	5	11
Males	9	17	4	8	6	7

Note. Classes 1, 2, 4 are non-manual.
1. Includes those not classified.
Derived from table 19, Sillitoe (1969).

Greater detail of the relationship between religious affiliation and practice is provided in an analysis of the Roman Catholic Pastoral Research Census data (Moulin, 1968). A door-to-door census was conducted in six parishes, four in Southwark and one in Westminster (both in London), and one in Northampton. This identified 15,851 Roman Catholics of whom 42 per cent were observed at Mass at their parish churches on the subsequent Sunday. Detailed analysis of the working men in the survey by social class is presented in Table 9.6. Note that among the Catholics social classes I and V are overrepresented in relation to the population of the areas in which the parishes were situated, while classes II and IIIn are underrepresented (compare the bottom two rows of the table).

TABLE 9.6 Church attendance and involvement of Roman Catholics,[1] by social class (percentages)

| | Social class (RG 60) | | | | | | |
	I	II	IIIn	IIIm	IV	V	All[2]
Attended Mass	61	51	49	37	36	36	42
Married to Catholic woman	79	74	72	67	70	77	73
Not confirmed	4	4	5	6	6	6	5
Member of Catholic organization	16	18	24	17	11	5	16
All education at Catholic schools	49	50	45	58	66	71	62
Social class distribution							
Catholics of 6 parishes	7	13	14	28	17	11	100[2]
Population of 3 areas	5	16	20	28	18	8	100[2]

1. Working males only.
2. Includes those whose occupation was not stated/classified.

Devised from tables 1, 2, 5 and 7 and pp. 27 and 28, Moulin (1968).

There are very apparent social class differences in attendance at Mass, which ranges from 61 per cent in social class I down to 36 per cent in classes IV and V, together with a noticeable difference between the middle classes, with attendance percentages of around 50 and upwards, and the working classes, with percentages around 36. Similar, though less marked differences can be observed in relation to Confirmation, where a slightly higher percentage of the working classes had not been confirmed, and in membership of Catholic organizations. In the latter case it is social class IIIn which had the highest percentage of members (24), and only classes IV and V which had noticeably lower rates than the other classes. Marriage within the faith shows some variation, though here (second row of the table) social classes I and V are very similar, and social class IIIm has the lowest percentage. A reversed situation is found in the case of Catholic school education, the percentages increasing across the social classes from 49 per cent for social class I to 71 for class V. While this may well reflect the provision of, and opportunity to attend, such schools, the survey also indicates that the majority of Catholics who were converts came from the middle classes, and obviously would not have attended Catholic schools. The study shows that all the factors outlined above (rows 2 to 5 in the table) are related to attendance at Mass. This supports Moulin's view that, since religious behaviour is a social act, only people integrated – through such factors as education, marriage and organizations – into the religious community will display such behaviour (in this case, attending Mass).

Even more local studies have been undertaken. For example, Burton (1975) compared social class profiles of two Midland Methodist churches with that of their locality. He found that members and leaders were predominantly middle-class, in contrast to the local population (see also Harris and Jarvis, 1979). In a suburban church 93 per cent of members and all leaders, compared to 46 per cent of the neighbourhood, were middle-class, while for an estate church the figures were: members 56 per cent, leaders 83, and locality 16 per cent. At the same time adherents – those who were involved in the churches' activities but who had not taken out membership – were 12 per cent working-class in the suburban church and 69 per cent in the estate church. Hence, while the general picture of churches as middle-class institutions may be sustained, local, and probably denominational, variations exist. A similar situation exists with respect to Sunday school pupils, the majority of whom have church-attending parents, and of their teachers, who are predominantly middle-class (Reid, 1979 and 1980a).

There are, of course, some sizeable non-Christian religious minorities in Britain. One of these, Anglo-Jewry, has had its social class structure investigated in a particularly novel way (Prais and Schmool, 1975). The study involved collecting information about Jewish burials and then securing social class information, via the Registrar General, from the death certificates of those involved. By comparing the top and bottom rows of Table 9.7 one can see differences between the social class structure of Jews and of the general population. What is very noticeable

TABLE 9.7 Social class profiles[1] of Jews, synagogue members and non-members (percentages)

| | Social class (RG 60) | | | | | |
	I	II	III	IV	V	Unclassified
Jews[2]	4	34	46	14	0	3
Synagogue members[3]	4	34	46	14	0	2
Non-members[3]	3	30	40	22	1	5
General population	2	14	46	22	13	3

1. Married women by husband's occupation.
2. Sample aged 15 to 64.
3. Sample aged 15 to 74.

Devised from tables 1 and 2, Prais and Schmool (1975).

is that none of the Jewish sample was in social class V, whereas 13 per cent of the general population were. Jews were also underrepresented in class IV (14 compared to 22 per cent), equally represented in class III, and overrepresented in classes I and II (34 compared to 14, and 4 compared to 2 per cent) in comparison with the general population. The table also reveals differences between the two-thirds sample (second row of table) who were Synagogue members and those who were not (third row). Non-members were rather more similar to the general population in social class than were members. In particular, the non-members were more likely to have been in social classes IV (22 compared to 14 per cent) and V (1 compared to 0 per cent) than the members. The authors suggest that this may be due to the greater difficulty encountered by these classes in meeting the expenses of membership.

The topics of religious membership, practice and belief continue to reflect Gaine's (1975) review conclusion quoted on page 326 above.

LAW

In this section we view three aspects – law-breaking, the use of legal services and the composition of the legal profession. The first presents some problems for research. The incidence of law-breaking is much greater than is revealed by statistics, for much crime goes unnoticed or undetected, or is not followed by prosecution. While most commentators recognize a relationship between crime and social class, the situation is far from clear because of variations in the detection and prosecution of different types of crime in our society. In particular, we can suspect that much 'white-collar' crime, associated with the middle classes, remains invisible to the official eye. In any case criminal statistics are neither recorded nor analysed by social class. However, Mays (1970) reported that of detected offenders in Liverpool, 86 per cent of those in employment were from the manual classes and 38 per cent from class V (RG), compared to the population of that city – 71 per cent manual and 16 per cent class V. Similarly, a study of the inmates of a prison in the South East showed that 75 per cent had manual last jobs, 18 per cent non-manual, and the remaining 7 per cent were not classified (Home Office Research Unit, 1978). The percentages in the population were 62 manual, 35 non-manual and 3 not classified.

The NCDS longitudinal study provided a unique opportunity to view the incidence of officially recorded delinquency, up to age seventeen years. Table 9.8 contains detailed figures for boys only, because delinquency among girls is very rare (see right-hand column of table). The first row, which refers to all police-recorded incidents, displays a rise of some sevenfold from upper middle to lower working class (2.7 to 18.7 per cent). The difference in the proportion committing more than one serious offence (row 4) is even more marked, there being no incidence in the upper middle and 5.6 per cent in the lower working

TABLE 9.8 Percentage juvenile delinquency rates,[1] by social class and sex

| | Social class (NS) | | | | | | |
	UM	LM	UW	LW	U/C[2]	All boys	Girls
Any offence	2.7	8.3	9.7	18.7	8.6	12	1.6
Non-indictable/trivial offence only	1.9	4.1	3.6	4.9	1.5	4	0.6
One or more indictable/serious offence	0.8	4.2	6.1	13.8	7.1	8	1.0
More than one indictable/serious offence	–	0.7	1.8	5.6	2.6	2.8	0.03

1. That is, either cautioned or sentenced for type of offence indicated.
2. Unclassified.

Derived from table IV, Douglas, Ross, Hammond and Mulligan (1966).

class. Obviously male delinquency, particularly repeated serious offences, has much higher rates in the working than in the middle classes and is specially pronounced at the lower end. Douglas, Ross, Hammond and Mulligan (1966) note that some 296 boys in the sample came from broken homes and these had a delinquency rate of 17 per cent (which is near the rate for the lower working class). Within this group those from homes broken by divorce and separation had a rate of 23 per cent compared to 12 per cent of those where death was the cause. The authors suggest that such a difference cannot be explained in terms of social class. A further analysis of these data is to be found in Wadsworth (1975).

Similarly, Rutter *et al.* (1979) found among fourteen-year-old boys in twelve Inner London schools that the percentage with a delinquency record (including caution) rose across the social classes (RG) from 16 for I and II to 46 for V and unemployed. For girls of the same age the respective percentages were 1 and 16. West (1982) used family income rather than occupation in his longitudinal study of four hundred males in a London working-class neighbourhood. Boys from low-income families were twice as likely to become juvenile delinquents as those from better-off families.

The clear sexual bias in law-breaking is not confined to juveniles: of those found guilty or cautioned on indictable offences in 1986, 83 per cent were male and 17 per cent female (*Criminal Statistics England and Wales 1986*). Some 27 per cent of offenders were aged under seventeen (males 26, females 32) and a further quarter were aged seventeen and under twenty-one (males 25, females 18). Of persons found guilty or cautioned on summary (less serious) offences (other than motoring), some 76 per cent were males. With some variation, this bias is evident in all types of crime other than in the sexually specific such as rape, prostitution and homosexual (for a review see Stratta, 1989). Law-breaking is not only a predominantly male activity but also one strongly related to age, just over half of offenders found guilty or cautioned being under the age of twenty-one years, and the rate per 100,000 males in 1986 dropped from 7573 at age fifteen, to 1352 at thirty to thirty-nine and 162 at sixty and over; the comparable figures for women were 1852; 301; 67.

The relationship between social stratification and crime is reflected (though not necessarily accurately, because of variations in detection, prosecution and sentencing) in the composition of the prison population, which in 1986 was almost 97 per cent male (*Prison Statistics England and Wales 1986*). Ethnic minorities are overrepresented in the prison as compared with the general population. In 1986 some 13.5 per cent of males and 18 per cent of females in prison were from ethnic minorities; the percentages for males and females were: West Indian/Guyanese, 8.5, 12; Indian/Pakistani/Bangladeshi, 3, 2; Chinese/Arab/Mixed, 2, 4. However as the commentary to the *Prison Statistics* points out, 'It is important to appreciate the limited explanatory value of these statistics in providing conclusive evidence, both as regards the involvement of particular ethnic groups in crime and in relation to the practices of the courts.' Rates for reconviction within two years of release are higher for males than females at around 60 per cent compared with 40 per cent.

Men are also more likely to be the victims of crime, twice as likely as women to be robbed, five times as likely to be seriously wounded and three times as likely to be a victim of minor assault. Such figures hide subcategory differences, for example, domestic violence, the victims of which are very predominantly female. Table 9.9 shows that one in eight of those interviewed were not only very worried about becoming a victim of violence but also had changed their life a lot because of it. Women were twice as likely to report this as men, the working classes more than the middle, and older people much more than younger. The overall relationship between the known incidence as opposed to anxiety displays interesting variation.

341

TABLE 9.9 Fear of being a victim of crime, by social class, sex and age (percentages)

	Social class (MR)					Age			
	ABC1	C2	DE	Males	Females	18–34	35–54	55+	All
Worry all the time about being victim	8	11	19	7	17	8	10	19	12
Have changed life a lot	9	10	19	8	16	7	7	22	12

Answers to:
How often do you worry about being the victim of violence, such as being mugged, or attacked in the street?
Has fear of violence made you change your way of life at all?

Devised from data supplied by National Opinion Polls Market Research Ltd, from a poll conducted 17–19 October 1985.

Unlike crime, problems for which legal advice is necessary or desirable face most people at some time. However, as Table 9.10 shows, the use of a lawyer's

TABLE 9.10 Use[1] and knowledge of lawyers' services, by social class[2] (percentages)

	Social class (RG SEG 70)						
	1	2	3	4	5	6	All
Used lawyers' services	25	21	19	13	11	10	15
Had heard of Law Society	87	75	76	62	52	45	64
Gave partly/wholly correct description of Law Society	64	48	41	28	21	14	32
Profile of sample	5	14	18	36	14	5	100[3]

1. During a year.
2. Of head of household.
3. 8 per cent were not classified.

Derived from tables 8.8, 8.19 and 8.58, Final Report, vol. 2, *Royal Commission on Legal Services* (1979).

services is closely related to social class. The percentage using the service ranges from one in four for class 1 to one in ten for class 6, with the manual classes below and the non-manual classes above the overall average. Similarly, as the Table also shows, knowledge of the system, in this case of the existence and function of the Law Society, also varies dramatically. Of course, the use of legal services is related to the type of problem, together with awareness of, and willingness to use, and ability to pay for, such services. The results of an analysis of people's legal problems are presented in Table 9.11.

TABLE 9.11 Social class profiles of persons reporting various legal problems

	I	II	IIIn	IIIm	IV	V	All[1]
			Social class (RG 60)				
Taking a lease	4	22	17	30	15	9	3
Repairs undone	1	5	9	45	22	15	19
Attempted eviction	–	7	7	32	33	15	4
Attempt to evict	6	22	11	28	11	17	1
Buying a house	11	26	19	20	9	9	5
Defective goods	3	10	10	41	17	14	16
Instalment arrears	–	1	4	51	18	18	4
Debtor would not pay	3	18	12	37	15	8	8
Taken to court for debt	3	6	6	51	9	15	2
Making a will	5	21	14	27	17	10	11
Accident	3	4	7	40	20	19	15
Social Security problem	1	7	16	42	17	14	6
Employment problem	2	9	12	54	10	7	6
Matrimonial problem	–	8	13	33	21	17	3
Other court proceedings	2	6	4	46	15	17	3
Juvenile court cases	–	3	5	38	24	27	2
Sample	2	8	11	37	20	15	

1. Includes unclassified (7 per cent of sample).

Derived from table 29, Abel-Smith, Zander and Brooke (1973).

Note that these are social class profiles of the problems. As will be seen by comparing each row with the bottom row, some problems appear with similar frequency in all social classes; these include purchase of defective goods, accidents, social security and matrimonial problems. Not surprisingly, the middle classes have more concern with houses, leases, the eviction of tenants, wills and debtors, while the manual are more involved with repairs undone, arrears in instalments, debts and employment, and juvenile court cases.

Many commentators, for example Zander (1978), suggest that part of the reasons for the lower use of legal services by the working class lies with the nature of the legal profession, which is better equipped to serve the middle classes. An interesting aspect of this thesis for our purpose is the social class composition of the profession, reviewed by the *Royal Commission on Legal Services* (1979). Table 9.12 shows that the backgrounds of law students are not markedly different from those of other university students on professional courses (see table's second section). However, it also reveals that while 66 per cent of young people are from manual homes this is true of only some 16 per cent of law students and an even smaller proportion of those becoming barristers (last section of the table). Some 85 per cent of those training to be solicitors and around 90 per cent of barristers are from non-manual, very predominantly professional and managerial backgrounds. Clearly the middle-class origins of the legal profession more than match the class composition of its clients! It also provides a further reflection upon the observation made in Chapter 8 that 83 per cent of High Court and Appeal judges were public-school-educated (see Table 8.14). It is interesting to note that a small survey (Cain, 1973) of the social class backgrounds of policemen revealed none from professional and managerial backgrounds, 23 per cent from class II (RG), 8 and 2 per cent from semi- and unskilled manual backgrounds and the remaining two-thirds from class III. Again this study

TABLE 9.12 Social class origins[1] of recruits to the legal profession (percentages)

| | Social class (RG 66 and SEG 70) | | |
	Professional/ managerial	Intermediate	Manual
Young People			
Aged 16–19	21	13	66
Aged 20–24 in full-time education	50	20	30
University Entrants			
Professional subjects	58	27	15
Law	54	30	16
Graduates			
Studying Bar examinations	59	30	11
Training for solicitor	56	29	15
Admissions to Bar			
Middle Temple	76	10	14
Gray's Inn	77	16	8

1. Based on father's occupation.

Derived from table 2.1, Final Report, vol. 2, *Royal Commission on Legal Services* (1979).

underlines the differences between the social origins of professionals and those of their clients.

POLITICS

As the epigraph at the beginning of this chapter suggests, the popular belief that politics is all about social class is shared by some academics. This is not to suggest that the situation is simple. If the working classes voted Labour, and the middle classes voted Conservative, then Britain would have had Labour government ever since the creation of the Labour Party, because the working classes are in a majority. In fact the situation is confounded not only by non-conforming voters, but also by the existence of other political parties, by shifts in allegiance, and by failure to vote. Some commentators have argued that class has become a less important factor in politics in post-war Britain. However, Heath, Jowell and Curtice (1985) in surveying the period up to 1983 conclude that while the shape of the class structure has changed, class in terms of objective inequalities, subjective values and party support has remained at the same level. Hence political as well as social explanations are necessary to explain the changing fortunes of political parties.

Voting behaviour is the most rigorously researched area of political activity. A growing number of commercial firms now conduct polls (or surveys) of the voting intentions of samples of the public, both continuously and during election campaigns. During campaigns the polls hope to predict, and some say they affect, the outcome. They bring out some of the problems involved in this type of social research: their predictive powers vary in accuracy, in relation both to other polls and to subsequent events. Overall, however, their track record is good. Table 9.13 shows the results of a large-scale survey conducted during the June 1987 general election campaign, won by the Conservative Party. The percentage unlikely to vote rises quite dramatically across the social classes from 5 to 13, is similar for both sexes and markedly higher for the youngest age group. Differences in major party support by men and women are small and those for the age groups far from marked and without discernible pattern. There are however clear class differences, though less marked than in the 1979 election (see Table 7.1, Reid, 1981 for parallel data). The proportion of Conservative and Alliance voters declines across the classes while that for Labour rises. In each of the middle classes the percentage of Conservative voters is larger than that of Labour and Alliance together. On the other hand in classes D and E the opposite is true, since 50 per cent intended to vote Labour. Breaking the mould is class C2 which follows the middle classes in

TABLE 9.13 Voting intentions[1] in general election 1987, by social class, sex and age (percentages[2])

| | Social class (MR) | | | | | |
	AB	CI	C2	D	E	All
Unlikely to vote	5	7	8	10	13	8
Conservative	59	52	41	28	30	43
Labour	14	21	33	50	51	32
Alliance	27	25	25	19	17	23
Nationalist	1	2	2	3	2	2
Other	0	1	0	0.2	0.4	0.4

| | | | Age | | | |
	Men	Women	18–22	23–44	45–64	65+
Unlikely to vote	9	8	20	9	4	5
Conservative	44	43	43	38	50	45
Labour	32	31	32	32	29	35
Alliance	22	24	20	27	20	20
Nationalist	2	2	2	2	1	1
Other	0.8	0	2	0.4	0	0

1. Except for top rows, based on replies from those who were definitely going to vote or had voted, excluding don't knows.
2. Over 1 rounded.

Devised from data supplied by Social Surveys (Gallup Polls) Ltd, from a survey conducted for the BBC during the June 1987 general election campaign.

having the highest percentage intending to vote Conservative, but this being lower than Labour and Alliance together. Nationalist and 'other' parties are supported equally by only very small overall percentages of each of the social classes. It is noticeable, however, that social class AB voters had little intention of voting for any party other than the three main ones. Only among the young and the men was there any intention to vote for 'other' parties, and even here it was extremely small.

Heath, Jowell and Curtice (1985) argue that economic interest is more important in voting behaviour than

TABLE 9.14 Percentage of each social class voting for the main political parties

| | Social class (HG/C) | | | | |
	I & II	III	IV	V	VI & VII
Conservative	54	46	71	48	30
Labour	14	25	12	26	49
Alliance	31	27	17	25	20
Other	1	2	0	1	1

Derived from table 2.3, Heath, Jowell and Curtice (1985).

income level and life-style, and used a modified social class classification, which separated the self-employed and foremen and technicians (classes IV and V on Table 9.14). As will be seen class IV was the most strongly aligned to the Conservative Party (71 per cent), a good deal more so than classes I and II at 54 per cent. Similarly, there is a clear difference in voting between class V and classes VI and VII, with almost half of the first voting Conservative and a similar proportion of the second voting Labour. The table also shows that Alliance voting is somewhat more class-based than other studies, using more common class scales, have indicated. Like the Conservative, Alliance voting is more popular in the middle than the working classes, but is least popular in class IV. In comparing the voting of the sexes the authors found a general similarity, with one exception – more working-class women than men voted Alliance (27 compared with 17 per cent). They also found few differences between the voting of married and single women.

In the past, however, many studies have shown women to be more inclined to vote Conservative than men, though often it has not been clear whether this was due to sex or to age – there being a larger proportion of older female voters, and older people being inclined to vote Conservative. A National Opinion Poll (1978) found an overall majority for the Conservatives over Labour, with clear sex differences in each age group, including those aged fifty-five years and over. While male voting intentions were Conservative 42 and Labour 44 per cent, females were 50 and 39 per cent respectively. The Conservative lead among women was 11 per cent compared to a Labour lead among men of 2 per cent. Social class analysis revealed similar differences; the Conservative lead, in percentage terms, was ABC1, all +34, men +32, women +35; C2, all – 11, men –22, women –1; and DE, all –16, men –21, women –10. It seems, as Campbell (1987) concludes, that 'men have been moving to the right and women have been moving away from the right'. In any case it seems unlikely that party allegiance is determined by sex alone (see Thomas and Wormald, 1989).

Fitzgerald (1984; 1987) reviews the political involvement and behaviour of ethnic minorities and looks at the implications of these for the parties. Black people are overwhelmingly supportive of Labour – a post-poll survey by CRE in selected Labour-held constituencies in the 1983 election found 81 per cent so voting, with 7 per cent Conservative and 11 Alliance. Other studies suggest this may exaggerate the extent, though the lowest, by Gallup, found the respective percentages to be 64, 21 and 15. According to self-report, Asians are more likely to have voted in 1983 (76 per cent), followed by Whites and Afro-Caribbeans (73 and 65 per cent: GLC research, 1984). There are also differences in the percentages of those eligible to vote who register to do so – Afro-Caribbeans, 76, Asians, 79 and Whites, 81 (CRE, 1984). Todd and Butcher (1981) found that in Inner London 25 per cent, and in England and Wales 14 per cent of ethnic minorities, were not on the register, compared with 12 and 13 per cent of Whites.

Levels of satisfaction with the government and leaders is monitored weekly by several commercial research agencies and, as might be expected, displays considerable variation over time. Table 9.15 contains data from a sur-

TABLE 9.15 Satisfaction/dissatisfaction[1] with the government, Mrs Thatcher and Mr Kinnock, by social class, sex and age (percentages)[2]

	Social class (MR)						Age			
	AB	C1	C2	DE	Males	Fe- males	18 –34	35 –64	65+	All
The government										
Satisfied	51	46	34	28	40	37	34	40	40	38
Dissatisfied	33	39	48	52	45	45	47	44	43	45
Mrs Thatcher										
Satisfied	54	49	41	33	43	42	39	44	46	43
Dissatisfied	33	39	44	51	44	42	45	43	40	43
Mr Kinnock										
Satisfied	27	31	31	40	37	30	36	31	34	33
Dissatisfied	55	53	48	38	46	49	45	50	45	47

1. Answers to questions:
   Are you satisfied or dissatisfied with the way (a) the government is running the country? (b) Mrs Thatcher is doing her job as Prime Minister? (c) Mr Kinnock is doing his job as Leader of the Labour Party?
2. Columns do not add to 100 because 'neithers' and 'don't knows' are not shown.

Devised from data supplied by National Opinion Polls Market Research Ltd, from a poll conducted 27 May–1 June 1987.

vey in the run-up to the 1987 general election. Around two in five of those interviewed were satisfied with government and Mrs Thatcher, and it is clear that class is the most important factor: the decline across the classes is most marked in comparison with the smaller rise over the age groups and the closeness of the sexes. While opinion about Mrs Thatcher was evenly split, that on Mr Kinnock was clearly towards dissatisfaction (overall 47 compared with 33 per cent). Again class is the major discriminator, though obviously opinion on leaders is likely to be related to party support.

Voting is for most people their only political activity.

Other political activities are very much minority affairs. NOP have conducted several inquiries into the public's political behaviour (1971, 1975b, 1977). In the last of these, some 74 per cent claimed to have voted in the previous general election and 55 per cent in the last local election. However, less than one in five had helped raise funds, about one in ten had presented their views to a councillor or MP; 7 per cent had paid a political party membership fee and only 4 per cent had taken an active part in a campaign. The NOP study developed a scale adapted from that of the Opinion Research Corporation of America, to identify 'political activists'. These were identified as those who had indulged in five or more of the following: voted in the last election; helped raise funds; been elected officer of, or made a speech to, an organization or club; urged someone to vote, or to contact a councillor or MP, written to an editor; taken an active part in a campaign or stood for public office.

Overall some 7 per cent of those surveyed were 'activists', of whom 56 per cent were men and 44 per cent women. The social class profile of 'activists'

TABLE 9.16 Social class and sex profiles of the politically active[1] and participants in local government[2]

	Social class (MR)				Males	Females	% of sample
	AB	C1	C2	DE			
Politically active[1]	40	22	22	16	56	44	7
Sample	16	21	34	29			100
Local government participants[2]	27	28	27	17			12
Sample	14	21	37	28			100

1. For definition, see text above.
2. Attended a public meeting/exhibition or completed a questionnaire.

Devised from p. 8, NOP (1977) and table 3b, NOP (1975a)

is given in the top row of Table 9.16. Clearly, the middle classes, particularly AB, are overrepresented, and the working classes, especially DE, underrepresented. Apart from being middle-class, 'activists' were also middle-aged, some 48 per cent being in the 35- to 55-year age group. 'Activists' compared to 'others' were also more likely to have voted in the last election (84 to 55 per cent), been to a trade union meeting (26 to 15 per cent), been a paid-up member of a party (42 to 6 per cent), attended a local party meeting (43 to 6 per cent) and to have been on a demonstration, march, picket or 'sit in' (13 to 3 per cent). Conservative supporters were more likely than Labour supporters to have indulged in most activities included in both the lists above.

Following the local government reorganization in 1974, local authorities took active steps to involve the public more in their affairs. In most areas this included mounting exhibitions, holding meetings and issuing questionnaires. NOP (1975a) investigated the level of public participation in these. Only 12 per cent of those surveyed had been involved, as can be seen in the second section of Table 9.16; the bulk of the participants were from the middle classes. For example, social class AB provided 27 per cent of the participants, but only 14 per cent of those interviewed. In contrast, social class DE provided 28 per cent of the sample, but only 17 per cent of the participants.

Phillips (1985) found that while three-fifths of respondents had signed a petition, only one in ten had ever attended a lawful demonstration, although a third 'might do so'. Social factors related to likelihood of, or favourable attitudes to, demonstrating were age, sex and class. Those most disposed were young middle-class males, those least disposed were working-class females aged sixty and over.

It is clear, then, that interest and involvement in politics vary along social stratification lines. These differences are even more dramatically marked among those who become politicians. A listing of the occupations of

MPs in 1974 (the last time they were so listed) revealed the following: 8 per cent had had what could be termed manual jobs – they had been trade union officials, or mine, rail or other manual jobs – another 8 per cent had had clerical, technical and engineering jobs, and the remaining 84 per cent had been professionals, managers, administrators or landowners (*The Times House of Commons*, 1974). Butler and Butler (1985) demonstrated differences in this respect between the political parties in the 1983 Parliament. The proportion of MPs who had or had had professional occupations was Conservative 45, Labour 42 per cent; those from business, Conservative 36, Labour 9 per cent; workers, Conservative 1, Labour 33 per cent; miscellaneous, Conservative 19, Labour 16 per cent. Butler and Sloman (1980) give the following breakdown of two Cabinets, both of which had twenty-five members: Labour Cabinet (1976), aristocrats 1, middle class 13, working class 7; Conservative Cabinet (1979), aristocrats 3, middle class 19, working class, none. Women are very underrepresented in the ranks of MPs. The Parliament elected in 1987 contained the record number of forty-one, some 6 per cent. The number of Black MPs is similarly token at three.

OPINION

The investigation of public opinion on a variety of matters has been a developing enterprise in Britain since the Second World War. Uniquely the government even held a referendum over the Common Market. Quite apart from academic research in the field, now enhanced by the annual British Social Attitudes surveys, there are a number of commercial concerns who regularly survey public opinion, particularly political, and also conduct sponsored research. The possible range of research that could be reported here is, then, extremely large. The small selection presented has been chosen with a view to topicality and relevance. Some other aspects of public opinion are dealt with elsewhere – social mobility (page 218), poverty measures (Table 5.6), the government and politicians (Table 9.15), religious belief (Tables 9.2–9.4).

It should be noted that the term 'opinion' is used here in preference to 'attitude' because of the nature of the research involved. The data have been produced from responses to direct questions – often with a choice of responses provided – and are therefore unlikely to illuminate or explain, in any depth, the phenomena of attitudes, beliefs and understanding. There is also the factor of social group variation in response to questions and their sensitivity to provide socially acceptable answers (discussed on page 245 above). Given the range of differences between the social strata we have viewed so far, it is somewhat surprising to find that public opinion contains relatively few sharp divisions along these lines – at least as measured by surveys. The reasons for this are none too easy to identify. It could be that opinion on these subjects, especially topical ones, is shaped by the media, or that other factors are more significant. As Jowell (1984) comments, 'The term public opinion is itself misleading . . . on nearly all issues there are actually several publics and many opinions . . . the population's attitudes steadfastly resist being divided neatly and consistently according to age, sex, class. . . . They divide very differently on different issues.'

Political and social issues The data in Table 9.17 derive from several sources and have been chosen to illustrate something of the range of topics covered. It would be tedious to describe these data in any detail and the reader is invited to explore the data looking for relationships and patterns. In many cases social differences are surprisingly small, and in a few cases quite different from what might be expected. The explanation of these differences, even leaving aside the nature of the questions involved, is complex. In some cases it could be argued

TABLE 9.17 Public opinion on a range of political and social issues, by social class, sex and age (percentages)

Note. Degrees of agreement/disagreement etc. have been combined. Other than where indicated, missing percentages are 'don't knows'. In the following cases they also include reply shown which is followed by overall percentage using it: (1) staying the same, 40; (2) not worried, 52; (3) neither, 42; (4) equally, 34; (5) equally, 38; (6) both, 27; (7) quite a lot, 13, only a little, 47; (8) about right, 30.

| | Social class (MR) | | | | | Age | | | |
	ABC1	C2	DE	Males	Females	18–34	35–54	55+	All
Stop all Future Immigration into Britain									
Support	58	71	75	66	68	58	64	80	67
Oppose	33	23	17	28	22	33	28	15	25
TU Membership Secret Ballots Before Call for Strike									
Compulsory	85	79	79	82	81	77	84	83	81
Not necessary	13	17	17	16	15	19	13	14	15
Use of Trade Union Subscriptions for Support of Political Parties									
Able to	44	40	42	57	29	39	41	47	42
Banned	49	50	46	38	59	49	53	44	49
Reintroduction of National Service									
Good idea	65	77	81	69	78	61	76	85	74
Bad idea	29	18	15	28	15	33	19	13	22
Task Force to Falklands									
Right	74	73	67	74	68	72	74	69	71
Wrong	21	21	25	20	24	22	22	22	22
British Society is Becoming (1)									
More equal	16	12	11	15	11	11	13	17	13
Less equal	35	35	36	36	35	39	38	29	35
How Worried if Questioned by Police (2)									
Very worried	11	17	20	17	14	16	15	15	15
Bit worried	33	25	27	31	27	37	27	22	31

TABLE 9.17 (contd)

| | Social class (MR) | | | | | Age | | | |
	ABC1	C2	DE	Males	Females	18–34	35–54	55+	All
Church Leaders on Political Issues									
Should speak out	38	30	31	37	30	36	33	32	34
Should not	58	64	62	59	63	56	63	64	61
Should People Get Married if they have Children?									
Yes	57	43	53	43	59	44	59	65	52
Does not matter	34	56	40	51	36	50	37	26	42
Divorce at the Moment (3)									
Too easy	53	51	66	49	63	44	54	71	56
Too difficult	4	5	5	6	4	9	4	2	5
Proportional Representation									
Favour	57	50	40	52	48	49	54	47	50
Against	29	27	31	34	24	23	30	34	29

	AB	C1	C2	DE	Males	Females	18 –34	35 –54	55+	All
People Entitled to Benefits Who do Not get Them										
A lot	59	65	73	73	–	–	72	70	64	69
A few	34	31	24	23	–	–	26	26	30	27
Most Money Lost Through (4)										
Social Security fraud	–15–		–21–		12	25	17	18	21	19
Tax evasion	–55–		–56–		66	47	68	56	44	56
Use of Available Money in 1988 Budget (5)										
To NHS, not tax cuts	45	54	57	58	–	–	50	59	54	54
To tax cuts, not NHS	11	4	3	4	–	–	3	6	8	5

356

TABLE 9.17 (contd)

	AB	C1	C2	DE	Males	Females	18 –34	35 –54	55+	All
Private Contracts to Run Public Services										
Good	66	49	34	27	44	36	40	43	36	40
Bad	29	38	53	56	45	47	47	29	46	45
Introduction of Poll Tax										
Favour	48	42	28	24	–	–	–	–	–	34
Oppose	40	51	61	69	–	–	–	–	–	54
Capital Punishment										
Reintroduce it	64	67	76	80	–	–	64	74	81	73
Leave as it is	31	28	20	16	–	–	30	23	14	23

		ABC1	C2	DE	Males	Females	18 –34	35 –44	45 –64	65+	All
Positive Discrimination in Jobs for:											
Coloured people	yes	13	11	15	12	14	15	10	12	13	13
	no	83	87	81	85	82	81	87	86	83	84
Women	yes	16	16	22	16	20	19	14	17	20	18
	no	82	79	73	81	76	76	84	80	75	78
Homosex-uals/gays	yes	6	6	9	6	8	10	4	7	3	7
	no	90	90	82	91	85	82	94	87	93	88
Disabled	yes	51	57	65	60	54	53	49	62	64	57
	no	43	40	32	37	40	42	46	35	32	39
Class Struggle in this Country											
Is		66	75	70	72	69	73	71	72	63	71
Is not		30	20	22	24	24	23	23	25	29	24
Reasons for Being Poor (6)											
Lack of effort		17	21	15	18	17	10	14	20	32	17
Circumstances		49	51	62	58	49	62	55	48	44	53

TABLE 9.17 (contd)

	Social class (MR)					Age				
	ABC1	C2	DE	Males	Females	18 −34	35 −44	45 −64	65+	All
Attitudes of Government Towards Poor (7)										
Cares a great deal	8	2	3	4	5	2	6	6	5	4
Cares not at all	24	34	46	32	35	31	33	35	36	33
Dole Money for Family with Two Children (8)										
Too much	8	6	8	7	8	6	4	8	12	7
Too little	53	58	59	59	55	63	62	57	37	57
Pornography Should be Available to Those Who Want It										
Agree	59	56	62	64	55	72	61	52	42	59
Disagree	29	35	28	27	35	19	26	39	45	31

Compiled from data supplied by National Opinion Polls Market Research Ltd, from a survey conducted 17–19 October 1985, *Political Social Economic Review* nos. 59, 63, 67, 68, 69, 70, and data supplied by Social Surveys (Gallup Polls) Ltd, from surveys conducted 26 February–3 March 1986, 3–8 April 1986, 29 October–3 November 1986.

that they reflect the differing experiences and/or level of involvement or responsibility of the strata, though little consistency is to be found. Hence, in the face of the lack of clear patterns, observations must remain speculative. Little evidence exists on which to claim that any particular stratum is consistently more liberal, radical or conservative than the rest.

Education Interest in education was almost certainly heightened by the media during the passage of the Education Reform Bill of 1988. Table 9.18 draws on a survey of parents with child(ren) in school from that time, which covered both issues from the Act and more general aspects. The national curriculum received support from around two-thirds of those surveyed and there were no social class differences. Opposition to it was voiced by less than a quarter, though in class AB it was almost a

TABLE 9.18 **Parents' views on and knowledge of education, by social class and sex (percentages)**

| | | Social class (MR) | | | | | | |
		AB	C1	C2	DE	Men	Women	All
National curriculum	Support	64	65	66	64	68	63	65
	Oppose	31	24	21	21	24	23	23
National testing at	Support	63	73	75	66	70	71	71
ages 7, 11 and 14	Oppose	34	24	20	26	26	23	24
Had heard of CTCs		48	39	21	16	36	25	29
% of those who had heard who would definitely apply for place for child		11	18	27	29	27	13	20
If voting on school to opt out of LEA	To move	25	20	24	13	23	19	21
	Leave as now	63	67	63	73	65	67	66
Switch from comprehensive to selective schools	Favour	54	52	52	40	51	49	50
	Oppose	43	40	42	50	45	42	43
Satisfaction with child(ren)'s education	Satisfied	79	79	81	73	77	79	78
	Dissatisfied	18	18	17	20	20	17	17
Receive enough information on child(ren)'s education	Do	65	57	57	54	62	55	58
	Don't	32	42	39	43	35	43	38
Member of PTA		47	36	25	15	28	30	29
Does not help child(ren)'s education at home		5	7	13	17	14	8	11

Devised from data supplied by Social Surveys (Gallup Polls) Ltd, from a survey conducted 26–30 September 1987.

third. Parents in that class were also much more likely to oppose the national testing of children. Overall, however, such testing received somewhat more support than the curriculum, particularly in classes C1 and C2. While the percentage of parents who had heard of CTCs declined markedly across the classes (from AB, 48, to DE, 16), working-class parents who had heard of them were much more likely than middle-class ones to say they would definitely apply for a place for their child(ren). There would appear to have been little overall support for schools to opt out of LEA control – about one in five. Opinion was clearly divided on the possibility of changing from comprehensive to selective secondary schools (50 per cent in favour, 43 against), the percentage in favour declining, that in opposition rising somewhat across the classes. Most parents were satisfied with their child(ren)'s education. Involvement in PTAs, like other forms of voluntary association, was predominantly middle-class, falling from almost half of class AB to 15 per cent of DE. Finally, the proportion of parents who reported not assisting their child(ren)'s education at home was much higher in the working than the middle classes.

Sexual relationships   In the past sex has appeared a more sensitive topic than religion for research. For example in 1973 Bone, investigating contraceptive use, wrote, 'It was not considered appropriate . . . to ask single women about their sexual experience,' and 'Exposure to intercourse was assumed in the case of married women.' Table 9.19 suggests that in the mid-1980s a large majority (80 per cent) saw marriage as an exclusive sexual relationship, though not as a precondition – since around half viewed sex before marriage as rarely or not at all wrong. In the latter case, while there is little difference between the classes (with the exception of IIIm), a greater proportion of females than males saw sex before marriage as wrong, and for both sexes the proportion rises over the age groups. Around seven in ten regarded sex between members of the same sex as always or mostly wrong: there was little difference between the sexes, the older age group and the manual class were somewhat more likely than others to see it as wrong. Airey and Brook (1986) in comparing these figures with those for 1983 note a rise in the proportion seeing homosexual relations as wrong and a fall in the proportion seeing them as right, and question whether this may be due to concern over AIDS. Such

TABLE 9.19 Attitudes[1] towards sexual relationships, by social class, sex and age (percentages)

	Social class (RG 80)							Age		
	I&II	IIIn	IIIm	IV&V	Male	Female		18–34	35–54	55+
Before marriage										
Always/mostly wrong	24	20	17	24	18	27	M	4	15	40
							F	9	24	50
Rarely wrong/not wrong at all	49	52	59	52	56	48	M	79	53	34
							F	74	47	19
Outside marriage										
Always/mostly wrong	80	81	84	84	80	84	M	77	76	87
							F	85	81	86
Rarely wrong/not wrong at all	2	2	3	4	4	2	M	7	5	2
							F	2	2	1
Same sex										
Always/mostly wrong	61	66	77	72	71	67	M	59	68	88
							F	59	61	82
Rarely wrong/not wrong at all	18	18	12	16	16	16	M	25	16	6
							F	26	18	5

1. Missing responses = sometimes wrong/depends/varies/don't know/no answer.

Derived from table 9.4, Airey and Brook (1986).

an assumption is not supported by parallel research in America, which showed no change.

An earlier study (Gallup Polls, 1977) of young persons' opinions found that 56 per cent of males thought pre-marital intercourse to be right and 68 per cent said they would indulge, but this was true of only 34 and 49 per cent of females. A larger proportion of both sexes in MR classes ABC1 than in DE saw it as right, though the opposite was marginally true with respect to indulging in it. The most common and helpful source of sexual knowledge was school, almost regardless of class and sex. Parents were a more common and helpful source for females than for males.

Racial prejudice Since few people are likely either to view themselves or admit to being very prejudiced (the

TABLE 9.20 Percentages believing there is prejudice against Asians and Blacks, and self-rated prejudice, by social class, sex and age

	Social class (RG 80)						Age		
	I&II	IIIn	IIIm	IV&V	Male	Female	18–34	35–54	55+
Prejudice[1] against Asians	92	93	91	88	91	88	95	91	83
Prejudice[1] against Blacks	91	92	87	85	90	86	92	87	81
More now than 5 years ago	26	23	17	17	22	19	21	21	18
Less now than 5 years ago	30	35	43	44	40	38	39	33	41
Self-prejudice[2]	– 36 –		– 34 –		39	30	37	34	32

1. A lot or a little.
2. Question used was: 'How would you describe yourself . . . as very prejudiced against people of other races, a little prejudiced, or not prejudiced at all?'

Derived from tables 9.1 and 9.2, Airey and Brook (1986).

'I have opinions, others are prejudiced' syndrome), British Social Attitudes surveys ask first about prejudice in society and then a self-rating question (see footnote to Table 9.20). About nine in ten people believed there was prejudice against Asians and Blacks, the young being most likely to. Over all, some 38 per cent thought prejudice was less and 20 per cent more now than five years ago. The level of optimism in this direction was higher in the manual than the non-manual classes, and in the youngest age group. Just over a third saw themselves as prejudiced, the only marked social difference being that more men identified themselves this way than women. Some associated aspects of this topic are in Table 9.17.

CHAPTER 10

Leisure and the Media

> Whichever way you turn this curse of class differ-
> ence confronts you like a wall of stone. Or rather it
> is not so much like a stone wall as the plate glass
> pane of an aquarium; it is so easy to pretend it is
> not here, and so impossible to get through it.
>
> GEORGE ORWELL (1937)

Leisure has a range of meanings. Literally it applies to all activities other than work, but this merely shifts the problem to defining work. In any case, many activities do not fall simply into the category of work or non-work, but span both. For many people leisure is a particular set of activities, or period of time, associated with pleasure. Clearly, for survey research purposes such broad and subjective definitions would be exceedingly difficult to operationalize. Much research therefore asks questions concerning participation in specific activities. The GHS uses a somewhat different approach. Those interviewed are informed that leisure time is when they are 'not working, at school, or looking after the house or family' (*GHS 1983*). Informants are free to decide what they see as work and, as a consequence, activities such as gardening, DIY and sewing are included as leisure by some and not by others. Several activities however are ignored by the GHS, such as 'just sitting and thinking', 'pottering about' and 'reading the newspapers'; while other activities are excluded in analysis – shopping, looking after children and short walks (less than two miles). Hence, neither space, nor our present purpose, nor available research allows for a comprehensive treatment of the topic, which has been approached in a selective way.

There is too an important, further factor to be borne in mind. All leisure activities demand time, many require money and some need skill and/or opportunity for their pursuit. While such factors are not necessarily the determinants of leisure behaviour, they obviously affect it and their distribution is related to the social strata. As we saw in Chapter 5, in general the manual classes spend longer at work and earn less money than the non-manual. The sexual division of labour in most homes is such that men are likely to have more time than women for leisure. Retired people may have more time than others, but may have less money for, or lack access to, certain activities, as well as possibly being physically more limited. The range of facilities for leisure activities is not evenly spread and neither is availability of transport to them (see pages 380–2 below).

Such considerations, and there are others, are very complex and have not yet received full and integrated treatment in respect to leisure. Here we have space only for a limited view of two aspects – money and time for leisure. Table 10.1 shows that the amount of money and the percentage of gross household income spent on leisure items increases with the amount of that income – 11.8 per cent of those up to £100, to 18.5 per cent for over £300. Table 10.2 shows, on the basis of self-report, the amount of free time available to people of different economic activity. Not surprisingly, retired people had the most free time per weekday, men in employment had more time than similarly occupied women, though housewives had almost as much as part-time male workers and more than male and female employees. It is worth noting that while employed women worked less hours than men (see also Chapter 6), they spent considerably longer at domestic work and personal care, and marginally longer asleep. At weekends men had more free time than women. Of course, these overall figures hide considerable variation on factors such as family size, composition and age; type of, and distance to, work; accommodation, etc.

TABLE 10.1 Expenditure on a range of selected leisure items,[1] by household income, 1984

| | Gross normal weekly income | | | | | |
	Up to £100	+£100 up to £150	+£150 up to £200	+£200 up to £250	+250 up to £300	+£300	All
Expenditure in £.p	8.05	16.09	22.10	27.09	34.50	54.18	24.08
Expenditure as % of total expenditure	11.8	13.5	15.1	15.5	16.8	18.5	15.8

1. Includes alcoholic drink and meals away from home, home-based media, materials for home repair etc., holidays, hobbies, cinema/dance/theatre/concert/sport admissions, sports goods (other than clothes), other entertainment.

Derived from table 10.17, *Social Trends 16* (1986), source *Family Expenditure Survey*.

TABLE 10.2 Weekday and weekend-day free time,[1] by economic status[2]

| | Full-time employees | | Part-time employees | | | |
	Male	Female	Male	Female	Housewives	Retired
Free time [1]						
Per weekday	2.6	2.1	4.5	3.1	4.2	7.9
Per weekend day	10.2	7.2	7.8	5.9	5.6	9.1

1. i.e. hours other than those spent at work and travel to and from work, asleep and domestic work and personal care (includes cooking, essential shopping, eating meals, washing, etc.).
2. Excludes self-employed.

Derived from table 10.1, *Social Trends 16* (1986), source *Leisure Futures* (Autumn 1985).

There are a number of dimensions on which leisure can be viewed; for example, popularity, regularity, where it takes place, who is involved. Here we start with those activities indulged in at home, which are by far the commonest and within which the media are most important.

Table 10.3 presents the self-reported involvement in a range of in-home leisure activities. Not surprisingly, given the near-universality of household ownership of TVs (see Table 7.28) and radios, watching and listening are by far and away the most popular. And it is with these we begin our review.

TABLE 10.3 Involvement in home-based leisure activities,[1] by social class, sex and age (percentages)

| | Social class (RG SEG 80) | | | | | | | | |
	1	2	3	4	5	6	Male	Female	All[2]
Watching TV	98	99	98	98	98	98			98
Listening to radio	93	91	91	84	83	81			87
Listening to records/tapes	79	66	70	60	56	50			63
Reading books	78	66	70	44	47	41	50	61	56
Gardening	61	58	47	46	39	38	50	39	44
DIY	67	51	35	45	28	23	51	24	36
Dressmaking/ needlework/ knitting	10	15	42	11	30	28	2	48	27
Hobbies/crafts/ arts[3]	21	9	7	8	6	2	15	6	7

1. Persons over 16 reporting activity in previous 4 weeks.
2. Includes full-time students and those not classified.
3. Includes cooking, wine/preserve-making and animal-keeping.

Devised from tables 10.31 and 10.32, *GHS 1983*.

Television

Research over the past two decades has shown TV-watching to be a, if not the, major leisure-time pursuit of the population as a whole (see, for example, Sillitoe, 1969; Young and Willmott, 1973; *GHS 1977, 1980, 1983*).

As can be seen in Table 10.3, there is virtually no social class variation from the overall 98 per cent of those interviewed who were viewers. However, the continuous and extensive research of the BBC makes it clear that there are social differences relating to the amount of viewing – overall average around 27⅓ hours per week in 1987 – and what is viewed. Table 10.4 shows that the amount of time spent watching television increases across the classes (row 5) from about 19⅔ hours for class AB to

TABLE 10.4 Average time per week spent watching TV channels,[1] by social class, sex and age

| | Social class (MR) | | | | | | |
	AB	C1	C2	DE	Male	Female	All
BBC 1	8:48	9:53	10:05	11:45	9:27	11:03	10:16
BBC2	2:48	2:59	3:00	3:39	3:08	3:10	3:09
ITV	6:17	10:12	11:58	15:45	10:21	12:43	11:34
Channel 4	1:49	2:03	2:19	2:59	2:10	2:32	2:21
All TV	19:43	25:07	27:23	34:07	25:06	29:27	27:21
BBC/ITV % viewing	59/41	51/49	48/52	45/55	50/50	48/52	49/51

| | Age | | | | | | | |
	4–15	16–24	25–34	35–44	45–54	55–64	65+	16 & over
BBC 1	8:55	6:25	10:22	9:32	10:58	12:23	13:54	10:33
BBC 2	2:12	1:55	2:59	2:50	3:30	4:26	4:34	3:22
ITV	9:00	6:41	10:47	10:01	11:25	15:51	18:02	12:05
Channel 4	1:41	1:40	2:27	2:03	2:31	3:11	3:12	2:30
All TV	21:48	16:42	26:35	24:25	28:25	35:51	39:43	28:30
BBC/ITV% viewing	51/49	50/50	50/50	51/49	51/49	47/53	47/53	49/51

1. In hours and minutes, by persons aged 4 and over, classified by head of household.

Derived and calculated from data supplied by the British Broadcasting Corporation, 1988, source British Audience Research Bureau/Audience GB.

just over 34 hours a week for class DE. These figures are, of course, averages, and the range of viewing time they represent is considerable. Viewing increases across the classes for all TV channels, but is particularly marked in respect to ITV, where the figure for DE is about two and a half times that for AB (just under 6⅓ compared with 15¾ hours). There is a clear divide between the non-manual and manual classes in choice of TV channel, as demonstrated by the percentages of viewing time spent on each (row 6) which decline from 59 to 45 for BBC and increases from 41 to 55 for ITV between classes AB and DE.

The table also shows that on average women spend more than four hours a week longer than men watching TV and that while men as a group divide their viewing time equally between BBC and ITV, women divide theirs 48/52 per cent. Length of viewing displays an uneven pattern up the age groups. Those aged fifty-five and over view more than the overall average, those forty-four and younger view less. Particularly heavy use of TV is made by those over the age of sixty-five – almost 40 hours a week and some two and a half times as much as people between sixteen and twenty-four, who in turn view considerably less than other groups including the four- to fifteen-year-olds. The latter together with those between thirty-five and fifty-four watch BBC slightly more than other channels (51 per cent of viewing), those aged sixteen to thirty-four divide viewing equally, those over fifty-five display a preference for ITV (53 per cent of viewing).

Radio, records and tapes

The patterns of radio listening which emerge from Table 10.5 are even more complex than those for TV-viewing. Overall listening time has an inverted 'U' shape with both class AB and DE spending less time at it than classes C1 and C2, and DE having the lowest listening time.

TABLE 10.5 Average time per week spent listening to radio channels,[1] by social class, sex and age. 1987.

| | Social class (MR) | | | | | | |
	AB	C1	C2	DE	Male	Female	All
BBC							
Radio 1	1:40	2:24	3:15	2:03	2:43	2:11	2:26
Radio 2	1:39	1:53	1:32	1:34	1:39	1:38	1:38
Radio 3	0:28	0:11	0:04	0:04	0:11	0:06	0:08
Radio 4	2:41	1:20	0:29	0:31	0:51	1:06	0:58
Local	0:33	0:52	0:56	1:09	0:51	1:01	0:56
Independent local radio	1:35	2:18	2:40	2:25	2:32	2:11	2:21
All radio[2]	8:59	9:18	9:18	8:08	9:12	8:32	8:52
% of listening BBC	81	74	69	68	70	73	72

| | Age | | | | | | | |
	4–15	16–24	25–34	35–44	45–54	55–64	65+	16 & over
BBC								
Radio 1	1:00	6:45	5:13	2:37	1:09	0:26	0:11	2:44
Radio 2	0:05	0:15	0:36	1:39	2:54	3:51	2:53	1:59
All radio[2]	2:07	11:26	11:09	10:20	10:04	10:24	8:44	10:20
% of listening BBC	59	66	65	67	73	80	84	72

1. In hours and minutes, by persons aged 4 and over, classified by head of household.
2. Includes others not listed.

Derived and calculated from data supplied by the British Broadcasting Corporation 1988, source BBC daily survey.

Probably because of the more distinctive differences between radio programmes than TV channels, social differences in listening are marked. While BBC Radio 2 is used for similar amounts of time by all classes, Radio 1 receives less use from class AB and more from C2 than from the other classes. Radios 3 and 4 are extensively used only by classes AB and C1, and most by the first – Radio 3 is barely listened to by classes C2 and DE (four minutes each), while AB listening to Radio 4 is over five times longer than both C2 and DE. On the other hand, BBC local radio displays increasing length of use across the classes – the average time for class DE being more than twice that for AB. Independent local radio displays a flatter, though irregular, pattern, with class AB listening less than the others. Of course, a complicating factor is the variation in availability and length of transmission time for the different services. Overall, the percentage of listening time devoted to BBC services as opposed to independent ones declines across the classes from 81 per cent for AB to 68 for DE.

In contrast to TV-watching, men as a group listen to the radio on average some forty minutes more per week than women. Only BBC Radio 2 has similar listening from both sexes; men make greater use of Radios 1 and 3 and Independent local radio than do women, while the latter listen longer to Radio 4 and BBC local radio. The second section to Table 10.5 shows that children spend relatively little time listening compared to others, and less than a tenth of the time they spend viewing. Young adults spend longest and those over sixty-five the shortest time with a radio. It also illustrates the age appeal of radio programmes, by contrasting the listening time for Radios 1 and 2. Radio 1 is listened to longest by those aged between sixteen and thirty-four, though four- to fifteen-year-olds spend about half their total radio time on it, and little by those over fifty-five. Radio 2, on the other hand, is used most by those over the age of forty-five and barely at all by children. The percentage of listening time devoted to BBC radio increases up the age groups, from 59 for those aged four to fifteen years to 84 for those over sixty-five.

No such detailed data on listening to records and tapes are available. What is clear from Table 10.3 is both its overall popularity and the quite dramatic decline of that popularity across the social classes, from almost four in five in class 1 to half of class 6.

Reading

The most comprehensively surveyed area of reading is that of newspapers and periodicals. The JICNARS produces regular *National Readership Surveys* which are widely used by advertising and commercial concerns. These are based on extensive and continuous research, involving around 30,000 interviews each year. The data in Tables 10.6 and 10.7 present the readership of selected titles (listed in order of their overall popularity) in two separate but related ways. The first shows the percentage of each social class which claims to have read or looked at a copy of the given title, in a period up to the interview corresponding to the length of time between publications; for example, in respect to weeklies, in the previous seven days. Hence, the top figure in the left-hand column of Table 10.6 shows that 5 per cent of class A claim to have read or looked at a copy of the *Sun*. Table 10.7 gives the social class and sex profiles of the readers of the same titles, hence the top figure in the left-hand column shows that class A provides 1 per cent of the readers of the *Sun*. The bottom row of each section in both tables gives the readership for each type of publication, while the last row to Table 10.7 gives the estimated class and sex profile for the population, which allows for comparison.

There is little consistent social class pattern to readership of types of publication in general. Sunday papers have a somewhat higher readership than daily ones (74 compared with 68 per cent of those interviewed). In both cases, only classes A and E have rates markedly different from the overall figure, A being higher and E lower than the other classes. The readership of evening papers rises across the classes A to D, while the percentage of all classes reading free weekly papers is similar at around 70, save for A which is 63. While the readership of general weekly periodicals declines from class A to E, that for women's weeklies, with the exception of classes A and B, shows a very flat pattern. Both general and women's monthlies exhibit a sharp decrease from around 50 per cent in class A to 20 per cent in class E.

It is fairly apparent that there are major social divisions in readership of particular publications. This is best illustrated by daily newspapers, where the social classes display quite different choices. It is common practice to distinguish between so-called 'quality' papers (*Guardian, Independent, Daily Telegraph, The Times*), which have overall readership figures of 2 to 6 per cent of the population, and 'popular' papers, which each have overall readerships of 9 to 25 per cent (see right-hand column to Table 10.6). While 'quality' papers can be characterized as middle-class – the non-manual classes constitute around 80 per cent of their readership – it is clear that the reading of such papers is only really widespread in class A. Adding together the percentage of each 'quality' paper (and thereby assuming that no individual reads more than one) reveals that 59 per cent of class A, 40 per cent of class B and 18 per cent of class C1 read such papers. Around a quarter of the members of these classes read the *Daily Mail* or *Daily Express* and constitute more than half the readership of these papers. In contrast, over three-quarters of the readership of the *Sun, Daily Mirror* and *Daily Star* are from classes C2, D and E; 71, 81 and 55 per cent respectively of the members of these classes claiming to read these papers (again assuming no individual reads more than one). Table 10.7 also reveals sex differences. Overall, women are somewhat underrepresented in the readership profile of any daily newspaper – males 51, females 49 per cent. While the sex profiles of readership of most 'popular' papers are similar to the overall, exceptions are the *Daily Star* and *Today* – females 41 and 38 per cent respectively. Women form only about a third of the readership of the 'quality' papers, with the exception of the *Daily Telegraph* where the figure is 46. Similar observations concerning the social class readership of 'quality' and 'popular' Sunday papers can be made, though it is interesting to note that sex differences in profile all but disappear.

TABLE 10.6 Percentage of each social class claiming readership of newspapers and selected periodicals

	Social class (MR)						
	A	B	C1	C2	D	E	All
DAILY NEWSPAPERS							
Sun	5	10	20	32	37	27	25
Daily Mirror	4	8	16	27	29	19	20
Daily Mail	14	14	14	9	6	5	10
Daily Express	9	12	13	10	6	6	10
Daily Star	2	2	6	12	15	9	9
Daily Telegraph	28	16	8	3	1	2	6
Daily Record	1	2	4	6	7	6	5
Guardian	9	10	4	1	1	1	3
The Times	16	8	3	1	1	1	3
Independent	6	6	3	1	1	[–][2]	2
Today	1	2	3	3	3	1	2
Financial Times	8	5	2	1	[–]	[–]	2
Any national daily[1]	74	67	67	70	72	52	68
EVENING NEWSPAPERS (any)	26	27	30	33	33	29	31
FREE WEEKLY NEWSPAPERS (any)	63	72	72	73	70	69	71
SUNDAY NEWSPAPERS							
News of the World	9	12	23	36	40	30	29
Sunday Mirror	5	10	17	27	27	18	20
People	3	8	16	23	25	17	18
Sunday Express	24	22	18	12	8	7	14
Mail on Sunday	16	16	16	11	7	4	11
Sunday Post	4	5	7	9	10	10	8
Sunday Times	35	22	10	3	3	2	8
Observer	14	14	7	3	2	2	5
Sunday Telegraph	19	11	7	3	2	1	5
Sunday Mail	1	3	4	6	7	6	5
Any national Sunday	78	75	74	76	76	64	74

1. Includes others not listed. 2. Less than 0.5 per cent.

TABLE 10.6 (contd)

	A	B	Social class (MR) C1	C2	D	E	All
GENERAL WEEKLIES							
TV Times	21	22	22	20	20	17	20
Radio Times	26	26	23	18	17	16	20
Exchange and Mart	3	3	3	4	5	4	2
Any general weekly[1]	46	45	41	38	36	29	38
WOMEN'S WEEKLIES							
Woman's Own	8	10	12	11	11	9	11
Woman	6	7	9	8	7	7	8
Woman's Realm	4	4	5	5	5	5	5
Just Seventeen	3	3	2	2	3	1	2
Jackie	1	1	1	2	2	1	1
Any women's weekly[1]	20	23	27	27	26	26	26
GENERAL MONTHLIES							
Reader's Digest	20	20	18	15	12	9	15
National Geographic	9	7	4	2	1	1	3
Practical Gardening	3	3	3	3	2	1	3
Do-It-Yourself	1	2	2	3	3	2	2
Mayfair	1	1	1	2	2	1	2
Penthouse	1	1	1	2	2	[–]	1
Practical Motorist	1	2	22	2	1	1	1
Any general monthly[1]	52	50	43	38	32	20	38
WOMEN'S MONTHLIES							
Family Circle	8	9	7	6	5	3	6
Good Housekeeping	15	12	7	4	3	2	6
Woman and Home	9	8	7	4	4	3	5
Cosmopolitan	10	8	6	4	3	2	5
Homes and Gardens	11	8	5	3	2	2	4
True Romances	1	1	22	3	4	3	3
Woman's World	3	2	2	2	2	1	2
'19'	1	2	2	2	2	1	2
Any women's monthly[1]	51	44	39	31	26	20	33

Derived from tables 6, 14, 22 and 30 of JICNARS's *National Readership Survey* Vol. 2, *January-December 1987* (1987).

TABLE 10.7 Social class and sex profiles of the readership of newspapers and selected periodicals

| | *Social class (MR)* | | | | | | | |
	A	B	C1	C2	D	E	Male	Female
DAILY NEWSPAPERS								
Sun	1	6	18	35	26	15	53	47
Daily Mirror	1	6	18	37	26	13	55	45
Daily Mail	4	20	32	26	11	8	51	49
Daily Express	3	18	31	28	12	9	52	48
Daily Star	1	4	16	37	30	14	59	41
Daily Telegraph	12	39	30	12	4	4	54	46
Daily Record	1	6	18	32	25	18	51	49
Guardian	7	43	27	12	7	3	58	42
Times	16	41	26	9	5	3	63	37
Independent	8	42	30	13	5	1	67	33
Today	1	14	25	31	22	6	62	38
Financial Times	12	40	33	8	5	1	73	27
Any national daily[1]	3	15	22	29	19	12	51	49
EVENING NEWSPAPER (any)	2	13	22	30	19	13	52	48
FREE WEEKLY NEWSPAPERS (any)	2	15	23	23	28	14	48	52
SUNDAY NEWSPAPERS								
News of the World	1	6	18	35	25	15	51	49
Sunday Mirror	1	7	19	37	24	13	52	48
People	[−]	6	20	35	24	14	52	48
Sunday Express	5	23	30	24	10	7	51	49
Mail on Sunday	4	21	33	26	11	5	50	50
Sunday Post	1	9	20	30	22	7	46	54
Sunday Times	12	40	28	11	6	3	53	47
Observer	7	40	28	14	6	4	54	46
Sunday Telegraph	11	34	31	15	6	3	53	47
Sunday Mail	1	7	19	32	24	17	50	50
Any national Sunday	3	15	23	29	18	12	50	50

1. Includes others not listed.   2. 15 years and over.

TABLE 10.7 (contd)

	A	B	C1	C2	D	E	Male	Female
			Social class (MR)					
GENERAL WEEKLIES								
TV Times	3	16	25	27	18	12	46	54
Radio Times	4	19	26	25	15	11	46	54
Exchange and Mart	2	13	22	37	18	8	73	27
Any general weekly[1]	3	17	25	27	17	11	53	47
WOMEN'S WEEKLIES								
Woman's Own	2	14	25	29	18	12	15	85
Woman	2	14	26	29	16	12	11	9
Woman's Realm	2	13	24	29	18	14	12	88
Just Seventeen	4	18	22	30	20	6	15	85
Jackie	1	11	18	33	23	14	10	90
Any women's weekly[1]	2	13	24	28	18	14	17	83
GENERAL MONTHLIES								
Reader's Digest	4	19	27	28	14	8	51	49
National Geographic	9	34	29	17	6	5	60	40
Practical Gardening	3	17	25	34	14	8	59	41
Do-It-Yourself	1	12	19	35	23	10	71	29
Mayfair	2	7	20	39	27	6	94	6
Penthouse	2	6	14	43	30	5	93	7
Practical Motorist	1	16	24	37	16	5	89	11
Any general monthly[1]	4	20	26	28	15	8	60	40
WOMEN'S MONTHLIES								
Family Circle	3	21	27	27	14	7	14	86
Good Housekeeping	7	36	28	19	10	6	17	83
Woman and Home	4	21	30	23	13	9	8	92
Cosmopolitan	6	25	32	22	10	5	23	77
Homes and Gardens	7	31	27	20	10	6	34	66
True Romances	1	7	14	32	26	20	6	94
Woman's World	3	14	24	32	18	9	18	82
'19'	2	14	31	29	16	8	15	85
Any women's monthly[1]	4	20	27	26	14	9	26	74
ESTIMATED POPULATION (%)[2]	3	15	23	28	18	14		

Derived from tables 125, 127 and 129 of JICNARS's *National Readership Survey 1987*.

Apart from the social differences noted above, which might be anticipated, the data also reveal considerable breadth of readership. Some members of all social classes read every newspaper: for example, 1 per cent of class D claims to read each of the 'quality' dailies and a small number (less than 0.5 per cent) the *Financial Times*. On the other hand 2 per cent of class A read the *Daily Star*. The readership of women's weeklies is 17 per cent male, and of women's monthlies 26 per cent, ranging from 6 per cent for *True Romances* to just over a third for *Homes and Gardens*. General weeklies have a predominantly male readership, though the *TV* and *Radio Times* claim a female majority. The class pattern to the readership of these two publications probably reflects differences in viewing and listening (see Tables 10.4 and 10.5 above). A general monthly is read by around half of classes A and B, but only one in five of class E. Their readership has a male majority (60/40) ranging from 51 per cent for *Reader's Digest* to 94 per cent for *Mayfair*.

In general it would appear that newspaper and periodical readership is declining. Since 1975 the overall percentage claiming readership of daily and Sunday newspapers both fell (from 75 to 68 per cent and 84 to 74 per cent respectively), as did both general and women's weeklies (from 50 to 38 and 37 to 26 per cent). In contrast there was a marginal 2 per cent increase in the readership of general monthlies (*National Readership Survey 1975 and 1987*).

Interest in types of news was explored in the *Royal Commission on the Press* (1977). Generally speaking, the middle classes were found to be more interested in most types of news and particularly in news concerning what the government was doing and about political parties. Less social class differentiation was apparent over the topics of trade union affairs and news about the locality and its council.

Book readership is not researched in the same detail as newspapers and periodicals. Table 10.3 shows that leisure-time reading of books is reported by more than half the GHS respondents and that such reading is higher among women than men (61 compared to 50 per cent), with marked differences across the social classes – from 78 per cent of class 1 to 41 per cent of class 6. Similar differences exist in book purchasing, as can be seen in Table 10.8, though, of course, some of these purchases will be for presents. In general book purchasing declines across the classes, with AB and C1 being above the overall average and the other classes below it. This decline was somewhat sharper in respect to non-fiction than fiction. Hardbacks were purchased by only about a third of those surveyed and were mainly non-fiction, paperbacks were bought by almost a half and were mainly fiction.

TABLE 10.8 Book purchases in the past twelve months,[1] by social class (percentages)

| | Social class (MR) | | | | | |
	AB	C1	C2	D	E	All
Hardback						
Fiction	13	12	10	10	8	11
Non-fiction	40	30	20	16	13	24
10 or more	3	3	2	2	2	2
3 to 9	20	15	11	9	8	13
2 or less	27	22	18	16	12	19
None	50	60	70	73	78	66
Paperback						
Fiction	52	41	28	25	20	33
Non-fiction	27	28	23	13	9	24
10 or more	13	9	6	7	6	8
4 to 9	26	21	13	12	10	16
3 or less	31	28	24	20	16	27
None	30	42	57	61	68	51

1. To interview.

Derived from pages 282, 284 , 286 and 288 of BMRB's *Target Group Index 1987*, vol 30.

Other home-based activities

As Table 10.3 shows, gardening and DIY activity both decline across the social classes and while male involvement is about a half, that for females is much lower. Of course, to some extent such activities are determined or affected by the type and tenure of the household's accommodation and whether or not it has a garden and/or an allotment. As was seen in Chapter 7, rented accommodation and that without a garden is more frequent in the manual than non-manual classes. Both sex and class differences in involvement in hobbies, crafts and arts are very much more marked than for other activities – from 21 per cent of class 1 to 2 per cent of class 6; male 15 and female 6 per cent. As would be anticipated, dressmaking, needlework and knitting displays a distinct female majority – 48 compared with 2 per cent for males. Unlike all the other activities, these do not decline across the social classes: classes 1, 2 and 4 have much lower incidence than the overall 27 per cent, 3 much higher (reflecting the large proportion of women's occupations in that class). In 5 and 6 similar, higher than average proportion.

Finally, entertaining, or being entertained, in the home approaches the popularity of TV-watching, 91 per cent reporting it in the four weeks before interview. Class differences are not very pronounced, though the non-manual classes had rates just above the overall, the manual below.

OUT-OF-HOME ACTIVITIES

Motor cars

The car itself can provide a leisure activity – cleaning, servicing and riding – but is probably most important in providing access to a range of other leisure pursuits. For example, some 72 per cent of all holidays in Britain during 1986 involved the use of a car (*The British on*

Holiday, 1986). Around two-thirds of households have a car or cars. Table 10.9 shows the social class variation, ranging from 91 per cent in class AB to 57 for D and 27 for E. While about four in every ten AB households have two or more cars, this is true for only one in ten for D and three in a hundred for E. It is also clear that company cars are primarily enjoyed by non-manual households.

While over all almost two-thirds of adults hold driving licences, markedly more men than women have them (79 per cent compared to 53) and the proportion declines across the classes – AB, 84 per cent, D 56 and E 35 per cent. Unpublished data from *GHS 1980* indicate that 90 per cent of men compared with 50 per cent of women who had

TABLE 10.9 Car[1] and licence ownership and average weekly mileage, by social class and sex (percentages)

| | Social class (MR) | | | | | | | |
	AB	C1	C2	D	E	Male	Female	All
Household car ownership								
None	9	22	25	43	73	–	–	34
One or more[1]	91	78	75	57	27	–	–	66
1 car	52	55	57	46	24	–	–	48
2 cars	34	21	16	10	3	–	–	17
3 or more cars	5	2	2	1	[–][2]	–	–	2
Company car	16	10	4	2	[–]	–	–	6
Adults with current driving licence	84	75	69	56	35	79	53	65
Adult's weekly driving								
Up to 179 miles	61	56	54	46	29	54	47	50
180 miles or more	22	17	13	7	2	22	4	13

1. Includes company cars.
2. Less than 0.5 per cent.

Derived from pages 4 and 6 of BMRB's *Target Group Index* (1987), vol. 27.

access to a car had a full driving licence (*GHS 1982*). The average weekly mileage driven shows a similar pattern. In particular women drive fewer miles than men, only 4 per cent compared to 22 clocking up 180 miles or more (see lower section of table).

Sports, games and physical activities

Involvement and participation in these types of leisure activity can be identified at several levels and in a number of ways. The 1983 GHS asked respondents an open-ended question and used an aide-memoire card about activities in the four weeks prior to interview. Table 10.10 provides a view of the level of participation in those activities undertaken by at least 1 per cent (for list see footnote to

TABLE 10.10 Participation[1] in sports, games and physical activity, by social class and sex (percentages)

| | Social class (RG SEG 80) | | | | | | | | |
	1	2	3	4	5	6	Male	Female	All[2]
Outdoor[3]									
At least one activity	53	41	34	30	22	20	39	24	31
Excluding walking	35	26	17	19	10	9	26	10	17
Indoor[4]									
At least one activity	34	27	27	28	18	15	33	18	25
Spectating[5]									
At least one sport	11	11	8	9	5	4	11	5	8

1. Persons aged 16 and over, who had taken part during 4 weeks prior to interview.
2. Includes unclassified and full-time students.
3. Only those activities undertaken by at least 1 per cent: walking (2 miles or more), swimming, football, golf, athletics/jogging, fishing, cycling, tennis, bowls, camping, horse-riding, cricket.
4. Snooker/billiards/pool, swimming, darts, keep fit/yoga, squash, badminton, table tennis, bowls/ten pin, gymnastics/athletics.
5. Excludes TV-watching.

Derived from tables 10.13, 10.14 and 10.21, *GHS 1983*.

table). As can be seen, some 31 per cent had undertaken an outdoor and 25 per cent an indoor activity – overall some 44 per cent had done at least one of either, 54 per cent of males and 35 of females. It is evident that, apart from walking, participation in sports, games and physical activities is low, declines across the social classes (class 1 stands out as most active) and is higher among men than women. Excluding walking reduces outdoor activity from 31 to 17 per cent and heightens social class and sex differences. Some 8 per cent of those questioned had watched a sport in the same period (excluding TV-watching). The pattern of spectating is similar to that of participation.

A separate view of the subject is provided in Table 10.11, based on the question, 'Which of these do you take part in or play yourself these days?' and for which a list is provided. Obviously such a question is likely to produce higher rates of participation. In general, as can be seen, most of the pursuits, particularly sports, exhibit a decline in participation across the classes and higher rates for men than women. There are, however, several exceptions to the overall pattern. More women than men take part in bingo and dancing, both of which are more popular with the manual than the non-manual classes. While the percentage of the sexes swimming and playing badminton are markedly more similar than other sports, horse-riding is the only one where female participation is much higher than male (3 per cent compared to 0.9). When considering the table, bear in mind that class E contains state pensioners whose age and economic circumstances, like casual workers who are also included, may preclude their taking part in many of the activities listed.

Clubs, voluntary work and classes

Most of the literature in this area suggests that joining is more characteristic of the non-manual than the manual classes. For example a national survey found that club

TABLE 10.11 Percentage of each social class[1] and sex participating in sporting and leisure activities

		Social class (MR)					
		AB	C1	C2	D	E	All
Jogging/training	Males	16	17	12	12	9	14
	Females	5	5	5	3	2	4
Rambling/hiking	M	16	15	7	5	9	10
	F	12	8	5	4	4	6
Swimming	M	29	29	21	17	14	23
	F	31	26	22	18	11	22
Tennis	M	14	10	5	6	5	8
	F	10	8	4	4	2	6
Badminton	M	11	12	7	6	4	8
	F	12	9	7	5	2	7
Squash	M	16	12	7	6	3	9
	F	6	5	3	2	1	3
Golf	M	20	14	10	7	5	11
	F	4	1	1	1	[−][2]	1
Skiing	M	8	5	2	1	1	3
	F	4	2	1	1	1	2
Horse-riding	M	1	1	0.8	0.8	[−]	0.9
	F	5	3	3	2	2	3
Cricket	M	10	9	6	6	5	7
Football	M	10	12	11	13	8	11
Fishing	M	5	6	9	10	6	7
Bingo	M	1	2	6	8	9	5
	F	1	4	10	15	12	9
Dancing	M	12	17	17	17	12	15
	F	13	17	20	22	12	17
Darts	M	11	13	17	21	15	16
	F	1	3	5	7	4	4
Football pools	M	28	36	45	46	37	39
	F	11	18	22	22	16	18
Betting (horse-racing)	M	8	10	14	19	18	13
	F	2	3	4	6	5	4
Bridge	M	6	3	1	[−]	1	2
	F	4	1	[−]	[−]	[−]	[−]
Chess	M	11	11	8	9	9	10
	F	2	2	2	2	1	2

1. Persons aged over 15.   2. Less than 0.5 per cent.

Derived from pages 44, 46, 52, 54, 56, 58, 60, 62, 64, 66, 68, 70 and 72 of BMRB's *Target Group Index* 1987, vol. 30.

membership among both sexes declined across the classes, both in terms of the percentage who were members and the average number of clubs per person (Sillitoe, 1969). Men were more likely than women to be members of all types of club, except for religious ones (see also Table 9.5). Similar sex and class differences have been observed in a study of youth club attenders (Bone and Ross, 1972). A survey of primary school children found 49 per cent of those from social class I (RG60) homes to be cubs or brownies, compared with 15 per cent of those from class V (Dearnley and Fletcher, 1968). However, as was seen in Table 6.7, manual workers are more likely to be members of trade unions than are non-manual.

The data at the first row to Table 10.12 are somewhat different in that they refer to activity in clubs and societies in the previous four weeks. However, it is clear that participation was markedly higher in class 1 and lower in classes 5 and 6 than overall. Sex difference is small. The rest of the table shows much higher participation in voluntary work and amateur music and drama among the non-manual than the manual classes and a rather similar

TABLE 10.12 Membership[1] of clubs, societies, classes, music, drama and voluntary work, by social class and sex (percentages)

| | Social class (RG SEG 80) | | | | | | | | |
	1	2	3	4	5	6	Male	Female	All[2]
Clubs/societies	17	11	12	11	9	9	11	12	11
Voluntary work	13	13	12	6	5	4	7	9	8
Leisure classes[3]	3	2	3	1	1	1	1	2	2
Amateur music/drama[4]	6	3	4	2	2	1	3	3	3

1. Persons over 16 reporting activity in previous 4 weeks.
2. Includes full-time students and those not classified.
3. Excluding sports and dancing.
4. Excluding classes.

Devised from tables 10.31 and 10.32, GHS 1983.

divide in the much lower attendance at leisure classes (excluding sports and dancing).

Entertainment, food and drink

The cinema, once a major form of entertainment in our society, has become a minority pursuit; only 7 per cent of those surveyed in 1987 reported going once a month or more – a marked decrease from the 10 per cent of only eight years earlier (*National Readership Survey 1979, 1987*). In fact, as Table 10.13 shows, almost two-thirds never attend, ranging from 45 per cent for class A to 87 for E. Not only is attendance related to social class, but also, as the lower section of the table shows, even more strongly to age. The percentage never attending rises dramatically from 27 per cent for those aged fifteen to twenty-four years to 93 for those over sixty-five years (and this despite concessionary entrance charges).

Going to the theatre is even more of a minority activity than going to the cinema, only 26 per cent overall

TABLE 10.13 Frequency of cinema attendance, by social class and age (percentages)

| | Social class (MR) | | | | | | |
	A	B	C1	C2	D	E	All
Once a month or more	8	10	9	6	6	2	7
Less than 1 per month, but at least twice a year	30	26	23	17	16	6	18
Less than twice a year	16	17	13	11	9	4	11
Never	45	48	55	66	69	87	64

| | Age | | | | | |
	15–24	25–34	35–44	45–54	55–64	65+
Never	27	52	61	75	85	93

Derived from tables 158 and 159 of JICNARS's *National Readership Survey 1987*.

TABLE 10.14 Frequency and type of theatre attendance, by social class (percentages)

| | Social class (MR) | | | | | |
	AB	C1	C2	D	E	All
Theatre Attendance[1]						
More than 3 times a year	12	8	3	2	2	6
2 or 3 times a year	19	15	7	5	5	10
Once a year	15	13	9	7	5	10
Type of Performance[2]						
Plays	48	33	15	10	9	23
Classical music, concerts/ recitals	28	16	6	6	5	12
Jazz, concerts/performances	14	10	6	6	5	7
Ballet	14	8	3	2	3	6
Opera	13	8	2	2	3	5
Contemporary dance	8	6	2	2	2	2

1. Based on answers to the question, 'About how often these days do you go to . . . ?'
2. Percentage who go these days.

Derived from pages 260, 264, 266, 268, 270, 272 and 274 of BMRB's *Target Group Index 1987*, vol. 30.

claiming to attend once a year or more. Table 10.14 displays very clear social class variation: among those attending at least three times per year the proportion in class AB is six times higher than that for classes D and E. The lower section of the table lists, in order of overall popularity, the types of performance seen. While social class differences are apparent in all types, it is noticeable that these are smallest for jazz and largest for the opera and ballet, together with classical music, in each of which class AB stands out in terms of attendance.

Eating and drinking can either be leisure activities in their own right or an aspect of other activities. The self-reported use of pubs, clubs, bars and restaurants is presented on Table 10.15. Public houses are frequented

TABLE 10.15 Frequency of use of pub, clubs, wine bars and restaurants, by social class (percentages[1])

| | Social class (MR) | | | | | | | |
	AB	C1	C2	D	E	Male	Female	All
Public house								
Any use	79	75	73	66	49	76	64	70
Once or more a day	2	2	2	2	1	3	0.7	2
2 or 3 times a week	14	16	18	16	10	23	8	15
More than once a month/at most once a week	26	24	24	23	17	25	21	23
Less than once a month	37	33	29	25	21	25	34	29
Licensed clubs	32	36	43	45	29	46	31	38
Wine bars	35	28	19	16	9	23	21	22
Restaurant								
Day	59	49	37	34	33	38	46	42
Evening	77	67	58	46	28	59	54	57

1. Over 1 rounded.

Derived from pages 204, 208, 212, 216, and 222 of BMRB's *Target Group Index 1987*, vol. 30.

by a declining proportion of the classes – from 79 per cent of AB to 49 of E – and by just over three-quarters of the men and less than two-thirds of the women surveyed. However, daily use is 2 per cent of all classes other than E, while class C2 has the highest proportion, claiming two or three times a week. The table clearly suggests that while wine bars are used predominantly by classes AB/C1 and by the sexes almost equally, licensed clubs are used most by C2/D and markedly more by men. Eating in restaurants declines across the classes, especially in the evening as opposed to the day, and men are more likely to eat at them in the evening and women during the day.

As might be expected, tastes in alcohol vary. For example, bottled wine is more popular among the middle classes – 68 per cent of those who drink at least three bottles of wine a month belong to classes ABC1 (MR) (*Target Group Index 1987*). In contrast, 73 per cent of 'heavy' (eight or more pints a week) lager drinkers and 63 per cent of 'heavy' draught beer drinkers are from classes C2DE. Similar class differences exist among all drinkers. Lager is somewhat more popular than beer in the younger age groups and among women. While men constitute 84 per cent of all beer and 65 per cent of all lager drinkers, the sex profile of wine drinkers is the same as the population at large.

Outings and holidays

Table 10.16 provides a view of the use of places of interest, listed according to their overall popularity. What is notable is not so much the perhaps expected social class differences in art gallery, stately home and archaeological site visits, but the lack of such differences in respect to safari parks and zoos whose appeal appears similar to all classes.

TABLE 10.16 Outings to places of interest,[1] by social class (percentages)

| | Social class (MR) | | | | | |
	AB	C1	C2	D	E	All
Beauty spots/gardens	51	42	31	25	21	34
Stately homes/castles	41	31	21	16	13	25
Art galleries/exhibitions	41	28	14	11	11	21
Zoos	16	18	17	16	10	16
Safari parks	9	9	8	8	5	8
Archaeological sites	15	9	5	2	3	7

1. In previous twelve months.

Derived from pages 254, 256 and 268, BMRB's *Target Group Index* (1987), vol. 30.

Six out of ten British adults took a holiday of four or more nights in 1986, 39 per cent in this country and 27 per cent abroad. (*The British on Holiday 1986*, 1987). Table 10.17 provides two views of holiday-makers by social class. The upper section shows that the proportion taking any holiday declines across the classes from 77 per cent of AB to 42 per cent of class E and that this pattern is more marked in respect to those going abroad than those

TABLE 10.17A Percentage of each class taking a holiday in the past year

	Social class (MR)					
	AB	C1	C2	D	E	All
Any holiday[1]	77	68	62	56	42	62
Holiday in the UK	45	45	43	40	29	41
Holiday camp	3	5	8	8	5	6
Holiday abroad	45	33	24	19	12	27
Package tour abroad	25	20	15	12	7	16

TABLE 10.17B Social class profile of holiday and non-holiday takers

	Social class (MR)				
	AB	C1	C2	DE	
British holiday[2]	19	23	31	28	each
Abroad holiday[3]	33	26	26	15	row
No holiday	9	20	29	42	=
Population	17	22	31	30	100

1. Excluding short visits to relatives.
2. 4 or more nights.
3. 1 or more nights.

Derived from (A) page 4 of BMRB's *Target Group Index* (1987), vol. 3. and (B) *The British on Holiday 1986* (1987), source British Tourist Authority's/English Tourist Board's *British Tourist Survey* (1986).

holidaying in Britain, where the use of holiday camps is highest in classes C2 and D. The lower section of the table provides the social class profiles of foreign and British holiday-makers, non-holiday-takers and the population. Comparing the profiles reveals again that people in class AB were overrepresented among holiday-makers, particularly abroad, and that holiday-making declines – class DE being overrepresented among those not taking a holiday.

CHAPTER 11

Social Differences into
the 1990s

> So to criticize inequality and to desire equality
> is not, as is sometimes suggested, to cherish the
> romantic illusion that men are equal in character
> and intelligence. It is to hold that, while their natu-
> ral endowments differ profoundly, it is the mark
> of a civilized society to aim at eliminating such
> inequalities as have their source not in individual
> differences, but in its own organization: and that
> individual energies, which are a source of social
> energy, are more likely to ripen and find expres-
> sion if social inequalities are, as far as practicable,
> diminished.
>
> R. H. TAWNEY (1931)

This book has presented what amounts to a catalogue of
social differences in Britain. This catalogue is based on,
and some would say limited by, the exclusive use of data
from empirical research. Its presentation is matter-of-fact;
for example, it does not present only those data which
exhibit the extremes of difference or inequality. It has
not elaborated either these or what might be seen as the
attendant injustices to the disadvantaged. It provides no
description or first-hand account of the varying situations
and conditions of the social strata surveyed. Doubtless
had this been done a much starker and more dramatic
picture would have been presented. Nevertheless, an abi-
ding impression must be that social strata in the Britain
of the 1980s experience not only differing life-styles but
also differing life-chances. Both the quality and quantity
of life of social groups are affected by their level of access

to forms of social wealth, particularly the economic and that of power. Further, however much the life-chances and -styles of the disadvantaged may have improved in absolute terms, relative differences have resolutely remained.

Indeed, it can be argued that relative differences between social groups have not only been sustained but are actually growing in importance. For example, as Runciman (1966) has argued, relative deprivation is likely to be a more serious social and political problem than abject deprivation since the disadvantaged in the latter situation have few concerns other than about survival. If the desirable aspects of life continue to grow in number and their desirability is heightened through political activity and advertising, then there may well be two consequences. First, on the assumption that such aspects of life remain scarce, competition for them will increase along with the feeling of deprivation by those without. Second, the mechanisms by which they are distributed will come under increasing scrutiny and the bases of inequality of opportunity will be questioned, and perhaps challenged.

In relying on social survey data our consideration of social differences has been constrained in a number of ways (see also Chapters 1 and 2). The major constraint has been the limited extent to which it has been possible to view the forms of social stratification other than separately. Obviously it is not possible to escape this constraint in what follows. It is worth reiterating, however, the fact that the dimensions and extent of the social differences revealed in this book are limited by this and other aspects of the approach of social researchers. As we have seen, where more than one stratum has been viewed simultaneously there is evidence of cumulative advantage and disadvantage and the exposed differences are extenuated. We have also recognized that our view of social differences is neither as comprehensive nor as detailed or continuous as might be expected or desirable.

This situation reflects the facts that much of the surveyed research was designed for purposes other than the exploration of social differences and that research is subject to both changes and inertia in fashion. In other words, like that which it studies, it is socially produced. To a great extent, shifts in social research mirror shifts in society's interest in, and recognition of, problems. This accounts for the rise in research activity in respect to sex and ethnicity, the slackening in class and the continued limited interest in age.

Those who have read this book are now in an informed position from which to judge both the usefulness of categorizing society into strata and the importance and nature of the exposed differences between them. For example, the actual differences between the separate classes have varied in magnitude and importance. What is clear is the very substantial extent of the differences between the middle (non-manual) and the working (manual) classes, and of the stark differences between the extremes – the professional and the unskilled manual classes. Readers would find it relatively simple to compile a list of contrasting differences from either a middle- or working-class perspective. Further, they have some knowledge both of the size of such differences and of the basis on which the evidence rests.

So equipped, they should have no difficulty in evaluating the following two statements made separately on the BBC Radio 4 programme 'Barriers' in January 1980 (*Listener*, 1980). The first is the opinion of Norman St John Stevas, then Leader of the House of Commons and a Conservative MP:

> I think that class is largely an irrelevancy in contemporary British society. Some people may use it as an excuse for their own failures, but I think we have very largely a mobile society, a society open to talent. The talented child or young person is able to reach the top of any profession or any activity to which that child sets his or her mind, provided that the ability is there. I think we're a much

more mobile society, for example, than the United States. We talk a lot about class in British society, but I think its significance socially is very small.

The second is my own comment:

> I think it's a pretty serious and important factor to the extent that we have a good deal of evidence to show that, right from the beginning of life, one's life-chances, the chance of surviving birth, of suffering from certain illnesses, the chances of living in certain types of accommodation, of receiving certain types of education and indeed the likelihood of earning a given income, are very much related to divisions in our society which we call social class. In fact, there seems to be very little of life in our society which isn't in some way characterized by differences between social classes.

In the face of the data contained in this book it would be difficult to deny that social class, in spite of the considerations discussed in the first two chapters, is a meaningful and useful concept. If it were only a spurious and artificial concept of social scientists it is difficult to imagine that its research application would so consistently turn up differences.

Similar opportunities are provided for the appraisal of sex, ethnicity and age, and these lead to parallel conclusions. However uncomfortable it may be, however incongruent with values concerning individuality and individual's responsibility, the evidence clearly shows that in reality most of life's opportunities and its experiences are vitally affected and mediated by the dimensions of social stratification. Of course, readers will form, or have formed, their own views and reactions to the social differences exposed in this book. As discussed at the outset, facts do not speak for themselves, they are available for differing interpretation and receive an almost infinite range of reaction. It seems unlikely, however, that many will be able to dismiss all or even the majority as inconsequential and of no concern to themselves or others.

As we have seen, there are intimate relationships between the forms of social stratification, much in the same way as we are all members of each. What remains somewhat contentious since it is not clearly demonstrated in research is whether the forms of stratification vary in their significance. As has been pointed out in various places in this book, the author is convinced that social class is the most fundamental. Mainly this is due to the fact that most of the vital social differences can be seen to have an economic base (see below). Just as important, however, is the clear indication that both the conditions of the other strata and their relationships vary according to class context. Put as boldly as possible, being Black, female or elderly *and* middle-class is different from being Black, female or elderly *and* working-class. Again, the relationships between the sexes, ethnic and age groups are not identical in the different classes. This is not to deny the importance of sex, ethnicity and age either objectively or subjectively, or to suggest that changes in class would necessarily end the differences between them. It is rather, again, to assert the necessity of properly viewing forms of social stratification as a single entity, and to underline once more the inherent dangers in ignoring class. It is to return to the basic claim in Chapter 1 that social groups are differentiated mainly by their ownership of or access to various forms of social wealth. Consequently, real change in their situations is dependent upon the redistribution of that wealth, however that may be achieved.

Our view has been of Britain in the immediate past (most of the data being from the 1980s) in empirical research terms, and, for all practical purposes, that is the here-and-now. At the same time it is clear that the differences both have a history of persistence and vary in the amount of change that can be discerned. It is difficult to escape from the realization that the basic facts of class are very far from being dynamic. For those with investment of hope in change, the lack of change observed in areas where the rhetoric for equality abounds – like education and health – may be galling. Indeed there is some evidence to suggest that class differences in such areas may be widening. At the same time, in some few cases change towards greater equality can be discerned. However, such changes do not relieve the overall picture of the stability of relative class differences within a context of general change in society – as witnessed by a conclusion of the *Royal Commission on the Distribution of Income and Wealth* (see page 170). It is difficult to see that political activity and social change in the 1980s has done much other than to sustain, or even increase, existing class differences. Indeed, the large body of unemployed, especially the long-term, may be seen as a new class whose deprivations are many and severe. There is, in short, no evidence to suggest that class differences are anything but alive and well at present and that they will feature prominently, along with those of sex, ethnicity and age, into the 1990s and beyond. Despite the cut-backs in academic and governmental agencies' research funding there will be more than enough data on which to base a further edition of this book.

In reviewing the findings of PSI surveys in respect to ethnic minorities, Brown (1984a) reaches similar conclusions:

> For the most part ... Britain's well-established black population is still occupying the precarious and unattractive position of the earlier immigrants. We have moved ... from studying the circumstances of immigrants to studying the black population of Great Britain only to find that we are still looking at the same thing. There is just the same need now ... for action to give black people access to widening economic opportunities and life chances; and there is just the same need to pursue equality between racial groups in Britain.

Despite the portrayal of the considerable and continuing disadvantages of being female in our society, it is here that some of the most dramatic changes have taken place.

Perhaps the most interesting are the changes in the educational performance of the sexes, especially as they are in some contrast to the continuing class differences (see Chapter 8). While the effects have yet to reach the areas of employment and earnings to the same degree, the fact that girls now out-perform boys at 16+ examinations and are closing the gap at 18+ and in higher education is a significant social change. And it has been achieved in a comparatively short time. While the precise ingredients and process of this change are not well understood, for those dedicated to greater equality this achievement serves as an encouragement.

The research reviewed has provided only a limited picture of age differences, and few grounds to anticipate much change. The association of being elderly and in poverty has not been destroyed by the advent of pensions and the welfare state (see Chapter 5). It seems unlikely that this will change now that Britain is an ageing society – an increasing proportion of the population is living longer – and where the demand for medical and other care affecting the quality of life for the elderly grows both with numbers and also with progress. What is interesting and unique here is that numerically at least the elderly have increasing political potential. In turn this raises the question of the roles of politics, legislation and ideology in the existence of social inequality. This is an extremely complex field, which is not relieved by much clear analysis. Certainly, as is clear from the fact that women have formed the electoral majority for sixty years in Britain, and the working class for longer, the realization of political potential hinges not so much on numbers as on the extent to which groups identify with common interests, and their power in comparison with the power of those established. As we have seen, the disadvantaged and advantaged often share a common view of the appropriateness and justice of each other's position. The co-existence of several forms of social group differences often causes conflict and division in each set of interests. Perhaps the assumed inevitability of inequality has had a profound effect on all, even on the proponents of equality. Certainly Le Grand (1982), having surveyed the effects of public expenditure on the social services, concludes:

> The strategy of equality through public provision has failed. It failed primarily because it implicitly accepted the ideology of inequality. Any alternative strategy has to have as an essential part an attack on that ideology; otherwise it too will fail. But if it does make the attempt and if the attempt succeeds, then there is a chance that the divisions which have plagued British society for centuries, and that have led to the inequalities documented in this book, will at last be eliminated.

It is ironic that the empirical approach to social class, which reveals so much by way of differences, at the same time disguises some. Though obviously effective in disclosing between-class variations, it can overlook within-class variation – which can be considerable. While this was illustrated, for example in respect to earnings and income, it needs to be borne in mind elsewhere. A further interesting effect of the approach is how little we know about the most powerful and rich – what we might call the upper class – of our society. Not only are they relatively rare in the population and hence extremely so in any sample, however drawn, but it is open to speculation how such people declare themselves, or are coded by researchers, in terms of occupation. Some have several 'occupations', none of which is necessarily revealing for, or within, a social class classification based on occupation. Other, perhaps less exotic, groups within the recognized classes – including the poor, the unemployed, the sick and the disabled, to mention the obvious, are similarly hidden. Both the strengths and limitations of operationalizing social class on the single criterion of occupation need, then, to be fully recognized.

In much the same way the operationalizations of ethnicity curtail a full and proper view of differences. Indeed, as we have seen, since research is a social activity so it incorporates many of society's values and assumptions. And these extend to sex and age. Hence to an extent both what is studied, the methods used, presentation and interpretation are all capable of embodying elements of classism, sexism, racism and ageism. The net effect of these factors, whether they heighten or disguise social differences, is difficult to ascertain and open to debate. What is necessary is to sustain an awareness of and sensitivity towards them.

Many, if not most, social differences can be seen to stem from, or be related to, basic economic inequalities, and their effects, both long- and short-term, on the people involved. In spite of changes in our society, the realities of life for people in different social classes have remained pretty constant. Field's (1973) comment in *Unequal Britain* still rings true: 'Despite the growth in national wealth the age-old inequalities remain. The position of the poor has improved. But so, too, has that of the rich.' Somebody who read an early draft of the first edition of this book remarked, 'What does it tell us other than that there are some very big economic differences in our society?' However tempting such a conclusion may be, it is almost certainly only partially true. Many social differences are difficult to explain directly, if at all, in such terms. It is by no means clear that we would all be middle-class if we could afford to be, or working-class if we could not afford to be middle-class. A study of affluent factory workers showed they were selective about which aspects of middle-classness they adopted and that they maintained some important aspects of traditional working-class life (Goldthorpe *et al.*, 1969). Again, the relative increase in wealth (in real terms) of many working-class people, together with increased opportunities for higher education, have not significantly affected the proportion of working-class university students. This proportion has remained stubbornly constant since the 1930s. If equality in the paid labour market or even economic equality between the sexes were to be achieved, it would profoundly affect the nature of sex differences and roles, but not necessarily heighten the similarity of the sexes. Much the same case could be made in respect to ethnic and age groups. What would be achieved, however, would be the removal of the economic constraints on life- chances, life-styles and choices – releasing them from the present level of economic determinism to become more the product of individuals and their society.

If social differences were related to the existence of closed groups with vastly different amounts of power, wealth and so on, within a political context of unmitigated self-interest, then they would be unremarkable and, perhaps, unexpected. However, as we have seen, there is social mobility in our society, and its social classes are not entirely closed, self-recruiting, stable and self-conscious groups. Very few institutions in our society completely exclude any social stratum, although representation and power in them varies greatly. Between the Second World War and the 1980s there were shifts in power between political parties which had apparently differing social interests and policies. Women have gained and are gaining access to many domains that were once exclusively male. However, the extent to which these facts indicate that our society is an open one is a subject for debate. What is clear is that such facts and changes are intriguingly related to the existence and persistence of social class differences. The fact that social differences are produced and sustained within relatively open, widely recruiting and dynamic social groups, in a context of apparent political diversity and democracy, yet show little if any sign of changing, is perhaps more than surprising. The evidence in this book clearly indicates that, however hazy the concept of class may be, the realities of social class, together with those of the other forms of social stratification, are obtrusive enough at present to be unavoidable.

It seems reasonable to conclude, then, by accepting

that a root factor in, or cause of, social differences is economic differentiation. At the same time, we can appreciate that such differentiation, on its own, is not a sufficient, let alone a complete, explanation. Only to a limited extent, then, may the continued existence of class and stratification differences be seen as due to the fact that the economic structure of our society has not changed dramatically and appears unlikely to do so. Even if it were to change, the concepts of class and stratification would still have considerable utility. In societies which claim more economic equality than our own – for example, the Soviet Union and China – social differences similar to ours have far from disappeared. Indeed the fundamentals of the existence of social stratification appear inescapable. What is almost infinitely variable and open to change are their cultural manifestations.

Finally, then, the book provides some basis for the identification of those areas in which change might or ought to be sought. Almost regardless of political or ideological belief, some aspects of social differences and inequality can be seen as undesirable or objectionable. As the epigraph used at the beginning of this chapter so aptly points up, to desire and work for social equality is not a romantic or idle pursuit, but a hallmark of civilized society. While few choose, or have the opportunity, to lead, all have a political role to play. We may all follow and support, and not to do so is either defeatist, an acceptance of the ideology of inequality, or a rejection of a main argument of this book – or some combination of the three. As society creates social differences so it can affect, change and abolish them. There seems little incapable of change or avoidance in the social manifestations of social class, sex, ethnicity and age. What appears crucial is that people should be freed from those inequalities, injustices, constraints or lack of choice imposed upon them by the structure of the society in which they live.

APPENDIX A

List of Abbreviations and Acronyms

BBC	British Broadcasting Corporation
BEC	Business Education Council
BMRB	British Market Research Bureau
BSAG	Bristol Social Adjustment Guide
CHES	Child Health and Education Study
CRC	Community Relations Council
CRE	Commission for Racial Equality
CSE	Certificate of Secondary Education
CTC	City Technology College
DES	Department of Education and Science
DHSS	Department of Health and Social Security
DOE	Department of Employment
EOC	Equal Opportunities Commission
ESN	Educationally Sub-normal
FES	Family Expenditure Survey
GB	Great Britain
GBA	Association of Governing Bodies of Public Schools
GBSA	Association of Governing Bodies of Girls' Public Schools
GCE	General Certificate of Education
GCSE	General Certificate of Secondary Education
GHS	General Household Survey
GLC	Greater London Council
GP	General Practitioner
HMC	Head Masters' Conference
HMSO	Her Majesty's Stationery Office
HNC	Higher National Certificate
HND	Higher National Diploma
ISIS	Independent Schools' Information Service
IUD	Intra-uterine Device
IQ	Intelligence Quotient
JICNARS	Joint Industry Committee for National Readership Surveys

LEA	Local Education Authority
LFS	Labour Force Survey
MC	Metropolitan County
MP	Member of Parliament
NC	New Commonwealth
NCDS	National Child Development Study
NDHS	National Dwelling and Housing Survey
NFER	National Foundation for Educational Research
NHS	National Health Service
NOP	National Opinion Polls Market Research Ltd
NSHD	National Survey of Health and Development
OAP	Old Age Pensioner
ONC	Ordinary National Certificate
OND	Ordinary National Diploma
OPCS	Office of Population Censuses and Surveys
PSI	Policy Studies Institute
PTA	Parent Teacher Association
RG	Registrar General
SC	School Certificate
SCE	Scottish Certificate of Education
SCOTBEC	Scottish Business Education Council
SCOTEC	Scottish Technical Education Council
SLC	Scottish Leaving Certificate
SMR	Standardized Mortality Ratio
SSC	Scottish School Certificate
SSD	Social Surveys Division
SUPE	Scottish Universities Preliminary Examination
TEC	Technical Education Council
TOPS	Training Opportunities Programme
UCCA	Universities Central Council on Admissions
UGC	University Grants Committee
UK	United Kingdom
USA	United States of America
YOP	Youth Opportunities Programme
YTS	Youth Training Scheme

APPENDIX B

Key to Qualifications

There is a considerable range of qualifications, with some changes over time. In some cases educational/academic and professional/vocational qualifications are separated; in others they are combined. The following outlines the terms used in tables and text and defines their equivalents. Appendix A is a key to abbreviations used.

16+ examinations
Until 1988 these were of two main types: O level GCE/SCE and CSE. Each of these had five grades of pass, A to E and 1 to 5 respectively. Until 1975 GCE/SCE O levels were pass/fail only. Subsequently CSE grade 1 was equivalent to an O level pass.

With the exception of Table 8.3 (see below), tables in Chapter 8 use the following:

Degree or equivalent
Degree; university or other diplomas/certificates/etc., of degree standard.

Higher education below degree
Qualifications above GCE A/SCE H level but not degree level, including: non-graduate teaching and nursing qualifications, HNC/HND, BEC/TEC, SCOTBE/TEC, higher.

GCE A level or equivalent
SC, SSC, SUPE, higher; ONC/OND; BEC/TEC, SCOTBEC/TEC, national/general/ordinary level; City and Guilds, advanced/final level.

GCE O level/CSE higher grades or *equivalent*
GCE/SCE grades A, B and C, CSE grade 1; SC, SSC, SLC, SUPE, lower/ordinary level; City and Guilds, craft/ordinary level.

GCE/CSE other grades/commercial/apprenticeship
GCE/SCE grades D and E, CSE grades 2–5.

Table 8.3 uses categories designed to rank both academic and vocational qualification, gained both in Britain and overseas.

Academic qualifications are as described in the table, but qualifications other than degrees and GCEs obtained overseas have been excluded.

The division between academic and vocational qualification is artificial and almost arbitrary (Brown, 1984a), in particular non-graduate teaching qualifications are in 'GCE A level and above', while all other professional, clerical, social work and nursing qualifications are in the top vocational category.

Table 6.9 *(LFS)* refers to level of qualification defined as:

Higher qualifications
First or higher degree; other degree level qualification such as graduate membership of professional institution; BEC/TEC, SCOTBEC/TEC, higher; HNC/HND; teaching and nursing qualification.

Other qualifications
Trade apprenticeship; BEC/TEC, SCOTBEC/TEC, national or general level; ONC/OND; City and Guilds; GCE/A and O levels and equivalents; CSE; any other professional or vocational qualification.

The census presently defines a *qualified person* as one who holds at least one of the following:

(a) Higher university degrees.

(b) First degrees and all qualifications of first degree standard and all qualifications of higher degree standard (other than such degrees which appear in (a).

(c) Qualifications that in general satisfy the following:
    (i) were obtained at eighteen or over;
    (ii) are above GCE A level;
    (iii) and below first degree level.

BIBLIOGRAPHY AND AUTHOR INDEX

All these sources are followed by page references which show where they are discussed or mentioned in the text. The figures in italic refer to tables. Works are referenced, wherever possible, by author(s)/editor(s) and otherwise by title or body responsible for publication. Appendix A is a key to abbreviations used.

Abbott, P. and Sapsford, R. (1987) *Women and Social Class*. London: Tavistock. **33**, **41**, **45**, **213**, **216**, *2.3B*, *6.14*, *A/B*, *6.15*.

Abel-Smith, B., Zander, M. and Brooke, R. (1973) *Legal Problems and the Citizen*. London: Heinemann. *9.11*.

Abercrombie, N. and Urry, J. (1983) *Capital, Labour and the Middle Classes*. London: Allen and Unwin. **18**.

Abercrombie, N. and Warde, A. (1988) *Contemporary British Society*. Cambridge: Polity Press. **18**.

Abrams, M. (1951) *Social Surveys and Social Action*. London: Heinemann. **122**.

Abrams, M., Gerard, D. and Timms, N. (1985) *Values and Social Change in Britain*. London: Macmillan. **418**, **426**.

ACORN (1979) *A New Approach to Market Analysis*. London: CACI Inc. International. **7**, **111**.

Airey, C. (1984) Social and moral values. In Jowell and Airey, 1984. **33**.

Airey, C. and Brook, L. (1986) Interim report: social and moral issues. In Jowell, Witherspoon and Brook, 1986. **361**, *9.19*, *9.20*.

Alderson, M. R. (1971) Social class and the health service. *Medical Officer*, 124. **151**.

Archer, C. (1988) *Qualifications of School Leavers 1983–1987*. Bradford: City of Bradford Metropolitan Council, Education, Research and Planning section. **303**.

Ashby, A. (1988) *Analysis of Applicants for Undergraduate Study with the Open University*. Milton Keynes: Student Research Centre, The Open University. **322**.

Atkinson, A. B. (1980) *Wealth, Income and Inequality*. Oxford: Oxford University Press. **174, 419**.

Atkinson, A. B. and Harrison, A. J. (1978) *The Distribution of Personal Wealth in Britain*. Cambridge: Cambridge University Press. **175**.

Atkinson, J. (1971) *A Handbook for Interviewers*. OPCS. London: HMSO. **89**.

Banks, O. (1968, 1971) *The Sociology of Education*. London: Batsford. **274**.

Barker Lunn, J. C. (1970) *Streaming in the Primary School*. Slough: NFER. **306**.

Barker Lunn, J. C. (1972) Length of infant school and academic performance. *Educational Research*, 14. **306**.

Barnes, J. (1975) *Educational Priority*, vol. 3, DES. London: HMSO. **300**.

Barry, J. and O'Connor, D. (1983) Costs and benefits of sponsoring the unemployed. *Employment Gazette*, March. **286**.

Beal, J. F. and Dickson, S. (1974) Social differences in dental attitudes and behaviour in West Midland mothers. *Public Health*, 89. **137**.

Bendix, R. and Lipset, S. M. (1966) *Class, Status and Power*, 2nd edition. New York: Free Press; London: Routledge and Kegan Paul, 1967. **17, 421**.

Benjamin, B. (1970) *The Population Census*. London: Heinemann. **89**.

Beral, V. (1979) Reproductive mortality. *British Medical Journal*, 2. **147**.

Beral, V. (1985) Long-term effects of childbearing on health. *Journal of Epidemiology and Community Health*, 39. **147**.

Berent, J. (1954) Social mobility and marriage; a study of trends in England and Wales. In Glass, 1954. **233**.

Bilton, T. *et al.* (1987) *Introductory Sociology*, 2nd edition. London: Macmillan. **18**.

Binstock, R. and Shanas, E. (1971) *Handbook of Aging and the Social Sciences*. New York: Nostrand, Reinhold. **429**.

Birth Statistics 1984 (1985), *1985* (1986) OPCS, Series FM1, no. 12. London: HMSO. **239, 7.10**.

Black, D. (1980) *Inequalities in Health*. Report of a Research

Working Group. London: DHSS. **122, 152**.

Blaxter, M. (1987) Self-reported health. In *The Health and Lifestyle Survey*, 1987. **133, 134**.

Blishen, E. (1969) *The School that I'd Like*. Harmondsworth: Penguin. **272**.

Bone, M. (1973) *Family Planning Services in England and Wales*. OPCS, SSD for DHSS SS 467. London: HMSO. **240, 242, 360**.

Bone, M. (1977) *Pre-school Children and the Need for Day-care*. OPCS, SSD for DHSS SS 1031. London: HMSO. **254, 267**.

Bone, M. (1978) *Family Planning Services: Changes and Effects*. OPCS, SSD for DHSS SS 1055. London: HMSO. **241**.

Bone, M. and Ross, E. (1972) *The Youth Service and Similar Provision for Young People*. OPCS, SSD for DES. London: HMSO. **385**.

Bottomore, T. B. (1965) *Classes in Modern Society*. London: Allen and Unwin. **17**.

Brierley, P. (1982) *UK Christian Handbook 1983*. London: Evangelical Alliance/Bible Society/MARC Europe. **327**.

Briggs, A. (1960) The language of class in early nineteenth-century England. In Briggs and Saville, 1960. **29**.

Briggs, A. and Saville, J. (1960) *Essays in Labour History in Memory of G. D. H. Cole*. London: Macmillan. **411**.

Britain's Children (1985) OPCS, Census Guide 2. London: HMSO. **121**.

Britain's Elderly Population (1984) OPCS, Census Guide 1. London: HMSO. **120**.

Britain's Workforce (1985) OPCS, Census Guide 3. London: HMSO. **202, 6.8**.

British Labour Statistics Year Book. Published annually by DOE. London: HMSO. **64**.

The British on Holiday, 1986 (1987) London: British Tourist Authority. **380, 390**.

Brittan, A. and Maynard, M. (1984) *Sexism, Racism and Oppression*. Oxford: Blackwell. **18**.

Britten, N. (1984) Class images in a national sample of women and men. *British Journal of Sociology*, 15. **45**.

Brooks, D. and Singh, K. (1978) *Aspirations Versus Opportu-*

nities: Asian and White School Leavers in the Midlands. Walsall CRC and Leicester CRC. **300**.

Brockington, F. and Stein, Z. (1963) Admission, achievement and social class. *Universities Quarterly*, 18. **317**.

Brotherston, J. (1976) Inequality: is it inevitable? In Carter and Peel, 1976. **149**.

Brown, A. and Kiernan, K. (1981) Cohabitation in Great Britain: evidence from the General Household Survey. *Population Trends*, 25. **225, 231**.

Brown, C. (1984a) *Black and White in Britain – the Third PSI Study*. Aldershot: Gower. **78, 81, 201, 232, 236, 283, 303, 397, 3.6, 5.4, 7.27, 8.3**.

Brown, C. (1984b) Patterns of employment among black and white people in Britain. *Employment Gazette*, July. **170, 206**.

Brown, G. W. and Harris, T. (1979) *Social Origins of Depression*. London: Tavistock. **139**.

Buchan, I. and Richardson, I. (1973) *The Study of Consultations in General Practice*. Scottish Home and Health Department, Study 27. Edinburgh: HMSO. **151**.

Bulmer, M. (1977, 1984) *Sociological Research Methods*. London: Macmillan. **51, 89**.

Burghes, L. (1979) The old order. In Field, 1979. **175**.

Burnhill, P. (1981) The relationship between examination performance and social class. *Centre for Educational Sociology Collaborative Research Newsletter*, 8. **8.7**.

Burt, C. (1937) *The Backward Child*. London: University of London Press. **272**.

Burt, C. (1943) Ability and income. *British Journal of Educational Psychology*, 13. **272**.

Burton, L. (1975) Social class in the local church: a study of two Methodist churches in the Midlands. In Hill, 1975. **336**.

Butler, D. and Kavanagh, D. (1984) *The British General Election of 1983*. London: Macmillan. **8.14**.

Butler, D. and Butler, G. (1986) *British Political Facts 1900–1985*, 6th edition. London: Macmillan. **353**.

Butler, D. and Sloman, A. (1980) *British Political Facts, 1900–1979*, 5th edition. London: Macmillan. **353**.

Butler, D. and Stokes, D. (1969) *Political Change in Britain*. London: Macmillan; Harmondsworth: Penguin. **34, 74, *2.2*.**

Butler, D. and Stokes, D. (1974) *Political Change in Britain*, 2nd edition. London: Macmillan. **36, 74.**

Butler, N. R. and Bonham, D. G. (1963) *Perinatal Mortality*. London: Livingstone. **63, 125.**

Butler, N. R. and Golding, J. (1986) *From Birth to Five*. Oxford: Pergamon. **250.**

Cain, M. E. (1973) *Society and the Policeman's Role*. London: Routledge and Kegan Paul. **344.**

Cambridge University Reporter (1985) vol. CXVI, Special no. 7. ***8.15*.**

Campbell, B. (1984) *The Iron Ladies*. London: Virago. **349.**

Carstairs, V. (1966) Distribution of hospital patients by social class. *Health Bulletin*, 24. ***4.6*.**

Carstairs, V. (1981) Multiple deprivation and health state. *Community Medicine*, 3. **7.**

Carter, C. O. and Peel, J. (1976) *Equalities and Inequalities in Health*. London: Academic Press. **412.**

Cartwright, A. (1978) *Recent Trends in Family Building and in Contraception*. OPCS, Studies on Medical and Population Subjects, no. 34. London: HMSO. **242.**

Cartwright, A. (1987) Trends in family intentions and the use of contraception among recent mothers, 1967–84. *Population Trends*, 49. **242, *7.12*.**

Cartwright, A. and O'Brien, M. (1976) Social class variations in health care and in the nature of GP consultations. In Stacey, 1976. **151, 152.**

Census 1981, *see under report title*.

Chapman, A. D. (1984) Patterns of mobility among men and women in Scotland: 1930–1970. Unpublished PhD thesis, Plymouth Polytechnic. **215.**

Chester, R. and Streather, J. (1972) Cruelty in English divorce. *Journal of Marriage and Family*, 34. **229.**

Classification of Occupations (1960, 1966, 1970, 1980) Published in the year before a census. OPCS. London: HMSO. **53, 54, 55, 56, 57, 58, 60, 68, *2.6*.**

Comprehensive Education (1978) DES. London: HMSO. **307.**

Congenital Malformation Statistics (1983) OPCS, Series MB3 (1). London: HMSO. **129**.

Consumer Council (1967) *Living in a Caravan*. London: HMSO. **264**.

Conway, F. (1967) *Sampling*. London: Allen and Unwin. **85**.

Cooper, A. (1989) Theorizing gender. In Reid and Stratta, 1989. **18**.

Cooper, J. (1979) *Class*. London: Eyre Methuen. **9**.

Cottrell, A. (1984) *Social Classes in Marxist Theory*. London: Routledge and Kegan Paul. **18**.

Country of Birth, Census 1971, Great Britain (1978) Supplementary Tables (10% sample), Part 2, OPCS. London: HMSO. **3.4**.

Cox, B. D. (1987) Body measurements (heights, weights, girth, etc.). In *The Health and Lifestyle Survey*, 1987. **142**.

Cox, P. R. (1976) *Demography*, 5th edition. Cambridge: Cambridge University Press. **89**.

Coxon, A. P. M., Davies, P. M. and Jones, C. L. (1986) *Images of Social Stratification*. London: Sage. **48**.

Coxon, A. P. M. and Jones, C. L. (1974) Occupational similarities. *Quality and Quantity*, 8. **47, 48**.

Coxon, A. P. M. and Jones, C. L. (1978) *The Images of Occupational Prestige*. London: Macmillan. **48**.

Coxon, A. P. M. and Jones, C. L. (1979) *Class and Hierarchy*. London: Macmillan. **48**.

Craft, M. and Craft, A. (1983) The participation of ethnic minority pupils in further and higher education. *Educational Research*, 18. **301, 303, 304**.

CRE (1984) *Ethnic Minorities and the 1983 General Election*. London: CRE. **349**.

Criminal Statistics England and Wales 1986 (1987) Command 233, Home Office. London: HMSO. **340**.

Crompton, R. and Mann, M. (1986) *Gender and Stratification*. Cambridge: Polity Press. **18, 433**.

Cullen, M. J. (1975) *The Statistical Movement in Early Victorian Britain*. London: Harvester Press; New York: Barnes and Noble. **30**.

Dale, A., Gilbert, N. and Arber, S. (1985) Integrating women into class theory. *Sociology*, 19. **49**.

Dale, R. R. (1963) Reflections on the influence of social class on student performance at university. In Halmos, 1963. **317**.

Davie, R., Butler, M. and Goldstein, H. (1972) *From Birth to Seven*. London: Longman. **125, 245, 246, 253, 270,** *7.14, 7.15, 7.16, 7.18, 8.6*.

Davis, H. H. (1979) *Beyond Class Images*. London: Croom Helm. **48**.

Dearnaley, E. J. and Fletcher, M. H. (1968) Cubs and Brownies – social class, intelligence and interests. *Educational Research*, 10. **385**.

Definitions, Census 1981, Great Britain (1982) OPCS. London: HMSO. **80, 89**.

Demographic Review 1977 (1979) A report on population in Great Britain. OPCS, Series DR 1. London: HMSO. **235**.

Demographic Review 1984 (1987) A report on population in Great Britain. OPCS, Series DR 2. London: HMSO. *7.8, 7.9*.

Donaldson, L. (1971) Social class and the polytechnics. *Higher Education Review*, 4. **323**.

Douglas, J. W. B. (1948) *Maternity in Great Britain*. London: Oxford University Press. **246**.

Douglas, J. W. B. (1964) *The Home and School*. London: MacGibbon and Kee. **291**.

Douglas, J. W. B., Ross, J. M., Hammond, W. A. and Mulligan, D. G. (1966) Delinquency and social class. *British Journal of Criminology*, 6. **340,** *9.8*.

Douglas, J. W. B., Ross, J. M. and Simpson, H. R. (1968) *All Our Future*. London: Peter Davies. **294,** *9.8*.

Driver, G. (1980) *Beyond Underachievement*. London: CRE. **302**.

Driver, G. and Ballard, R (1979) Comparing performance in multi-racial schools: South Asian pupils at 16+. *New Community*, 8. **300**.

Dunnell, K. (1979) *Family Formation 1976*. OPCS, SSD. London: HMSO. **223, 242**.

Durkheim, E. (1952) *Suicide*. London: Routledge and Kegan Paul. **272**.

Economic Activity, Census 1981, Great Britain (1984) OPCS. London: HMSO. *3.1, 3.2, A/B, 3.7, 3.8, 3.9, 3.10, 3.11, 8.21, Fig.3.1*.

Education: A Framework for Expansion (1972) London: HMSO. **288**.

Education for All (1985) Command 9453 (The Swann Report). Report of Committee of Inquiry into the Education of Children from Ethnic Minority Groups. London: HMSO. 77, **275**, **300**, **304**, *8.11*.

Education Statistics for the United Kingdom, 1984 (1985) DES. London: HMSO. **309**, *8.15*.

Education Statistics for the United Kingdom, 1986 (1986) DES. London: HMSO. **286**.

Education Statistics for the United Kingdom, 1987 (1987) DES. London: HMSO. *8.10*.

Education Tables (10% sample) (1966) Census 1961 England and Wales, General Register Office. London: HMSO. **276**.

Edwards, E. G. and Roberts, I. J. (1980) British higher education: long-term trends in student enrolment. *Higher Education Review*, 12. **318**, *8.20*.

Eliot, T. S. (1932) *Sweeney Agonistes: Fragments of an Aristophanic Melodrama*. London: Faber. **122**.

Employment Gazette (1982) November. DOE. London: HMSO. **205**, *6.10*

English Life Tables 14 (1987) OPCS, Series DS no. 7. London: HMSO. *4.16*.

EOC (1978) *Second Annual Report 1977*. London: HMSO. **5**.

EOC (1980) Women and government statistics. *EOC Research Bulletin*, no. 5. Manchester: EOC. **14**, **423**.

EOC (1983) Sex differences in sickness absence from work: evidence from the General Household Survey and other sources. Manchester: EOC. **199**.

Essen, J. and Ghodsian, M. (1979) The children of immigrants: school performance. *New Community*, 8. **300**.

Family Expenditure Survey Report for 1986 (Revised) (1988) DOE. London: HMSO. **65**, **88**, **172**, **186**, *5.12*, *5.13*, *5.14*.

Fenner, N. (1987) Leisure, exercise and work. In *The Health and Lifestyle Survey*, 1987. **142**, **143**.

Field, F. (1973) *Unequal Britain*. London: Arrow Books. **400**.

Field, F. (1979) *The Wealth Report*. London: Routledge and Kegan Paul. **412**.

Field, F. (1983) *The Wealth Report 2*. London: Routledge and Kegan Paul. **427**.

15–18. (1960) (The Crowther Report) Central Advisory Council for Education. London: HMSO. **306**.

Fitzgerald, M. (1984) *Political Parties and Black People*. London: The Runnymede Trust. **349**.

Fitzgerald, M. (1987) *Black People and Party Politics in Britain*. London: The Runnymede Trust. **349**.

Fogelman, K. R. and Goldstein, H. (1976) Social factors associated with changes in educational attainment between 7 and 11 years of age. *Educational Studies*, 2. **291**.

Fogelman, K., Goldstein, H., Essen, J. and Ghodsian, M. (1978) Patterns of attainment. *Educational Studies*, 4. **291**.

Fogelman, K. and Gorbach, P. (1978) Age of starting school and attainment at school. *Educational Research*, 21. **305**.

Forster, D. P. (1976) Social class differences in sickness and general practitioner consultations. *Health Trends*, 8. **151**.

Gaine, J. J. (1975) *Young Adults Today and the Future of the Faith*. Upholland: Secretariat for Non-Believers. **326, 338**.

Gallup Polls (1977) *BBC Survey – Sexual Attitudes of Young People*. London: Social Surveys (Gallup Polls) Ltd. **362**.

Gallup Polls (1979) *Report No. 662*. London: Social Surveys (Gallup Polls) Ltd. **333**.

Gavron, H. (1966) *The Captive Wife*. London: Routledge and Kegan Paul. **223**.

General Household Survey, Introductory Report (1973) OPCS Series GHS, 1. London: HMSO. **90, 263, 264, 267**.

GHS 1972 (1975) OPCS Series GHS, 2. London: HMSO. **264, *8.5***.

GHS 1976 (1978) OPCS Series GHS, 6. London: HMSO. ***8.12***.

GHS 1977 (1979) OPCS Series GHS, 7. London: HMSO. **198, 262, 264, 265, 367**.

GHS 1978 (1980) OPCS Series GHS, 8. London: HMSO. **277, 367, 381**.

GHS 1979 (1981) OPCS Series GHS, 9. London: HMSO. ***4.5***.

GHS 1980 (1982) OPCS Series GHS, 10. London: HMSO. **133, 282, *4.4*, *7.29***.

GHS 1981 (1983) OPCS Series GHS, 11. London: HMSO. **133, 136, 151, 199, 367, *6.3*, *10.3***.

GHS 1982 (1984) OPCS Series GHS, 12. London: HMSO. **382, *4.5*, *7.26*, *7.29***.

GHS 1983 (1985) OPCS Series GHS, 13. London: HMSO.**143, 199, 206, 364, 382, *4.10*, *6.6*, *6.7*, *6.11*, *7.2*, *10.10***.

GHS 1984 (1986) OPCS Series GHS, 14. London: HMSO. **90, 130, 145, 146, 243, *4.4*, *4.8*, *4.9***.

GHS 1985 (1987) OPCS Series GHS, 15. London: HMSO. **82, 90, 130, 172, 225, 231, 260. *4.4*, *4.5*, *7.24*, *7.25*, *7.27*, *8.1*, *A/B*, *8.2*, *A/B*, *8.4*, *8.9***.

George, V. (1970) *Foster Care*. London: Routledge and Kegan Paul. **244**.

Gerard, D. (1985) Religious attitudes and values. In Abrams, Gerard and Timms, 1985. **333**.

Gibson, C. (1974) Divorce and social class in England and Wales. *British Journal of Sociology*, 25. **226**.

Giddens, A. (1973) *The Class Structure of the Advanced Societies*. London: Hutchinson. **15, 18**.

Giddens, A. and Mackenzie, G. (1982) *Social Class and the Division of Labour. Essays in Honour of Ilya Neustadt*. Cambridge: Cambridge University Press. **18**.

Glass, D. V. (1954) *Social Mobility in Britain*. London: Routledge and Kegan Paul. **32, 33, 208, 410, 424**.

Goldberg, E. M. and Morrison, S. L. (1963) Schizophrenia and social class. *British Journal of Psychiatry*, 109. **139**.

Goldsmith, O. (1770) *The Traveller*. London: Carnan and Newbery. **325**.

Goldthorpe, J. H. (1983) Women and class analysis: in defence of the conventional view. *Sociology*, 17. **45**.

Goldthorpe, J. H. and Hope, K. (1974) *The Social Grading of Occupations: a New Approach and Scale*. Oxford: Clarendon Press. **70**.

Goldthorpe, J. H., Llewellyn, C. and Payne, C. (1980) *Social Mobility and Class Structure in Modern Britain*. Oxford: Clarendon Press. **71, 208, 212, *6.12*, *A/B*, *6.13***.

Goldthorpe, J. H., Llewellyn, C. and Payne, C. (1987) *Social Mobility and Class Structure in Modern Britain*, 2nd edition. Oxford: Clarendon Press. **208, 212, 213**.

Goldthorpe, J. H., Lockwood, D., Bechhofer, F. and Platt, J. (1969) *The Affluent Worker*. Cambridge: Cambridge University Press. **43, 67, 400**.

Goldthorpe, J. H., Payne, C. and Llewellyn, C. (1978) Trends in class mobility. *Sociology*, 12. **212**.

Gorer, G. (1971) *Sex and Marriage in England Today*. London: Nelson/Panther. **223**.

Gray, P. G. and Russell, R. (1962) *The Housing Situation in 1960*. London: HMSO. **264**.

Gray, P. G., Todd, J. E., Slack, G. L. and Bulman, J. S. (1970) *Adult Dental Health in England and Wales in 1968*. OPCS SSD for DHSS. London: HMSO. **137**.

Greenhalgh, C. and Stewart, M. B. (1982) *Occupational Status and Mobility of Men and Women*. Warwick Economic Papers, no. 211. Warwick: University of Warwick. **215**.

Grey, E. (1971) *A Survey of Adoption in Great Britain*. Home Office Research Studies, 10. London: HMSO. **244**.

Grimes, J. A. (1978) The probability of admission to a mental hospital or unit. *In-Patient Statistics from the Mental Health Inquiry for England 1975*. **138**.

Hall, J. and Jones, D. C. (1950) The social grading of occupations. *British Journal of Sociology*, 1. **46, 66**.

Halmos, P. (1963) Sociological studies in British university education. *Sociological Review*, monograph 7. **415, 421, 426**.

Halsey, A. H. (1972, 1988) *Trends in British Society since 1900*. 1st and 2nd editions. London: Macmillan. **14, 20**.

Halsey, A. H. (1978, 1981, 1986) *Change in British Society*. 1st, 2nd and 3rd editions. Oxford: Oxford University Press. **20**.

Halsey, A. H., Heath, A. F. and Ridge, J. M. (1980) *Origins and Destinations*. Oxford: Clarendon Press. **71, 311, 319, 8.13**.

Hanks, P. (1979) *Collins Dictionary of the English Language*. London: Collins. **75, 219**.

Harbury, C. D. and McMahon, P. C. (1980) Inheritance and the characteristics of top wealth leavers in Britain. In Atkinson, 1980. **176**.

Hare, E. H., Price, J. S. and Slater, E. (1972) Parental social class and psychiatric patients. *British Journal of Psychiatry*, 121. **139**.

Harris, J. and Jarvis, P. (1979) *Counting to Some Purpose*. London: Methodist Church Home Mission Division. **336**.

Harrison, G. A. and Boyce, A. J. (1972) *The Structure of Human Populations*. Oxford: Clarendon Press. **431**.

Harrop, M. (1980) Popular conceptions of social mobility. *Sociology*, 14. **218**.

Hart, J. T. (1971) The inverse care law. *The Lancet*, 1, 405–12. **149**.

Haskey, J. (1983) Social class patterns of marriage. *Population Trends*, 34. **222, 233, 7.1, 7.2**.

Haskey, J. (1984) Social class and socio-economic differentials in divorce in England and Wales. *Population Studies*, 38. **227, 7.3**.

Haskey, J. (1986a) One-parent families in Great Britain. *Population Trends*, 45. **231**.

Haskey, J. (1986b) Grounds for divorce in England and Wales – a social and demographic analysis. *Journal of Biosocial Science*, 18. **229, 7.4**.

Haskey, J. (1987) Social class differentials in remarriage after divorce: results from a forward linkage study. *Population Trends*, 47. **230, 7.5**.

Haskey, J. and Coleman, D. (1986) Cohabitation before marriage: a comparison of information from marriage registration and the General Household Survey. *Population Trends*, 43. **225**.

Hatch, S. and Reich, D. (1970) Unsuccessful Sandwiches? *New Society*, 15, 389. **322, 323**.

The Health and Lifestyle Survey (1987). London: Health Promotion Research Trust. **133, 138, 142, 143, 411, 414, 416, 4.4, 4.7**.

Health and Personal Social Services Statistics for England 1986 (1986) DHSS. London: HMSO. **138**.

Heath, A. and Britten, N. (1984) Women's jobs do make a difference. *Sociology*, 18. **49**.

Heath, A., Jowell, R. and Curtice, J. (1985) *How Britain Votes*. Oxford: Pergamon. **72, 346, 348, 9.14**.

Higher Education (1963) (The Robbins Report) Command 2154. London: HMSO. **313, 315, 317, 322, 8.8, 8.16, 8.17, 8.18**.

Hill, M. (1975) *A Sociological Yearbook of Religion in Britain*, 8. London: Student Christian Movement. **412**.

Hodge, R. W., Trieman, D. J. and Rossi, P. H. (1966) A comparative study of occupational prestige. In Bendix and Lipset, 1966. **47**.

Holman, R. (1975) *Trading in Children*. London: Routledge and Kegan Paul. **244**.

Home Office Research Unit (1978) *Research Bulletin*, 5. London: HMSO. **339**.

Hospital In-Patient Inquiry 1983, Summary Tables (1985) DHSS/OPCS Series MB4 no. 22. London: HMSO. **141, 153**.

Household Composition Tables (10% Sample), Census 1971, England and Wales (1975) OPCS. London: HMSO. **7.1**.

Household and Family Composition, Census 1981, England and Wales (1985) OPCS. London: HMSO. **5.5**.

Husband, C. (1984) *Race in Britain, Continuity and Change*, 2nd edition. London: Hutchinson Educational. **18**.

Hymns, Ancient and Modern (1950) Revised 1950 edition; original 1861. London: Clowes. **219**.

Immigrant Mortality in England and Wales 1970–78 (1984) OPCS Studies on Medical and Population Subjects, no. 47. London: HMSO. **4.15**.

In-Patient Statistics from the Mental Health Inquiry for England 1975 (1978) DHSS. London: HMSO. **138**.

In-Patient Statistics from the Mental Health Inquiry for England 1982 (1985) DHSS. London: HMSO. **138**.

James, W. P. T. (1979) *Research on Obesity*. DHSS Series no. 23. London: HMSO. **142**.

Jenkins, R. (1985) Sex differences in minor psychiatric morbidity. *Psychological Medicine*, monograph supplement, 7. **139**.

Jenkins, R. and Clare, A. W. (1985) Women and mental illness. *British Medical Journal*, 1. **139**.

Jones, D. C. (1934) *Social Survey of Merseyside*. Liverpool: Liverpool University Press. **66**.

Joseph, K. and Sumption, J. (1979) *Equality*. London: John Murray. **180**.

Jowell, R. (1984) Introducing the survey. In Jowell and Airey, 1984. **354**.

Jowell, R. and Airey, C. (1984) *British Social Attitudes: the*

1984 Report. Aldershot: Gower. **409, 421**.

Jowell, R. and Witherspoon, S. (1985) *British Social Attitudes: the 1985 Report.* Aldershot: Gower. **362**

Jowell, R., Witherspoon, S. and Brook, L. (1986) *British Social Attitudes: the 1986 Report.* Aldershot: Gower. **409**.

Kahan, M., Butler, D. and Stokes, D. (1966) On the analytical division of social class. *British Journal of Sociology,* 17. **33, 38**.

Kelsall, R. K. (1963) Survey of all graduates. In Halmos, 1963. **317**.

Kelsall, R. K., Kelsall, H.M. and Chisholm, L. (1984) *Stratification: an Essay on Class and Inequality,* 2nd edition. London: Longmans. **19**.

Kelsall, R. K., Poole, A. and Kuhn, A. (1972) *Graduates: the Sociology of an Elite.* London: Methuen. **317, 322, *8.19***.

Kiernan, K. (1980) *Patterns of Family Formation and Dissolution in England and Wales in Recent Years.* OPCS Occasional Paper 19/2. London: HMSO. **225**.

Kipling, R. (1902) 'The Wage Slaves', reprinted in *Rudyard Kipling's Verse.* London: Hodder and Stoughton, 1940. **191**.

Knight, I. (1984) *The Heights and Weights of Adults in Great Britain.* OPCS SS 1138. London: HMSO. **142**.

Labour Force Survey 1983 (1985) OPCS Series LFS, no. 3. London: HMSO. **286**.

Labour Force Survey 1985 (1987) OPCS Series LFS, no. 5. London: HMSO. **116, 191, 201, 203, 262, *3.13, A/B, 6.9, 7.25***.

Lambert, L. and Streather, J. (1980) *Children in Changing Families.* London: Macmillan. **244**.

Leete, R. (1979) *Changing Patterns of Family Formation and Dissolutions in England and Wales 1964–76.* OPCS, Studies on Medical and Population Subjects, no. 10. London: HMSO. **220, 221, 233**.

Leete, R. and Anthony, S. (1979) Divorce and remarriage: a record linkage study. *Population Trends,* 16. **231**.

Leete, R. and Fox, J. (1977) Registrar General's social classes: origins and uses. *Population Trends,* 8. **53**.

Le Grand, J. (1978) The distribution of public expenditure: the case of health care. *Economica,* 45. **149, 150, *4.11***.

Le Grand, J. (1982) *The Strategy of Equality*. London: Allen and Unwin. **152, 399**.

Little, A. (1981) Education and race relations in the United Kingdom. In Nisbet and Hoyle, 1981. **299**.

Lomas, G. B. G. and Monck, E. (1977) *The Coloured Population of Great Britain*. London: The Runnymede Trust. **100, 3.5**.

Maby, C. (1981) Black British literacy. *Education Research*, 23. **300**.

McCrossan, L. (1984) *A Handbook for Interviewers*. OPCS. London: HMSO. **90**.

McDowall, M. E. (1985) *Occupational Reproductive Epidemiology*. OPCS Studies on Medical and Population Subjects, no. 50. London: HMSO. **4.1**.

Macfarlane, A. (1979) Child deaths from accidents: place of accident. *Population Trends*, 30. **129**.

Macfarlane, A. (1980) Official statistics and women's health and illness. In EOC, 1980. **124, 139**.

Macfarlane, A. and Mugford, M. (1984) *Birth Counts: Statistics of Pregnancy and Childbirth*. National Perinatal Epidemiology Unit and OPCS. London: HMSO. **4.1**.

McGregor, O. R. (1957) *Divorce in Britain*. London: Heinemann. **226**.

McIntosh, M. E. and Woodley, A. (1974) The Open University and second chance education. *Paedagogica Europaea*, 9. **8.23**.

McKay, D. L. and Reid, G. L. (1972) Redundancy, unemployment and manpower policy. *Economic Journal*, 82. **206**.

McNeil, P. (1985) *Research Methods*. London: Allen and Unwin. **89**.

McPherson, A., and Willms, J. W. (1987) Equalization and improvement: some effects of comprehensive reorganization in Scotland. *Sociology*, 21. **275**.

McPherson, A., and Willms, J. W. (1988) Comprehensive schooling is better and fairer. *Forum*, 30. **275**.

McPherson, B. D. (1983) *Aging as a Social Process*. Toronto: Butterworths. **19**.

Mack, J. and Lansley, S. (1985) *Poor Britain*. London: Allen and Unwin. **183, 5.11**.

Madeley, R. J. (1978) Relating child health service to needs by use of simple epidemiology. *Public Health*, 92(1). **7**.

Main, B. and Raffe, D. (1983) The transition from school to work. *British Educational Research Journal*, 9. **286**.

Marriage and Divorce Statistics 1985 (1986) OPCS Series FM2, no. 12. London: HMSO. **220, 227, 230**.

Marsh, C. (1982) *The Survey Method*. London: Allen and Unwin. **89**.

Marsh, D. C. (1965) *The Changing Structure of England and Wales 1871–1951*. London: Routledge and Kegan Paul. **20**.

Martin, F. M. (1954) Some subjective aspects of social stratification. In Glass, 1954. **32, 33**.

Martin, J. (1978) *Infant Feeding 1975: Attitudes and Practice in England and Wales*. OPCS SS 1064 for DHSS. London: HMSO. **246**.

Martin, J. and Monk, J. (1982) *Infant Feeding in 1980*. OPCS SSD. London: HMSO. **246, 7.13**.

Martin, J. and Roberts, C. (1984) *Women and Employment: a Lifetime Perspective*. DOE/OPCS Studies on Medical and Population Subjects, no. 47. London: HMSO. **215**.

Marwick, A. (1980) *Class, Image and Reality*. London: Collins. **30**.

Marx, K. and Engels, F. (1848) *Manifesto of the Communist Party*. Moscow: Foreign Languages Publishing House. **18**.

Matthijsen, M. A. J. M. (1959) Catholic intellectual emancipation in the Western countries of mixed religion. *Social Compass*, 6. **327**.

Mays, J. B. (1970) *Crime and its Treatment*. London: Longman. **338**.

Miller, W. L. (1983) *The Survey Method in the Social and Political Sciences*. London: Frances Pinter. **89**.

Mingione, E. and Redclift, N. (1985) *Beyond Employment*. Oxford: Blackwell. **426**.

Monk, D. (1970) *Social Grading on the National Readership Survey*. London: Joint Industry Committee for National Readership Surveys. **6, 27**.

Monk, D. (1985) *Social Grading on the National Readership Survey*. London: Joint Industry Committee for National Readership Surveys. **73**.

Monthly Index of Earnings. DOE. London: HMSO. **165**.

Morbidity Statistics from General Practice 1981–82 (1986) OPCS Series MB5, 1. London: HMSO. **138, 153**.

Morison, M. (1986) *Methods in Sociology*. London: Longman. **89**.

Morris, J. N. (1975) *The Uses of Epidemiology*, 3rd edition. London: HMSO. **163**.

Mortality Statistics 1985a (1987) OPCS Series DH1, no. 17. London: HMSO. **138, 3.12**.

Mortality Statistics 1985b, Perinatal and infant: social and biological factors (1987) OPCS Series DH3, no. 18. London: HMSO. **4.2**.

Mortality Statistics 1985c, Childhood (1987) OPCS Series DH3, no. 19. London: HMSO. **4.2**.

Mortality Statistics 1985d, Cause (1987) OPCS Series DH2, no. 12. London: HMSO. **4.3**.

Moulin, L. de Saint (1968) Social class and religious behaviour. *Clergy Review*, 53. **334, 9.6**.

Murgatroyd, L. (1982) Gender and occupational stratification. *Sociological Review*, 30. **49**.

Musgrove, F., Cooper, B., Derrick, T., Foy, J. M. and Willig, C. J. (1967) *Preliminary Studies of a Technological University*. Mimeograph. Bradford: Bradford University. **322**.

National Dwelling and Housing Survey (1979) Department of Environment. London: HMSO. **77, 81, 7.27**.

National Opinion Polls (1972) *Bulletin No. 109*. London: NOP Market Research Ltd. **32, 33, 329, 2.4**.

NOP (1975a) *Political Social Economic Review*, 1. **352, 9.16**.

NOP (1975b) *Political Social Economic Review*, 3. **351**.

NOP (1977) *Political Social Economic Review*, 13. **351, 9.16**.

NOP (1978) *Political Social Economic Review*, 16. **348, 2.3A, 9.2**.

A National Health Service (1944) Command 6502. London: HMSO. **146**.

National Readership Survey 1975 (1976) London: JICNARS. **378**.

National Readership Survey 1979 (1980) London: JICNARS. **386**.

National Readership Survey 1987 (1988) London: JICNARS. **10.6, 10.7, 10.13**.

New Earnings Survey 1979 (1980) Part D, Analysis by Occupation, DOE. London: HMSO. **166**.

New Earnings Survey 1987 (1988) Part D, Analysis by Occupation. DOE. London: HMSO. **166, 5.1, 6.1, 6.2**.

Newfield, J. G. H. (1963) Some factors related to the academic performance of British university students. In Halmos, 1963. **317**.

Newson, J. and Newson, E. (1963) *Infant Care in an Urban Community*. London: Allen and Unwin. **245, 7.23**.

Newson, J. and Newson, E. (1968) *Four Years Old in an Urban Community*. London: Allen and Unwin; Harmondsworth: Penguin (1970). **25, 245, 252, 7.17, 7.19, 7.23**.

Newson, J. and Newson, E. (1976) *Seven Years Old in the Home Environment*. London: Allen and Unwin. **245, 257, 7.20, 7.21, 7.22, 7.23**.

Newson, J. and Newson, E. (1977) *Perspectives on School at Seven Years Old*. London: Allen and Unwin. **245**.

Nisbet, S. and Hoyle, E. (1981) *World Yearbook of Education*. London: Kogan Page. **422**.

North, G. (1948) *Matters of Life and Death*. London: HMSO. **1**.

Northern Ireland Census, 1981. Religion Tables (1984) OPCS. Belfast: HMSO. **207, 327**.

Novitski, E. (1977) *Human Genetics*. London: Collier Macmillan. **113**.

Oakley, A. (1972) *Sex, Gender and Society*. London: Temple Smith. **18**.

Oakley, A. (1981) *Subject Women*. Oxford: Blackwell. **18**.

Occupational Mortality (1971) The RG's *Decennial Supplement for England and Wales 1961*. OPCS. London: HMSO. **57, 155**.

Occupational Mortality (1978) The RG's *Decennial Supplement for England and Wales 1970–72*. OPCS Series DS, 1. London: HMSO. **153, 161, 4.3, 4.16**.

Occupational Mortality (1986) The RG's *Decennial Supplement for England and Wales 1970–72*. OPCS Series DS, 2. London: HMSO. **153, 4.12, 4.13, 4.14**.

OPCS (1987) *The Family*. Occasional Paper 31 (British Society for Population Studies, Conference papers). London: HMSO. **219**.

Open University (1979) *Analysis of Applications for Under-*

graduate Study with the Open University 1980. Milton Keynes: The Open University. **323**.

Orwell, G. (1937) *The Road to Wigan Pier*. London: Gollancz. **19, 364**.

Osborn, A. F., Butler, N. R. and Morris, A. C. (1984) *The Social Life of Britain's Five Year Olds*. London: Routledge and Kegan Paul. **260**.

Osborn, A. F. and Morris, T. C. (1979) The rationale for a composite index of social class and its evaluation. *British Journal of Sociology*, 30. **7.49**.

Ossowski, S. (1963) *Class Structure in the Social Consciousness*. London: Routledge and Kegan Paul. **29**.

Oxford University Gazette (1984) Supplement (1) to no. 3966. **8.15**.

Pahl, R. and Wallace, C. (1985) Household work strategies in economic recession. In Mingione and Redclift, 1985. **49**.

Penrose, L. S. (1973) *Outline of Human Genetics*, 3rd edition. London: Hutchinson. **113**.

People in Britain (1980) Census Research Unit, Dept of Geography, University of Durham OPCS and General Registry Office (Scotland). London: HMSO. **115**.

Phillips, D. (1985) Participation and political values. In Abrams, Gerard and Timms, 1985. **352**.

Pierce, R. M. (1963) Marriage in the fifties. *Sociological Review*, 11. **223**.

Platt, J. (1971) Variations in answers to different questions of perceptions of class. *Sociological Review*, 19. **43**.

Playford, C. and Pond, C. (1983) The right to be unequal: inequality in incomes. In Field, 1983. **171**.

Pond, C. (1983) Wealth and the two nations. In Field, 1983. **174, 175, 176, 179**.

Prais, S. J. and Schmool, M. (1975) The social-class structure of Anglo-Jewry, 1961. *Jewish Journal of Sociology*, 17. **337, 9.7**.

Prison Statistics England and Wales 1986 (1987) Command 210. Home Office. London: HMSO. **341**.

The Public Schools Commission: First Report (1968) DES. London: HMSO. **311**.

Pulzer, P. G. J. (1968) *British Government and Politics*. London:

Allen and Unwin. **325**.

Pumfrey, P. D. (1975) Season of birth, special educational treatment and selection procedures within an LEA. *Research in Education*, 14. **306**.

Registered Blind and Partially Sighted Persons at 31 March 1986 England (1987) DHSS. London: HMSO. **135**.

Reid, I. (1969) An analysis of social factors in children's educational experience between 11 and 17 years of age in two LEA areas. Unpublished MA thesis, University of Liverpool. **299**.

Reid, I. (1977a) *Social Class Differences in Britain*, 1st edition. London: Open Books. **1**.

Reid, I. (1977b) Your chance to have a say. *Homes and Gardens*, 4. **33**.

Reid, I. (1978a) *Sociological Perspectives on School and Education*. London: Open Books. **274**.

Reid, I. (1978b) What you had to say about life in Britain today. *Homes and Gardens*, 9 (59). **33**, *2.4*.

Reid, I. (1979) Sunday schools as socialization agencies. In White and Mufti, 1979. **337**.

Reid, I. (1980a) *Sunday Schools: A Suitable Case for Treatment*. London: Chester House. **337**.

Reid, I. (1980b) Teachers and social class. *Westminster Studies in Education*, 3. **42**.

Reid, I. (1981) *Social Class Differences in Britain*, 2nd edition. Oxford: Basil Blackwell. **1**, **291**, **346**.

Reid, I. (1986a) *The Sociology of School and Education*. London: Fontana. **274**.

Reid, I. (1986b) Who's afraid of social class? *Education and Society*, 4. **276**, **303**.

Reid, I. (1989) Vital statistics. In Reid and Stratta, 1989. **147**, **153**.

Reid, I. and Stratta, E. (1989) *Sex Differences in Britain*, 2nd edition. Aldershot: Gower. **17**, **414**, **430**, **431**, **432**, **433**.

Reid, I. and Wormald, E. (1982) *Sex Differences in Britain*. Oxford: Basil Blackwell. **17**.

Report of the Committee on the Working of the Abortion Act (1974) vol. 2. Command 5579–1. London: HMSO. **243**.

Rex, J. (1983) *Race Relations in Sociological Theory*, 2nd edition. London: Routledge and Kegan Paul. **18**.

BIBLIOGRAPHY AND AUTHOR INDEX

Rex, J. (1986) *Race and Ethnicity*. Milton Keynes: Open University Press. **18**.

Rex, J. and Mason, D. (1986) *Theories of Race and Ethnic Relations*. Cambridge: Cambridge University Press. **18**, **434**.

Riley, M. (1971) Age strata in social systems. In Binstock and Shanas, 1971. **19**.

Roberts, H. (1981) *Women, Health and Reproduction*. London: Routledge and Kegan Paul. **148**.

Roberts, H. (1987) *Women and Social Classification*. Brighton: Wheatsheaf. **49**.

Roberts, K., Cook, F. G., Clark, S. C. and Semeonoff, E. (1977) *The Fragmentary Class Structure*. London: Heinemann. **18**, **33**, **36**, *2.2*.

Roberts, K., Noble, M. and Duggan, J. (1983) Young, black and out of work. In Troyna and Smith, 1983. **302**.

Rogers, R. (1980) The myth of 'independent' schools. *New Statesman*, 4 January. **309**.

Rosser, C. and Harris, C. C. (1965) *The Family and Social Change*. London: Routledge and Kegan Paul. **33**.

Routh, G. (1965) *Occupation and Pay in Great Britain 1906–60*. Cambridge: Cambridge University Press. **20**, **57**.

Routh, G. (1980) *Occupation and Pay in Great Britain 1906–79*. London: Macmillan. **20**, **57**, *5.2*.

Royal College of Psychiatrists (1986) *Alcohol: Our Favourite Drug*. London: RCP. **145**.

Royal Commission on the Distribution of Income and Wealth (1979) Report no. 7, Command 7595; Report no. 8, Command 7679. London: HMSO. **170**, **175**, **397**, *5.3*.

Royal Commission on Legal Services: Final Report (1979) vol. 2, Command 7648–1. London: HMSO. **344**, *9.10*, *9.12*.

Royal Commission on the National Health Service: Report (1979) Command 7615. London: HMSO. **157**.

Royal Commission on the Press: Attitudes to the Press (1977) Command 6810–3. London: HMSO. **378**.

Runciman, W. G. (1964) Embourgeoisement, self-rated class and party preference. *Sociological Review*, 12. **33**.

Runciman, W. G. (1966) *Relative Deprivation and Social Justice*. London: Routledge and Kegan Paul. **393**.

Rutter, M., Maughan, B., Mortimore, P., Ouston, J., with

Smith, A. (1979) *Fifteen Thousand Hours*. London: Open Books. **294, 340**.

Salaman, G. (1972) Major theories of stratification. Unit 9 in D283, *Sociological Perspectives, Block 3, Stratification and Social Class*. Milton Keynes: The Open University. **17**.

Sampson, A. (1982) *The Changing Anatomy of Britain*. London: Hodder and Stoughton. **20, *8.14***.

Searle, P. M. A. and Stibbs, A. (1985) The participation of ethnic minority students in post-graduate teacher training. *Collected Original Researches in Education* (CORE), 10. **321**.

Seglow, J., Pringle, M. K. and Wedge, P. (1972) *Growing Up Adopted*. Slough: NFER. **244**.

Shaw, C. (1988) Latest estimates of ethnic minority populations. *Population Trends*, 51. **117, *3.14*, *7.2***.

Sillitoe, K. (1969) *Planning for Leisure*. Government Social Survey. London: HMSO. **61, 367, 385, *9.5***.

Sillitoe, K. (1987) *Developing Questions on Ethnicity and Related Topics for the Census*. OPCS Occasional Paper 36. London: HMSO. **79, 80, 81**.

Silver, H. (1973) *Equal Opportunity in Education*. London: Methuen. **272**.

Skeggs, B. (1989) Gender differences in education. In Reid and Stratta, 1989. **297**.

Small Area Statistics (Ward Library) (1985) Census 1981. England and Wales, OPCS. London: HMSO. **111**.

Small Area Statistics, Census 1981. OPCS London: HMSO. ***Fig. 3.2***.

Smee, C. H. and Stern, J. (1978) *The Unemployed in a Period of High Unemployment*, Government Economic Service, working paper no. 11, Economic Adviser's Office, DHSS. London: HMSO. **206**.

Smith, D. J. (1980) Unemployment and racial minority groups. *Employment Gazette*, June. **206**.

Social Security Statistics 1986 (1986) DHSS. London: HMSO. **138**.

Social Trends 15 (1985) CSS. London: HMSO. **297**.

Social Trends 16 (1986) CSS. London: HMSO. **169, 182, *5.6*, *10.1*, *10.2***.

Social Trends 17 (1987) CSS. London: HMSO. **148**, **219**, **226**, **231**, *4.10*, *5.7*, **7.27**.

Socio-Economic Group Tables (1966) Census 1961, England and Wales, OPCS. London: HMSO. *8.18*, *8.19*.

Sparks, J. (1986) Marital conditions estimates 1971–85: a new series. OPCS. *Population Trends*, 45. London: HMSO. **231**.

Stacey, M. (1976) The sociology of the National Health Service. *Sociological Review Monograph*, 22. **413**.

Stanworth, M. (1984) Women and class analysis: a reply to John Goldthorpe. *Sociology*, 18. **45**.

Stanworth, P. and Giddens, A. (1974) *Elites and Power in British Society*. Cambridge: Cambridge University Press. **434**.

Statistics of Education 1961, Supplement (1962) Ministry of Education. London: HMSO. **294**.

Statistics of Education 1979 (1981) DES. London: HMSO. **289**.

Statistics of Education 1982 (1984) DES. London: IIMSO. **321**.

Statistical Bulletin 13/84 (1984) DES. London: HMSO. **298**.

Statistical Review of England and Wales 1967 (1971) Part 3, Commentary. RG. London: HMSO. **226**, **233**.

Stratta, E. (1989) Involvement in crime. In Reid and Stratta, 1989. **340**.

Stevenson, T. H. C. (1928) The vital statistics of wealth and poverty. *Journal of Royal Statistical Society*, 91. **30**, **46**, **53**, **122**.

Stone, J. (1985) *Racial Conflict in Contemporary Society*. London: Fontana Press. **18**.

Stott, D. H. (1963) *The Social Adjustment of Children*. London: London University Press. **250**.

Target Group Index (1987) Vols 27, 29, 30, 32 and 33. London: British Market Research Bureau. **389**, *5.8*, *7.28*, *10.8*, *10.9*. *10.11*, *10.12*, *10.14*, *10.15*, *10.16*, *10.17A*.

Tawney, R. H. (1913) Poverty as an industrial problem. In *Memorandum on the Problem of Poverty*. London: William Morris Press. **164**.

Tawney, R. H. (1931) *Equality*. London: Unwin. **19**, **272**, **392**.

Teitelbaum, M. S. (1972) Factors associated with the sex ratio in human populations. In Harrison and Boyce, 1972. **113**.

431

The Times House of Commons (1964/84). London: Times Newspapers. **353**, **8.14**.

Thomas, L. and Wormald, E. (1989) Political participation. In Reid and Stratta, 1989. **349**.

Thomas, T. (1988) *The British*. London: Routledge and Kegan Paul. **432**.

Thompson, D. (1971) Season of birth and success in the secondary school. *Educational Research* 14(1). **306**.

Thompson, K. (1988) How religious are the British? In Thomas, 1988. **327**.

Thompson, K. and Tunstall, J. (1971) *Sociological Perspectives*. Harmondsworth: Penguin. **17**.

Titmuss, R. M. (1968) *Commitment to Welfare*. London: Allen and Unwin. **148**.

Todd, J. and Butcher, R. (1982) *Electorial Registration in 1981*. OPCS SSD. London: OPCS. **349**.

Todd, J. and Dodd, T. (1985) *Children's Dental Health in the United Kingdom 1983*. OPCS SSD Series SS 1189. London: HMSO. **137**.

Tomlinson, S. (1980) The educational performance of ethnic minority children. *New Community*, 8. **301**.

Townsend, P. (1974) Inequality and the health service. *Lancet*, 1. **158**.

Townsend, P. (1979) *Poverty in the United Kingdom*. Harmondsworth: Penguin. **33**, **44**, **68**, **180**, **196**, **267**, *2.1*, *2.2*, *2.4*, *5.9*, *A/B*, **6.4**.

Townsend, P., Corrigan, P. and Kowarzik, V. (1987) *Poverty and Labour in London*. London: Low Pay Unit. **171**, **184**.

Townsend, P. and Davidson, N. (1982) *Inequalities in Health*. Harmondsworth: Penguin. **152**, **158**.

Trieman, P. J. (1977) *Occupational Prestige in Comparative Perspective*. London: Academic Press. **47**.

Troyna, B. (1984) Fact or artefact? The educational under-achievement of black pupils. *British Journal of Sociology of Education*, 5. **302**.

Troyna, B. and Smith, D. (1983) *Racism, School and the Labour Market*. Leicester: National Youth Bureau. **429**.

Turner, B. S. (1986) *Equality*. Chichester: Ellis Horwood/London: Tavistock. **19**.

UCCA (1984) *Statistical Supplement to the Twenty-first Report 1978–9*. Cheltenham: UCCA. **8.15**.

UCCA (1988) *Statistical Supplement to the Twenty-fifth Report 1986–7*. Cheltenham: UCCA. **8.21, 8.22**.

Unemployment and Ethnic Origin (1984) *Employment Gazette*, June. **205**.

Unemployment Unit (1986) *Bulletin*. London: Unemployment Unit. **202**.

UGC (1987) *University Statistics 1986–7*. Vol. 1, *Students and Staff*. Cheltenham. Universities Statistical Record. **321**.

Victor, C. R. (1987) *Old Age in Modern Society*. London: Croom Helm. **18, 183, 5.10**.

Wadsworth, M. E. J. (1975) Delinquency in a national sample of children. *British Journal of Criminology*, 15. **340**.

Walby, S. (1986) Gender, class and stratification. In Crompton and Mann, 1986. **45**.

Webb, D. (1973) Some reservations on the use of self-rated class. *Sociological Review*, 21. **41**.

Webb, M. (1989) Sex and gender in the labour market. In Reid and Stratta, 1989. **191, 286**.

Wells, N. (1987) *Women's Health Today*. London: Office of Health Economics. **115, 124, 143, 148, 163**.

Werner, B. (1984) Fertility and family background: some illustrations from the OPCS Longitudinal Study. *Population Trends*, 35. **236**.

Werner, B. (1985) Fertility trends in different social classes; 1970 to 1983. *Population Trends*, 41. **240, 7.11**.

Werner, B. (1988) Birth intervals: results from the OPCS Longitudinal Study 1972–84. *Population Trends*, 51. **238**.

West, D. C. (1982) *Delinquency. Its Roots, Careers and Prospects*. London: Heinemann. **340**.

West Indian Children in Our Schools. (1981) (The Rampton Report) Interim report on the education of children from ethnic minority groups. Command 8273. London: HMSO. **275, 300**.

Westergaard, J. and Resler, J. (1975) *Class in a Capitalist Society*. London: Heinemann. **18**.

Whitaker's Almanac 1984 (1984) 116th edition. London: Whitaker. **8.14**.

Whitburn, J., Mealing, M. and Cox, C. (1976) *People in Polytechnics*. Guildford: Society for Research into Higher Education. **323**.

White, G. and Mufti, R. (1979) *Understanding Socialisation*. Driffield: Nafferton. **428**.

Whitely, R. (1974) The city and industry: the directors of large companies, their characteristics and connections. In Stanworth and Giddens, 1974. *8.14*.

Who's Who (1984). London: A and C Black. *8.14*.

Woolf, M. (1971) *Family Intentions*. OPCS SS. London: HMSO. **62**.

Yarrow, M. R., Campbell, J. D. and Burton, R. V. (1964) Reliability of maternal retrospection: a preliminary report. *Family Process*, 3. **245**.

Yinger (1986). Intersecting strands in the theoryization of race and ethnic relations. In Rex and Mason, 1986. **76**.

Young, M. and Willmott, P. (1956) Social grading by manual workers. *British Journal of Sociology*, 7. **47**.

Young, M. and Willmott, P. (1973) *The Symmetrical Family*. London: Routledge; Harmondsworth: Penguin, 1975. **367**.

Zander, M. (1978) *Legal Services for the Community*. London: Temple Smith. **344**.

SUBJECT INDEX

Numbers in italics refer to tables